PREVENTING

WORLD WAR III:

Some Proposals

EDITED BY QUINCY WRIGHT
WILLIAM M. EVAN
MORTON DEUTSCH

SIMON AND SCHUSTER / NEW YORK / 1962

PUBLISHED BY SIMON AND SCHUSTER, INC.
ROCKEFELLER CENTER, 630 FIFTH AVENUE
NEW YORK 20, N. Y.

FIRST PRINTING

ACKNOWLEDGMENTS

The editors wish to thank the following publishers for permission to reprint material which has appeared elsewhere:

Roger Fisher, "Constructing Rules that Affect Governments," reprinted from *Arms Control, Disarmament and National Security,* edited by Donald G. Brennan, © George Braziller, 1961. By permission of George Braziller, Inc.

Erich Fromm, "The Case for Unilateral Disarmament," reprinted from *Arms Control, Disarmament and National Security,* edited by Donald G. Brennan, © George Braziller, 1961, by permission of George Braziller, Inc., and © 1960, 1961, The American Academy of Arts and Sciences, in whose journal, *Daedalus* (Vol. 89), this article first appeared. By permission of George Braziller, Inc.

Robert Gomer, "Some Thoughts on Arms Control" (called "The Armed Arbiter" in this book), reprinted from the *Bulletin of the Atomic Scientists,* April, 1961, pp. 133–7.

David Riesman, "The Nylon War," reprinted from *Individualism Reconsidered,* The Free Press, Glencoe, Ill., 1954, pp. 426–34.

T. C. Schelling, "Arms Control: Proposal for Special Surveillance Force" (called "A Special Surveillance Force" in this book), reprinted from *World Politics,* October, 1960, pp. 1–18.

LIBRARY OF CONGRESS CATALOG CARD NUMBER: 62–12416

MANUFACTURED IN THE UNITED STATES OF AMERICA

BY BOOK PRESS, INC., BRATTLEBORO, VT.

To the Next Generation

CONTENTS

PREFACE

NUCLEAR WAR is not inevitable. The belief that it is inevitable can help make it so.

For centuries, most societies have allocated enormous resources to the development of the technology and strategies of war. The technology and strategies of peace are virtually nonexistent. Whereas the military is an old and respected profession, there is no comparable profession concerned with the maintenance of peace.

The United States and the Soviet Union both spend approximately half of their annual budget on preparations for a possible World War III. By comparison, their yearly outlay of funds to prevent war and to increase our knowledge of how to resolve international conflicts without war is infinitesimal. The present disparity in the use of human and physical resources is particularly dangerous in view of the magnitude of the catastrophe that could befall mankind in the event of an all-out nuclear war. To prevent such a disaster, novel social and cultural innovations are imperative.

The dangers in our present world situation are many indeed. Especially serious are such threats to peace as the arms race between the United States and the Soviet Union; the continuing disputes about territories divided by controversial boundaries or supposedly temporary armistice lines; the gap in the standard of living between the technologically advanced and the underdeveloped countries of the world, coupled with the demand to eliminate this inequity; the revolution in military technology with such attendant dangers as surprise attack, accidental war, "escalation" of small-scale wars into a nuclear war, and the likelihood that the present "nuclear weapons club" will be greatly increased in membership in a decade or two.

The unparalleled risks confronting us, as well as the belief that a nuclear war is not inevitable, prompted the editors to initiate this book. These essays represent a modest effort to increase our understanding of the agonizing problems of war and peace. All the contributors are scholars—whether in the sciences or the humanities—who, in their capacity as private citizens, bring their intelligence to bear on ways of averting a nuclear catastrophe.

Each contributor has sought to develop an original and significant proposal which, if implemented, would lessen the chances of World War III. The book as a whole does not purport to be a full treatment of the complex problems of war and peace. Nevertheless, the editors believe that if only some of the proposals advanced in this book could be taken into account in policy making in East and West, the likelihood of a nuclear war would be diminished.

The book is divided into three parts. Part I deals with the immediate and urgent problem of stopping the arms race. The increase in international tensions, both a cause and an effect of the arms race, is considered in Part II. Here our contributors offer proposals aimed at the reduction of international tensions and the development of policies and orientations which could provide a basis for fruitful negotiations. The essays in Part I and Part II deal with the short-range problems which will have to be tackled in the next decade if we are to prevent World War III. If these problems are not to recur, a fundamental change is required in the thinking and social organization of human beings. This, then, highlights the long-range problem of building a world society, which is the focus of the essays in Part III.

In the Epilogue, each of the editors, in the light of the various contributions, presents a general essay from the vantage point of his own field: psychology, sociology or international law.

The editors' decision to include a given contribution should not be taken to mean that they agree with the proposal advocated by the author but rather that they believe it to be worthy of serious attention; nor are the contributors necessarily in agreement with the proposals of the editors. It should be clear that each contributor as well as each editor bears sole responsibility for the views expressed in his essay.

Preventing World War III represents only one of the many intellectual efforts that will be necessary if new pathways to an enduring peace are to be found. Our hope is that these proposals will stimulate discussion and will further efforts to find alternatives to the "balance of terror" now confronting us. Clearly, we need a worldwide research effort—preferably under the auspices of the United Nations—on the most urgent problem of mankind, the preservation of peace in the nuclear age.

We dedicate this book to the next generation. If world peace is preserved for the next generation, the chances of eliminating war may well be brighter than they have ever been in the history of man.

October 1961

Q. W
W. M. E.
M. D.

PART I

STOPPING THE ARMS RACE

INTRODUCTION

THE INCREASING AWARENESS of the dreadful implications of modern military technology has stimulated considerable thinking and discussion about how to reduce to a minimum the dangers inherent in modern weapons. In contemporary discussions, some scholars place their emphasis on *unilateral* and some on *bilateral* actions; some stress *arms control,* while others stress *disarmament* as an objective. To understand much of the current discussion, the meaning of the foregoing terms must be grasped.

Unilateral action is action that can be taken by either side, with or without the agreement or cooperation of the other side. Thus, the likelihood of war would diminish if either side were to develop sufficient control over its military forces so as to lessen the possibilities that nuclear weapons would be used as a result of accident, insanity, mischief, or misunderstanding. Similarly, the chances of a nuclear catastrophe would lessen if either side were able to make its military forces relatively invulnerable so that the other side would not be tempted to initiate a surprise attack. Invulnerability would also lessen the need for hasty decisions to use one's weapons before they were destroyed by the other side. Efforts to achieve better control over one's forces and to increase their invulnerability are often referred to as *stabilizing the deterrent.* (The term "deterrent" is used by some authors as a shorthand to express the questionable notion that war can be deterred by making a potential aggressor afraid of the possibility of a devastating nuclear retaliation.)

Most authorities doubt that the nuclear "deterrents" can be stabilized by unilateral actions alone. Agreements with the other side appear to be necessary to end the arms race and to prevent unexpected technological developments from unstabilizing the "stable deterrent." For the past fifteen years, the East and the West have attempted unsuccessfully to negotiate arms control and disarmament agreements. The phrase *arms control* is sometimes used broadly to refer to any type of agreement to limit or eliminate the dangers inherent in the possession of military weapons. In this usage, *disarmament* is one of many possible types of arms-control agreements. A narrower usage distinguishes between "arms control" and "disarmament." Here, "arms control"—which some view as a step on the road to total disarmament and others view as an ultimate objective—refers to those agreements which would allow each side to maintain a sufficient amount of invulnerable nuclear weapons to deter the other side from cheating. Some writers view arms control, in this latter sense, as an ultimate objective because they consider that the temptation to cheat and develop nuclear weapons secretly in a disarmed world would be very great. Others view arms control as a preliminary to total disarmament because, realizing that disarmament cannot be instantaneous, they believe that there must be carefully defined agreements on the control of arms during the process of disarmament.

Arms control and disarmament negotiations between East and West have, so far, foundered on the hard rock of suspicion. The United States has been unwilling to disarm unless it could make sure, through careful inspection, that the Soviet Union was also doing so. The Soviet Union has been unwilling to allow itself to be inspected, unless the United States were more or less disarmed. It fears that inspection would give the United States valuable military information which it has not been able to obtain through espionage; it also probably believes that inspection procedures would give little information about the United States that it could not get otherwise. The Soviet Union also suspects that it cannot get fair treatment in an international authority if it disagrees with the United States; in the United Nations it has been consistently outvoted when its position differed from that of the United States.

The papers in this section of our book are directed at preventing World War III by eliminating the dangers inherent in the arms race. None of the papers attempts to deal comprehensively with the various problems involved in working out ways of coping with the horrors of modern military weapons. Each focuses on an important aspect of the total problem and offers an imaginative approach to its solution.

The papers by Melman, Bohn, Karl Deutsch, and Gerard confront a basic difficulty that has made many informed people despair of the hope of achieving a disarmament agreement which contains adequate safeguards against attempts to violate it. There is considerable doubt that *physical inspection* techniques can ever be developed which would enable reasonably certain detection of clever, clandestine cheating. For example, despite an agreement to destroy all nuclear weapons, the United States or the Soviet Union could probably conceal from well-equipped inspectors enough weapons to devastate the other if they so desired. Melman, Bohn, Karl Deutsch, and Gerard start from the fundamental fact that a hidden weapon is useful only if somebody knows about it. Thus, if clandestine violations are occurring, knowledge of them must exist in certain people. Each makes stimulating and unique suggestions with regard to detecting the *knowledge* of cheating, if cheating occurs. Their papers represent contributions to the development of a new approach to the problems of inspection. This new approach, which is still in a rudimentary state of development, is often referred to as *psychological inspection.* Karl Deutsch supplements his proposals for psychological inspection with suggestions for the inspection of the mass media and of national budgets, each of which might provide clues of warlike intent.

Gomer's proposal of an armed arbiter makes use of a well-known principle: trust between two parties is often made possible because each of the two parties has trust in a strong third party. Indirect or mediated trust is, of course, a most common form of trust in interpersonal relations. Since we exist in a community in which various types of third parties—the law, public opinion, mutual friends, etc.—can be mobilized to buttress an agreement, we can afford to be trusting, even with a stranger in most circumstances. This suggests that *neutral* nations might play a crucial role in the development of a trustworthy disarmament. Unfortunately, in a bipolar world community, it is difficult to find nations that both sides would regard as truly neutral. This difficulty may reflect, in part, the common psychological tendency to view others who are not clearly on one's side as being sympathetic to the opposing side.

Morton Deutsch's proposal also makes use of an ancient practice: the use of hostages to deter aggressive action. There are many variants of the hostage notion—e.g., locating the government of the United States on Soviet territory and vice versa (modern communication technology might make this feasible), or locating a large part of one's strategic air force in the other's territory. "Hostages" might be used not only to reduce the fear of surprise attack but also to overcome some of the suspicions that impede disarmament.*

* If the leaders of the Soviet Union could be persuaded to live in Washington, D.C., and the leaders of the United States could be persuaded to live in Moscow during the execution of a crash program of disarmament (during which time the strictest inspection and control procedures would be instituted) the current impasse in disarmament negotiations might be resolved. Let us arbitrarily assume that 100,000 people on each side would have to be relocated and that it would cost 100,000 dollars per person per year to create the

The paper by Schelling starts from a pessimistic but perhaps realistic assumption: namely, that an intense enough motivation for arms control may not arise until a general war seems imminent. He reasons that if this is so we must prepare ourselves now for the opportunity and difficulty of instituting radical measures of arms control, quickly, in a tense situation. His paper proposes a general orientation for preparing to cope with such an emergency situation and offers several novel proposals for action in such an emergency.

Kelman's essay is based upon the unusual assumption that an army is too dangerous an institution to be characterized by strong national loyalties. From this novel assumption, he goes on to develop a proposal for internationalizing military force. His proposal does not presuppose the existence of a world government and yet provides nations with protection against military aggression.

Like Kelman's paper, the essay by Naess challenges some of the widely held assumptions concerning military defense. He indicates that the selection of methods of defense cannot be separated from the thing that is being defended. He points out that we are interested in defending a certain "way of life" and that an emphasis on military methods distorts rather than defends the way of life we wish to preserve. Naess, then, examines what nonmilitary methods can be used to strengthen a "way of life" and how it can be defended and preserved even under adverse conditions of a military occupation by a foreign power. His paper draws upon the Norwegian experience under Nazi occupation in World War II. It should be noted that Naess's proposal for an emphasis on nonmilitary defense does not require *both* sides to de-emphasize the military—although unilateral actions of this sort may very well reduce international tensions and lead to reciprocation.

The paper by Benoit examines the question of whether the economy of the United States is too dependent on armaments for disarmament to be a feasible policy. He discusses the kinds of problems and dislocations which might result from disarmament. On the one hand, his analysis indicates that adequate planning and research would enable the United States to cope readily with the economic changes involved in the transition to a disarmed world. On the other hand, his analysis suggests that without such planning and research, there may be severe problems indeed. There are, of course, large numbers of people who have careers, skills, special privileges, or financial interests

---

necessary facilities: the annual cost would be 10 billion dollars per side. Assume that it would take five to ten years to disarm. Would 50 to 100 billion dollars and the personal inconvenience of the leaders of each country be too outlandish a cost for each side to pay to achieve disarmament?

that are dependent upon military expenditures. Special efforts must be made to develop plans which will assure these people that they will not suffer as a result of disarmament. Benoit points out that this may "remove the opposition to disarmament which the existence of a politically potent bloc with a large interest in the defense program tends to create." Clearly, the fear of disarmament must be dealt with constructively or else it may produce defensive adherence to views which justify a hostile, armed world.

M. D.

NONPHYSICAL TECHNIQUES OF DISARMAMENT INSPECTION

By LEWIS C. BOHN

LONG BEFORE MOST OF US will have died of natural causes, many more countries will have many more thermonuclear explosives and rockets; and biological, chemical, and perhaps still other means for the mass extermination of mankind will come within the reach of petty tyrants and even of revolutionaries, adventurers, criminals, and ordinary madmen.

The problem is so to arrange our affairs that our species can survive its technology. This may involve efforts not only to prevent war, but also to reduce the arsenals available to national governments today, and the more modest but perhaps still more dangerous products of scientific research available to individuals tomorrow.

It has come to appear to many who have struggled with this problem that there is an ultimate obstacle to its solution. As arsenals grow and as new kinds of weapons become easier and easier to manufacture, there has appeared to be no satisfactory way of telling who may have hidden them, and who may be producing them, and from where a new danger may threaten. If international agreement could be reached to reduce or eliminate national nuclear stockpiles, for example, there has seemed to be no adequate means of checking whether all governments or all people are obeying its prohibition. No scientific device is available or apparently even conceivable that can track down hidden nuclear weapons, biological agents, lethal chemicals, or even large ballistic rockets. Science appears to have got us into a fix from which science offers us no way out.

This ultimate obstacle of inspection has tended to focus attention on very modest steps toward arms limitation agreements. These have the additional attraction of a certain political realism implied by their very modesty. But the same feature means they can offer only limited improvement in the present outlook for the species (though every gain is surely welcome).

Those brave enough or rash enough to continue to take seriously more thoroughgoing disarmament agreements have felt constrained to envisage "balancing" the dangers of undetectable hidden capabilities with permitted, "legal" military forces, national or international. Since under conventional inspection concepts the hidden forces can apparently be large, the "balancing" ones must be also. And we are left still under the physical threat of immediate death to tens of millions from legal forces, illegal forces, or both.

The present paper discusses nonphysical techniques of inspection, a novel approach to disarmament inspection.[1] Nonphysical inspection conceives the problem in human rather than physical terms. Because its operation is not directly controlled and determined by the physical nature of the concealed object or forbidden activity to be detected, it achieves (in principle, at least) a type of coverage and effectiveness not possible for the conventional "physical" inspection techniques. When used to supplement these, it may hold real promise for the effective detection even of the most easily concealed violations of an arms limitation agreement.

If nonphysical inspection fulfills its apparent promise, it may make technically reasonable complete disarmament not requiring large "balancing" military capabilities. By providing supplementary coverage and assurance that agreements are being observed, it may also facilitate acceptance of the more modest arms limitations more likely in the immediate future. And it may help deal with the long-run problem of major destructive capabilities in the hands of nongovernmental groups, by allowing the greater society at least to know by whom it is threatened.

Basic Principle

The principle—though not the practice—of this approach is basically simple. The search for violations of an arms-control agreement is to be pursued not in places but in people: in the minds and actions of policy-makers, and in the minds and actions of those below the policy level who may have some knowledge of activities, weapons, or installations forbidden by the agreement.

In most thinking on the problem of disarmament inspection, the objects of inspection have been regarded as the prohibited weapons themselves, and the task of devising effective inspection has appeared to be the task of developing various kinds of scientific instruments that can detect and locate these prohibited weapons: better radiation detectors to locate nuclear materials, better seismographs to detect nuclear test explosions, better photography from aircraft or earth satellites to locate missile sites or airfields, better radar or infra-red systems to detect rocket flights, etc. In contrast, we advocate that instead of conceiving the problem in terms of better "hardware" to hunt out hidden bits of uranium or plutonium, nuclear tests, or missile components in basements, caves, deserts, ocean bottoms, or lunar mountains, one attempt to devise political and psychological methods to discover the men who know of the existence of these things, and to exploit this discovery to detect evasion. Our stress is not on seismographic, photographic, or electronic engineering, but on political and psychological engineering. We wish to detect not things, but the possession of information about things.

It is useful to distinguish two levels at which nonphysical techniques operate: the policy-makers and the non-policy-makers. As for the first, the essential point is that a national political leader intending to exploit violations of an arms-control agreement for political or military ends must have some form of knowledge of the violation. The task then becomes somehow to get at this knowledge of the violation that exists in the leader's mind, either to expose it to the rest of the world or else by the threat of exposure to deter even the attempt at violation.

Let us assume that inside the Soviet Union (for example) there are secret stocks of weapons or secret military activities which are forbidden by an arms-control convention. If these violations of the control agreement are to be of any use to Soviet policy-makers, then knowledge of them *must exist in some form* in the minds of the Soviet policy-makers. For unless and until the policy-makers have this knowledge, there is no way in which they can use the forbidden weapons or activities for national, political or military purposes.

This is not to say that if the Soviet government were to attempt evasion of control, Khrushchev (for example) would have to know precisely what forbidden weapons were hidden where, which missiles were being readied in forbidden launch sites, or the like. He might not even be aware of just who did know the physical details. But *if he were to base any national decisions on the fact of violation,* he would have to know that fact, and with considerable confidence. He would have to know the general dimensions of the violation if these dimensions were of any significance. And he would have to know the chain of command by which the military potential represented by the violation could be brought into use.

Could there exist a violation of the control agreement of which the Soviet rulers were unaware? Such a violation does not appear impossible: it might be undertaken, for example, by a rival for Khrushchev's power; or possibly by a friendly associate who felt that insurance was necessary and chose not to inform his chief; or perhaps by a more subordinate person or group whose motivation might be ultraconservative, revolutionary, or pathological.

However, if the violation represented a significant military capability, a Communist leader would have the strongest incentive to know of its existence. No governmental leaders can countenance the existence of significant military capability that is beyond their control and that might therefore be used against them; that a ruler of the Soviet Union or of China would permit such a possibility seems all the less likely. Even if the violation were not accessible to the international control system it appears unlikely to be inaccessible to the internal political control system, especially in a relatively autocratic state. And in any case even if the ruler were unaware of it for a certain period of time, he would have to have knowledge of a violation before he could exploit it for military or political purposes.

Application to Policy-Makers

But if we know that knowledge of evasion must exist in the minds of the policy-makers, our task is just beginning. The big problem is obviously whether anything useful can be done with the knowledge of "where to look."

One approach is physiological. If a Communist ruler were to know of a violation, then questioning about the possibility of such violation, or perhaps other material relating to it, would produce certain physical and mental reactions which would not be produced in the absence of such knowledge. Instruments can be arranged as a "polygraph" to measure and record chemical and electrical responses of the individual being questioned, as has of course been done for some years in psychological research, as well as with the "lie detectors" used in domestic crime detection. A major research effort might well bring these techniques to a level of reliability far beyond the present one, so that the polygraph, carefully and legally applied with the consent of all concerned, could gain a respectability that has rightly been denied the "lie detector."[2]

The conditions for presenting questions, the kind of questions that would be permissible, the means of recording and interpreting the results, and the use which would be made of such results—these would all have to be carefully worked out and specified in the control convention, with full attention to safeguards against abuse of legitimate personal rights, secrecy, and other matters outside the direct and proper concern of the agreement.

If a country were not attempting to violate the control agreement, then measurements of its leaders' reactions would have to be made to give no misleading or otherwise unacceptable indications. But assuming this can be done, there seems to be no reason why the leaders of such a country would find the procedure inherently unacceptable, once they had been accustomed to the whole idea. This is not to say that Premier Khrushchev—or President Kennedy—would necessarily welcome such an innovation. But would either of them necessarily reject it, if (a) he genuinely desired the arms limitation it was designed to inspect, and (b) it could be shown to hold no dangers except for a violator of the agreement?

The degree to which reliable data could be expected from a procedure that was acceptable on all counts is impossible to estimate without thorough study. But despite its novel and rather drastic appearance, this physiological approach should not be ruled out. The decision-makers are the one "place" where there would have to be evidence, if a violation that could threaten the international community were being undertaken. If modern scientific techniques can be employed to uncover such evidence, then possibilities for their use must be considered seriously.

A related but somewhat more traditional approach would be a sort of controlled "cross-examination" of the decision-makers without polygraph measurement. Again, the circumstances would involve a variety of safeguards, but the main purpose would be to discover by thorough questioning, rather in the fashion of a legal cross-examination and without physiological measurements, whether evasions of the control agreement were in fact being attempted. The results of the questioning might be interpreted in a formal manner by an international tribunal for the purpose; also, it might be helpful to have the proceedings themselves televised internationally.

In the absence of physiological measurements, the interpretation of the results becomes necessarily less "objective" and scientific. However, it still might have considerable value. Political leaders, especially if they have attained top power in totalitarian countries, may be highly experienced in the art of public deception. But it is not automatically the case that the acting ability of the present leaders, or of those in power when a control agreement became effective, would be adequate to the task of completely successful deception under repeated examination and under close scrutiny in controlled conditions by a variety of able observers or even (via television) by whole populations.

Application to Non-Policy-Makers

There are many persons who would not inevitably have knowledge of violations, but who nevertheless might gain such knowledge, perhaps by virtue of their position or occupation. These include top-level military planners, who might have to be brought in on the secret before effective military use could be made of the violation; other individuals near the top policy levels or near the ruler himself who might gain knowledge by chance, by virtue of opportunities to investigate their own suspicions, or perhaps through a desire to blackmail or even supplant their bosses; members of the families of the policy-makers or of those near to them; military personnel in lower positions who might be involved in preparations or activities related to the violation; scientists; technicians; clerical personnel and accountants, especially those involved in budget preparation, auditing of government accounts, and the like; airplane pilots, seamen, explorers, or others whose work might present special opportunities for chance observation of secret installations or activities; and members of the secret police (if any), public police forces, private investigative agencies (if any), intelligence services, or the like.

One approach to inspecting individuals in such groups is to adopt techniques similar to those described for the top-level policy-makers. Where the number of individuals is small—for example, the top-level military planners, rivals for political supremacy, or top scientists—it might be possible to have formal interviews at reasonable intervals, and perhaps to investigate physiological responses as well. For larger groups—for example, accountants and technicians—any such procedure would have to be very streamlined, would probably be a severe burden to individual rights and privacy, and might have little effectiveness.

It is a rather different approach to the nonpolicy groups that appears to hold more promise: if you can't find the man, have him find you. In the case of those below the policy level, we have the chance that a knowledgeable element will "speak up."

When one thinks in terms of "physical inspection," there seems to be no chance under the sun of making, for example, a remote desert dune concealing illegally buried plutonium call its secret to the attention of a control agency. It is perhaps primarily the impossibility of this which stacks the odds so much against discovery; the plutonium could be in any of literally billions of places, and there is no way physical inspection can distinguish the hiding place from its empty fellows. But a human being with knowledge of illegal activities is not hopelessly passive like a rock or a sand dune. If he decides to do so, he is quite capable of initiating the action necessary to inform the control agency. However few the individuals possessing the crucial information might be among the hundreds of millions of their fellows, there is at least the theoretical possibility that—whoever they were—they could be motivated to take such action. There is at least the theoretical possibility, lacking in a purely physical approach, of improving the odds in favor of discovery, by providing an effective motivation.

A national policy-maker contemplating violation of a control agreement for his own ends will have a very direct interest in concealing his violation. If he fails and the violation is exposed, his schemes for aggression or national advantage will presumably collapse, and his personal power may be jeopardized as well. But the viewpoint of a person in a subordinate position is basically different. The decision to attempt the violation would not be his, and if the matter were put to him he might not be at all in sympathy with an attempt at evasion. Its success might appear to be a grave threat to himself and his family, and the only chance for continued peace and national survival might seem to lie in its detection and exposure.

Whether or not a subordinate knowing of an attempt at evasion would wish to help expose it depends on a number of factors, including the danger of arrest or other penalty by his government which he considered likely to be incurred by disclosure; his view of whether war (and its resulting peril to him or his family) would result if the violation were *not* discovered; his patriotism, and how he would view successful evasion of the control agreement in terms of his country's interests; his belief that other countries were violating the agreement or adhering to it; his ideology; his personal heroism; his grudges against the regime; his desire to escape from his government and country; and probably still other considerations.

The task in designing the nonphysical inspection system below the policy level is primarily the task of maximizing the factors that could encourage reports, and minimizing those that could discourage it. Obviously there is no hope of achieving perfection here, any more than in the different job of getting at the policy-maker's knowledge of violation. But the total number of "uncommitted," nonpolicy individuals who in one way or another might learn of a violation may be appreciable—tens, hundreds, or (for some types of violations) even thousands. If any one of these should, on balance, decide to report the violation to the international control agency, then the inspection system would have done its job. Perhaps more important, if those at the policy level considering a violation were to recognize a real chance of one such report, which they could not completely control and eliminate, then they might be deterred from attempting violation in the first place. A purely physical inspection system seems to leave the violator a multitude of possibilities for escaping detection; a nonphysical inspection system may instead present him with a multitude of possibilities for being caught.

Some Critical Questions

In the section that follows, we raise some of the problems involved in nonphysical inspection techniques. We have put these matters in the form of questions to emphasize that we do not have solutions. At this stage, this is no more than an *approach* to arms inspection (though I believe it a promising one); it is by no means a plan or (still less) a solution.[3]

1. *Policy-Makers.* Which national leaders would necessarily have direct knowledge of clandestine activities? How many might suspect, or have indirect knowledge? How precise would this knowledge have to be?

2. *Lesser Officials, Guards, Accountants, Engineers, etc.* What categories of people might automatically be involved to a greater or lesser degree? How might specific individuals be identified? To what extent is past association with specific military projects a helpful guide?

3. *Scientists.* Would some have to be involved in hiding past production? In diverting current production? In developing delivery methods? Would they be good sources of tips on other personnel who might be involved—or on how evasions might still be attempted—or detected?

4. "*Average Citizens.*" In what ways might average citizens gain knowledge or suspicion of hidden stockpiles or related activities?

5. *Lie Detectors.* What is their present degree of reliability? Could they be used for large-scale personnel survey operations, to develop leads? Are there technical obstacles to their use on policy-makers and perhaps selected officials? Is it inconceivable that policy-makers would volunteer for lie-detector examination, regardless of their knowledge of evasions?

6. "*Truth Serums.*" Might these be used instead of, or as an adjunct to, lie detectors?

7. *Hypnosis.* Can hypnosis be applied (under carefully specified and controlled conditions and safeguards) to elicit information from promising individuals? Can it also be used to invalidate nonphysical methods such as lie detectors? What is the significance of the fact that

most individuals cannot be hypnotized deeply? That some who can, might be made poor subjects by posthypnotic suggestion?

8. *Interviews of Policy-Makers.* Should interviews be conducted in public or in private? What should be the composition of the interviewing board? Should attempts be made to discover contradictions among the accounts of different officials? Should the interviews be at regular preannounced intervals? Should the results of physiological measurements (if any) be displayed to the interviewers, or only recorded for later study? Should specific questions be submitted in advance, and perhaps approved by an appropriate body as being "legitimate," or should only the general range of permitted questions be specified in the original control convention? What provision should there be for a "second round" of questioning of the policy-makers or of others whose names may have been raised? What provisions should be made to prevent forced or inadvertent disclosure of legitimate military and political secrets?

9. *Top-Level Intrigue.* Can the power struggle at the top of a Communist or other government be made to work in favor of a control system? Might not an actual or aspiring ruler be particularly interested in making sure there were no hidden nuclear weapons at the disposal of any potential rival? Would there be ways for him to gain this assurance other than thorough support of the official inspection system? If one ruler could demonstrate deliberate violation of a control agreement by one or more other rulers, he might gain from this demonstration decisive support from lesser officials and the public (as well as eliminate a potent weapon that might be used against him). Could the possibility of such a bid for support be exploited to deter violation by any or all of the rulers?

10. *Personnel Exchange.* Can trips or extended visits of individuals or groups to other countries develop leads on evasions? For instance, might Soviet policy-makers be interviewed fruitfully by U.S. newsmen? Might the inclination of, say, Soviet physicists to feel a bond with their Western counterparts be developed by visits in ways to promote the uncovering of forbidden activities? Might officials or ordinary citizens be afforded safer ways to disclose useful information on evasions, if travel restrictions were minimized?

11. *Promoting Favorable Attitudes.* How might officials and others be discouraged from feeling that measures to hide stockpiles could provide insurance against violation by other countries? How could ordinary citizens be made to feel a personal stake in revealing to international authorities information that might come to them of attempted violation by officials of their own government?

12. *Dead Men Tell No Tales.* Can an autocratic ruler completely

"cover his traces" by simply killing all those involved in preparing the evasion or who may otherwise have knowledge of it? Can he get at these individuals without arousing the suspicions of a still wider circle? Can potential victims be made so aware of their danger that they can take some effective action to avoid recruitment in the first place?

13. *Exploiting Propaganda.* Can past Soviet characterizations of "mass destruction" weapons as basically evil, for example, be used to encourage reports to foreign inspectors of activities concerning nuclear stockpiles? If a government accepted a weapons-control plan in which hidden stockpiles were illegal, could it be forced by its own propaganda position to proclaim domestically the obligation of any citizen to report outlawed activities through the agreed channels? Could this kind of publicity have any real effect on Soviet or Chinese citizens, who may have become largely inured to government propaganda?

14. *Exploiting Police State Controls.* Can the Communist internal control system and the attitudes toward official authority which it encourages operate in favor of weapons control? Can a situation be promoted in which the citizen feels that failure to report information on hidden stockpiles in the officially approved ways might lead to his arrest? In which involvement of the whole Secret Police would be a prerequisite for a conspiracy to evade control?

15. *Constitutional Obstacles.* Would nonphysical inspection entail changes in national constitutions?[4] Could individual rights be protected? Would infringements of national sovereignty necessarily be involved?

16. *Tips: Different Types.* What channels could be arranged for tips on clandestine activities? Could an office in each city receive anonymous telephone calls involving minimum risk to the caller? Could use of ordinary mail be made a more certain route with less risk of interception? What possibilities might there be for getting tips in individual interviews conducted under conditions designed to safeguard the informant and his family?

17. *Tips: What to Do with Them.* Should information on clandestine activities be carefully guarded while at least preliminary investigation is made by foreign inspectors? Or should a public declaration be made, alerting other nations and also putting the government directly concerned on the spot? How might the informant best be protected (if he is known)—by public declaration of his identity and demand for his immunity, by attempting to conceal his identity, or in other ways?

18. *Tips: Preventing Effective Counteraction.* If tips on violations become known to the attempting violators as well as to the inspectors for whom they are intended, what can be done to prevent hiding the

evidence of violation? Could the danger of such leaks be minimized by careful selection of inspection personnel? Could hiding evidence of violation be made very difficult if complete access of inspectors to suspect areas and personnel were guaranteed in the control agreement?

19. *Tips: Rewards and Penalties.* What rewards, such as large sums of cash or guarantees of job security and asylum, might encourage tips? Could systems of penalties be devised for failure to report? How could we make most effective such intangible inducements as the conviction that only reporting forbidden activities related to "mass-destruction"weapons could prevent a world war which would involve the eventual use of these weapons against one's own nation and family?

20. *Dangers of Overload.* Could means be found to handle a large number of tips, many of them perhaps deliberately introduced to jam the inspection system, or perhaps resulting from the eagerness of Communist-bloc citizens for asylum?

21. *Testing.* Could hidden weapons or other apparent violations be "planted" by an international inspectorate, (a) as a means of checking the operation of the control system or, perhaps more important, (b) as a means of tightening up operation of the system? Could "plants" be devised in some way directly by opposing states, to test operation of controls on their potential adversaries? Can useful testing procedures be devised other than "plants"?

22. *Combination with Other Inspection Activities.* Nonphysical inspection methods would in all probability be combined with physical methods (direct searches for hidden stockpiles, for illegal diversion of nuclear material, for manufacture of weapons, etc.). In what ways might leads uncovered in one type of search be developed through the other? For example, what forms of physical inspection, rights of access, etc., might be required to follow through effectively on leads first developed by nonphysical methods?

23. *Political Prerequisites.* Must the inspectorate be international, or "neutral," or might it consist of United States citizens in the USSR and Soviet citizens in the United States? Might some techniques of nonphysical inspection be usable even if there existed considerable suspicion that the potential opponent might be evading control and hence that security lay only in "hedging" rather than giving unreserved support to an operating control system?

24. *BW-CW Inspection.* Inspection for biological or chemical warfare agents and facilities for their production is even more difficult than the detection of hidden nuclear materials. Can this task be approached effectively by nonphysical methods, concentrating for

example on (in addition to policy-makers) scientists, physicians, or technicians with relevant backgrounds?

Workability of Nonphysical Techniques

The single problem at the heart of the foregoing questions is just this: can nonphysical techniques be made to work? Can there be found solutions to all of the technical, political, and other difficulties which will enable the setting up of a nonphysical inspection system with a real capability of discovering violations of an arms-limitation agreement? The answer can only be determined by large-scale organized research in the development of nonphysical inspection measures, with a view to making such an inspection system do what it is supposed to do, and preventing it from doing what it is not supposed to do. Such research should be pressed.

Even now it is worth pointing out, however, that if these methods can be made to work, their performance might be greatly superior to purely physical inspection techniques. In principle at least they can detect the fullest possible range of forbidden activities or objects, regardless of how carefully these are hidden. For physical inspection we have long since passed the point of no return in concealment of nuclear materials, and are in process of passing it for long-range missiles. But while there is no physical device able to ferret out buried nuclear materials or missiles, nonphysical methods have a real chance of doing just that, provided only that the existence of these items is known to those who might be tempted to use them, or that all who participated in their concealment or otherwise learned of it are not dead. Nonphysical methods can even cope with products of scientific ingenuity not dreamed of when the inspection system is set up, provided only that those concerned with them realize that these products constitute violations of the agreement; no physical methods are likely to be able to do this. Even violations that occur before nonphysical methods are instituted can be inspected: if there had been nuclear tests during the East-West moratorium, for example, these would be known at least to some scientists and policy-makers in the country concerned. Even a violation that has not yet occurred, that exists only as a plan in the minds of a tiny group, is subject to discovery, perhaps many months before it could be implemented and detected by physical inspection.

Acceptability: Existing Parallels

But there is a grave question that must be raised in connection with this approach to inspection. Even if it is technically feasible, do we want it? Is it worth it? Are the kinds of things that would go on under a nonphysical inspection scheme things that we would like to see introduced into human society in the future?

The first point here is that it is only the context that is novel; many (at least) of the methods are not. Although the detection of violations of an arms-limitation agreement has predominantly been regarded as a problem for physical inspection, this is not true for the detection of violations of ordinary domestic law. It has been recognized for many centuries that murder, for example, can be uncovered satisfactorily only through the use of nonphysical detection methods. The physical evidence may show only that someone is dead—sometimes not even that. To tell whether a deliberate crime has been committed, and if so, by whom, frequently requires the testimony of witnesses, information received from "tips," the interviewing of suspects, and sometimes their careful cross-examination first by the police and then in court before the jury that will have to decide their truthfulness. Locating individuals with knowledge of the crime, motivating full and accurate reports of this knowledge by involuntary witnesses to the crime, and getting at the knowledge of those who would prefer to conceal it, perhaps through finding inconsistencies or contradictions in their accounts—these nonphysical techniques must often play a much greater role than the discovery and analysis of purely physical evidence.

Because the latter does not suffice in dealing with crime, there have been evolved over the centuries combinations of effective nonphysical approaches and safeguards against their misapplication and abuse. Police investigators may welcome anonymous tips, rewards may be offered for information, and the personal safety and even legal immunity of witnesses may be guaranteed; but even the accused normally has the right to confront his accusers, their testimony may be subjected to the closest scrutiny, and witnesses who are shown to be testifying primarily for personal gain may be discredited. As for the accused himself, his confession of guilt may be given great weight, unless it is obtained by force; his account of his actions and whereabouts at the time of the crime will be closely studied and given much weight if supported by other nonphysical evidence of witnesses; and he cannot be required to testify against himself. The impossibility of developing totally unambiguous evidence, physical or nonphysical, combined with the grave penalty for conviction, has required the complex and costly procedure of trial by jury for major crime, in which the necessary element of judgment will at least be the judgment of one's peers. "Lie detectors," since they are recognized to be very far from completely reliable and since they have sometimes been used maliciously to encourage "confessions," are rightly regarded with much suspicion in established legal procedures; their evidence is admitted (if at all) only to corroborate, or to raise questions about other findings.

Nonphysical inspection techniques in fact have wide application well beyond the context of capital crime. In the United States, an informant whose tip leads to the recovery of income taxes can collect a percentage of the amount recovered. The intended victims of racial violence, or perhaps of underworld revenge, may receive anonymous tips helping them to safety. The credit manager may give as much weight to the manner, carriage, and references of a loan applicant as to his bank deposit record. Newsmen may find their secret informants so valuable as to prefer jail to revealing their identity. A candidate for public office may be judged by millions of television viewers as much for his shifting eyes or fidgeting hands as for what his record may indicate of dishonesty and mendacity. The parent may come to put less weight on concrete evidence of good or bad behavior than on the child's manner of reporting what he has been up to. Lie detectors are used to screen applicants for certain positions and in other connections in private industry where their indications may be very helpful even though not foolproof.

What is needed for the inspection provided for in arms-limitation agreements is the rapid evolution of nonphysical inspection techniques and methods of applying them that will do this new job as well as the more traditional ones. The same sorts of balance must be found between results and safeguards. Appropriate institutional and social arrangements must be developed and given legal status. Since murder (for example) has clearly required more than purely physical techniques for its discovery and control, society has found ways to use nonphysical methods that are both very helpful and on the whole acceptable; the new job is to find similarly effective means for the detection and control of arms-agreement violations.

New Personal Burdens

The application of nonphysical techniques of arms-limitation inspection does not promise to lay too great a burden on the average citizen. The number of violations which he might witness or otherwise gain knowledge of would have to be very small, or else the arms agreement itself would soon be denounced by the participating nations and collapse. The great majority of citizens in any country would probably never find themselves called upon to weigh the gains and drawbacks of reporting violations to the international control authority. They would have no need to avail themselves of the various safeguards, such as the anonymity of their reports (if they wished this), the rewards of money or asylum or the assurances of personal safety for themselves and their families; they would not have to face the possibility that, if they did report, the safeguards would not work. However, if occasion did arise and if they did not report, they might not only lose the possibility of great reward, but also have on their consciences some responsibility for the successful violation of the control agreement and perhaps for the resumption of the uncontrolled arms race, the ascendancy of a global tyranny, or the outbreak of a new war.

Imagining oneself faced with these or other dilemmas is easy, and sobering. But there is the possibility that we may face just as sobering dilemmas today if we should somehow witness a murder or become involved in blackmail. We live with this possibility partly because, for most of us, it will never happen. Still less likely would be our personal involvement in the violation of an arms-limitation agreement, or our personal confrontation by the demand that we report it.

For certain groups the situation would be different. Scientists in certain fields, political leaders with national responsibilities, and some others might be subjected periodically to private interviews by the international inspectors, polygraph interrogation (if the equipment and techniques can be sufficiently perfected), and even to public questioning by an international board established for the purpose. Precisely because people in these special groups are more likely to be involved in violations, or may even be certain to know of violations if they occur, they would, under a psychological inspection system, be required to bear these additional burdens. The political leader, at least in the Western democracies, must already expect severe limitations on his family privacy, his personal finances, the public behavior of his friends and relatives, etc. The scientist, though not so directly burdened, may well be aware of a special social responsibility, and in particular may be concerned that the fruits of his researches shall not be misapplied by others. An arms-limitation agreement that establishes explicitly what may and may not be done with regard to military weapons and activity may help the scientist share the burden of his conscience. And on the whole I would argue that the extra burdens imposed on members of these special groups are a reasonable price for them to pay for their special positions of responsibility and (often) public recognition and personal reward.

International Trust

We have so far been considering possible complications and drawbacks on the national and personal level. But it is unfortunately clear that a nonphysical inspection system would also impose certain burdens on the international environment as well.

Any inspection system, even one relying entirely on purely physical techniques, can contribute to international distrust as well as trust. Communist governments frequently interpret Western inspection proposals as designed primarily to expose political and military weaknesses rather than to contribute to the general welfare. Moreover, any inspection system may uncover data that gives grounds for suspicion rather than reassurance; for example, a nuclear test inspection post may signal a seismic disturbance inside the USSR which may or may not be a prohibited nuclear test, and which without the inspection post would go entirely undetected. And frictions may arise over a variety of matters such as the objectivity of inspection personnel, whether the host country is providing the agreed access and facilities, whether commercial or private secrets are being violated, and many more.

Nonphysical inspection in particular can raise further difficulties. By taking advantage of the necessary involvement of political leaders in deliberate national violations, it brings into question explicitly and publicly the integrity and veracity of these individuals, where ordinary inspection does this only by implication. By exploiting the fact that a violation that may escape physical inspection is likely to be known to some citizens besides those responsible for its initiation, it circumvents traditional channels of international contact and communication. Extending the reach of inspection to these areas is at first likely to be objected to because of its simple novelty. Disarmament negotiations have shown that new inspection concepts have always been questioned at the start, though often accepted in the course of time. To propose any kind of increased coverage for inspection may be interpreted, especially by Communist governments, as evidence not only of aggressive intent to jeopardize military and political secrecy but also of extreme Western suspicion and distrust; this may produce new resentments. But as the objective needs for nonphysical inspection of certain kinds of arms limitations are explained and understood, this effect may diminish. It is a central axiom in inspection that anything that does a better job of checking veracity must in a sense do more to bring veracity into question. But where there is a technical reason for better checking, the subjective reactions and misgivings can in time be overcome.

On the positive side, the very fact that nonphysical techniques can get at possible violations that physical inspection cannot reach reduces the "shadow area" of uncertainty and suspicion. If the countries involved are scrupulous in their adherence to the arms-limitation agreement, merely apparent evidence of evasion will eventually be tracked down and proven false, and in the course of time there will accumulate a vast body of evidence demonstrating the effective functioning of the agreement. The distrust that presently exists, especially between East and West, cannot be surmounted without effective inspection. Only if the United States government, for example, comes to believe that the Soviet proposals for general and complete disarmament provide for reliable inspection is there any chance that we will agree to such proposals. And if in their operation nonphysical (and other) techniques showed that all countries were adhering to an arms agreement in every possible way, then the high levels of mutual distrust and suspicion that exist today and that might easily continue into the early stages of a disarmed world would gradually diminish, as evidence of the good faith of all participants accumulated.

The Balance of Gains and Drawbacks

The various burdens and inconveniences of nonphysical inspection are only a means to an end. We are not interested in developing, proposing, or implementing nonphysical techniques because of any desirable effects these have in themselves—far from it. We should not imagine that the many drawbacks and problems of this approach to inspection are to be added to the burdens of our present world. Rather, the purpose in giving them serious attention is to change that world for the better, through internationally agreed-upon arms limitation. Far more important than advantages or drawbacks of nonphysical techniques themselves would be the balance of gains and drawbacks of the arms limitations they would help to inspect. For centuries we have intended through trial by jury and the acceptance of certain police activities—and safeguards—to diminish the chance that individual citizens will be violently attacked or otherwise mistreated by their fellows. In our new era of mass weapons we hope by international arms agreements (and the necessary inspection systems) to diminish the chance that whole nations will be destroyed or mistreated by other nations—or more precisely, that millions will be killed or enslaved by a power-hungry few. If nonphysical inspection techniques encroach on our personal lives and even (at first) on international harmony, their ultimate purpose is the preservation of our lives and homes from nuclear destruction and of our political freedoms from complete foreign domination.

It is therefore in this broader context of their possible contribution to achieving and maintaining international arms agreements that the various costs, complications, burdens, and inconveniences of these techniques must be evaluated.

This is not to say that arms limitation or even complete disarmament is necessarily a panacea that is certain to achieve the high objectives we hope for from it. Still less does it mean that one must necessarily accept any and all proposals for inspection to achieve such agreements. From the standpoint of the United States and from the standpoint of the world as a whole, one can unfortunately conceive of many arms agreements whose benefits would be questionable and whose drawbacks would be many and serious. There are many more questions to be asked of a disarmament proposal than "How much will it reduce armaments?" and "Can it be inspected?" What can be done in the case of deliberate, overt violation to counter it effectively? How can disputes over the interpretation of the evidence turned up by the inspection system be settled? What provision could be made for the peaceful adjustment of international disputes over borders, trade, revolution, racial discrimination, etc.? Could the agreement survive a limited war? How could the transition be made smoothly and equitably from the preagreement situation to full operation of the limitations and their control system?

Controlled arms limitation by international agreement is itself only one possible approach to a just and stable world peace. It presents many intrinsic difficulties, and the record of movement toward it is so far highly unimpressive. At the same time, in the light of the prospects for the human species without arms reduction, very many people in all countries believe that it has a promise that must not be neglected. The larger task facing those with this conviction is the discovery and development of arms-limitation arrangements that, all things considered (including inspection systems), will be advantageous. Moreover, before there can be more grounds for optimism, arrangements must be developed that also appear advantageous to the governments of the United States, our allies, the USSR, China, and their allies, and at least most of the "neutral" and uncommitted nations. This is certainly a tall order, in the light of wide-ranging national differences in weapons programs, strategic positions and doctrines, secrecy, aggressiveness of ideologies, economic and political expectations with and without arms limitation, and internal political structures.

Whether nonphysical inspection techniques should or should

not help monitor disarmament agreements, we at this time simply cannot judge. Despite the efforts of a handful of scholars and diplomats over the years, our understanding of disarmament needs and possibilities is today clearly little more than rudimentary. And if our grasp of this larger context is defective, our understanding of the possibilities and difficulties of nonphysical inspection is far more limited still.

But for all the reservations and questions that must now surround it, the subject surely deserves close study by all who might contribute to it, and who see any hope at all for improving the human outlook by controlled arms limitation.

NOTES

1. Nonphysical inspection has also been designated "knowledge detection" and "psychological inspection." The latter term was first used in an internal Rand Corporation memorandum by the author dated January 12, 1956. The present paper is based in part on a later version of that memorandum, "Psychological Inspection," P-1917, The Rand Corporation, Santa Monica, Calif., February, 1960. Some of the points touched on here are developed more fully in "Knowledge Detection: A Non-Physical Inspection Method for Arms Control," PP-2, Lockheed Electronics Company, Systems Research Center, Bedminster, N.J., January, 1961; this appears also in a chapter in *Arms Control, Disarmament, and National Security,* edited by Donald G. Brennan (New York: George Braziller, 1961).

   Some of the same concepts were developed independently in the study edited by Seymour Melman, *Inspection for Disarmament* (New York: Columbia University Press, 1958), especially in the section by Melman on "Inspection by the People," pp. 38–44. Similar concepts are also present in Grenville Clark and Louis B. Sohn, *World Peace through World Law* (Cambridge: Harvard University Press, 1958), especially pp. 261–2 (revised edition, 1960, pp. 267–8), and in Tom Slick, *Permanent Peace: A Check and Balance Plan,* (New York: Prentice-Hall, 1958), especially the section on "Human Inspection," pp. 79–80.

   Some discussion of nonphysical inspection is contained also in various papers of the 1960 Summer Study on Arms Control of the American Academy of Arts and Sciences.

2. The first mention of using "lie detectors" in arms inspection that has been brought to my attention is in a privately circulated paper by D. R. Inglis, D. A. Flanders, H. S. Freedman, and A. H. Jaffey dated December 1, 1952.

3. The numbered items that follow are taken almost verbatim from the author's 1956 Rand memorandum, and are therefore a little anachronistic in flavor. For further discussion of many of them, and of the re-

search needed to evaluate their promise, see the paper on "Knowledge Detection . . ." cited earlier.

4. In his very valuable study, *Arms Control and Inspection in American Law* (New York: Columbia University Press, 1958), pp. 186–7, Louis Henkin indicates that changes would not be required in the Constitution of the United States.

INSPECTION BY THE PEOPLE

By SEYMOUR MELMAN

FEAR AND DISTRUST of the opposing nation in the arms race has generated the problem of guarding against secret evasion of disarmament. Plans for evasive behavior are prepared, justified in each case by confidence that the other side will surely evade. Organization for controlling disarmament agreements must therefore take into account the possibility that secret evasion of disarmament agreements has been prepared in important countries. These would consist of secret caches of weapons and secret organizations of men committed to use them against an enemy.

In the United States it is held that with this country's tradition of law-abidingness, it would disarm, and that the disarming process could be easily verified to the satisfaction of the Soviets. But this would only be the occasion seized upon by Soviet agents to threaten the United States Government with secret weapons and thus compel surrender.

Under conditions of an arms race it would be feasible for secret groups to be formed in each of the major powers for the purpose of preparing an underground evasion of a possible disarmament agreement. The arms race has required each of the major governments to set up extensive internal security systems which include major departments of the government and a large proportion of the scientists and engineers of the society. And the arms race with its fearful distrust generates and reinforces justification for evasion of disarmament.

A will for secret evasion of disarmament can be made into an organized system with serious capability, by virtue of the available technology in weaponry and in organization. When we conducted the study on *Inspection for Disarmament* at Columbia University during 1957 and 1958, we were interested in the possibilities of such evasion operations. We found that physical systems of inspection all have their limits and that these limits could be exploited by men who understood the art of secret operations on a large scale. I thought it would be helpful for our understanding of such processes to set up three evasion teams charged with devising methods of evasion. I thought that we could thereby at once test for the feasibility of such action and also test the appropriateness of inspection systems. The reports of these teams were published in the volume *Inspection for Disarmament*.[1] Indeed, I found the activities of these three evasion teams so "successful" that an additional approach to the inspection problem was needed. This method we have called "inspection by the people." Essentially, this involves an effort to organize the population of the inspected countries to constitute a random, far-flung network of people who would report to the international inspection organization any evidence of evasion activity. It should be possible by such means to socially isolate an evasion group and to eliminate opportunity for organized action on their part; for the method of inspection by the people, put into action in a vigorous manner, would surround the prospective evaders with sustained, undefinable hazard for their violation of a disarmament agreement.

Who Would Try to Evade?

The main build-up for evasion of disarmament is circulation of the idea that the other side is certainly doing it, not only because it is possible, but because they have engaged in similar acts of deception in the past.

There are policy lines on the Soviet and on the American side which include such estimates for the people who take such analyses seriously. The fear then is that the other side would surely upset the disarmament *status quo* in order to turn it to political account. Accordingly, there is a pressure to prepare a military evasion of disarmament for fear of political debacle. In the United States, such fearful speculation is heightened by the existing sense of weakness toward Soviet political-economic operation.

One of the same assumptions of inspection for disarmament is that the primary area of inspection consists of weapons and military organization. While that is true, even the elimination of all of these would leave a residual military capability in the form of knowledge about destructive methods in the hands of men who might be prepared to use them. Thus, "in a totally disarmed world, even a small number of secreted or clandestinely manufactured nuclear weapons could disrupt the international order and allow one power to dominate its more trusting adversaries . . . It is highly unlikely that a 'foolproof' arms control can be devised."[2] Herman Kahn has declared that

"It would be child's play for one of these nations to hide completely hundreds of these bombs . . . This surely means that even if all nations should one day agree to total nuclear disarmament, we must presume that there would be hiding of some nuclear weapons or components as a hedge against the other side doing so . . . The problem of the clandestine nuclear cache in itself makes total disarmament especially infeasible."[3]

Once these fears and predictions of evasion exist, then there also begins to be discussion about doing it. In an unpublished communication one of the theorists of arms control has said:

> I do not think that violating secretly an arms control treaty would be the blackest crime, or the most wilfully irresponsible action, the action I could most deplore, that my government might take. In fact, there are policies that for all I know may be in existence now that I think may be just as hard on the fate of the world as a decision to violate secretly an arms control agreement.
>
> This may sound as though I have no morality and therefore do not appreciate that an arms control treaty would bring into play moral obligations that transcend selfish national security. That may be true; but that does not account for my position. I think there may be decisions that might be taken by this government or governments of other countries that would be at least as serious in their consequences for the fate of the world, potentially just as "immoral," as violating an arms control agreement. (But I should confess that I can at least conceive of circumstances in which I would favor my government's cheating on arms control; and to some people this might seem like a disqualification of my judgment.)

In my opinion, the kind of dehumanized militancy that has been generated by the arms race will also continue to be in some degree a danger for the disarmament process. Some of the men who have been so moved will surely be persuaded to change their attitude. Others, however, may not, and these must be socially isolated, so that organized evasion can be prevented.

Methods of Secret Evasion

Successful evasion of disarmament agreements by underground methods has been studied in several countries.[4] These investigations show that three conditions must be satisfied for the successful operation of a clandestine military organization, and especially for clandestine production of weapons.

1. A group of men exists which is prepared to carry out the clandestine production even at the cost of considerable personal sacrifice and risk. These men have strong allegiance to a guiding ideal.

2. The central working group is backed by a substantial part of the population, including a government or quasi-government, which backs up the operating group and shields them from the inspecting authorities.

3. The operators of the clandestine production system learn how to simulate appearances that will seem to be ordinary and innocent in the eyes of the inspectors.[5]

Practical possibilities for the implementation of evasion schemes exist because of the large quantities of weapons with high destructive capability available in many countries. This could include not only atomic warheads in various forms, but also biological and chemical warfare material. It is possible to conceive of two general systems of operation for an evasion effort. One is an evasion effort involving coordinated operations by many people; the second, evasion by a few.

Evasion of a disarmament system by a few men could take the form of a weapons system put in place well before an international inspection organization has begun to operate. In that case, even a few men could conceivably control a far-flung network of nuclear warheads. In that situation, they could at some moment decide to make their bid for power. A crucial feature of evasion by a few men, however heavily armed, is that a few men cannot make a military campaign. Neither can they undertake control of a government administration, let alone the whole society. For that purpose evasion and military action by large forces are required.

A large-scale military organization can hardly be assembled and set in motion without exposing itself. Furthermore, such an effort requires considerable time not only for organization and training but even to set it in motion. Thus, a major evasion effort on a large scale would surely require the collaboration of thousands of men. Even a plan for evasion by a few would, in the preparatory stages, require the collaboration of large numbers of men.[6]

Any sizable evasion activity would probably lend itself to direct exposure by the inspectorate. Accidents with weapons would reveal their presence. Unexplained exposure to radiation could be a basis for suspecting illegal handling of nuclear material and processes. Secret organizations often have problems of coping with defectors; thus political murders are important indicators of evasion operations.

In my opinion, the crucial aspect of evasion operations, their

Achilles' heel, is the requirement for substantial backing by the surrounding population and by an important section of the government. This is essential if no aspect of a complicated secret military organization is to be exposed to the international inspectorate in some way. This feature of any potential evasion of disarmament can be exploited to strengthen a system of inspection for disarmament.

The Method of Inspection by the People

Inspection by the people is an invitation to the populations of the participating countries to participate in the disarmament process by making known to the inspectorate any evidence of evasion of disarmament.[7]

The principal legal requirement for inspection by the people is the proviso that each country shall require in its code of law that every citizen of the country report to the inspectorate any evidence of evasion of the disarmament agreement. Failure to report such information is punishable under the law, national as well as international. To be sure, this type of provision invites allegiance to a supranational authority, to peoples and organizations that are removed from one's immediate and normal circle of allegiances.

Included in the disarmament agreement would be provisions for the right of the inspectorate to address itself to the population. These legal obligations would include a minimal use of facilities in the press, on the radio, and on television, and arrangements for addressing the population face to face by members of the inspectorate. In addition, the requirements would include participation by the leaders of each country in the public statements of the inspectorate to the population.

The inspection organization would devote itself, in part, to being a voice for the ideals of international disarmament and peaceful living.

The international agreement would also include means for the population of each country to reach the inspectorate. The postal system, which could be constantly monitored by the sending of test mail to the inspectors, could be used as an ordinary way of sending information to the international inspection organization.[8]

Lewis Bohn has suggested that the facilities of the inspection organization, including inspection posts and other United Nations premises, be given diplomatic immunity. Any person who wished to report evidence of evasion of disarmament could then do so with the assurance that if he wanted the protection of the international organization, even to the extent of being moved abroad, he could have it. It might also be possible to arrange for inspection posts and officers of the international inspectorate to be connected with information centers and technical libraries to which the population has free access. By such means, too, confidential access to the inspectorate would be possible.

The regulations of the inspectorate would include rewards for reporting on evasion activities and guarantees for the protection of persons submitting information in good faith.

One of the crucial features of known evasion operations is the requirement of collaboration by at least a part of a government. Therefore government officials must be regarded as priority personnel for inspection.[9] Even one man's defection from an evasion group could suffice to expose a larger design. Information useful to an inspectorate would include not only past actions but plans for future behavior. This could include evidence on underground organizations, their members, rules, plans, and time schedules.

Would the Public Support Inspection by the People?

Obviously, a key aspect of this method is the requirement that a wide section of the public be prepared to report their own countrymen in the interest of protecting the disarmament agreement as man's shield against war and for a peaceful life. In 1958 a special survey of public opinion in six countries was carried out (mainly by the American Institute of Public Opinion and its affiliates abroad) to discover public readiness to cooperate in inspection for disarmament in these countries. The full report of this survey was prepared by William Evan for the Columbia University study of *Inspection for Disarmament.*[10]

Three major questions in this international survey elicited extremely interesting and important responses.

> To the question, "Would you favor or oppose setting up a world-wide organization which would make sure, *by regular inspection,* that *no* nation, including Russia and the United States, makes hydrogen bombs, atom bombs, and missiles?" replies of the following percentages of the population were in favor:

United States	70 percent
Great Britain	72 percent
France	85 percent
West Germany	92 percent
India	78 percent
Japan	91 percent

To the question, "If this inspection organization were set up, would you favor or oppose making it each person's *duty* to report any attempt to secretly make atom bombs, hydrogen bombs, and missiles?" replies of the following percentages of the population were in favor:

United States	73 percent
Great Britain	54 percent
France	74 percent
West Germany	86 percent
India	71 percent
Japan	80 percent

To the question, "If you, yourself, knew that someone in (name of country) was secretly attempting to make forbidden weapons, would you report this to the office of the world-wide inspection organization in this country?" replies of the following percentages of the population were in favor:

United States	80 percent
Great Britain	50 percent
France	63 percent
West Germany	73 percent
India	63 percent
Japan	83 percent[11]

The results of this poll indicate that major proportions of the populations of these countries express a willingness to cooperate in inspection by the people. It may be reasonable to expect that a substantially smaller proportion than the number shown here would actually act in this way. It remains, however, that even if a very small minority in a population were prepared to report violation of disarmament, that would give great strength to an inspection system. Accordingly, these results add measurably to our confidence in the feasibility of these methods.

One of the most important results of the international poll of public opinion, and of special surveys conducted by William Evan, was the finding that scientists and engineers supported inspection by the people in larger proportion than did the general population.

Obviously, the American reader would want to know about the attitudes in the Soviet population toward questions of this sort. I do not know of any such public opinion polls in the Soviet Union. However, many persons who are knowledgeable about Soviet society, and several well-informed Soviet citizens (not government officials), have indicated to me that there is a high probability that the Soviet population would welcome participation in inspection by the people for disarmament. Such participation would be especially forthcoming if Soviet leaders were required to and did urge the population to cooperate. It may be significant that Khrushchev recently indicated that he would approve of an arrangement whereby the population of a country was invited to report on violations of disarmament to an international inspection organization.[12]

Effects of Inspection by the People

These methods would, I believe, immensely strengthen the whole process of protecting an international disarmament agreement. Every effort for evasion of the agreement would have to reckon with the likelihood of being exposed. Its people would have to operate in the constant knowledge that someone, anyone, might expose their activity to the international inspectorate. Clearly, the direction of effort would also include encouragement of supranational loyalty by every population.

Most important, perhaps, inspection by the people would contribute mightily toward giving general confidence that military activity as a mode of national policy is unnatural and unthinkable. This tendency would be a direct reversal of the whole pattern that has been built up during the last decade of the arms race. I regard the existence of groups of able, technically trained men, with readiness to use their knowledge for large-scale destruction, as the hard-core danger of the arms race. As the condition of society changes, and men who are so inclined find less approval for their type of activity, then that isolation of military thinking and practice serves as the final line of defense for mankind against warlike activity.

Once military activity, and evasion of disarmament, is widely regarded as unnatural and unthinkable, then the people who attempt such evasion would be regarded as "mad bombers" and treated accordingly—as the object of necessary police measures for protecting the whole community. A large-scale underground organization would be highly vulnerable to exposure under an inspection process that included inspection by the people. A small evasion organization consisting of no more than a handful of people might very well keep itself intact, and, under certain conditions, might try to score a political victory by threatening a military attack. The response of the society would be essentially different if these men represented another government, or represented an unknown power-seeking group of individuals. Under such extreme conditions, high social morale and a readiness to treat such an attempt as a police problem could make a major difference in the response of a community, and in readiness of secret plotters to make such an attempt. After all, the actions of people are not random. Capability for acting is in good measure controlled by what is regarded as reasonable and acceptable behavior.

Time is a major factor on the side of the inspection organization and against evasion. With the passage of time the original reasoning that gave force to the formation of evasion groups, and even to the preparation of secret arms caches, would lose strength. As disarmament proceeded, international arrangements would be developed which maintained a peaceful world while major disputes were settled through international machinery, and a United Nations force armed with police-type weapons would be available and functioning to preserve the peace. As the atmosphere that once justified an evasion organization changed, the readiness of the original evasion group to perform such action would also be affected. With the passage of time under disarmament, the whole point of evasion plots would gradually lose their force. As men in the evasion group died and had to be replaced, the difficulty of replacement would grow. Under conditions of the arms race, one can find, without great difficulty, men who are prepared to risk an evasion effort. If the arms race were terminated and disarmament became the operative condition, it would become more difficult to find such men.

None of this means that international competition of social systems would be curtailed. It would mean, however, that military methods of such competition would gradually tend to lose their force and their point.

In my opinion, negotiating inspection by the people as an early and integral part of disarmament would be a major contribution to the reliability of inspection systems. This becomes an important criterion in considering the framework of negotiation with the Soviets, even in the immediate future. Inspection by the people clearly involves a major break in internal security systems, and abrogation of major parts of long-cherished ideals of national sovereignty.

Inspection by the people can also be an important feature of special types of international disarmament arrangements. Thus, inspection by the people in the regional disarmament of Central Europe suggested by the Rapacki plan deserves special attention. The population of Eastern Europe, for example, would probably cooperate generously with an international inspection organization for disarmament of that area together with Germany.

Including provisions for inspection by the people in an international agreement should be one of the governing considerations of the agreement and of the frame of reference in which it is negotiated.

Conclusion

Present conditions include preparation for the destruction of entire populations, and all manner of evasive devices, as regular features of national policy. The strategy of disarmament is designed to change present conditions, by removing the proximate cause of the real threat to our very existence, and by replacing the war system for settling international disputes.

The core of our present danger is the willingness of so many people to regard evasive behavior for destructive ends as natural, laudable, and manageable. The strategy of disarmament is designed to cause evasion and destructiveness to be regarded as unnatural and reprehensible. It is the particular task of an inspection system to prevent any schemes for evasion. Inspection by the people is part of the process of causing members of an evasion group to be regarded not as patriotic heroes, but as "mad bombers," as enemies of the whole community. Under such conditions, a large evasion group could not remain long concealed, and even a small group would be subject to all of the moral and police powers which an intelligent and determined community can wield against "mad bombers."

It is a measure of the terrible and growing danger to mankind that we should have to regard such operations of madmen as part of the real dangers that we must now overcome. This brings home to us the nature of the choice before us: to continue the arms race with its sure result in a holocaust, or to undertake a process of leading men into peace, with its risks of evasion that come from the long practice of the arms race. I believe that all men who want to live, and are politically optimistic about the strength of freedom in society, will choose the latter course—with the knowledge that making it work will require and deserve the best alert intelligence that we can muster.

NOTES

1. S. Melman (ed.), *Inspection for Disarmament* (New York: Columbia University Press, 1958). See the reports of evasion teams A, B, and C.

2. From a report presented to the U.S. Senate Foreign Relations Committee by the Washington Center of Foreign Policy Research of the Johns Hopkins University. The principal authors of the report were Arnold Wolfers, Director of the Foreign Policy Research Unit, Paul H. Nitze, and James E. King, Jr. See *The New York Times,* December 6, 1959.

3. H. Kahn, *On Thermonuclear War* (Princeton: Princeton University Press, 1960), pp. 4–5.

4. Melman, *op. cit.,* pp. 27–30, 191–219. Two papers in this book concern underground military activities, in Germany under the Weimar Republic and in Palestine under the British mandate.

5. *Ibid.,* p. 27.

6. See the report of the evasion team in Melman, *op. cit.*

7. There are two papers of major importance for this field by Lewis C. Bohn: "Psychological Inspection," Paper No. P-1917, prepared for the Social Science Division of the Rand Corporation, February 19, 1960; and "Knowledge Detection: A Non-Physical Inspection Method for Arms Control," Lockheed Electronics Company, Systems Research Center, Bedminster, N.J., January 3, 1961. In these two papers, Bohn sets forth a highly imaginative analysis of the possibilities of controlling against evasion of disarmament by inspecting for knowledge which people have, as against direct inspection of physical objects and activities. Bohn has also given extensive discussion to the possibilities of developing sophisticated methods for discovering indications of knowledge withheld by individuals. See pp. 20–39 of this volume.

8. Professor Jay Orear has suggested that a most reliable method for checking against tampering with sealed letters would be microphotography of the letter-seal before mailing. This could be compared to the seal upon delivery and any attempt to open and then close the letter again would surely be revealed by imperfection in the second sealing.

9. Some of the people who have looked into these matters have concluded that the use of special truth-testing and information-seeking methods on government officials would be an important part of the operation of inspection organizations. From one standpoint, special controls on government officials may be justified by the assumption that an important evasion is unlikely without their knowledge and complicity. However, the use of methods of "psychological inspection" which would incorporate methods that have come to be regarded as police methods, could alienate the inspectorate from at least a part of the population. After all, police-type methods are not usually well regarded in the West and the attempt to use such methods in the Soviet sphere might very well alienate the population from the inspectorate, for many of the efforts of freedom-seeking people in the Soviet sphere have been precisely toward reducing the operation of such methods. For papers and discussions on such techniques, see "Non-Physical Inspection Techniques," American Academy of Arts and Sciences, Summer Study on Arms Control, 280 Newton Street, Boston 16, Massachusetts, 1961.

10. William M. Evan, "An International Public Opinion Poll on Disarmament and 'Inspection by the People': A Study of Attitudes Toward Supranationalism," in Melman, *op. cit.,* pp. 231 ff.

11. Melman, *op. cit.,* pp. 42–3.

12. *The New York Times,* September 27, 1960.

TRUTH DETECTION

By RALPH W. GERARD

THE ARGUMENT IS SIMPLE: given matched power, at any level from maximal armament to none at all, opposing nations will resort to actual warfare overwhelmingly as a result of mistrust of the other or of misunderstanding resulting from false information—either suspected or actual.[1]

My solution is to insure that public or other official statements made by key figures are indeed true. This can be done with available lie-detection techniques if national leaders will submit to them. Given an agreement to try, the operational procedures and instrumental techniques could readily be tested and perfected in real life situations of lesser moment than international warfare.

The resounding close to Archibald MacLeish's preamble to the charter of UNESCO, "Since wars begin in the minds of men, it is in the minds of men that the defenses of peace must be erected," is no less true for having become hackneyed. Wars generate and develop and are released from the minds of men, and their objective is to change the minds of other men. Wars are always the result of opposed wills and terminate when one will yields to the other. Death and destruction are unfortunate concomitants to the goal of making an opponent change his mind. Subversion, trickery, threat, political intrigue, riot, and revolution—all the familiar techniques studied and used by revolutionaries throughout time—may serve the same ends, and sometimes less disastrously. Above outright villainy come the techniques of rabble-rousing, propaganda and hidden persuasion, and the adroit use of mass communication techniques. As behavioral science increasingly reveals (as it rapidly is doing) the springs of human behavior and the means of manipulating them, including the direct attack on the brain by drugs and electrodes and other well-understood biological channels, it will become progressively easier to control men's desires and behaviors.

If men are not successfully induced or seduced into reasonably peaceful situations, when conflicting wills and interests remain insufficiently resolved, resolution of the conflict by force is the eventual outcome. Force cannot be equated, however, with nuclear weapons nor with missile control and range nor with any combination of these and other triumphs of physical science. Other sciences have also offered, and are further developing, their own means of vast and terrible persuasion. The "nerve gases" of chemical warfare, the extraordinarily toxic products of bacteria, even more the possibility of disseminating live virulent organisms able to kill off plant or animal life in great areas, make any solution of world stress limited to atom bomb control an untenable one.

Limitations of Alternative Proposals

Physicists are now quarrelling about the possibility of detection of bomb explosions, and intergovernmental conferences are haggling over the conditions of disarmament and inspection for carrying out such agreements. A solution along hardware lines seems doomed to failure, because of the continuous emergence of new devices and because of the continuing game of each antagonist outsmarting the other. No matter how extensive and practiced the security measures, prisoners continue to escape from jails, and disturbed children to evade control. Attack and defense, move and countermove, cross and doublecross allow the game to go on indefinitely.

If the control of weapon development is unrealistic, what about some regulation of their use? The proposal that a mathematics of destruction be agreed upon—if you bomb Minneapolis I may bomb Minsk, without further retaliation—is psychologically unrealistic. When emotions are raised to the destruction of one major city they will not ebb with the counter-destruction of another. Given, again, a real equality of power (or what is effectively the same thing, the power for total destruction of the enemy, and the ability to release a counterblow after receiving an initial one) no rational man or nation would throw his boomerang.

Alas, most human behavior is irrational, and even rational judgments are subject to error. Unbalanced or insane individuals or groups have come to power in human history, men and mobs have committed incredible acts on the swell of emotions—anger, fear, despair, even exuberant abandon. The ruthless egotist is rather likely to ascend the power ladder and, at the showdown, is often enough willing to yield his life rather than his goal, let alone the lives of others. And even men well within the range of normal can be misinformed, or misperceive, or misinterpret an event—especially under conditions of heightened fear and mistrust. So did Othello come to choke Desdemona.

Some see safety in increasing the membership of the atoms club. That not two or four but dozens of nations own and can deliver the atom bomb is seen as a deterrent to action by any one. I see only increased opportunity for a fatal blunder as more potential blunderers are on the scene. If lethal retaliation by one country is possible, what more can be added by further attack by others? If Castro had nuclear weapons at his disposal would this constitute an additional restraint on Russia and the United States, or would there be just a trigger-happy source of danger thrown in?

International controls and a United Nations police force? In principle, certainly fine; but always potentially dangerous and seemingly impracticable at present. There is always the question of who shaves the barber; when one *force majeure* exists, human beings are still in control of it and what is to prevent their usurpation of this naked power for their own purposes? This is the recurring experience of Latin America, where the military turns on the state it is supposed to protect. But such military or police revolutions are rare in North America and Western Europe.

Certainly efforts to discover the controlling factors and to achieve and apply new political and social inventions are of high desirability; but I cannot feel that any result will come soon enough to have a practicable impact in the desperate decades ahead of us. This stricture applies to such concrete suggestions as the following:

1. Instead of mass warfare, abide by the outcome of a limited combat, Hector-Achilles type of solution, on the sport field, over the chessboard, in the actual gladiatorial arena, or what not. Nonsense! Exchange members of the families of the rulers of hostile nations; allow opponents' inspection teams to destroy any violating installations; have an enemy observer sit in the decision-making centers of each country so as to be able to relay back immediate warning of any missile release, etc., etc. These are all gamesmanship moves and all can be circumvented.

2. Manipulate the brains of whole populations, by pills and the like, so as to prevent the build-up of hostile emotions. Perhaps scientifically possible; socially and politically unrealistic and probably unenforceable.

3. Allow individuals in any country to sacrifice national citizenship and voting rights and taxability in favor of United Nations citizenship and vote and taxes. A well-directed political invention; but possible, if at all, only in the far future and with many additional adjustments.

4. Manipulations of the communication channels in various ways —turn over the communication media to an opposing control when war tension reaches a certain measurable level, raise standards of truthfulness and coverage in the mass media, condition the citizenry toward action for the good of mankind rather than for more selfish national goals so that negotiators could no more act selfishly than they could appear without clothes on. All these are goals rather than means; they are not presently possible and are even theoretically dubious.

A brief digression is now necessary, before considering a more promising approach. A pivotal issue in the raging public debate on nuclear warfare is, "What price freedom?" Violent polar positions have been taken by outstanding men from all areas of human excellence. Patrick Henry said, whether or not he meant it, "Give me liberty or give me death." In unvarnished terms, freedom for me means getting my way, just as freedom for you involves getting yours. If our ways are in opposition, some freedom must be lost. If a person wants his way badly enough, and is willing to sacrifice enough for it, he is likely to get it. The bantam fighter who tears in without thought of pain or odds often enough whips his heftier opponent. The ferocious vole attacks and kills animals many fold its size and strength. An animal, cat or rat or monkey, low in the pecking order of its group, will rapidly rise to the top after a brain operation that makes it more ferocious. The story of the Black Connallys of Canada (or that of the Doones of Devonshire) exemplifies an entirely comparable socially induced ferocity, and success.

I am satisfied that the wild and tough animal or man or nation, willing to pay the greater price to get its way, will mostly overcome the tamer and more civilized. Only two or three things can prevent it: (1) biological manipulation or social reconditioning of the aggressor; (2) greater power at the disposal of the tamer antagonist; and perhaps (3) the certain knowledge of death or annihilation to the one who starts the fight. The first solution is far in the future; the second cannot hold when more than one nation has the ability to wreak total destruction on the other; the third returns to the problem of belief.

I have often thought of a Bret Harte story that perfectly illustrates the point. Two pals in a village in the old West were crack shots, a great influence for good and beloved of their townsmen. A minor quarrel sprang up between them, grew into a feud, and culminated in a challenge to a duel. Their many friends tried in vain to dissuade them and the whole town turned out unhappily at the appointed rendezvous. The sheriff made a last minute plea. "Bill and Jack, you are good men and really good friends, and you are damn good shots. You know perfectly well that at ten paces you will both fall dead on the word 'fire.' " They remained adamant; honor demanded satisfaction. "Well," said the sheriff, "I can't stop you; but if it does happen that one of you is alive at the end, I swear as sheriff of this township to string him up then and there for murder." The duel was called off.

The problem here is to create such an inescapable power or, if it exists, to convince the potential aggressor that it is there and will be used—whether by the attacked nation or by a United Nations is immaterial. And, even then, as a wild animal may kill itself in trying to escape or as Samson pulled down the temple of the Philistines upon his own body, there may still be situations in which nations would commit suicide.

I think the direction toward a real solution must be not by countervailing force or guile or other move in the strategy of overcoming the opponent; the hope, rather, is in decreasing and eliminating the gamesmanship. Conflicting interests there will always be; the problem is the manner in which they are handled. A few wild men will always appear on the world scene, but unless large masses of men go with them—in which case the situation is indeed hopeless—these can be controlled by force by the greater society, if they are identified in time. Just so are the criminal and insane forcefully controlled by their larger societies. The problem is to identify individuals with hurtful goals and methods. So far as aberrant individuals are concerned, they are relatively few in number and can be identified with reasonable success by available scientific resources of behavioral science, especially psychiatry. It seems not entirely quixotic to expect the leaders of major nations to subject themselves to psychiatric examination by an international panel of psychiatrists at the time of taking office and at occasional intervals thereafter. Their reports could at least give warning to the rest of the world of impending trouble. But this proposal is only on the margin of feasibility and, fortunately, would be important only at the fringe level. A much simpler, more dependable and acceptable, and easily instituted applied maneuver is the heart of my proposal.

Potentialities of Truth Detection

It is possible today, by simply attaching a few measuring instruments to the surface of the body, to detect a deliberate lie. The polygraph has had a wide and increasing success in crime detection, although relatively little scientific effort has been devoted to this field. Besides respiration and heart rate and blood pressure, regularly used, such other physiological responses as skin resistance and potential, pupillary size, muscle tension, eye blinks, brain waves, and so on, register emotional responses of a person. A detailed analysis of vascular and respiratory responses, involving not only over-all rate and amplitude and shape of the waves in the continuing train, but also the changes in individual waves or groups in relation to particular questions, or other situations, yields a plethora of information. An inversion of the galvanic skin response, an early phasing of waves from the front of the brain,[2] increased pupil and lid responses, are related to certain emotional states, and could be harnessed for further differentiation. And the whole situation can be further shifted by innocuous drugs in particular cases.

Although lie detection has found its greatest use so far in crime detection, many other areas have been touched with highly promising results; indeed, one of the early applications was to the psychiatric examination and treatment of problem children.[3] These techniques have been used successfully in personnel selection, performance checking, claim examination, and the like, by banks, merchandisers, insurance firms, and others.

A department store, suffering great losses from petty thieving, had all employees take a polygraph test. They were told that this was to convince them of its efficacy, and the findings would remain confidential but that the test would be repeated in six months and would then be the basis for action. On the first test, three-fourths of the workers were found to be pilfering; the subjects must have been convinced of its effectiveness, for on the second round only 3 percent showed guilt.[4] In straight criminal work results have been outstanding; Inbau and Reid[5] report a series of over 4,000 cases, over 95 percent of which were definitively and accurately judged guilty or innocent. Only three cases were known to be in error.[6]

The main limitations in the technique are associated with a general physiological sluggishness of all responses or with an emotional indifference when the test is not really important to the subject. Both of these can be overcome in many instances by existing maneuvers,[7] and there is no reason to doubt that further research could encompass essentially all situations.

The broad problem is to "titrate" human beings so that the inner state can be assessed in other ways than by the spoken word. The flush of anger or cold sweat of fear are familiar indices; and experienced "menschenkenners," let alone trained psychiatrists, become expert at reading the paralanguage of the body. A labor negotiator knew when he had pushed his bargaining opponent to the last concession by observing pulsations in a neck vessel. In a group of hospital patients it proved possible for six observers to rank some thirty individuals for anxiety level; the raters agreed with fantastic accuracy ($P<.001$) and were checked by an entirely objective drug test.[8] All such measures, plus judicious interview and questioning techniques, can certainly be developed far beyond their present efficiency. Probably at present, certainly in the immediate future with an appropriate effort, adequate lie-detecting techniques are or will be available.

As stated, such techniques cover only conscious lies. A psychotic, with the delusion that he was George Washington but knowing that the others did not accept this, replied "No" when directly asked if he were George Washington—and the polygraph showed he was lying! But such situations occur in the truly psychotic; even hardened criminals, with very distorted value hierarchies, are caught up by the lie detectors. To what extent a zealot, starting with deliberate falsification, may come to really believe his oft-repeated lies, and how such pseudo-truth can be exposed remain to be explored. I am satisfied that wise testing would reveal the situation, would probably expose particular misstatements, and would point to other persons or cases in which certain answers could be obtained.

The proposal is simply this: all key men, speaking officially for their country in private negotiations or public addresses, subject themselves to lie-, or better, truth-detection procedures administered by technicians from an opposing country or from the UN. More positively, when a statesman wished to convince the world that he was making a true statement he would subject himself to truth detection.

Since each antagonist would be able to tell very soon when his own lies were caught, he would soon develop confidence in a technique that revealed them. With growing conviction that false statements would be caught up, spokesmen would tell the truth publicly and their hearers would come to have some trust in the truth of these statements. Do not misunderstand. I am not suggesting that a country can have no secrets from another or that governmental conversations be "bugged." All that is necessary is that statements made to the public or to the adversary be certified as true. In the heat of a speech, one may well make untrue statements and believe them; but this self-hypnosis will not endure through a lie-detection interview. Here the public statements can be explored and their truthfulness determined. If the speaker chooses to refuse an answer to a question, this would also be revealing, as when certain witnesses in our courts have taken the Fifth Amendment.

Even true lack of knowledge can be noted and made a point of departure. Physics and engineering cannot quite detect the explosion of an atom bomb underground. But if a head of state declares that no bomb tests are being made and also gives the source of his information with proven veracity, then his source, say the head of a nuclear development program, can also be queried on the same point. If those who know assert, truly, that no tests have been made, no tests *have* been made. But in many cases the issue is simpler and sharper; Kuznetsov or Lodge must have been knowingly lying before the UN on what happened when our RB-47 plane was shot down by Russia in Arctic waters.

Conclusion

Whether the lie-detector technique or another device be agreed upon, it is not necessary to wait for world-wide acceptance before moving. These techniques could be applied at once to less universal and vital situations, and so their possibilities and limitations can be discovered and improvements made. Labor relations decisions, chancery decisions in court, legislative hassles, even lesser international disagreements—as over the twelve-mile territorial limit—could be handled with such techniques on an experimental basis.

My assumption is that men are overwhelmingly of good will, that altruism at least balances selfishness, and that most fracases result less from legitimate conflict of interest than from exaggerated mistrust and fear and the resultant counter-measures. I have presented elsewhere[9] at length the evidence for these convictions. Unless cooperation among individuals exceeds conflict, no group or society can survive; and the whole panorama of evolution documents the survival value of cooperation and altruism and its progressive increase in the living world. I do not know whether war is inevitable or not; but the only sensible approach to the problem is to assume that sooner or later it can be eliminated from human action. The other assumption leads only to a fatalistic surrender to annihilation as man comes to exercise ever greater control over the energy and material resources of his world. Man differs from all other animals in the effectiveness of his cerebral cortex, the tool of reasoned behavior; I cannot but believe that a mastery of man comparable to mastery of nature will allow men to live together rather than die together.*

* This paper, written originally for the present volume, was published in *The Journal of Conflict Resolution* (V [1961], pp. 212–17), with the generous consent of the volume editors. The manuscript was also circulated earlier and, by one avenue or another (including some personal effort in Washington), the government became interested in further exploration of the ideas here presented. Further, correspondence soon revealed that the idea was not entirely novel; Bohn (in D. G. Brennan [ed.], *Arms Control, Disarmament, and National Security* [New York: George Braziller, 1961]), Orear ("A New Approach to Inspection," *Bulletin of the Atomic Scientists,* XVII [1961], pp. 107–10), and

NOTES

1. "Truth is too precious a commodity to be bandied about lightly; it is rather a courtesy reserved for one's friends" (Townsend Harris, ca. 1860).

2. C. W. Darrow, J. P. Wilson, R. N. Vieth, and J. M. Maller, *Acceleration and Momentum in Cerebral Function Reflected in EEG Phase Relations: Recent Advances in Biological Psychiatry* (New York: Grune and Stratton, 1960, pp. 51–9.

3. J. A. Larson and G. W. Haney, "Cardio-Respiratory Variations in Personality Studies," *The American Journal of Psychiatry,* XI (1932), pp. 1035–81.

4. C. D. Lee, *The Instrumental Detection of Deception: The Lie Test* (Springfield, Ill.: Charles C Thomas, 1935).

5. F. W. Inbau and J. E. Reid, "Lie Detection," *The American Journal of Police Science,* XXX (1939), pp. 848–81, and *Journal of Criminal Law and Criminology,* XXIX (1939), pp. 104–19.

6. D. L. Lykken distinguishes "guilt detection" from "lie detection" and reports full accuracy for the former in "The Validity of the Guilty Knowledge Technique: The Effects of Faking," *Journal of Applied Psychology,* XLIV (1960), pp. 258–62.

7. See Lee, *op. cit.*

---

others had considered lie detection in connection with "nonphysical" inspection methods.

This subject is now being studied by interested workers in many fields. The subjects which have been examined are: lie-detection techniques; their use in arms inspection procedures; and their modification to permit a statesman to demonstrate the truth or sincerity of his statements. On the technique side, there is a strong feeling that both the instrumental and the interview facets are now quite satisfactory, perhaps at the 95 percent level of confidence, and can be further improved in precision and extent of application by a modest research program. For inspection procedures, there is enthusiasm for the lie-detection technique on all counts—cost, speed, flexibility, acceptability, and reliability. Used on a population sample, reliability probably could be pushed to any desired level (certainly far beyond that attainable by physical inspection methods now in sight) without excessive cost.

The use of various physiological responses (galvanic skin reaction, pulse rate, respiration, blood pressure, etc.—the mainstays of lie detection) to permit a subject to demonstrate the subjective truth, or sincerity, of his statements is quite different from lie detection. A single person will usually be involved, he wishes the truth to come out rather than to be hidden, the antagonist or some neutral group would be invited to make the test, major national figures would be involved, etc. With the many aspects not yet explored, the experts examining this use are more reserved than are the other groups; but here, also, the judgment is definitely that this approach deserves prompt exploration.

8. R. W. Gerard, "The Schizophrenia and Psychopharmacology Project," *Proceedings* of the 1959 Detroit Divisional Meeting of the American Psychiatric Association, 1960.

9. R. W. Gerard, "The Biology of Ethics," *Society and Medicine,* No. 17 of the New York Academy of Medicine Lectures to the Laity (New York: International Universities Press, 1955), pp. 20–45.

COMMUNICATIONS,

ARMS INSPECTION, AND NATIONAL SECURITY

By KARL W. DEUTSCH

IT IS BECOMING QUITE WIDELY RECOGNIZED that any decision about the acceptance or rejection of any scheme of international arms limitation and inspection involves the balancing of two types of risk. One class of risks consists of those incurred from continuing a competitive policy of national armaments without any limitation or inspection, formal or informal. Since a growing number of countries are very likely to acquire during the 1960's a supply of nuclear weapons and eventually the means for their delivery, these risks must be considered as not only substantial but growing.[1] The second class of risks consists of those incurred from complying in good faith with an agreed-on policy of arms limitation and inspection—the risk of being deceived by other powers who might sign the agreement and promise to conform to it without in fact doing so. In the total absence of inspection risks of the second kind could be vast; in the presence of some inspection arrangements they would be smaller but would still remain real. It seems very likely that there is no inspection agreement—nor any physical or political method of inspection—under which these risks of inspection could be reduced to zero.[2]

If these considerations are valid, then there is no policy available to the government of the United States, nor to the government of any other major power, that would be completely free from risk. The best that could be done would be to select that policy that promises to be appreciably less risky than its alternatives. The risks of a continuing policy of competitive armaments, including the risks of the entry of additional countries, the risks of misunderstanding and false alarms through failures of personnel or electronic equipment, the risks of political crises or the coming to power of extremist leaders in some country, and other risks of this general kind might be considered as growing and as exceedingly hard to control. In the absence of any international agreement there is little the United States could do about reducing these risks in the case of another country, though we could do something to keep these risks as small as possible within our own political and military establishment.

The risks from the inadequacies or malfunctioning of an international inspection system, on the other hand, including the risks of deliberate evasion, could be reduced to some extent by making any international arms limitation or inspection agreement as realistic as possible. The following pages are dedicated to suggesting in rough outline some policy considerations that might be useful for making international arms limitation and inspection somewhat more effective and somewhat harder to evade, and, it is hoped, to make it a policy that would be safer to pursue in the interests of the United States than its alternative of relatively unchecked qualitative and quantitative competition in the field of armaments.[3]

Starting from this background we may ask: What kinds of arms limitations might come to be agreed on by the main powers, and policed by a mutual inspection system, capable of giving all participants early warning of any large-scale violations?

Possibilities of Arms Limitation and Inspection

One possible agreement might consist in limiting all major powers, and the lesser ones as well, to quotas of rockets suitable for the delivery of nuclear weapons. These quotas would have to be kept well below the saturation level for any large country. In other words, if a country should decide to use some rockets in violation of the agreement and if it should choose to equip them with warheads, the arms-limitation agreement might have seen to it that there might not be sufficient rockets available for completely saturating any major country that might be chosen as a victim of attack. In pursuit of the same goal, the agreement might well specify that no nuclear warheads may be installed in rockets, that no practice and training flights with nuclear weapons may be undertaken, and that stockpiles of warheads might be limited to stringently inspected quotas. An important part of any such agreement would consist in having no nuclear warheads in any objects put into outer space by any power.

Other parts of the agreement might specify that no organized target files, guidance grids, and other paraphernalia for the effective direction of nuclear bombardment would be maintained by any major power. Finally, and perhaps most significantly, the participating countries would undertake not to maintain any large organized military rocket forces or other military forces above certain agreed-on levels of capabilities.

The over-all result of such measures should be to leave no country with a capability of waging total war quickly after it had begun to violate the agreement, but to force any violating country to spend considerable time in acquiring the needed capabilities for large-scale nuclear war, so as to give other countries ample warning time of the threat confronting them. Given such warning time, other countries would, of course, prepare for countermeasures of defense or retaliation against the violator; and after the arms race had been resumed by all the major powers, the world might be not much worse off than it is now or than it would be by, say, 1984 if no scheme for arms limitation had been attempted.

Under the conditions just envisaged, much would depend upon the competence and effectiveness of the inspection system. If such a system should be enforced by 1984, it might well have developed from its beginnings as a system of inspection by professional staffs, recruited in considerable part from the military, police, and intelligence forces of the participating powers. Inspection within each country might be carried out either by mixed teams, recruited in terms of parity between the home country and foreign countries, or in accordance with some other agreed-on formula for composition. An alternative would be reciprocal inspection under which, for instance, American teams would carry on in the main the inspection in Russia, and Russian teams in the main inspection in the United States. Compromises between reciprocity and mixed inspection teams might well develop, but the principles of parity and reciprocity—in contrast to any as yet unacceptable schemes of majority voting—would remain essential.

The main object of inspection, in any case, would be maintenance of mutual confidence so that no country would be tempted to return to the arms race. The sanction would be, of course, the loss of such confidence. A power dissatisfied with the results of the inspection system, or with what it might consider the imperfect degree of compliance of some other country, would have a double problem. It would have to make credible its own threat of withdrawing from the arms limitation agreement and of resuming the arms race; and it would at the same time have to convince its rivals that it had not merely seized on a pretext in order to take up a course which it had desired in any case. The diplomatic problems thus posed to any great power might be difficult, but they should not be insuperable. If the scheme should have succeeded for a number of years, governments and peoples by 1984 might well have come to take it seriously, as well as to take seriously the complaints or objections of any nation suspicious of violations on the part of its rivals.

The technical capabilities of inspection teams might well be increased by 1984 by further developments in such areas as reconnaissance satellites, infrared photography, the analysis of seismograph readings, and other techniques of this kind. The greatest increase, however, in the capabilities of inspection teams, or of an agreed-on inspection authority of the type of the United Nations (with powers limited to reporting and recommendations, and with sanctions through threats of national returns to the arms race limited to the major powers) would consist in a shift of emphasis in regard to the activities inspected.

Possibilities of Inspecting the Social and Communication Aspects of Armament

The concealment of hardware is a technical problem, and it may be one that might actually have become somewhat easier by 1984, for instance by means of putting some installations under the surface of the ocean on the continental shelves, or putting them on space objects in orbit around the earth. Detection, on the other hand, is also a technical process, and we have already suggested that its efficiency in at least some respects is very likely to increase. The large-scale preparation of war, however, is a social process and so would be its concealment. Neither of these social processes will be particularly facilitated by technical developments. Rather it should on the whole become easier, as time goes on, to detect major changes in the activities and communications of a large community, such as a modern industrial nation. In order to be successful, arms inspections, therefore, will have to be an activity carried out by professional teams but oriented in significant part to the monitoring of human relations and social activities.

Clandestine preparations for large-scale war may well require major preparations in the climate of opinion and legitimacy within the country carrying on these violations of its arms-limitation agreement. The presence or absence of such psychological preparation can be readily monitored from the statistical analysis of the content of mass media of communication, as well as of the materials used in the institutions of indoctrination within each country, such as schools, armies, police forces, national service organizations, and the rest.

Content analysis of mass media might well center on three points. The first of these would be the absence of excessive amounts of inflammatory material. This might involve an agreement of putting quotas on the amount of space which the mass media in each country might devote to particular controversies or disputes. This might relate in particular to space on the front pages of newspapers, lead bulletins in broadcasts, prime viewing time on television, and so on. The upshot of this might be an agreement to maintain in all countries freedom to whisper, but not freedom to shout. Each country, in other words, might well be limited to devoting not more than 2 percent of its news space on any day and not more than 1 percent of its news space during any week to controversies focused on any one particular country, and these limitations might then hold for each particular newspaper or broadcasting station in the country. A consistent violation of these quotas, perhaps by hammering on one particular inflammatory incident or chain of incidents, or on a succession of different quarrels with the same country, could hardly fail to come to the attention of inspectors. If persisted in, this practice in itself would provide the early warning of an impending violation of the arms-limitation agreement which the inspection system is designed to provide.

In the United States, a policy of limiting the freedom of the press to engage in an inflammatory *volume* and *manner* of expression, in a potentially dangerous situation of international conflict, would raise constitutional issues similar to those referred to by Justice Holmes when he said that no man who shouted "Fire!" in a crowded theater could invoke the constitutional freedom of speech. As this well-known "clear and present danger" doctrine (cf. *Schenck* vs. *United States,* 249 U.S. 47, 1919) suggests, the American constitutional tradition would have ample means of invoking legal remedies to defend the public interest against the irresponsible and inflammatory use of mass media of communication in situations that could lead to thermonuclear war and vast tragedy for the American people. Radio and television stations are legally held to even closer limits of responsibility, insofar as they must show that they have been using their allocated channel frequencies in the public interest, when their licenses are to be renewed.

The question would be one of will and motivation to use the legal means of control that are available. Given this desire on the part of the government and of a substantial part of the community, experience shows that even informal suggestions as to what the mass media should or should not play up in the national interest have a way of being heeded to a remarkable extent by the bulk of American newspapers and radio and television networks. If all these safeguards should fail, the President and the administration could still fulfill the United States commitment to moderate any large-scale domestic agitation, by explicitly appealing to the people, as well as by deliberately "making news" and creating alternative foci of attention. Finally, if not even this remedy should prove effective, the violation of the agreed-upon quantitative threshold in the mass media would at least provide an early warning to all parties concerned.

A corollary of this inspection of mass media and of institutions of indoctrination might consist in an agreement to make it illegitimate to advocate violations of the agreement or to conceal them. Individuals might thus be taught by their own governments, acting in concert with their partners to the arms-limitation agreement, that it was their duty to refrain from advocating violations, as well as their duty to denounce any violations of which they should acquire knowledge. A number of opinion polls held in different countries on the question of "inspection by the people" have disclosed among all audiences, including samples of members of the American Legion, a sufficiently high number of people who expressed their willingness to denounce any violations even on the part of their own government, of which they should gain knowledge, to make it very unlikely that any large-scale violations could be carried on in secret for any length of time. Another corollary of the same type of agreement would be the passing of national legislation in all participant countries making it explicitly legitimate to disclose any relevant facts or doubts to inspectors. Suitable offices of such inspectors, perhaps under the United Nations, might well be maintained in most of the scientific and industrial centers of the participating countries.

Another corollary might be an agreement providing not only for the absence of objectionable material from the mass media of communication in the participating countries but also providing for the presence of material agreed on as helpful to their implementation. Such material, setting forth either the obligation of compliance or the undesirability of violation, might well be carried in the national media of each country over the signature or with the picture of the leaders of the national government and in conjunction with the strongest symbols of political legitimacy accepted in that country. That is to say, the obligation to comply with inspection agreements might have to be publicized within the Soviet Union as a resolution of the Politburo, and embodied in the May Day slogans and in all similar ceremonial settings; in England it might be made a part of the annual speech from the throne; in the United States it might be carried by Presidential proclamation and Congressional resolution.

An agreement to pass suitable national laws, implementing the illegality of concealment and the legitimacy of denunciation of all secret armaments, might be further supplemented by such ancient devices as that of having all judges, as well as all offices of the armed forces and police forces of the participating countries, take a specific oath to uphold the arms limitation agreements.

None of all these and similar devices, singly or together, will insure complete compliance, but they might go very far indeed in facilitating timely leaks, so as to permit the system to fulfill adequately its early-warning function. By making it so extremely unlikely, furthermore, that any large-scale violation could be carried on in secrecy for any great length of time, these measures might very well discourage would-be violators from attempting any such practices.

Mobility of Scientific Personnel as an Aid to International Inspection

Another part of the arms-limitation and inspection agreements might provide for the mutual or international registration of all scientific and technical personnel, such as perhaps all holders of the masters and doctors degrees in the natural sciences and of corresponding degrees of engineering. Professional inspectors might then be able to make sure, at least in the case of samples, of the whereabouts and the accessibility of scientific personnel. The agreement might then explicitly protect the scientist's freedom to travel and to gossip—two propensities which have long been the despair of security officers—and any attempt on the part of any country to conceal the whereabouts of its scientists, to keep them inaccessible to inspectors, or to interfere with their freedom of travel and communication, might serve as prima facie evidence of bad faith in the carrying out of the arms-limitation agreement, and might hence provide another item of early warning. Incidentally, any power proposing such international guaranties for the freedom of scientists might make it hard for its rivals to refuse to agree to them.

Other Control Techniques

Another method of inspection, already proposed by some Western governments in the 1950's, might be the inspection of budgetary allocations. The national incomes of the United States and the USSR were already sufficiently well known by 1959 to make it doubtful that the large percentages devoted in each of these countries to national defense would have been concealed for any great length of time. If the participating powers should agree to publicize their budgets and permit inspections in their budget-making organizations, in addition to agreeing gradually to shorten their work week and step up their spending on nonmilitary uses, either in terms of consumer goods or in productive or public-service installations of various types—it might become very difficult indeed to mobilize, segregate, and conceal the very large financial resources, as well as the large amounts of manpower and material, required for the preparation of total war.

All forms of inspection discussed thus far have been social, economic, or psychological, rather than being oriented toward military hardware. All of them could be made even more effective by agreements for widespread personnel interchange, particularly in the scientific fields, and in the budgetary organizations, among the participating powers. Conventional ground inspection or air and ground inspections by military experts, on a reciprocal or international basis, would then supplement the measures just outlined.

The Problems of Steps and of Spill-Over

Once in operation, the system would amount to the abolition of military secrecy in the participating countries. A complex, but not insoluble, problem would consist in finding an acceptable sequence of steps by which secrecy could be abolished in the participating countries at a time during which each of them still possessed the capability of utilizing the newly acquired knowledge of potential targets in the other countries for striking at one or more of its rivals.

The first steps should deal with matters that cannot be kept secret in any case, and that are thus practically self-inspecting. Agreements on the banning of nuclear weapons tests in the atmosphere, as well as agreements in regard to the content of mass media, the content of national indoctrination, and the general institutional apparatus of legitimacy and legality in all countries all might well lend themselves to implementation in the early stages. Mutual sample tests of opinions and attitudes in the participating countries, as well as the compilation of the personnel roster of scientists and technicians, might then follow. Budgetary controls might come still later, followed by controls of all new installations and all new output. Putting the inspection system into operation might then be completed finally by the disclosure of the last remaining older launching facilities and weapons stockpiles.

Another problem might be that of containing the possible spillover effects of the abolition of military secrecy into a possible erosion of other social, economic, and political institutions in the participating countries. This problem is likely to be minor in the case of the Western democracies, but may well be serious for a dictatorship such as the Soviet Union. If the system were worked in such a way as to convince the Soviets that they must either continue the arms race, or else sacrifice their type of dictatorship and substitute for it a Western-style private enterprise democracy with complete freedom of the press and freedom of private-interest organizations, they might very well prefer an arms race, somewhat as the governing elites of some other countries might feel, if they should come to believe that the inspection system were used as a lever to force otherwise unacceptable social and political changes upon them. There seems no reason to assume, however, that such difficulties will prove insuperable. It should be possible for the participating powers to develop an inspection system, and particularly an inspection staff, that would concentrate on the business of inspecting and not attempt to reform from the outside the societies which it would be trying to keep from returning to an arms race.

Some Possible Areas for Experimentation and Research

Even under the best conditions, however, schemes for agreed-on arms limitation and inspection will require a good deal of experience, which might best be acquired by carrying on some experiments among like-minded powers within the Western community of nations. This might hold in particular in regard to such matters as the content of mass media, the registration and interchange of scientific personnel, and the disclosure of budgetary data.

In regard to all these matters, more knowledge will be needed. From the perspective of 1961, five areas for desirable studies seem indicated as an aid for a better understanding of the problems of 1984:

1. A study of capabilities in fundamental science and in technological application and innovation, in regard to the probable rapid increase in scientific opportunities resulting from activities in outer space.

2. Problems of reciprocal or automatic inspection systems, as regards the technological aspects of such inspections.

3. Problems of social and political inspection, through such techniques as media surveys, monitoring of legitimacy and loyalty of institutions and practices, and the allocation of economic resources to unconcealed locations and uses.

4. Registration, inspection, freedom of mobility, and interchange of scientific personnel.

5. Experiments in regard to both supranational and reciprocal experiments or arrangements in regard to arms limitations, as well as to the joint conduct of nuclear, scientific, and space activities among like-minded countries within the Western bloc of nations, but includ-

ing notably the United States. Studies as to the possible feasibility and the expectable problems resulting from such arrangements between the United States and its closest allies, might go far to throw some light on the problems to be expected in the negotiation, as well as the putting into practice of any agreements, however limited, with less like-minded powers.

The scientific and technological opportunities of 1984 will have demanded in all likelihood a substantial expansion of our capabilities in science and technology. The problem of coping with some of the political consequences of these changes may well require a substantial increase in our capabilities in the field of social science.

Some Problems of United States Security Policy for 1961–1985

Such an inspection policy would be compatible with American national security and strength.

Perhaps the most effective way of strengthening United States security in the space age might consist in amplifying the scientific and innovating capabilities of the United States by a very substantial margin. This policy might be supplemented then by substantial improvements in early-warning capabilities, and by deep-shelter programs for substantial parts of the civilian population. The increase in capabilities for scientific research and technical innovation, however, might well be decisive in the long run. The basic principle for such a policy of raising national capabilities might well be the notion that the learning capacity of a society is in some way proportional to that proportion of its resources that has remained available for a wide range of recommitments, such as might be suggested by future information as soon as it becomes available.

Possible steps toward accomplishing this increase in such capabilities might well form suitable topics for research. Such possible steps might include the following:

1. A substantial enlargement of the pool of trained scientific talent in the United States by means of broad practices of early talent identification and broad fundamental training. This would be a policy aimed at maintaining a relative abundance of high-level technical talent, so as to permit the country to afford giving its young scientists several years of broad fundamental training before letting them commit themselves to specialized applications. It would thus be the opposite of recent Soviet policies, which still appear to have been tailored to a situation of a relative shortage of technicians and which seem to

have emphasized very early specialized training for relatively narrow applications.

2. A change in the cultural and educational climate of the United States, particularly in regard to private and public education on the primary and secondary school levels. The climate to aim at would be one stressing scientific and cultural achievement (rather than minimizing it as a departure from general equalitarianism) but at the same time a climate stressing the values of playfulness and curiosity and supporting the intellectual forays of the young with well-founded expectations of early support and follow-up.

3. A partial shift of material resources from relatively sterile military end-products, such as nuclear warheads, bombardment rockets, tanks, etc., to intermediate capital goods that can make a contribution to the economic growth of a society and to its standard of living in peacetime, and that are available for recommitment to a wide range of different needs. Intermediate capital goods of this type might include power stations, machine tools, communication and transport facilities, etc.

Among such intermediate capital goods available for wide ranges of reallocation two categories should stand out:

4. A greatly enlarged scientific-instrumentation industry, capable of turning out a wide range of advanced scientific instruments at low cost to users. It might conceivably be worth while to shift some national resources, both capital and labor, from currently protected industries such as the wrist watch industry, to a program of federal support for the re-equipment of American universities, colleges, and secondary schools with a wide range of scientific and laboratory instruments, perhaps with the aid of an enlarged National Science Foundation. A by-product of such a program would be an increase in the pool of manpower trained in the use of scientifically advanced instruments.

An even more important category of intermediate capital goods might be found in:

5. Greatly increased capability and installations for electronic computation. Such electronic computing equipment might be developed beyond the current profitable applications of engineering and commercial bookkeeping and payrolls. In particular it might aim at developing a broader range of more flexible tools of thought, like electronic desk computers for designing trend graphs and distribution graphs, fitting and testing them against any set of data put into a computor, and extrapolating them for possible trends or other regularities. Other intellectual tools might be abundant and inexpensive electronic indexing and searching equipment, and cheaper, smaller,

and less clumsy devices to take the place of current punched-card techniques. The development of such devices would require the creation of large pools of very broadly trained programing personnel and of far broader and more readily accessible libraries of program routines.

The essential point of such a program would be a substantial increase in the intellectual capabilities of the United States, through creating the conditions for attaining a new level of intellectual teamwork between human beings and man-made computing, searching, and information-processing devices.[4]

None of these suggestions for a possible national security policy during the coming decades can be developed here, but each of the points just sketched might deserve some serious study.

NOTES

1. Howard Simons, "World-Wide Capabilities for Production and Control of Nuclear Weapons," *Daedalus* (Summer, 1959), pp. 385–409.

2. Seymour Melman (ed.), *Inspection for Disarmament* (New York: Columbia University Press, 1958).

3. Samuel P. Huntington, "Arms Race: Prerequisites and Results," *Public Policy: A Yearbook of the Graduate School of Public Administration* (Cambridge: Harvard University Press, 1958), pp. 41–86.

4. It is perhaps not an accident that some of the early suggestions in the area were made in 1945 by Vannevar Bush, who at the same time was very interested in the defense capabilities of the free world. See Bush, "That Men May Think," *Atlantic Monthly,* CLXXVI (July, 1945), 105–108, and his pamphlet, "Arms and Free Men," deriving from the same general period.

THE ARMED ARBITER

By ROBERT GOMER

THE LAST HALF-CENTURY has seen a radical change in the general attitude toward war. Most people take it for granted today that a peaceful solution of international conflicts is intrinsically desirable, and even aggressors pay at least lip service to this principle. The idea of some form of arms control as one of the requisites for maintaining peace has also been gaining ground.

While the desirability of arms control seems to be accepted in principle and as an abstract aim, like goodness, there is little unanimity on the possibility or even the desirability of achieving it now or soon. It is not enough to tell the world to disarm or face the consequences. It is necessary first of all to inquire whether arms control is really necessary for peace (there is a school which holds the opposite view) and if so to indicate how disarmament can be brought about. A clarification of what would be involved in disarmament should make it easier to see whether we really want arms control, and may provide a yardstick with which to measure present or future proposals.

Modern War

It has become a commonplace to assume that a major war now or in the near future would be destructive beyond anything hitherto imagined, but it may be well to examine its technical aspects in more detail. The weapons available for use in a general war now consist of fission and fusion devices, large and small, and of biological and chemical agents in addition to conventional high explosives. Some idea of the power of nuclear weapons can be gained from the fact that the total bomb load dropped on Germany in the Second World War was considerably less than the explosive capacity of a five-megaton bomb.

At present all the nuclear weapons can be delivered by manned aircraft and probably by intermediate-range ballistic missiles; massive delivery by ICBM's is universally expected to be a reality within a few years. The present large missiles require liquid fuels and large installations. From published reports it appears that newer ones like the *Minuteman* and *Polaris* will be solid-fuel devices, capable of being launched from mobile or hidden land or marine sites within minutes.

The defensive means in a modern major war can be divided roughly into three categories: active defense, passive defense, and counterforce. The first consists of destroying the enemy's offensive weapons after they have been launched—that is, shooting them down. The second consists of protecting oneself from their effects, and the third of destroying them at their source before they are fired. At present there does not seem to be any active defense against ballistic missiles and it does not seem likely, on general physical grounds, that an active defense is in sight, which cannot easily be saturated by sheer weight of numbers.

Counterforce depends on the ability to hit an enemy's offensive means before these can be put into action. Consequently speed is essential and it seems clear that only missiles with flight times of fifteen to thirty minutes provide any possibility of it. If they can reach their target without warning, missiles can be effective against all immobile unprotected installations of known location, such as bomber bases or fixed missile-launching sites. There are no physical reasons against potential increases in missile accuracy to the point where the missiles could provide counterforce even against hardened and dispersed sites, although direct hits and consequently a large number of missiles would be required.

At present there exists almost no large-scale passive defense against the direct effects of large nuclear weapons. It is probably impractical to protect more than small and isolated installations against blast, overpressure, and prompt radiation. Thus it seems unlikely that cities or present industrial complexes can or will be protected. On the other hand, it does seem feasible, at least in principle, to protect survivors of initial attacks against the radiation hazards of fallout. However, at least in the United States, only token steps have been taken or seem imminent.

In summary, it seems likely that both the USSR and the United States will possess in the near future offensive means capable of massive destruction of cities, unprotected populations, livestock, and crops. It seems unlikely that an active defense against these weapons will be devised in the foreseeable future, or that they can be destroyed at their sources before launching with a high degree of probability. Passive defense against primary effects of nuclear explosions seems possible only for very small installations and can be extended on a large scale only to protection from secondary effects.

In view of the above it must seem that a general war would or could result in the annihilation of a substantial fraction of the wealth and population of the participants and probably of the close by-standers as well. Estimates of the consequences of an all-out nuclear exchange between the United States and the Soviet Union involve casualties on the order of 50 to 100 million people on either side, not counting Europe, which might be almost completely destroyed in addition.

Deterrence and Stability

It might therefore be argued, as it has been, that the terrible consequences of an all-out nuclear war are adequate in themselves to prevent its occurrence if each side constitutes a sufficient threat to the other. Certainly this has been the case until now, but it is well to examine also the arguments against stability.

To begin with it is vitally necessary for both sides to keep up with each other in arms quality (and to some extent quantity) as long as the consequences of falling behind can be so lethal. Since technological developments are continually taking place, generally somewhat out of phase with planning, let alone production, temporary disparities in armaments are likely to occur cyclically. The first reaction of the lagging side is an increase in the quantity of its existing weapons until it can catch up with or surpass the other side in quality.

Since arms technology seems to be developing offensive or counterforce devices much more effectively than defensive ones, it may become increasingly hard to convince the other side of one's peaceful intentions. Weapons intended for deterrence and retaliation may look remarkably like the means of blackmail, surprise, or pre-emption. In fact, even purely defensive weapons, such as anti-ICBM devices, have definite offensive implications; if one is able, by active defense, to neutralize the opponent's deterrent threat, one can take the offensive.

Despite these facts it is often argued that these are the chances we must take and that the dangers of disarmament are even greater for the United States. These arguments boil down to the assumption that we are weaker than the Communist world, and that the possession of nuclear weapons restores the balance.

It is implicit in this reasoning that the nuclear stand-off between us and the USSR, which will likely come about in a few years if it has not come already, will provide enough mutual deterrence to prevent Communist adventures on a large scale.

Mutual deterrence may or may not be stable when only two powers possess modern weapons, but its stability is doubtful indeed when more than two can play at this game. It is quite conceivable that China would be perfectly willing to involve the United States and Russia in a major war if she were able to do so. If no way can be found of imposing controls, the binuclear power situation will certainly give way to a multinuclear situation.

Profits of Peace

It therefore seems reasonable to conclude that we have more to lose than to gain from a continuation of the arms race. It must be asked if this is also true of the Communist world, or at least of the Soviet Union. Much of the thinking in the United States has tended to regard the USSR solely in terms of our own fears, inevitably committed to an expansionist doctrine. We seem to regard the USSR as committed to world revolution, when her own interests may in fact be the opposite. She has entered the ranks of the "have" nations, abruptly and violently, but quite unequivocally. Her real problem, for many decades to come, is to cope with this change in status, to assimilate and digest it. Thus, her strongest desire must be for peace. Even if she could "win" a war, the absolute gains of peace far exceed any relative gains of "victory." Despite bluster and threats, there is mounting evidence that Khrushchev is very much aware of this fact.

This is not to say of course that given the opportunities to enlarge its sphere of influence, for instance in Africa, the USSR, like most other nations, would not seize them. It is not even implied that the USSR is not doing its best to create such opportunities. However, this is a far cry from the monomaniacal determination to enforce the triumph of Communism everywhere, even at the risk of war and annihilation, which is frequently attributed to the Soviet Union.

The situation seems to be quite different with China. However, it is well worth noting that China today is making all the noises the USSR made when she was weak and afraid. Thus, even if the Chinese mean every word they say now, increases in strength and security will have much the same effect as in the USSR. But this will take considerable time and there is a real danger that China will concentrate in the meantime on purely military strength. If she should succeed in acquiring, despite the USSR's quite obvious reluctance, nuclear weapons and long-range missiles while still belligerent, she might well involve us in a major war, even if the USSR stayed out of it.

Thus a strong case can be made that the USSR and America are continuing the arms race principally in fear of each other and that it would be to the advantage of both to come to an agreement before China becomes a nuclear power. If both sides were convinced of the desirability of arms control, it would still be impossible for them to disarm unilaterally, which is just what a power living up to any of the currently talked-about agreements would be doing as far as it could tell. The USSR is extremely reluctant to permit detailed inspection because she believes that one of her principal strategic advantages consists of being *terra incognita*. Further, there are probably no iron-clad inspection and detection systems even for the West. In any case, even if the USSR and America acted in good faith both would have to worry about nonsignatory nations.

A Control Proposal

It follows that both powers would have to retain strong safeguards for their security during and after disarmament before they could seriously consent to any control scheme. From the previous discussion it appears that the only reasonable safeguard is a strong deterrent threat. This paradox can be resolved if a third power can be found to whom both sides are willing to transfer the job of deterrence. Given this protection both sides could discard nuclear weapons, refrain from the race for more deadly weapons, and feel safe from residual sneak attacks.

To be effective the armed arbiter would have to meet the following requirements: he must command the trust of both sides, be capable of massive and prompt retaliation against any aggressor, be determined to retaliate, be impervious to surprise attack, be able to detect and identify aggression and have some inspection rights. It will prove illuminating to examine these points more carefully.

In order to have the trust of the USSR and the United States, the arbiter must be disinterested, free from ambitions, and not subject to undue pressure or manipulation by either side. This excludes immediately a multi-nation group, including the representatives or allies of the opponents, but there are a number of small countries with stable populations and relatively high economic standards whose principal interest is the prevention of a general war which would surely engulf them. The Scandinavian countries, Switzerland, and possibly some non-European countries fall into this category. I believe that neither nation would have real reasons to distrust these.

In order to be effective, the arbiter must be able to inflict speedy and severe damage on any aggressor. To this end, he must be equipped with ballistic missiles and nuclear and biological warheads. Railroad-based and fixed, hardened sites could be used for launching, in combination with sea-based weapons.

Since the possible arbiter nations do not now have weapons or delivery systems of their own, these would have to be supplied by the United States and the USSR, along with technicians for their firing and maintenance. If it is understood that our weapons would point at the USSR and theirs at us, the crews would have every incentive for maintaining them at maximum efficiency. The effectiveness of the arbiter's deterrent threat depends to some extent on the assumption that neither side will discover an efficient active defense against ballistic missiles. An attempt to circumvent the agreement in this way would have to be carried out on so large a scale that it would be discovered at an early stage and could be dealt with accordingly.

The arbiter must be impervious to surprise attack. This could be accomplished by mobility and dispersal of land-based missiles. If these are supplemented by a number of ship- and submarine-based IRBM's there is little reason to suppose that any country would develop adequate means of knocking out this striking power. If the arbiter is granted even limited inspection rights the possibility of a surprise attack against him becomes even more remote.

In order to detect aggression the arbiter would require a warning network of some kind. This could be satellites (e.g., Midas), a radar network of the BMEWS variety and manned aircraft on surveillance missions. If the other conditions discussed here could be met, the aim of inspection would be reduced from detecting all violations to detecting those on a large scale only. Given the arbiter's protection, it is quite likely that both sides would agree to inspection schemes adequate for this purpose.

If one believes Lord Acton's dictum on the effects of power, the possibility of its misuse by the arbiter must be considered. In my opinion, it is technically feasible to arrange the command in such a way that both the arbiter and the United States or Soviet staff must be convinced that aggression has occurred before firing could be accomplished. It would then be rather difficult for the arbiter to convince both sides that they had been attacked. If arbiters included more than one country, the chances of misuse would be even slimmer.

The responsibility of acting as custodian of the world's peace under this scheme carries with it danger as well as inconvenience. Would the arbiters be willing to serve? Since the countries in question are liable to severe fallout hazard as well as to the dangers of epidemic and starvation in the case of an all-out war, chances are good that they would be more than willing to do their share.

A cunning aggressor might agree to the plan and after its implementation reveal hidden strength with the threat to use it against the arbiter unless the latter submitted to blackmail. This eventuality could be circumvented only if the arbiter's strength were adequate to blanket possible hidden threats and if he were determined to risk its use.

One of the major dangers of a continuing arms race is the possibility of other powers, notably China, acquiring substantial nuclear ballistic missile strength. China may well refuse to cooperate in ending the arms race. It is probable that China could be forced to submit to some inspection as long as she is substantially weaker than the USSR and the West; consequently there is added incentive for putting the proposal into effect as soon as possible.

This disarmament scheme would clearly be expensive. On the other hand, an accelerating arms race is even more expensive, and it is by this criterion that costs must be measured. Since it involves mainly offensive and detection rather than defensive schemes, its cost would certainly be small relative to serious efforts at passive defense.

Why It Won't Work

In my opinion, this plan is technically feasible and logically sound. Nevertheless, I do not believe that it is likely to capture the imagination of statesmen or that it will be put into effect in the foreseeable future. The most frequently voiced objection—distrust of the altruism and determination of the arbiter—contains only a hint of what I consider the real obstacle: unwillingness to surrender the essence or even the symbols of national autonomy to the degree required by *any* effective scheme.

It is probably inescapable that any solutions of our conflict with the Communist world will have to deal not only with its symptoms (among them the arms race) but with its basic causes. It has been pointed out that the latter seem largely based on mutual fear and are by no means irresolvable. Consequently all steps which tend to diminish distrust should be welcomed and actively pursued. Unfortunately, and this has been traditionally hard for Americans to accept, this is not wholly up to us. But there is much we can do and the more clearly we recognize the limits of our power to shape events the more effectively we can act.

Realistic Action Now

The things we can do may seem small at the moment: abstention from petty propaganda triumphs, particularly in the field of disarmament; a more sober acknowledgment of the difficulties confronting both sides in reaching any arms-control agreement; a maximum of cooperation with the Soviets in nonmilitary spheres; and a gradual understanding with them about our joint interests in preventing a major war.

In effecting this shift from mutual to joint deterrence, the United Nations may well play an important, if not always recognized role. The United Nations has become a useful device for compromising or at least airing conflicts too important to be ignored and not important enough for war. In fact, it may become a means, even for the large powers, of saving face and accepting with passing good grace inevitable but unpalatable facts.

It will probably be impossible to prevent China from becoming a nuclear power by any means short of world-wide enforced disarmament. The uncertainties of a nuclear China constitute, in my opinion, the greatest and least predictable dangers of war. As long as the USSR and the United States see each other as dangerous enemies their hands are tied with respect to China; the USSR cannot then afford to relinquish so important an ally and could be dragged, against her better judgment, into a war with the United States, much as Germany was so impelled by Austro-Hungary in 1914. America cannot deal rationally with the fact of a powerful Asian Communist entity as long as she feels already so threatened by the USSR.

Summary

This essay has advanced the following ideas: The conflict between the U.S. and the Soviet Union, appearances to the contrary, is not fundamental or irresolvable enough to make war inevitable. Despite this fact the stakes are so high and the dangers of defeat so enormous that a rapid, explicit termination of the conflict by contract and agreement is impossible without a judge and a policeman. While these could be found and equipped to adjudicate and enforce, neither side considers war sufficiently imminent to make it willing to surrender the degree of national autonomy required for any effective control scheme.

In contrast to any other time in history, the dangers of war are being realistically understood by both sides, and probably do provide an adequate restraint, barring the real possibility of accidents. In order to minimize the latter, and to provide for more stable long-term relations, a gradual understanding of their joint interests by the major powers is essential. In achieving this, and in making concomitant abridgments of national autonomy tolerable, a supranational organization like the United Nations may come to play, not always very obviously, an increasingly important role. Such an organization also provides the large powers with the obvious means of dealing with the multinuclear problem. It is to be hoped very strongly that they will avail themselves of it.

REDUCING THE RECIPROCAL FEAR OF SURPRISE ATTACK

By MORTON DEUTSCH

IMAGINE A SITUATION in which two adversaries may be able to blow up each other's house by pressing a button. Further, let us assume that if one of the adversaries presses his button, there will be an explosion in the other's house; the explosion will possibly make the other unable to strike back and is likely to damage his house. Moreover, let us assume that each is afraid that the other will press the button first, either in anger or in fear. Each person's fear of what the other fears (namely, that the other will strike first) enhances the reciprocal fear of surprise attack.[1] What might these adversaries do to lessen the possibility, during a particularly tense period in their relations, that temptation or fear might lead one or the other to strike first?

Consider the possibility that each adversary has a family of children and grandchildren. Might not each feel considerably safer if they worked out a continuing exchange which would always have some of the adversary's children or grandchildren residing in his own house? Presumably, knowledge that pressing the button would destroy loved ones would eliminate much of the temptation to a surprise attack and would also eliminate much of the fear that the other would initiate an attack. Moreover, one could assume that the wife and other relatives of the potential aggressor (the mother, grandmother, sisters, and brothers of the children living in the adversary's house) would keep him under constant surveillance to insure that the button was not pressed accidentally or in a fit of rage.

I suggest that the development of modern military weapons has placed the United States and the USSR in a situation comparable to the one described above. We are each afraid of a surprise attack by missiles and hydrogen bombs. Each feels the other side may be tempted into an attack that has some possibility of crippling one's own military force or may be frightened into an attack to prevent being crippled by a surprise attack. The reciprocal fear of surprise attack, and the military steps taken to increase one's capacity to retaliate after such an attack, tend to increase international tension which, in turn, tends to increase the fear of surprise attack. How can we break out of the vicious circle without disadvantaging either the United States or the USSR in the process? The proposal presented below outlines a feasible exchange program which might lessen the reciprocal fear of surprise attack and might be mutually advantageous in other respects.

The main features of the present proposal are the following:

1. Some arbitrary, large number (e.g., 10,000) of American and Russian students would be interchanged annually or biannually. The scheduling of the interchange would be such as to maintain approximately equal numbers of exchange students in the host countries.

2. The students would be selected so as to represent a stratified sample of the children and grandchildren of the people holding important positions in each country. It would not be difficult to develop a listing of such positions for each country. Illustratively for the United States, one would include the President and his Cabinet, the various under- and assistant-secretaries, admirals and generals, members of Congress, governors, mayors of cities over a certain size, leading industrialists, leading members of the political organizations, leading scientists, and so on.

3. For the student, the interchange year's objective would be purely educational. He (or she) would be given the opportunity to learn the language of the host country and to become familiar with its culture and its people. To alleviate fears of harmful "contamination" or undue indoctrination, the administrative control of the student's educational program would remain with the student's native country—as in embassy schools. Mutual agreements would specify the location of students in the host country, their rights to travel, etc.

4. The student-interchange program could be supplemented by a similarly oriented teacher-exchange program and by a cultural-exchange program which would place a small proportion of the leading scientists, artists, politicians, industrialists, etc., in each other's countries at the same time.

5. The gross cost of such a program, estimated at 10,000 dollars per exchanged person per year, would be from 100 to 200 million

dollars per year for each country. Net costs (subtracting normal living and other expenses that would have been incurred by the exchanged person in his native land) would be somewhat smaller. This is a small cost for a program which has merits apart from its value as a means of mutual prevention of surprise attack.

The Merits of the Proposal

1. It places a severe penalty on the initiation of a surprise attack —to achieve surprise one has to kill one's own children.

2. Even if a segment of the ruling groups of a country is willing to sacrifice its children for the advantages to be incurred from a surprise attack, it is highly unlikely that there would not be some internal resistance which would frustrate or forecast a surprise attack. That is, it is very unlikely that all of the leading groups of people that have to be involved in the planning and execution of a surprise attack will be willing to sacrifice their children. The resistance of these unwilling people could serve as an internal restraint which would either prevent a surprise attack or give sufficient clues to warn of its possibility. The legitimacy of resistance to the preparations for a surprise attack might be encouraged by a formal agreement between the United States and the USSR which would require their respective governments to make periodic announcements in the mass media that participation in preparations for a surprise attack is a crime which should be denounced publicly. Neither the United States nor the Soviet Union could afford *not* to make such an agreement.

3. It decreases the likelihood of a surprise attack upon either the United States or the USSR by any third country. Any country which attacked either the United States or the USSR would automatically incur the hostility of both countries—of the country whose children were killed, as well as of the country that was attacked.

4. The exchange program would over a period of years be likely to increase the friendship and understanding between the two countries. Assuming that the host countries can arrange favorable experiences for the exchange students, in a few years there would be a large group of people that have developed favorable reactions to the other country either through their own direct experiences or, indirectly, through the experiences of loved ones. Moreover, the development of knowledge of each other's language and culture is likely to be stimulating and productive for each country.

5. Unlike other programs to prevent surprise attack, it will not become technologically obsolete.

NOTES

1. T. C. Schelling coined the phrase "the reciprocal fear of surprise attack" to characterize the type of situation discussed in this paper. See his *The Strategy of Conflict* (Cambridge: Harvard University Press, 1960) for an insightful discussion of such situations. My proposal, which was stimulated by Schelling's suggestion of an exchange of kindergarten children (a suggestion which he rejected as impractical), was widely circulated in 1958.

A SPECIAL SURVEILLANCE FORCE

By T. C. SCHELLING

THIS ARTICLE PROPOSES that there be discussed with the Russians the establishment (for each of us, separately, and perhaps for other countries) of a *Special Surveillance Force*. Its function would be to observe the enemy's behavior, at the enemy's invitation, and to report home instantly through authentic channels. The purpose is to help tranquilize crises that threaten to erupt into general war, particularly crises aggravated by the instability of strategic deterrence—by the urgency, if general war seems imminent, of starting it before the enemy does.

The special feature of such a force would be its readiness, through advance preparation, to take advantage of motives and political circumstances as they might be in a sudden crisis, rather than as they are during the normal ups and downs of the cold war. It should be prepared to do, with the sudden acquiescence of the enemy (host), things that the latter might never dream of permitting except in extraordinary circumstances, when some kind of arms control—even if only a temporary monitoring of some synchronized withdrawal or relaxation—becomes urgently required as an alternative to war or to the rapid deterioration of a strategic crisis. The attributes of the force should be readiness, speed, reliability, self-sufficiency, versatility, and ability to improvise.

Underlying Premises

This suggestion rests on two premises.

The first is that any real stimulus to arms-control or arms-tranquilization measures would likely come in an unforeseen crisis that developed rapidly. There is not now a powerful belief in arms control as a necessary alternative to general war; but events could occur—technological events or political events—that would make the balance of deterrence much more unstable than it is now, or that would cause a drastic reappraisal of the instability that has existed all along—events that would make "measures to safeguard against surprise attack" (to use the current terminology) needed instantly as an alternative to war. At such a moment the motives for arms control, the political feasibility of various control measures, the willingness to incur costs, to break precedent, and to infringe the rights of other countries, might be strikingly different than in the circumstances of the cold war. In other words, the demand for disarmament may come suddenly when it comes, and not be able to wait. Advance intellectual preparation, and material and personnel preparation, may be essential to meet that contingency.

The second premise is that there are things that the United States and the USSR might do cooperatively in anticipation of a possible sudden need to meet unforeseen emergencies. In the course of such emergencies the ability of each side to see reliably, with its own eyes, and with authentic capabilities for communicating home, certain things that either are going on or are not going on in the other country may be essential to the avoidance of misunderstanding or to the negotiation of practical arrangements—even very temporary arrangements—that would help to stabilize mutual deterrence. (The possibility of a nuclear accident, or of nuclear mischief by some third party, suggests one type of situation for which stand-by observation teams of a versatile and flexible sort could be useful in the process of mutual reassurance.)

Nature of the Contingency

In considering the crises that may arise, and how they may arise, we should distinguish between (1) the crises that we should anticipate unilaterally and (2) those whose possibility or likelihood we can acknowledge to the Russians and discuss with them as mutual problems susceptible of cooperative preparations.

For example, we can think unilaterally about the "crises" that would occur if we received evidence that the Russians were preparing to launch an attack on American strategic forces. Just what to do under the circumstances, particularly if the evidence is ambiguous, and especially if our capability to forestall it by a surprise blow of our own is not terribly reassuring at the time, is not obvious. As an important possibility, one might consider some kind of disarmament ultimatum, a demand for "measures to safeguard against surprise attack" of a potency and rigor suggested by the term "preventive disarmament."

Whether there would be any military restraint or sacrifice that the Russians and we could undertake and that we could adequately monitor under the demanding time schedule, of a sufficiently irreversible and advantageous form to satisfy us and yet not intolerably susceptible of double cross from the Russian point of view, is a vital technical question. The answer will depend, among other things, on the facilities for monitoring compliance—Soviet compliance and United States compliance—with whatever arrangements can be negotiated. Facilities and personnel may be needed instantly and continuously so that there is no lapse, even a momentary one, in the synchronized process of withdrawal, tranquilization, redeployment, submission to inspection, disarmament, or whatever we call the arrangement. This particular contingency, however, is not the kind that we would discuss with the Russians or make a basis for overt cooperation prior to the event.

In contrast, certain contingencies are suggested by the notion of "accidental war," particularly in its more mechanical and psychological connotations. This is the possibility of a war that might result from the triggering effect of an accident or error in the literal sense, or from electronic and other false alarms, or from the calculated mischief of a strategically irresponsible third party.[1] There may be a legitimate basis for considering with the Russians the possibility that we and they might want to respond cooperatively in the face of certain events, certain uncertainties, certain "crises." At least this may be true of those contingencies in which there is a strong presumption that neither side is on the verge of premeditated war. It may be important to each side to reassure itself of this fact and to provide reassurance to the other side, which might otherwise be tempted to respond explosively to the uncertain potentialities of the situation.

In between would be crises of the kind that could occur in the course of a violent limited war, or in a political crisis where the piling up of strategic threats had gotten both sides so committed that withdrawal without submissiveness seemed impossible, and in which general war began to seem imminent. If it were part of the strategy of each side to reassure the other that it was not about to launch all-out war momentarily, on condition that it could satisfy itself that the other was not about to do so either, it might be possible to specify a sufficient set of actions to be taken and actions to be abstained from to constitute such reassurance—on condition that they could be instantly, continuously, and reliably observed, with the observers reporting through channels known to be authentic. This might be the kind of crisis that, while not readily susceptible of overt acknowledgment and discussion between us and the Russians, could be in the backs of our minds as we talked or negotiated about some of the less sensitive contingencies.

Pre-Emptive Instability

This whole notion rests on a single premise about the character of the strategic problem: that there is likely to be, during most of the foreseeable future, an enormous advantage in striking first in the event that war occurs, and that each side will not only be conscious of this but be conscious of the other's preoccupation with it. In any circumstances in which the likelihood of early or immediate war rises above a certain threshold, the urge to pre-empt, to pre-empt the other's pre-emption (and to pre-empt his attempt to pre-empt our pre-emption, and so on *ad infinitum*), may become a dominant motive. This implies that crises could develop very suddenly. And when they do, both sides may fervently wish that the premium on first strike did not exist; both sides may recognize that they are both trapped by the unstable technology of attack and defense; both may recognize that each is, from its own point of view, tempted to attack first in "self-defense"; and both may wish that there were adequate cooperative measures to be taken ("measures to safeguard against surprise attack") to tranquilize the situation.

Aggravating Factors

There are some special technical considerations here. One is that the things that each side does to make its own strategic force more secure—to be more alert, to be less vulnerable to surprise, and to be better able to strike quickly if that is the way the decision goes—are likely to be the kinds of actions that can be interpreted as preparations for attack. They are likely to be actions that increase the danger of "false alarm" on both sides and that could lead to a succession of decisions aggravating each side's perception of the need to pre-empt. Thus the things that each side does in the face of uncertainty and instability may, by mutual feedback, aggravate the instability.

A second consideration is that each side may take extraordinary measures in a crisis that could not be maintained indefinitely. Sooner or later there comes a need to withdraw, recuperate, disalert, or otherwise respond to the "fatigue" produced in the strategic force by the crisis itself. It may be that each side could much more readily relax into something like normal alert status if there were a means available for monitoring a synchronized relaxation on both sides. It would be exceedingly difficult to work out a reasonable plan for a synchronized relaxation of that sort; but it may be more than difficult—it may be impossible—to monitor compliance within the time available unless certain ingredients of the inspection system are prepared and pre-positioned before the crisis.

Irreversible Destabilization

Once we imagine crises that might require some kind of *temporary* strategic cooperation, it is not much farther to the notion of a crisis that *irreversibly* changes the basic political premise that we and the Russians work on. At the present time our mutual deterrence probably gets some stability from our both working on the premise that general war, though terribly possible, is rather unlikely; that we will both try hard to prevent it; that we are both deterred by the "mutual suicide" possibilities; and that neither of us has yet come demonstrably close to triggering the other's pre-emptive decision. It is possible, of course, that today's (relative) tranquility reflects only that the enemy has taken the decision to launch an attack, has computed that his advantage will be greatest at a date still in the future, and is lulling us in the interim. But the contrary judgment seems to prevail. If, however, we really get to the brink of all-out strategic war; if we display to ourselves and to the Russians our willingness to take extraordinary risks; if the Russians demonstrate the same; and particularly if the crisis is one that leads us to readjust our estimate of how likely general war has been all along, then we may at that point revise our basic operating premise and expect the Russians to do the same. We may have to stop relying on *inertia* as a supplement to mutual deterrence, and plan to live on the brink of general war. At such a point we might decide that nothing the Russians could ever do would reassure us, since efforts to reassure us would naturally be associated with definite plans to attack us; we might also conclude that no *moderate* arms-control measures could be of any significance. At that point drastic disarmament, negotiated under the threat of immediate general war, with drastic implications for the political balance of the world and without regard to the sensitivities of neutrals and allies, may suddenly be recognized as the alternative to war.

"Crash Disarmament"

It would be a shame if in such a contingency, in spite of powerful and unprecedented motives on both sides to negotiate drastic disarmament as an alternative to war, the possibility were precluded by the sheer technical inability of both sides to monitor, instantly and continuously, each side's compliance with whatever arrangement for synchronized crash disarmament could be worked out. It would be particularly disgraceful if the possibility were precluded by the failure of both sides to think seriously and imaginatively about such contingencies in advance and to make certain basic and flexible preparations for them, such as procurement, training, pre-positioning, and the establishment of a degree of coordination with each other.

The notion of "crash disarmament," suddenly motivated and demanding facilities for negotiation, observation, and communication on a time schedule wholly different from that of normal cold-war disarmament discussions, may seem strange and unreal, implausible and unrealistic, unprecedented and improbable. But any idea of general war between the United States and the USSR is somewhat strange and unreal, implausible and unprecedented; any idea of disarmament that goes beyond the most innocuous sort of diplomacy seems politically unrealistic. Perhaps a few concepts like massive retaliation or limited war have come to seem real, plausible, and consistent with the motives of one or both sides only because we have gained more familiarity with such ideas during the last several years. Thus the need for a technical capability to engage in sudden disarmament is not to be judged for its plausibility or probability in the ordinary sense of historical familiarity; it is to be judged for its relative likelihood in comparison with the drastic and unprecedented, strange, and unreal contingencies that are involved in any discussion of our strategic relation to the Russians in the years to come, such as war itself.

Unilateral Actions

Unilaterally, there are a number of implications that flow from such a contingency if we take it seriously. One is to *design our own strategic forces,* and to deploy them and to control them, and to provide them with an operating doctrine, in a manner consistent with the *need to endure crises,* and with emphasis on their potential strategic role of *policing disarmament* (in addition to their strategic role of deterring attack or fighting a war). A second is the need to think about, to plan for, and to war-game in detail the question of what we should (could) demand of the Soviets if we did reach the point where, in the interest of averting imminent war, we were willing to use the threat of imminent war to support a disarmament ultimatum (including one that might put the Soviets at a real disadvantage). A third is to think about the problem of actually negotiating with the Russians in such a crisis, and making preparations for communication and inspection, not only so that we can monitor their compliance but so that—equally essential to the success of a negotiation—they can monitor ours. And a fourth is the question of what we might, in advance of any such crisis, talk about with the Russians, and do with them, either by way of reaching understandings with them or by way of exchanging facilities and practicing their use. It is mainly the fourth and, to a lesser extent, the third that relate to our bilateral negotiation with the Russians ahead of time.

The Positive-Evidence Concept

In considering the kind of surveillance scheme that could be mounted in a hurry, and especially in considering what could be accomplished by a small but adaptable elite group of potential inspectors and communicators, it is necessary to keep in mind the motives that would be brought to bear on the kind of crisis being discussed. There is only one premise about these motives that can make sense of the scheme discussed in this article: that is, that both sides would be emphatically eager, desperately eager, to convey the truth if in fact the truth were reassuring, and to behave in ways that facilitate observation of the truth. In a crash scheme of disarmament, or arms restraint, or mutual withdrawal and tranquilization, both sides would require *positive evidence* of compliance, rather than just an absence of evidence that the other is cheating. In these contingencies the inspectors would not look for evidence about what the other side was not doing; they would demand to see what it *was* doing.

As mentioned elsewhere,[2] there are two quite distinct criteria for judging an inspection system. One is how well the system gets at the truth in spite of the subject's best efforts to conceal it; the other is how well it helps the subject to display the truth when it is in his interest to do so. (The difference is a little like that between a scheme for discovering the guilty and a scheme for permitting the innocent to establish their innocence.)

To give an artificial illustration, if the Russians told us that a particular submarine was not within a thousand miles of the United States, and we did not know where the submarine was, it would be looking for a needle in a haystack to discover whether they were lying. But if *in fact* the submarine is not within a thousand miles of the United States and the Russians wish to prove it, they always have the option of producing the submarine for us to take a look at.

I am not trying to propose in a simple-minded way that the truth is easy to document if only the motive is there, or that in a crisis each side's sole interest will be to convey the truth and there is no need to worry about cheating. I am simply saying that while cheating and deception are problems even in the best of circumstances, and while authentic evidence of the truth may be difficult to convey even if one wants to, there is nevertheless an enormous difference between discovering the truth in spite of the enemy's best efforts to conceal it, and creating facilities for his provision of satisfactory evidence on the assumption that he is powerfully motivated to reassure us and knows that we can be reassured only if we are presented with overwhelming evidence that passes our most skeptical scrutiny.

Take a case that involves less military technology and tactics than the submarine, the question of where Khrushchev and other important members of the Russian government are at any moment. If they have just gone deep underground in Siberia, or on a sustained airborne alert, or have taken some other action that might suggest they were preserving their command and saving their skins in preparation for general war, and if they alleged that they were doing no such thing but were minding their own ordinary business somewhere in the USSR, it could be nearly impossible to discover the truth. We could not know with certainty everywhere they were not, in order to deduce (or prove) where they momentarily were. But if in fact they have not absented themselves, and badly want to prove it, all they have to do is to produce Khrushchev—if we have somebody available who can recognize him on sight and report home instantly through authentic channels.

What I am trying to emphasize is that the ways they could prove to our complete satisfaction the *truth* about something they *are* doing, when in fact they are doing it and badly want us to know it, are much simpler than the ways that we would have to discover the falsehood of the same proposition if in fact it were false and we had to search for our own evidence. I emphasize this point not because it makes the problem easy, but because it may keep the problem from being utterly insoluble.

Nature of the Arms Control

Ordinarily arms control is thought to depend on some minimum of mutual trust; and it could be argued that cooperation between enemies on the brink of war is out of the question because mutual trust would be nil. But any scheme of negotiated behavior would have to rest on the premise of absolute mistrust. In fact, it seems certain that unless thoroughgoing distrust were acknowledged on both sides, no understanding could be reached. The sheer intellectual clarity required to recognize the nature of the common interest would be incompatible with the pretense that there was any basis for mutual trust. Commitments would have to be entirely physical, not verbal or legal or moral. Each side must *do things* in an observable way, simultaneously with the other's doing corresponding things in an equally observable way, according to a plan sufficiently synchronized that neither acquires an attractive opportunity to double-cross the other.

In the case for which I have used terms like "withdrawal from the brink," "relaxation," or other words suggesting return to the *status quo ante,* the negotiated scheme may have a limited horizon. The scheme succeeds in a matter of days, if not hours, or at most in a few weeks, or it fails altogether. But in the case of a crisis that irreversibly aggravates strategic instability, permanently changing each side's expectations about the other, and in which the *status quo ante* is militarily intolerable to both sides or at least to one of them, a more heroic negotiation is involved; and the requirements for surveillance are more varied.

To fix ideas, consider an extreme case. Suppose we get evidence that the Russians have decided to launch a surprise attack either when a good opportunity occurs or on some specified planning date. Suppose the circumstances—the ambiguity of the evidence, the motives we ascribe to the Russians (including their fear that we might attack first someday if they do not do it first), and the military balance between us—make it not only intolerable just to sit still and wait but unattractive to pre-empt ourselves, and not altogether satisfying just to announce to them that we know what they are up to and are prepared for it. It is conceivable that one alternative course available to us, one worth considering seriously, would be an ultimatum demanding that the Russians instantly begin to disarm themselves sufficiently, in conjunction with measures for our observation of what they are doing, so that they could not at any time (with good prospects of success) attack us by surprise. Suppose that, in the interest of making this course succeed, we consider certain similar (not necessarily equivalent) concessions that we might make in order to reduce Soviet vulnerability to a surprise attack by us while preserving or even enhancing the security and potency of our retaliatory forces. In other words, suppose that we decided that drastic and "permanent" disarmament of some sort (aimed mainly, but not necessarily exclusively, at the surprise-attack problem) would be our objective and that we would seek it through the threat of all-out war. ("Permanent" means, I suppose, not that we or they or both of us would be physically incapable of rearming, but that neither could take steps to rearm or to evade the scheme in other ways except through a time-consuming process that would give the other side sufficient warning for it to take heroic measures for the security of its own retaliatory forces or to initiate war quickly on terms corresponding to those existing under the disarmament scheme.)

Under these circumstances, it is apparently necessary to negotiate under extreme duress, and very quickly, a drastic permanent readjustment of the world military situation, of such a sort that both sides can move by stages from something exceedingly temporary to something slightly less temporary and so on by degrees into something reasonably durable. Presumably one adopts suddenly the most extraordinary alert and readiness posture, delivering the ultimatum that (hopefully) initiates negotiation; the enemy does the same as he sends his response; and what is now required is to withdraw from the very brink of general war by some synchronized process that not only avoids instant war but leads by degrees into a durable system, with each side recognizing that if the synchronized process fails to work, or if no satisfactory solution can be discovered, each side will be tempted to initiate war if only because it expects the other to do so. And all of this has to be monitored!

The near-hopelessness of such an attempt to divert the course of history might justify the reader's giving up the article at this point, if it were not for two attenuating considerations, one hopeful and the other not. The first is that the very gravity of the situation, the heroic nature of the accommodations required, the unprecedented seriousness of the moment, might make certain courses of action feasible that ordinarily would not seem to be, by making leaders on both sides aware of the demands of the situation, of the risks in not trying as well as in trying, and of the enemy's seriousness in seeking a conservative outcome. The second consideration is that, however modest the prospects of finding a solution on the brink of war, the gravity of the problem suggests that we should do what we can to keep open the possibility.

The Scheme and the Resources Required

If the philosophy is accepted, the next question is what can be done. The internal answer is, first of all, that we should think about it seriously; second, that we should work out articulate, detailed, sequential descriptions of such kinds of crises as we can imagine and experiment with them to see what personnel and material ingredients might be required ahead of time, in the event that we wished, in a crisis, to pull out the plan and examine it as a basis for action. The most important preparation is intellectual; and if the things we might wish to do involve human and material prerequisites, and we can foresee to some extent what they are, we can begin to provide them. If in addition the likely success of any scheme would depend on some prior understanding, formal or informal, tacit or explicit, vague or precise, that we had worked out with our enemies, we should think about the best way to concert with them in advance at least on the kinds of communication that we might need for a sudden negotiation, and on some of the concepts and ideas that it would be good for us to share in the event we had to reach agreement on a crash scheme in a hurry. This is a tall order, and implies research within our own government, and, ultimately, some kind of formal or informal communication with the Russians.

There is then the question of what we might begin to do now, in cooperation with the Russians, to prepare for some of these eventualities, and particularly for those eventualities that can bear to be acknowledged and talked about. I suggest that we consider the general idea of two versatile, flexible, adaptable observation and communication forces, one for each side and each located in the other's country, whose main function is to be available to meet whatever demands are placed on them in a crisis—recognizing that in a crisis improvisation will be needed, and that improvisation may be enormously facilitated by the instant availability of some adaptable resources or ingredients physically located near the points on the earth where they will be required.[3]

In trying to imagine what would go into these versatile emergency forces, there are at least three lines of inquiry that may be helpful. One is to think about some of the *tasks* they might be called on to perform in an emergency. A second is to think about the *capabilities* they need, whatever their tasks may be. And a third is to think, in a practical way, about what they can be doing meanwhile, about what current excuses there are for bringing them into existence, about the tasks they could be used on *in the interim* for purposes of practice and as a means of supplementing the justification for their existence.

The last point is a sufficiently important one to deserve a moment's emphasis. If anything makes a force "adaptable," "resourceful," "versatile," and so forth, it is probably exercise—doing novel jobs, meeting unforeseen situations, being continually tested and, most important of all, doing this as serious work and not in the form of make-believe. Any inspection-observation-communication force that might be established with a view to its potential usefulness in unforeseeable contingencies should if possible have operating functions during the interim. Thus an important criterion, perhaps the most important in thinking about the creation of resourceful facilities, is what is currently going on, or can be initiated, that would yield as a by-product adaptable teams and facilities so located as to be useful in an emergency.

For example, in the event that there is some formal agreement on nuclear-test suspension or a jointly monitored nuclear-test program, there will be required teams of observers with equipment for inspection and for communication home, of a kind that could be exploited in an emergency. Their location may be useful; some of their communication equipment may be useful; the transportation they have available may be useful; their mobility, their knowledge of the terrain, and the operating procedures they will have worked out for themselves and with the host country could be enormously helpful if they were called on to do something of an analogous sort in the approximate area where they were. Thus one promising line of approach is to inquire how we can design and deploy and operate our nuclear-test surveillance forces, and give them experience, and test their competence, and increase their resourcefulness, with the deliberate idea that they may, in unforeseen contingencies, be the best means we have for letting home governments see with their own eyes certain things that the host government may want them to see.

Take an example. To avoid technical or classified-information difficulties, consider a nonmilitary aspect of an effort by the Russians to reassure us that they were not about to attack us, on an occasion when we thought (or they thought that we thought) that they might be about to. Suppose they wanted to claim (among other things) that they were not evacuating cities. How would we substantiate this claim?

The idea is that they might, in case of our attack, save lives by getting people out of the target area, particularly if fall-out protection were available in the countryside; so the people still in cities and unable to get out before our attack amount to "hostages" in our hands. Depending on the city, on whether the city would be attacked by aircraft or missiles, and so forth, the time for evacuation might be anywhere from a fraction of an hour to a few hours. And we would like to know, to within the nearest fifteen minutes, whether or not the Russians had begun to evacuate most of their cities.

They say they have not; how do we find out? To make it interesting, suppose that the crisis is one in which both sides have taken security measures and ordinary communication is cut off between the United States and various newspaper correspondents and officials in Russia. In Moscow it may be only necessary for somebody in the Embassy to look out the window; but even he will not necessarily see all of Moscow, nor under the circumstances would he necessarily be permitted to travel around Moscow in a special car equipped with its own electric generator and transmitting equipment. Nor could he necessarily recognize evacuation if he saw a sample of it, given the confusion of the crisis already postulated. It may take some analysis, and advance thinking, to discern what is going on. Outside of Moscow, we might not have, on thirty-minute availability, observers who could authentically report reliable information about the evacuation of Soviet cities. But suppose we had mobile observers available at widely dispersed spots in Russia, whose loyalty and reliability to the United States were beyond question, who could communicate authentically to us, identifying themselves beyond question through cryptographic or other devices, who could in fact proceed to various Soviet cities and observe what was going on and let us know within a very few minutes. In that case, if the Russians in fact were not evacuating their cities and badly wanted us to know that they were not, they could take advantage of the resources we had available in Russia by asking us to dispatch our people to cities of our choice, providing our observers with police escort, helicopters or the right to use their own, and anything else that would facilitate the job.

(This illustration, incidentally, may be a good example of a principle that can often be applied to positive-evidence schemes—to schemes where there is a presumption that the enemy will comply or that his failure to comply settles the question—namely, the use of random sampling. Ordinary probability theory suggests that if the Russians tell us that they are not evacuating any of their cities, and out of two hundred cities that we might be interested in we can select a dozen at random, and if we find that of the dozen we examine none shows signs of evacuation, the odds are exceedingly small that the Russians are evacuating more than an insignificant number of their cities; and the risks to the Russians of cheating are high.)

So much for the example, which the reader can elaborate from here as well as I. The example does help to identify a few of the characteristics that the force should have. Most important of all is that these versatile observers be able to establish *communication* with their own governments in ways that are quick and reliable, and in ways that are unquestionably authentic. They must, in other words, solve the problem of identifying themselves so that the enemy cannot intercept the messages and change them, or physically commandeer the facilities, without its becoming evident back home that something is amiss. (Whether the observers require privacy of communication—i.e., cryptographic facilities—is a different question, the answer to which would depend on the job at hand.)

What they need by way of communication equipment—their own generators or access to electric power, transmitters, receivers, relay stations, and all that—is an interesting technical question, of which a part concerns the division of responsibility between themselves and their hosts. Probably, the more opportunity there is during normal times for these observers to simulate, in cooperation with their hosts, the kinds of things they would do in a crisis—or, better still, to engage in actual jobs that are similar to what they might be called on to do in a crisis—the more opportunity there would be to work out routines and procedures and methods of coordination so that they could utilize the facilities of the host country. If instead there is little for them to do but sit in their shacks under blackout waiting for the great moment, they may have to rely more on working out procedures for self-contained and independent communication than on trying to improvise sudden collaboration with the host country at a critical moment.

In addition to communication, *mobility* is a prerequisite. It has several dimensions. One is the ability to move sizable distances fast, navigating and avoiding hindrances. Another is being located initially at strategic points, dispersed to keep portions of the force within quick travel time of the places where they might be demanded. A third dimension is fine-grain mobility—the ability to move about within a city, to pass check points, to avoid molestation, and to enjoy immunity—in short, to have the equivalent of police protection and political authority, immunity to language barriers and other nuisances, and good guidance, road maps, knowledge of vantage points and access to them, and whatever else is required. Additionally they need practice—practice not only in the functioning of their own equipment and in their own capabilities to navigate, but in coordinating with their hosts, in overcoming obstacles and nuisances, in recognizing the kinds of occurrences that are "normal" so that they can be distinguished from abnormal obstructions on those occasions when abnormal obstructions might have a strategic interpretation.

In looking about for other jobs that observation teams might perform, and that would consequently be an excuse for such teams and an opportunity to experiment with them, some of the suggestions for monitoring space activity may become relevant. Even a rather innocuous program for inviting each other's observers to attend launchings, particularly those involved in programs of a more scientific and less military sort, might provide an activity at which observation and communication techniques could be tested and developed. Considering, for example, how much the Russians can observe in this country without the help of formal invitations from our military establishment, there might not be a great deal to lose in inviting them to places like Cape Canaveral from time to time. So if we thought it might someday be useful to have in this country some Russian observers of undoubted loyalty to the USSR whom we could call on to help Khrushchev see with his own eyes something that we wanted him to see, there may be several activities that are not so terribly sensitive or dramatic that they would commit us too much, and that would give us a chance to see just how hard it might be, on a few minutes' notice, to get a Russian to a spot 1,000 miles from Washington to see something significant, establish an authentic line of communication home, and persuade his own government that he had seen it. A little practice may go a long way, at least in overcoming such simple things as language difficulties, traffic regulations, how to find the Russians on short notice, means of communication, and even the personal and emotional problems that bear on such questions as the size of a team and the kinds of escorts they need.

Perhaps the newly initiated agreement on the status of Antarctica provides, under interestingly rigorous climatic conditions, some opportunities for seeing what the problems are in looking over an enemy installation, at the enemy's invitation, and reporting home what is seen.

Some Reservations

It may be difficult to persuade a reader that the concept is valid and relevant, and nearly impossible to persuade him that there is anything to be done about it. Beyond that, it has to be admitted that even if something can be done, it is by no means obvious that we and the Russians both have an interest in it, or even that we do whether the Russians do or not. It may go without saying, for most of us, that if drastic disarmament should ever become the only alternative to imminent war, and the war that is imminent looks pretty unpromising, a scheme to facilitate disarmament efforts would be all to the good. But there are at least two kinds of problems that reduce the advantages of such a scheme and that have to be acknowledged even if we decide on reflection that they are not of controlling importance.

One is that measures to avert war and to facilitate disarmament, even measures to avert accidental war, may reduce the potency of some of our deterrent threats, may reduce the Russians' fears of the consequences of their own aggressive actions, may remove some of the inhibitions on limited war by suggesting that the likelihood of explosion into bigger war is not as serious as it might have been. An important deterrent to Soviet aggression may well be the fear of "accidental war," an unpremeditated war, a war that does not begin with a cold-blooded determination by the United States to retaliate massively but rather comes out of the complex interaction of the fears and commitments of both sides—a war that results from false alarm, panic, mischief, human error, or a dynamic process of decisions whose consequences cannot be entirely foretold even by those who make them.[4] Reduce the fear of all-out war, including the fear of inadvertent war—perhaps *especially* the fear of inadvertent war—and an important deterrent to Soviet or Chinese aggression may be gone. Provide facilities for avoiding war at the eleventh hour and the Soviets may enjoy increased confidence that, whatever they do beforehand, they can always be saved at the eleventh hour and that the eleventh hour will be recognizable when it comes. Establish procedures and facilities that suggest that, when we might have launched all-out war, we will launch all-out negotiations instead, and the Russians may enjoy a new sense of immunity to American retaliation.

These are reservations that attach to any of the so-called "measures to safeguard against surprise attack," and that may similarly apply to measures to forestall general war at the last minute. How important they are depends on whether one is mainly concerned with the consequences of general war and the probability that it will occur, or with the need to intimidate and inhibit and discipline an aggressive enemy in circumstances short of total war.

The second sort of considerations that give one pause are of a lesser order. A flexible and adaptable observation system of the kind hinted at so sketchily here could be abused if one side or the other wanted to abuse it. One can feign alarm and demand reassurance as a means of using an observation force to get information not intended under the scheme, either information about how the enemy responds to dramatic events or just snapshot information about his posture that might be obtained by putting an observation force in action. The enemy can "spoof"; he can engage in spectacular actions that activate the system and play on our nerves but that, because of the system, are less risky than they might have been. He can accuse us of abusing the system for purposes of espionage. It is even conceivable that if we had our own trusted observers in Soviet territory who could see things that we knew existed but preferred not to acknowledge, we would find it more difficult not to acknowledge them. (If, for example, either side occasionally intruded into the other's territory and pretended not to, or if either liked to accuse the other of engaging in activities whose occurrence would be embarrassing to the other, it might be difficult or equally embarrassing to continue this once one's own observers could be called on to witness the truth.) These are in addition to all the other diplomatic and propaganda dangers that can readily be imagined.

How to Get Started

If it is decided that there is something to this idea and that the dangers are outweighed by the advantages, and that there may be programs of action that allow us to give a stand-by scheme some exercise, the immediate question is how to open up the subject with the Russians and how to formulate the problem.

One possibility is to shift our approach to "safeguards against surprise attack." There are, broadly speaking, two different aspects to the surprise-attack problem. One is premeditated surprise attack; the other is pre-emptive attack, false alarm, accidental war, and the like. The two are tied together, but in a rough way the distinction can be made. If one makes the distinction, it looks as though discussions and negotiations with the Russians on the subject of surprise-attack schemes have so far been oriented, at least implicitly, toward the problem of premeditated attack. I say "implicitly" because there has been no explicit agenda or agreement on the point; but what has been discussed seems to imply long-term surveillance rather than schemes to cope with crises. And the United States has generally deprecated discussion of "accidental war."

I imagine that some of our reluctance to talk to the Russians about measures to forestall "accidental war" stems from our sensitivity to public opinion, particularly opinion abroad, and an unwillingness to acknowledge that there could be any basis for the Soviet contention that "accidental war" (however defined) is a real possibility. But that phase of our public relations may be past, and maybe we need not be quite so defensive about it. Furthermore, there are special difficulties in discussing measures to safeguard against premeditated surprise attack; it must be a serious embarrassment to both sides to talk about the kinds of vulnerabilities they are most preoccupied with. The very information needed to make progress is the most sensitive kind.

One might say that the *presumption of mutual interest* is stronger in the prevention of unpremeditated war (the so-called "accidental war") and that one may possibly discuss the subject without getting too close to the touchy question of just where he is most vulnerable and just what kind of surprise he would least like his enemy to engage in.

If, then, we acknowledge that unpremeditated war, or inadvertent war, or accidental war, or war resulting from a crisis of some sort is a significant possibility, and that the existence of a premium on striking first aggravates the possibility, we can assimilate this possibility to the general problem of surprise attack; and there may be a basis for discussing fairly openly just what kinds of joint measures could be taken to reduce misunderstanding in those cases where war caused by misunderstanding is imminent. It may be possible to begin with a list of reasonably innocuous hypothetical occurrences that could lead to a misunderstanding of each other's strategic intentions, and to discuss the kinds of measures that might lead to mutual reassurance and improved understanding.[5]

If, to take an example, there were no propaganda disadvantages in adopting the hypothetical premise that an accidental nuclear-weapon detonation might occur somewhere on the face of the earth, and specifically in the United States or the USSR, it might be a useful exercise to think with the Russians about the way that each of us could reassure the other that we were not misinterpreting the event as the harbinger of general war, and were not so afraid of the other's misinterpretation as to feel obliged to initiate a pre-emptive attack. (Perhaps events blamable on mischievous third parties would be a noncommittal way to begin discussions.) We could at least discuss such simple questions as how to establish a line of communication between Washington and Moscow, and how to get inspectors not only to the scene of the accident but to vantage points where they could see that the nation was calm rather than frenzied and that strategic forces were not being readied for attack.

At least it is worth thinking about.

NOTES

1. Regarding the possibility of "accidental war," and its deterrence, see T. C. Schelling, "Meteors, Mischief, and War," *Bulletin of the Atomic Scientists,* XVI, No. 7 (September, 1960), pp. 292 ff.
2. T. C. Schelling, "Surprise Attack and Disarmament," in Klaus Knorr (ed.), *NATO and American Security* (Princeton: Princeton University Press, 1959), pp. 176–208; see also T. C. Schelling and Morton H. Halperin, *Strategy and Arms Control* (New York: The Twentieth Century Fund, 1960), pp. 97 ff.
3. There is a prerequisite that, if not now provided, should come at the head of this proposal. It is that facilities and arrangements, of a mobile and versatile sort, for communication between the Soviet and American governments be worked out and in some way concerted on, and that each side have adequate communication and other arrangements within its own government and military services to make sudden negotiation possible in the circumstances that would surround a crisis of this sort.
4. For an elaboration of this point, see T. C. Schelling, *The Strategy of Conflict* (Cambridge: Harvard University Press, 1960), ch. 8, "The Threat that Leaves Something to Chance."

5. The arms-control significance of such communication with the enemy is discussed further in T. C. Schelling, "Reciprocal Measures for Arms Stabilization," in Donald G. Brennan (ed.), *Arms Control, Disarmament, and National Security* (New York: George Braziller, 1961), pp. 167 ff.

INTERNATIONALIZING MILITARY FORCE

By HERBERT C. KELMAN

SOCIAL-PSYCHOLOGICAL WRITINGS on international relations have pointed to the need for the discovery and promotion of wider and more inclusive values among opposing nations. Chances for peace would be enhanced if it were possible for conflicting nations to redefine the priorities of desired goals in such a way that certain "superordinate goals" became dominant—that is, shared goals, derived from a larger system that embraces both parties, and attainable only by their joint effort.[1] The problem, however, is not merely to discover superordinate goals, but to create a situation in which the existence of such goals and their shared character are recognized by the competing parties, and in which there is sufficient trust and institutional support for the translation of these goals into stable cooperative patterns.

Disarmament

The current relationship between East and West is, in fact, characterized by the existence of a very powerful superordinate goal—the avoidance of nuclear war. There are many indications that both parties recognize the priority of this goal and are governed by it.[2] Yet this shared goal has not led to any noticeably successful efforts at cooperation. It has been translated, primarily, into a policy of mutual nuclear deterrence and a competitive increase in nuclear arms by both sides.

A policy of multilateral disarmament would represent a much more stable approach to the avoidance of nuclear war because—unlike a deterrence policy—it would help to lessen the possibility of attack, to decrease tension, and to facilitate cooperative actions. Before such a program could be instituted, however, both sides would have to feel reassured that it did not represent a decline in their relative level of "national security."[3] This requirement presents many realistic obstacles,[4] which are further enhanced by the existing state of tension and distrust between the two sides. The atmosphere in which disarmament negotiations are typically carried out is conducive to a "biased perception of what is equable,"[5] and a readiness to suspect and dismiss the other side's proposals. We are faced with the dilemma that disarmament cannot proceed without some degree of trust, but trust cannot develop until there has been some experience with a workable disarmament program.[6]

To get around this dilemma, it is necessary to find some way of *beginning* the process of disarmament without giving up a significant amount of national security. Such a beginning might be made with a minimum of trust. Once the process has been initiated, however, it is likely that there will be a gradual increase in trust, which in turn will make possible an increasingly widened disarmament agreement.[7] However, even if ways are found to break through the barrier of distrust and to negotiate an agreement, disarmament in and of itself does not represent a stable solution. While it helps to create the atmosphere for more far-reaching political settlements, it does not eliminate the underlying conflict of interests between the two sides, nor does it remove all threats to national security. If the disarmament is partial, there remains the possibility of attack—although, presumably, a less destructive attack. If the disarmament is total, there remains the possibility of evasion or circumvention. Mutual suspicions are thus likely to continue while the slow process of negotiating political settlements is under way. It is even conceivable that these negotiations may, at times, reinforce suspicions by bringing the genuine conflicts in national goals and ideologies into sharper focus. Under these circumstances there is always the danger that a spiraling process of rearmament might be set into motion as soon as one side suspects the other of gaining some military advantage.[8]

The instability of disarmament is inherent in the fact that it derives from an essentially "negative" superordinate goal. While both sides share the desire to avoid nuclear war, they continue to be concerned with national security in the traditional sense and to pursue it in the traditional way.[9] The agreement to disarm is a cooperative effort designed to prevent these individual quests for national security from resulting in mutual annihilation. There is no question that, despite its essentially negative character, such an agreement is a necessary condition for any resolution of the current nuclear impasse. Alongside of disarmament, however, there is also a need for the development of certain "positive" superordinate goals. There is a need, in other words, for conflicting nations to redefine their quest for national security and to join in the development of new goals, anchored in a larger system of values that embraces both sides. The existence of such positive superordinate goals would not eliminate the possibility of conflict—a state of affairs which is neither attainable nor desirable—but it might eliminate highly destructive resolutions of conflict.

The concept of *international security* represents one promising direction for the development of such positive superordinate goals. It would seem best to formulate superordinate goals in terms of concrete superordinate structures, rather than in terms of ultimate values. A specific institutional structure may be accepted on pragmatic grounds without requiring, in the first instance, a radical reorganization of national and individual values (although such a reorganization may evolve from the institutional structure in action). In line with this assumption, this paper proposes the *internationalization of all armed forces, armaments, and espionage systems* as a specific institutional arrangement through which the goal of international security would find expression.[10]

The present proposal views disarmament and the internationalization of military force as two mutually facilitative policy directions that have to be pursued simultaneously. On the one hand, it will be apparent that the arrangement I am proposing—at least in its full-blown form—could not be instituted at the present high level of armament. On the other hand, I would argue, the development of this institutional arrangement would help to lower the current barriers to a disarmament agreement, and to increase the stability of such an agreement once it is achieved.

There is no question that the proposal, as presented here, is not easy to implement and, in fact, working out the details of implementation requires many kinds of expertise that I do not possess. My purpose in presenting this proposal is not to offer a precise blueprint ready to be put into action, but to develop certain general principles which can conceivably be applied in various specific arrangements.

The Army of Your Choice

The original conception of the present proposal was stimulated by a comment by Kenneth Boulding. Pointing to recent publicity that advises people to "visit the church of your choice" and to "give your bucks to the party of your choice," he wondered what it would mean if young people were urged to "join the army of your choice" and "fight for the country of your choice."

I do not react very favorably to advertisements that tell me to support the church or the party of my choice. Such advertisements imply that differences between religions and between political parties are really quite unimportant. Politics and religion, I feel, ought to be areas of controversy, involving strong loyalties and emotional commitments, and not matters of indifference. But armies are an altogether different story. *An army is entirely too dangerous an institution to be embroiled in controversy and to be characterized by strong loyalties and identifications.*

Boulding's playful vision implies a far healthier definition of the role of the armed forces than is common today. It serves to pose the problem to which the present proposal addresses itself. How can we manage to achieve a state of affairs in which the armed forces are no longer agents of international conflicts of interest and ideology, and in which military might is no longer tied to considerations of national loyalty, national survival and the preferred way of life? Ideally, I would like to get rid of armies and armaments altogether. But if we accept the notion that this is a utopian solution—worth striving for but not attainable in the foreseeable future—is there perhaps an interim solution whereby armies are maintained but neutralized, that is, eliminated as instruments for carrying on international conflicts? The internationalization of military force is proposed as a solution that might meet these requirements.

The Final Stage

Careful phasing and the gradual introduction of partial and intermediate steps will be essential before the proposed arrangement can take final shape. I shall return to these problems below, but at this point a tentative description of the envisioned final stage will help to concretize the proposal and bring out its salient features.

1. The basic feature of the proposed plan is that the function of maintaining security becomes internationalized. It is removed from the domain of national governments and relegated to a special international body. No nation maintains an armed force, military weapons (aside from small weapons for internal police use), or an espionage system of its own. These functions are all handed over to a central agency whose range of power is strictly limited to military matters.

2. Ideally, participation in the plan would be universal, but it can become operational once all the nuclear powers have ratified the agreement. It would probably be wise to include a popular referendum as part of the ratification process in each country in order to underscore the principle that the plan's operation is free from the control of national governments. The plan is binding only on those states who

have ratified it, but it is open to all states who subsequently decide to join and are prepared to accept its provisions.

3. Each nation participating in the plan gradually turns over its armaments, its facilities for arms production and research, its troops, and its espionage network to the central agency. The individual gradual steps would presumably include both agreements to disarm along specified lines and agreements to internationalize specified aspects of security and defense. These two types of agreements could be combined along the lines of a proposal by Singer that certain specified national weapons be "transferred—slowly, cautiously, but regularly and in accordance with a pre-arranged schedule—to previously designated United Nations depots, where trained members of an international gendarmerie [are] prepared to receive, account for, and man such weapons."[11] In any event, the participating nations cumulatively gain experience in disarming, turning armaments over to the international agency, and relying on this agency for partial protection. The relative emphasis on international security thus increases gradually until—in the final stage of the plan—it completely replaces national security, and all military operations are controlled by the central agency.

4. Troops and weapons are reassigned in such a way as to meet the particular defense requirements of each participating nation. Details about deployment of troops and weapons within each country are negotiated by the central agency with the national government in question. The agency also takes over the production of whatever weapons are necessary. Wherever possible, it uses existing plants, but care is taken that facilities for the production of armaments are distributed fairly evenly over the participating countries. Finally, the central agency also takes over all "espionage" functions and, again, negotiates details about inspection procedures with the individual governments.

5. The troops assigned to each country—both enlisted men and officers—are *mixed* with respect to nationality. *It is essential that the army stationed in a given country include some nationals of the country itself, and some nationals of its traditional "enemy" countries.* Wherever possible, individual soldiers should be allowed to choose the country in which they want to serve (in which case the enlistment posters could literally urge young men to "join the army of your choice"). However, because of the need of following—at least in the beginning—some formula for the national distribution of the troops stationed in each country, it will not always be possible to meet these requests. As far as career personnel is concerned, and especially officers, it will be necessary to discover the optimum amount of time

that a man should serve in a given foreign country. The success of the plan depends in part on the development of a delicately balanced pattern of identifications in these men. They must have a certain amount of identification with the country in which they are stationed without, however, losing their identification with their country of origin; neither of these, in turn, must dominate their primary identification with the international agency for which they work.

6. The functions of the troops stationed in each country are threefold. First, they are committed to the *protection* of the country in which they are stationed from any outside attack. Secondly, they are responsible for the regular *inspection* of the country, with the aim of discovering any secret weapons development or organization of underground armies. Thirdly, they spend at least some proportion of their time in various *public service* activities, along the lines envisioned in President Kennedy's Peace Corps proposal. The specific nature of these activities depends on the needs and the facilities of the host country. Men stationed in countries that are at a high level of industrial development may spend more of their time on activities that have educational value for themselves, although even they should spend some of their time on activities that benefit the host country.

7. The international agency is governed by a central command whose function it is to formulate general policy and to decide on military operations. The latter includes both decisions about assignment of troops, distribution of weapons, and so on, that are required in the regular operation of the system, and decisions in cases of emergency. The composition and selection of the central command, as well as the rules for decision, present very difficult problems. On the one hand, members of the command should not be agents of individual governments, acting under their instructions, and juggling for competitive advantage within the agency—as is the case, for example, in the United Nations. Otherwise the agency might easily become converted into an instrument of the power struggle between states and blocs of states and lose its independent status as protector of world security. On the other hand, however, the agency cannot function unless it provides a sense of security to the individual nations which have given up their own defense systems. This sense of security depends on the extent to which they regard the central command as a legitimate and trustworthy organ in which they are in some sense represented and which does not neglect their national interests.

One possible way of meeting these different needs is to have each participating government select its representatives to the central command from a list of nominees prepared by an international body. The initial list could perhaps be prepared by a special committee of the

United Nations, and subsequent lists by a special committee of the central agency itself. The list of nominees would include men who possess some of the expertise relevant to the functions of the central command, and men of international stature who have made their careers in science, art, literature, etc., rather than in national politics. The representatives are not instructed by their governments and act as individuals. Their method of selection and the supranational definition of their roles should offer the necessary assurance that members of the central command are relatively independent agents who can be trusted across national boundaries, and who are not likely to use their positions to gain advantages for their respective countries or blocs. At the same time, these representatives can be expected to look out for the interests of their own country and to be especially sensitive to matters of concern to it.[12]

The number of seats in the central command assigned to each nation is determined by some formula that takes into account both the size of the population and other criteria of national power (such as the military capability that the particular nation gives up to the central command).[13] This formula will have to be worked out through negotiation and compromise. The leadership of the central command is selected by the representatives themselves. Many of the details of the command's operations are carried out by an international civil service, resembling the current U.N. Secretariat.

8. The relationship between the army stationed in a country and the national government has to be worked out carefully. On the one hand, the troops cannot be under the control of the national government, for this would defeat the whole purpose of the plan. The government must be prevented from using the troops for international adventures or for internal control of its own population. On the other hand, it is essential that the troops serve as a source of security for the government, and that the army does not become an independent political power within the country. The following provisions are designed to meet these conflicting requirements:

a) Under peacetime conditions, the government cannot *order* the army to engage in any kind of military action. It can *request* the army to take action only in a situation in which it is necessary to counteract a clandestine build-up of arms or organization of an underground army which threatens international peace. The local army command can turn down such a request if it deems military action unnecessary, thus reducing the likelihood that the army would be used by the government at will to subdue political opposition. If the army turns down the request for action, the government can

call on the central command to investigate and make a final decision.
b) In case of an attack from the outside, the national government can order the army to take immediate action. The army remains essentially under the control of the government until the central command can investigate the situation and take over. The central command, after consultation with the government, may decide to provide additional weapons and troops to meet the emergency and may undertake supportive action.
c) The local army command cannot take military action against any segment of the local population on its own initiative. If the army discovers secret build-ups of arms or troops, it reports these to the government, which in turn can ask the army to take action. If the government refuses to act in the light of the information brought to its attention, the local army command can call on the central command to investigate and make a final decision. The decision of the central command is binding and can be backed up, if necessary, by the imposition of sanctions.
d) If the government has any grievances against the local army command (e.g., grievances stemming from the way the inspection is being carried out), these can be referred to a special appeals board attached to the central command. Similarly, grievances of the local command against the government (e.g., if the command feels that the government is interfering with the inspection process or is engaged in an arms build-up of its own) can be referred to the appeals board.

Acceptability of the Plan

Despite its radical features, there is a good chance that the present plan would be acceptable to the individual governments. It must be kept in mind that the plan does not involve any extensive loss in security for the participating nations. Each country continues to have troops and weapons at its disposal in case of external attack, and if necessary it can call on the central command for further military assistance. The only difference from the present situation is that the function of maintaining security is delegated to a supranational organization, i.e., that nations arrange for their security on a cooperative basis. In a sense, the plan resembles a world-wide alliance and, in fact, precedents for some of its features can be found in some of the existing alliances. Furthermore, the fear that the other side will arm secretly—which blocks disarmament agreements—is reduced in the present plan since the army stationed in each country is authorized to undertake inspection and control. Thus, the plan provides for protection against attack on both ends—control at the source of a potential attack, and defense if an attack occurs nonetheless.

Another factor favoring the acceptability of the plan is that it does not require a radical reorganization in the goals and values of the participating nations. It does not represent the kind of threat to national identity that is often aroused by the concept of world government. Individual states have to yield sovereignty only in the military area, and can maintain and develop their national identity in all other respects. For example, each state can maintain its own political institutions and compete with other systems on economic and ideological levels. Similarly, the plan does not demand a transfer of loyalty from the individual nation to a supranational world society. The new loyalty that it is designed to foster is not competitive with national loyalty and should not create an issue of split allegiances. Nor does the plan demand a complete commitment to nonviolence.

In short, the plan does not start out with a commitment to radically new ends, but a commitment to certain new means. It is essentially a pragmatic commitment to a particular institutional structure, not because it embodies an ideal state of affairs, but because it represents the most promising arrangement in the context of existing values. There is no question that the plan will meet with resistance, since it represents a sharp break with the traditional conception that security is in the national domain and that an independent military establishment is essential to national sovereignty. Nevertheless, it should be easier to gain acceptance of such a structural arrangement as the best safeguard of security under the prevailing circumstances than to induce a basic reorganization of values.

The Prevention of War

The proposed arrangement contains a number of special features that are likely to help prevent the outbreak of war.

1. The plan continues to provide whatever deterrence against attack can be derived from military force. If a country is attacked, the army stationed within its borders is ready to go into immediate action and the central command is able to send additional troops if necessary. The central command has at its disposal an independent, integrated, nonnational army that *replaces* national armies; troops are available whenever they are needed and cannot be supplied or withheld at will by the national governments in pursuit of their own policies. Such an army can intervene more effectively than the type

of U.N. force we have known so far in a situation that might otherwise deteriorate into full-scale war.

2. The inspection procedures built into the plan make it possible to detect secret build-ups of arms and weapons, and thus to prevent surprise attacks by nipping them in the bud. Inspection thus fulfills, in an open and above-board manner, some of the positive functions of espionage—it becomes, in short, a form of *cooperative espionage*.[14] The fact that inspection in any given country is carried out by the very army that is responsible for its defense has some rather important implications. It should serve to minimize the perceived threat to security that is so often associated with inspection by an outside agency. At the same time, it should help to reassure other nations of the adequacy of the inspection process, since it is carried out by an agency that is always on the scene and familiar with the country's military and strategic situation. Thus, combining the functions of protection and inspection in the same agency—which represents the interests of both parties—should make inspection procedures more acceptable and less likely to deteriorate into mutual suspicion.

3. The plan facilitates progressively greater steps in disarmament. Its very enactment and operation can be expected to reduce tension, suspicion, and the threat of attack and thus to create an atmosphere favorable to further cuts in armaments. Moreover, the mechanisms for planning and administering disarmament steps are readily available, since all military facilities are centralized and inspection mechanisms are already in operation. Disarmament thus becomes largely a technical problem rather than a problem for delicate negotiation. Disarmament will have to be carried out gradually in order to assure the sense of security of the individual nations who would be looking to a strong central agency for protection. As the level of trust continues to rise, however, more and more drastic steps can be introduced. Eventually, if the plan operates successfully, war will lose its meaning and the function of arms and armies will become so different from what it is today that radical forms of disarmament will be possible.

4. The plan contains powerful psychological barriers to attack because of the nationally mixed composition of all armies. For example, if a clandestine army in country A intended to attack country B, it would face the prospect of war with B's army—which includes men and officers from A itself, from A's allies, and from neutral countries. Even if there is a group sufficiently psychopathic to overcome the barriers against such a war, the likelihood is that they would be fighting for a highly unpopular and unpalatable cause and that they would find little support in their own and other countries. It is particularly unlikely that such an attack would be sanctioned by the

government of A.[15] Similar barriers would arise if the government of A succeeded in subverting the army stationed on its territory, gaining its loyalty, and transforming it into the equivalent of a national army. Any attempt to use this army in an attack on country B would face not only the obstacle of a defending army which includes men from A and its allies, but also the obstacle of an attacking army which includes men from B and its allies. Even if their loyalty to the central agency had been subverted, it is not likely that the men from B would relish a war against their own country, nor would the government of A feel safe in entrusting a war to a force with such built-in ambivalences.

The Elimination of War

In the long run, the arrangement of nationally mixed armies should make war as we know it impossible. The entire plan is based on the supposition that armies and weapons and inspection systems located in different countries are not posed against each other, but are all part of a world-wide cooperative enterprise. The fact that the men stationed in each country represent the whole range of nationalities helps to reinforce this lack of opposition. Under these circumstances, it becomes difficult to imagine what kind of war would occur. Who would be fighting whom? Who would be protecting whom? Who would be spying on whom? Everything would be hopelessly mixed up, and herein precisely lies our hope for peace. For, given this state of affairs—along with the basic fact that the supranational agency holds a monopoly on armed force—war should become impossible as a meaningful way of achieving national goals, just as violence *within* most modern states has become impossible as a way of achieving power or status. As in national affairs, violence would then become merely a technique for the deviant, which would represent a military problem of a rather different nature than the one we face today. It is important to stress that the present plan is designed to achieve this condition not by eliminating nations or national loyalties, but by breaking up the traditional relationship between nationhood and military force.

The conception of military force as an instrument in international conflict is likely to be further undermined by the effects of service in nationally mixed armies on the military personnel itself. As they participate in the operation of the plan, officers and soldiers are likely to undergo gradual changes in their patterns of loyalty and identification which may have far-reaching implications. Men stationed in a foreign country are not expected to abandon their loyalty to their country of origin. As a matter of fact, the continued maintenance of this loyalty is necessary to the successful operation of the plan; on it rests the expectation that these men will report and resist any aggressive moves on the part of the country in which they are stationed. While maintaining their national loyalties, however, the soldiers are also likely to develop a certain amount of identification with the country to which they are assigned. Such an identification would derive in part from the very fact that they are living in that country, as is often the case with members of the diplomatic corps. More powerful forces in that direction are likely to arise from the fact that the soldiers have the job of defending the country in which they are stationed and are involved in various public service activities for its benefit. This kind of participation in some of the vital concerns of the country and opportunity to serve its interests are especially likely to create loyalty to it.

The officers and men are also likely to develop an identification with the supranational agency that provides the context for their roles. The soldier *qua* soldier is acting as a functionary of the agency rather than as a national of his particular country. Given the supranational definition of his task and the supranational setting in which he functions, a special loyalty to the agency must, almost of necessity, develop. This loyalty does not compete with national loyalty: to be a good functionary of the agency one need not be alienated in any way from one's own society. National loyalty is simply less relevant as far as the job itself is concerned. The soldier's allegiance to the agency, along with his allegiances to his own country and to the country in which he is stationed, produce a diffusion of loyalty which should have an effect on the whole conception of military force and should help to create an atmosphere in which conflicts between nations are no longer settled by resort to military means.

The anticipated effects of the proposed plan—reduction of tension and the sense of threat, increase in the general level of trust, progressive cuts in armaments, experience in extensive international cooperation, diffusion of national identifications, and gradual abandonment of the concept of military force as an instrument of national policy—are likely to create the necessary conditions for a fundamental redefinition of values. I have argued that the plan does not presuppose such a value reorientation. Yet, in the long run, an institutional structure designed to eliminate war cannot maintain itself without the emergence of widely held values that support its basic assumptions. Without eschewing conflict and competition, men will have to develop a commitment to the value of nonviolence in the settlement of conflicts. Without denying and eliminating differences, men will have to accept a responsibility for human welfare that cuts across national boundaries. While the plan does not assume an initial commitment to these higher-order superordinate goals, its operation is likely to favor their development and reinforcement.

Aside from creating the conditions for the emergence of these new values, it is also important to build into the structural arrangement itself certain features that express these values in a concrete way. An example of such a feature is the requirement that the soldiers stationed in each country spend at least some proportion of their time in public service activities that are of direct benefit to the country (and in addition may have some educational value for themselves). This concrete expression of the concept of mutual aid should foster a commitment to it among both the soldiers and the population that benefits from it, especially if these activities meet the needs of the host country in a significant way. At the same time, involvement in such activities should help to "demilitarize" the role of the soldier. By giving a broader definition to the function of the troops, it would set up both the necessary patterns and the necessary attitudes for a gradual transition to the more desirable state of affairs when the strictly military functions are relatively unimportant. It should then become increasingly possible to assign soldiers to different countries not on the basis of military considerations, but by matching their skills to the needs of the host country and matching their educational needs to the facilities of the host country. As time goes on, then, perhaps a complete redefinition of armies will become possible. Under the present plan, they have already lost their national character and their function as instruments in the pursuit of national policies. In the end, perhaps, even their military character may go by the wayside.

Preliminary Stages

I have argued that the proposed plan is more likely to gain acceptance than certain other proposals because it does not involve an extensive loss in security for the participating nations and does not require a radical reorganization in their goals and values. Nevertheless, it would be quite unrealistic to claim that such a plan can be implemented at the present time. Many questions arise when one imagines how national governments would react to the key features of the plan and to its various details.

Would it really be possible to overcome the barrier of distrust sufficiently to initiate such a program? Despite the assurance of protection and inspection, would national governments regard armies that are not entirely under their control as sufficient guarantors of security? And, even assuming that security requirements could be met to everyone's satisfaction, would governments be prepared to give up the various other functions that an independent military establishment fulfills? Could such a plan be acceptable to totalitarian regimes, which need a national army to maintain internal control? To colonial powers, which need an army to maintain their empires? To newly emerging countries, which need an army as a symbol of independence and prestige? To expanding powers, which rely on their military establishment for advancing their ambitions? Moreover, would it be possible to reach agreement on the various details of the plan? With respect to the central command, for example, would it be possible to negotiate a formula for representation and to set up rules for selection and decision-making that are acceptable to all participants? Would it be possible to develop adequate guarantees to prevent a national government from taking over the army stationed in its territory? To prevent a powerful nation or a bloc of nations from taking over the central command? To prevent a local army from usurping power and establishing a military dictatorship? To prevent the central command from establishing a military dictatorship on a world-wide scale?

These and other questions make it abundantly clear that the complete internationalization of military power cannot serve as a basis for negotiations at this time. A comprehensive plan of the kind proposed here must be preceded by considerable experience with partial and intermediate programs, incorporating one or more of the general principles that underlie the plan. These programs must represent relatively small steps, which are not confronted with as many difficulties as the total program, and they must also be self-contained so that no nation would find itself at a relative disadvantage in the event that no further steps are taken. As experience with such partial programs accumulates, it may become possible to find a basis for resolving some of the knotty issues that block the comprehensive plan. Whether or not a comprehensive plan of some kind materializes, these partial programs themselves may make important contributions to the prevention of war.

One direction worth exploring, in the development of partial programs, is a limited exchange of officers and men within the context of existing national armies. For example, a regular arrangement might be worked out whereby a certain number of American soldiers serve in the Russian army and vice versa. This program might be expanded to include troops from other countries, thus creating nationally mixed units within various national armies. These units might be assigned to nonsensitive tasks at the beginning, and to increasingly sensitive tasks as time goes on. The latter would have to be linked with a second type of program, involving some arrangement for mutual inspection or "cooperative espionage." For example, it might be possible to negotiate an agreement to share all military information that is necessary for the prevention of surprise attacks. This information would be gathered or verified on a regular basis by inspectors representing the participating countries or a special international agency. Once such an agreement has been established and secrecy has declined in importance, it should be possible to broaden the program of exchange of troops and officers. Such exchanges may, in fact, be tied directly to the mutual inspection program. For instance, nationally mixed armies stationed on nuclear bases might contribute to the prevention of surprise attacks. It may even be possible to have American representatives sitting in on meetings of the Russian general staff, and vice versa. These exchange generals would be in a position both to gather and to supply information highly relevant to mutual security problems.

A third direction in the development of partial programs might involve experimentation with various independent supranational military agencies that do not replace national armies, but operate in addition to them. It may be possible, for example, to establish a permanent U.N. emergency force in which both the small and the big powers participate (a proposal approved, incidentally, by the majority of Americans in a recent Gallup Poll). Such a force would be particularly valuable if it were to consist of nationally mixed units under a unified command. Another possibility is to develop a supranational agency with armies regularly stationed in each participating country (alongside the national armies) and carrying out certain special functions assigned to them. Gradually, these armies may take over more and more responsibility for the maintenance of security, without however completely replacing the national armies. The continuation of even a small national army for limited purposes may make the idea of an international security force more acceptable. Finally, a related possibility is the proposal by Singer, mentioned earlier, for the combination of disarmament with a regular and gradual transfer of weapons to a United Nations agency, charged with the task of using these weapons for the protection of signatory nations under specified conditions.

Because of the nature of modern weapons and the resulting elusiveness of national security, governments have shown a certain willingness to consider *specific* plans that are quite radical in their implications for national sovereignty. The steps that I have proposed here—and similar ones that have yet to be invented—are small enough and specific enough to serve as bases for negotiation in the present international context. The importance of these steps, and of the comprehensive plan that they are designed to mediate, rests in the fundamental principle that they embody. This principle states that security is not a commodity in the national domain, to be attained on a competitive basis. The only possible security in the nuclear age is *international security*. If we internationalize military force, we can hope that the *practice* of war will become impossible and will be eliminated from the repertory of nations. With time, perhaps, the supranational agency responsible for the maintenance of world security will have to depend to a lesser and lesser degree on the backing of the military force under its monopolistic control. This will happen when even the *idea* of war as an acceptable institution is rejected by the majority of mankind.

NOTES

This paper was written while the author was on leave at the Institute for Social Research in Oslo. I benefited greatly from the opportunity to discuss these ideas with Norwegian and American colleagues in the course of a seminar on international relations held at the Institute. I am particularly grateful to Christian Bay and Robert Noël for their encouragement and their many helpful comments.

1. For a discussion of this point, see Gordon Allport's chapter in *New Knowledge in Human Values,* and Muzafer and Carolyn W. Sherif, *Groups in Harmony and Tension* (New York: Harper, 1953), especially p. 307.

2. This discussion refers primarily to the relationship between the United States and the USSR. There is some question whether China is governed by the same goal at this point.

3. I am using the term "national security" here in the traditional sense, which emphasizes military power. For a discussion of this and related concepts, see Donald G. Brennan, "Setting and Goals of Arms Control," *Daedalus,* LXXXIX (1960), pp. 681–707.

4. See, for example, Robert R. Bowie, "Basic Requirements for Arms Control," *Daedalus,* LXXXIX (1960), esp. pp. 713–14.

5. Charles E. Osgood, "Suggestions for Winning the Real War with Communism," *Conflict Resolution,* III (1959), p. 305.

6. For a discussion of this dilemma, see J. David Singer, "Threat-Perception and the Armament-Tension Dilemma," *Conflict Resolution,* II (1958), pp. 90–105.

7. Osgood's proposal for graduated unilateral disengagement (*op. cit.,* pp. 315–21) presents an excellent and convincing approach to the problem of making a beginning.

8. See Singer, *op. cit.,* pp. 101–3.

9. I am speaking of partial disarmament here. Total disarmament presupposes that certain other changes have already taken place.

10. It will soon become clear that what is proposed here differs from a United Nations force or from an army tied to a world government, although there are, of course, some overlaps.

11. Singer, *op. cit.,* p. 103.

12. In order to meet the needs of the participating governments more adequately, it may be advisable to have only some of the representatives selected by the method described above, and others by the reverse method. That is, a certain proportion of the representatives might be selected by the international agency from a list of nominees prepared by each government. These nominees would, of course, have to meet certain agreed-upon qualifications. Another possibility is to have a *second* chamber in the central command whose members represent the individual governments more directly. Yet another possibility is to set up an advisory council whose members are appointed by the governments and who work with the central command without, however, having a vote. They would be in a position to bring the concerns of their governments to the attention of the command and to keep their governments informed of important developments.

13. The principle of one vote per nation would be entirely inappropriate here for two reasons. (1) It is highly unlikely that the big powers will want to turn over their arms and troops to an agency in which their representation is not somehow commensurate with their size and the amount of military force that they have given up. (2) The proposed agency is not an association of nations, but an organization with a world-wide mandate; the nation is thus not a relevant unit. Ideally, the central command should be selected on a world-wide basis, without regard to national representation, but such an arrangement would not be feasible at first.

14. There is some precedent for the notion of legitimizing and cooperating on espionage in Eisenhower's open-skies proposal, and in his reaction to the U-2 incident. In essence, Eisenhower argued in the U-2 incident that espionage is a proper activity which can be admitted and should be accepted because of its function in preserving peace. The present plan just goes one step further by proposing that the nations of the world arrange for this activity on a cooperative basis.

15. Similar considerations are involved in the proposals for exchange of hostages. See Morton Deutsch, "Reducing the Reciprocal Fear of Surprise Attack," pp. 83–86 of the present volume. See also Jules Feiffer's semiserious proposal that points up various advantages of an exchange of armies. *The Village Voice,* IV (March 30, 1960), p. 4.

NONMILITARY DEFENSE

By ARNE NAESS

THE TRADITIONAL MEANS of defending life and freedom have included a major emphasis on the military. Because of technical developments, the use of these traditional means may have the result that in ten or fifty years there may be few human beings left to enjoy freedom or to struggle against tyranny. But there also exist nonmilitary methods of struggle. It is the aim of this article to explore to what extent these nonmilitary methods might be developed to serve more adequately the need for means of defending life and freedom, and along what general lines such a change might operate. I do not claim to offer a panacea, a detailed blueprint, a final answer to every single aspect of the problem, and certainly not an easy way without risks. There is no realistic response to the present crisis which does not involve risks. What I am seeking to do here is to establish a reasonable case why there should be serious consideration of an alternative method of defense which has, relatively speaking, been ignored. Having in mind the defense of the way of life of peoples with whom I identify—primarily Norwegians, but also many others in many countries—I shall attempt to broaden the traditional concept of defense and defense institutions. It is my belief that thinking in terms of the broader concept will strengthen the possibilities of peace and freedom.

The Inadequacy of Military Defense

The need for defense is greater today than ever before. The decline in the importance of military defense does not reduce the importance of defense in general.

To defend Norway today means to defend our independence, our freedom to shape our lives within the framework of Norwegian social traditions and culture and to change them as we wish. It is to defend a way of life against all external forces that would alter it without our consent. From experience we know that events in another country can endanger our freedom. Throughout the world there exist dictatorships or power concentrations under various labels which for ideological, economic, military, and other reasons may threaten the freedom of other countries. The Soviet Union is one of them, and I share the view of those who are convinced that a continued advance in power and influence of the Eastern bloc sooner or later may reach the point at which Norway could be taken within that bloc's sphere of influence and possibly be occupied. This would clearly threaten our ability to form our own institutions, and might even mean the deportation of our people to the expanses of northern Asia.

In the event of nonnuclear war Norway might hold out for hours or even weeks, but in any war between the major blocs we must expect occupation under a more or less benevolent or malevolent military dictatorship. If the war should end with (so-called) victory of those states introducing a way of life we despise and a totalitarian state machinery, conditions resembling those of the occupation during World War II would again exist. Even in the event of the establishment of a world state, it will be necessary for the peoples of the world to develop means by which to check the possible abuses of power and dictatorial tendencies which could arise from such an extreme concentration of power.

What means of defense happen to be most effective is relative to what is to be defended. In defending a way of life, those means must be avoided which will undermine or destroy the way of life to be defended and the very people who cherish it.

For hundreds of years the world was such that the defense of Norway could be identified with the defense of Norway's geographic borders. Defense of a territory against physical invasion was often to defend a way of life, a culture pattern, or an ideology. In this context, military forces strong enough to keep the invader out were conceivable and possibly were effective. Today, however, we recognize that the relative independence that we enjoy is the result of many forces and conditions outside of Norway. It is these forces and conditions which we must seek to influence in order to preserve our independence. Military preparations are inadequate to the task.

Against a powerfully armed totalitarian state, military defense of Norway's geographical boundaries by its three and a half millions alone might be heroic, but it would inevitably be futile and quixotic. Allied with NATO, our military resources are increased, but they are not in the long run more effective. As well as increasing the likelihood of occupation during a major war, alliance with nuclear powers makes more acute the danger of annihilation by nuclear weapons.

Though not a single enemy soldier crossed our borders, our existence could be terminated. It is also possible that strong alliances will force Norway to fight nuclear wars for aims which most of its inhabitants do not consider basic or of supreme value.

Hence the very notion of defense needs clarification. Simply *to call* something a "defense" measure does not make it capable of defending anything whatsoever. Let us therefore read "military defense" as meaning "military preparation for the eventuality of war." Military preparation is the most thoroughly institutionalized means of defense, but there is no good reason for narrowing down the concept of defense by identifying military defense with defense in general.

Nonmilitary Defense

As wars have become increasingly more destructive there has grown up a conviction that the use of modern weapons is justified only, if at all, in the service of fundamental values. But at present, foreign policies are generally shaped not in order to protect and extend fundamental values, but to uphold or change existing power-relations in favor of this or that nation. Military means may still to some degree be effective for such customary aims. A foreign policy shaped mainly to protect and extend fundamental values could scarcely make use of modern weapons, and thus risk a nuclear war, because a war would violate some of those values which are to be defended.

However, immediate dissolution of military defense organizations is not likely to realize the aims of those who believe in substituting more or less completely nonmilitary methods for military defense. If at present the military organizations were to be greatly reduced unilaterally or even universally, it is probable that many people would feel more insecure, threatened, and helpless than ever; the passive state of despair and fatalism would actually be reinforced. If one takes away the only means of defense a person *believes* to be truly effective, he certainly has every reason to feel frustrated. Thus, a reduction of reliance on the military must be preceded by *the development of increased confidence in and the gradual adoption of alternative means of defense.*

Let it be quite clear that I do not advocate what is usually called "pacifism" as an alternative to present policies. As an organized movement centering around individual conscientious objection to participation in war, pacifism must from the political scientist's standpoint be regarded mainly as nonpolitical. It is also clear that although pacifists are not always without political influence, they have no common platform. What I am interested in exploring is a primarily nonmilitary defense policy determined by the political and military realities of our day. In light of the present political situation, such a policy cannot call for immediate disarmament.

Commitment to Freedom

Since a nonmilitary defense policy depends upon the active participation of the populace in times of emergency, it is vital that the citizens understand what it is that they are trying to defend. The first stage of a nonmilitary defense policy is therefore the clarification of the principles which we value and of the qualities of the way of life we wish to pursue, so as to increase our commitment to these principles.

Various steps might be taken which would further this understanding and commitment. The most apparent need is for a national self-examination by all parts of the population as to what it is in our way of life that we cherish and wish to extend and to preserve. Discussion groups, panels, debates, articles, books, essays, and radio and television, on both local and national levels, must be enlisted to facilitate this self-examination. Every scholar interested in the question should be provided with the opportunity of obtaining funds for study and publication. Schools, universities, churches, and other educational institutions could serve as local centers for this national program.

This program might be called ideological, but the term must not be confused with ideologies which are detailed systems seeking to force compliance and converts. What is needed is work on the ideas, ideals, and moral convictions associated with freedom, not with force. It is of course possible and desirable that an effective program of this kind might influence other countries and contribute to the liberalization of potentially aggressive dictatorial regimes. This would be one demonstration of the direct relation of this program to the problem of defense. On the home front, it would strengthen the motivation for defense and assist in the mobilization of defense energy in times of crisis.

International Service

The second general policy which would in the long run contribute to a fulfillment of our society's ideals and the meeting of human needs as well as to defense is *international service*—service to friendly countries, "neutrals" and potential enemies alike.

Thanks to Henrik Wergeland, Fridtjof Nansen, and others there is in Norway a tradition stressing world-wide solidarity and responsibility. If the opposition to the programs advocated by Nansen had not found such strong backing in various powerful countries, there might have developed forms of cooperation on the international level which would have reduced the likelihood of wars. Since 1945 Norway has organized help to countries in which physical disasters have occurred (floods in Italy and Holland, earthquake in Agadir, etc.). Fisheries in India have been supported in various ways with combined government aid and voluntary contribution, and a variety of other activities have been carried out, all of which might be said to exemplify international service. Other countries have made similar efforts, sometimes more comprehensive and better organized.

It is now time to show the close connection between such measures and defense, and to try to make such international service more effective on a larger scale. Such enterprises need to be integrated into the country's normal economic system, for instance, by lowering import duties on products from areas which we assist and encouraging an expansion of trade with them. In addition, it is important that there be some kind of reciprocal aid, such as cultural programs with the countries receiving assistance. It is cooperation and *mutual* aid that will reduce tension in the long run, and not simply humanitarian help.

International service should be undertaken for its own sake, to relieve suffering and meet human needs.[1] It is also important as a means of expressing and implementing our nation's way of life and principles, particularly the concern for human dignity and justice and freedom upon which we like to think that our society is based. To undertake international service purely from the "ulterior" motive that it will assist our own defense effort will reduce or destroy many of its intrinsic values and its contributions to that effort. However, it is important to recognize the relation between such efforts and the defense problem.

First, in relieving suffering and poverty, international service will contribute to the removal of important causes of conflicts and wars. The relationship of poverty, gross inequality, and suffering to violent conflicts, hatred, and war is too widely recognized to require detailed elaboration.

Second, such programs increase "man-to-man" contacts and contribute to the development of personal loyalties between individuals of various countries. These "crisscross" loyalties can contribute to international solidarity and make it more difficult to obtain popular support for international conflicts with countries with which such contacts have been rich.

Third, international service can contribute to the creation of a more sympathetic attitude toward our country and way of life which would reduce the chances of aggressive action against us. The potential attacker would have clear evidence of our nonaggressive intentions; and the fear of alienating "world opinion" would make him hesitate before invading. And in case of a crisis our plight would receive more attention, publicity, sympathy, and concrete aid than might otherwise have been possible.

Fourth, carrying out an international service program will make our own country better prepared to meet crises. It will help to create a positive sense of purpose and mission comparable to that which often accompanies military efforts, but without certain of the disadvantages of such measures; and in giving our citizens experience in working cooperatively in a common altruistic cause it will enhance their ability to practice this cooperation in other tasks in times of crisis.

Fifth, knowledge of international service conveyed to the troops and population of a potential enemy might reduce their motivation to take aggressive action against us, cause them to carry out repressive orders inefficiently, and increase the chances of their deserting and mutinying in support of freedom.

Areas of Service

A wide program of international service would include a multitude of tasks. Emergency help in cases of natural catastrophes and famines[2] and aid to refugees[3] would be vital. Technical help adapted to meet the needs and culture of the countries desiring it is an obvious means of international service. Another is various types of educational aid, particularly assistance to students who wish to study in other parts of the world.

A service of a somewhat different type is to provide independent observers and investigators to assist in the study and resolution of specific international conflicts and perhaps of certain national political crises such as civil wars. This service would include operational research aimed at contributing to the solution of such conflicts and more general and fundamental research on conflict, war, and nonmilitary means of conducting and resolving conflicts—in short, on much of the nonmilitary defense program advocated here. The results of such research should be widely distributed. Other countries wishing to adopt a similar type of defense policy could be provided with special defense liaison officers, lecturers, and consultants to assist in the adoption of such a program.

Such a program of international service would of course require considerable resources, which I am convinced should be provided mainly through the government budget. There would also be a large demand for manpower, including both untrained workers and specialists. In addition to a highly trained long-term technical staff, there would be an important role to be played by persons serving for one or two years. Volunteers alone could not fill the demand. Manpower should therefore be supplied by conscription from the country's youth of both sexes. This form of service ought to be a full or partial alternative to the usual military conscription or alternative service for conscientious objectors. Essential training would include language skills as well as knowledge and techniques required for particular jobs.

It would be by far preferable if such service corps could be organized on an international basis and made available to the United Nations or some other international body. The experience of several countries' corps working together—the Americans and Russians cooperating in building a steel plant in India—would contribute to closer understanding and develop the ability to cooperate in service projects. This might make resolution of other issues between such countries less difficult.

A considerable part of such a service program could be carried out through existing organizations which are already operating along the same general lines, such as the Red Cross, Save the Children, and War on Want. Other services could be conducted through national branches of international organizations, others through contributions of men and resources to such international organizations as UNESCO, UNICEF, WHO, and FAO.

Improving Our Own Society

Another aim of a nonmilitary defense program would be to make our own society more worthy of defense and more capable of being defended by nonmilitary means. It must be frankly admitted that there are many aspects of our own society and others which many people would not wish to defend and would certainly not make great sacrifices to defend. The victims of racial segregation and discrimination, for example, and those subjected to economic and political oppression, will not be eager to defend their societies against foreign aggressors who may claim to be "liberators." Neither will the more idealistic members of such societies, even though not victims of such policies, be eager to sacrifice heavily in the defense of such conditions.

At the time of Hitler's annexation of Austria, for example, Schuschnigg had already established a one-party system, had built concentration camps on the German model, had abolished individual liberties, and had carried out the principle of authoritarianism to its ultimate implication. There remained in Austria little basis for ideological resistance to Hitler. A similar though perhaps less severe condition existed in other European countries such as Poland and Yugoslavia; apart from the warnings of psychological warfare, there was in many cases no basis for universal and determined resistance to Hitler. Societal house cleaning is a prerequisite of effective nonmilitary defense.

Another necessary improvement is the decentralization of decision-making power. Citizens must be more accustomed to making decisions individually and in small groups and less dependent upon the government or leaders of organizations. Admittedly, technical developments seem to have made inevitable a certain amount of centralization. However, if the opportunity for local initiative and responsibility is destroyed rather than actively cultivated and nurtured, then the ability of citizens to resist encroachments on their freedom will be disastrously affected. Needed is a general strengthening of those institutions in our society which can train the individual to make decisions in times of crisis in the absence of the top governmental hierarchy and of all other major organizations. This would prevent demoralization if the state apparatus were seized by opponents of liberty and yes-men placed in key positions in all major organizations.

Nonmilitary Resistance

All of the above components of a nonmilitary defense policy will contribute to the ability of the nation to cope with crises; and at the same time they will enrich and improve our own society. They will also reduce the chances of invasion and occupation. It is nevertheless necessary that we have an adequate program for dealing with the latter eventuality, for with modern weapons it will always be possible to invade and occupy territories for shorter or longer intervals. Unhappily, the customary identification of military defeat with total defeat prevents discussion at government levels of problems of occupation and suppression, such discussion being identified with defeatism or lack of "defense-mindedness." The opposite is actually nearer the truth; those who identify military defeat with total defeat neglect a sector of defense of vital importance.

Perhaps the most positive way in which a small country like Norway could contribute to the prevention of a nuclear war would be to say "no thank you" to an offer from a friendly superstate to stop an invasion of her territory by using nuclear weapons. Such a policy is, however, irresponsible so long as the populace is no better trained to meet the problems of occupation than it was in 1940. As I have indicated previously, reliance on military methods of defense cannot be diminished until other means of defense are generally recognized as equally effective. It is therefore my proposal that, for the present, side by side with conventional military preparations, there be instituted a program of preparation for nonmilitary resistance in case of invasion. As popular confidence in such measures gradually grew, it would be possible and desirable to reduce the military preparations and to rely in greater degree upon nonmilitary training.

In the event of invasion by an army possessing nuclear weapons, relatively little could be done by military means to prevent the invader's disbanding major organizations and eliminating known leaders of opposition. Our citizens must understand that this military failure does not mean defeat; it does mean that the struggle is entering a new phase of more direct confrontation of human forces. The struggle ought not to be waged on a front where the opponent already has overwhelming superiority. Rather it must be waged by nonmilitary weapons and by techniques which can continue to function regardless of the invader's control of communications, ammunition, and supplies, and despite his power of mass deportations. Also, there is likely to be an inverse relationship between the degrees of military and of nonmilitary preparedness for defense. For precisely those humanitarian values which give rise to spontaneous loyalty and affection for a way of life are likely to become undermined to the extent that military preparedness is maximized.

Techniques of Resistance

It must be kept in mind that our ultimate goal is to preserve our way of life. Hence, even under enemy occupation *certain fundamental principles must be upheld,* regardless of what the opponent does and regardless of the cost. *No human being is to be sacrificed by others to achieve an end; each person must be something of a goal in himself. No goal can justify destruction of respect for truth.*[4] *And under no circumstances may any human being be mistreated or tortured.*

It is important to distinguish this kind of a program from psychological warfare, which may resort to all types of threats and deception in verbal propaganda. It must also be distinguished from a program of general noncooperation, a program focused on the invaders. The weakness of a policy of general nonviolent resistance is that it should not be upheld at all costs; if repression gradually stiffens it is impossible to continue defending, for instance, the major organizations of a democratic government. Automatic refusal to cooperate with the invaders in food distribution may result in a famine. Self-inflicted hardships for nonessential goals cannot easily be asked or expected of a populace except in critical periods of very short duration.

Techniques of resistance which would serve to defend the above principles could include many types of noncooperation: strikes, boycotts, civil disobedience, refusal to operate and participate in the existing governmental agencies and other major organizations once they had been taken over by the enemy, and refusal to provide him with labor, transportation, information, and so on.[5] Wherever the invader sought to extend his power by forcing the inhabitants to violate the basic principles, he should be met with those forms of nonviolent resistance best adapted to each case. Let there be no pretense that the enemy would not retaliate and inflict repression. But this is no argument against nonmilitary resistance, for it is at least as true of military means. The question is *how* to do the job, not whether it should be carried out.

At the same time a large variety of efforts could be undertaken to encourage the occupying soldiers not to carry out measures which must be resisted by the inhabitants. These efforts would of course include no acts of terrorism against the soldiers themselves. Rather, by means of posters, underground newspapers, secret radios, acts of resistance and defiance, personal contact where possible, the soldiers could be convinced of the pervasive and tenacious nature of the resistance offered. The history of recent occupations—for instance, that of Norway—shows that it is possible for occupying soldiers and even high officials to be actively sympathetic with the occupied populace, to be lax or even negligent in carrying out orders, and to pass important information on to the underground. While maintaining the noncooperation and defiance, the resistance should be aimed at maximizing the amount and degree of this support from the occupying forces.

It is vital in such resistance movements for people to be willing and able to continue their customary ways of life in small units when the public life of a democracy is absent. During the occupation of Norway, for example, the teachers successfully prevented the schools' being used for spreading false information in the interest of the invaders. Further, by mass nonviolent noncooperation they openly refused to participate in the teachers' organization Quisling was creating as a part of the foundation of his corporate state. When the schools were closed they taught in homes. The price was months in concentration camps for hundreds, but both the organization and the corporate state were stillborn and the schools remained free of control.

During the German occupation of Poland, the pressure on schoolteachers was in part so heavy that direct resistance at the schools and within the school organizations was impossible. But teaching was conducted "privately" in tiny groups, a form of *microresistance.*[6] In Norway repression and brutality did not reach such a high pitch that all large organizations, "legal" or "illegal," were destroyed. But with another five years of occupation, under steadily worsening conditions, the resistance might have disintegrated into microresistance. This would also happen in case of large-scale deportation. But if the citizenry were thoroughly prepared, even microresistance could be a weapon far more powerful than any military means used against it.

Research

Military defense methods have for centuries been carefully studied. Nonmilitary methods cannot be improvised. In fact we do need study and clarification of nonmilitary methods and training and preparation in the use of such methods in specific situations. And we need it now.

There has already been sufficient practical experience to indicate that, in the light of the obvious limitations of possible alternatives, such nonviolent resistance constitutes the best available means for combating an occupation. There has, on the other hand, been little academic study of these phenomena; our knowledge about them, as compared to techniques of war, for example, is extremely limited. Therefore a first requirement is the initiation of a large-scale program of fundamental research on nonviolent resistance. In addition to this basic research, specific attention must be paid to the application of such methods against totalitarian opponents. This must include study of totalitarian systems and of the experiences of previously occupied countries under such regimes. Much of the research could be conducted through existing institutes for social research, defense academies, and universities, though it might also be desirable to establish a special institute or academy for coordination of such projects. This program of study cannot wait until a nonmilitary defense program is adopted; it could begin immediately. It will also be necessary to train and develop a core of specialists in such methods, theoreticians and strategists, coming from the military and from a variety of academic disciplines, including sociology, political science, and psychology, and from devotees of nonviolent philosophies.

Conclusion

These then are certain aspects of a nonmilitary defense program whose primary purpose is to preserve and extend liberty and to prevent invasion and expansion of suppressive systems, a program also capable of dealing with invasion and suppression.

It is of course important to recognize that such a program of nonmilitary resistance depends upon popular acceptance of the probability that the invader will inflict severe repression, torture, and executions, and that the nation will neither be in a position to retaliate in kind, nor be willing to do so. Only such a program, however, could keep alive and active both those principles which furnish the ultimate basis of freedom and the willingness to fight for freedom.

Implementation of a nonmilitary defense policy could be cumbersome, it is true. Such a defense policy involves a reorganization of the existing defense department, and a broadening of the tasks of the department of foreign affairs. It is possible that the two might effectively be combined under one or the other auspices, or a new arrangement created. The cost of a nonmilitary program would be considerable, and at the start it might have to be an addition to the present military budget.

This is admittedly not a program that will be adopted in a day. But whereas initial adoption of the policy may be difficult, once the program is worked out in fuller detail and put into practice its adoption by many countries will be facilitated and accelerated. As more and more countries adopt such a program, the dangers of war will be further reduced as greater pressure is exerted for the abandonment of military aggression. In short, it may well be that the only direct means to achieve the fundamental social change required for the permanent prevention of war is the widespread and immediate implementation of the policies of nonmilitary defense.

NOTES

1. It is probably true of most nonmilitary methods of defense that the actions recommended are more effective, the more they are engaged in as ends in themselves—as parts of a way of life rather than as means for defense.

2. Examples: the earthquakes in Agadir and Chile, floods in India or England, famine in China or India. Such help should be available on an adequate scale as soon as the need is known. Hence there must be reserve resources available on instant call.

3. Had adequate help been ready for the 900,000 refugees from the Palestine conflict in 1945–48, it is possible that the present tensions in the Near East would have been of lesser intensity. The U.N. General Assembly appropriated the small sum of five million dollars and requested all countries to contribute to a fund for a peaceful solution of the refugee problem; but few governments responded and

only thirty-five million dollars was collected—about one-tenth of the cost to Britain and France of the Suez invasion. Despite energetic efforts, the agencies involved could do relatively little. Now the problem is complicated by rigid official positions adopted by the Arab States and Israel and the constructive program is shoved into the background, while propaganda and fruitless discussions on the question of guilt occupy the foreground. This is only one of the many cases of refugee crises throughout the world, from China to India, Africa to Hungary.

4. This does not imply always providing the invader with all of the information he requests.

5. For a classification with examples of sixty-five techniques of nonviolent resistance (in the sense of resistance without weapons), many of which would be applicable in such a situation, cf. G. Sharp, "The Methods of Non-violent Action" (mimeo., Olso, Institute for Social Research, 1960).

6. Microresistance: resistance by individuals and tiny, temporary groups carried out in such a way that exposure and annihilation of larger organizations and institutions do not affect it, at least not directly.

ECONOMIC STEPS TOWARD PEACE

By EMILE BENOIT

THE SYSTEM OF NATIONAL DEFENSE which Western societies have employed for several centuries, and which has come to be accepted as part of the "order of nature," is, in fact, in the process of rapid breakdown. This breakdown arises from the technological revolution in the arts of destruction, which has liberated forces too vast, protean, and unstable to serve reliably any rational human purposes. Thus national defense can no longer provide its chief *raison d'être,* physical security. Some people have concluded that they would be safer without a defense program, and there has been considerable popular agitation in some countries against rearmament, or against nuclear weapons in particular. Without exaggeration, one can agree that the risks of unilateral defense programs mount alarmingly, and that it is urgent to find some better type of security system.

It is difficult, however, to visualize a positive alternative to the defense system we know. Clearly a great intellectual effort will be required to develop a workable alternative in the form of a system of international security, and thereafter a great educational, political, and diplomatic effort will be needed to obtain its acceptance.

Economic—Political Issues

The first step is to recognize that we are not irrevocably committed to the existing system. Here we must face and dispose of two widely accepted misconceptions—that capitalist countries are economically too dependent on the making of armaments to be *able* to disarm, and that the Communists are politically too dependent on the use of them to be *willing* to disarm. Both of these ideas have a certain surface plausibility, but little real substance.

On the first point the negative evidence is compelling. The United States actually carried out the largest unilateral disarmament program in history from 1945 to 1948, and put through another pronounced defense cut from 1953 to 1957. Since 1957 the program has continued to decline as a percentage of the gross national product, and now absorbs less than a tenth of all goods and services produced. While the existence of a program even of this size creates a significant group interest in the continuance of that program, this interest is not as large relatively as it was when overridden before. Our society is, in any case, accustomed to balancing interests and to subordinating a special group interest to the general welfare when the two conflict.

Furthermore, the interests of defense contractors are not absolutely tied to a continuation of the arms race. Profits on war contracts, while more dependable as long as the contracts last, are likely to be lower (especially after renegotiation) than on nondefense business. Moreover, the stability of defense business is highly uncertain. Some defense-centered businesses have begun to study ways to diversify into nondefense lines. This is viewed as "insurance" and usually strengthens their appeal to investors. There are other profitable things for most defense contractors to do; and defense contractors, like other people, have an interest in staying alive and keeping their families and their country from harm.

Sometimes the argument is put in broader form, involving an assumption that the prosperity of our economy as a whole requires the maintenance of a large armaments program. As we shall see, this assertion has a certain plausibility under a particular set of conditions. But wiser economic policies could change these conditions. Rapid growth and full employment should not depend on a large defense program, nor does a large defense program automatically produce full employment and rapid growth.

As for the Russian attitude, there is little evidence up to this point that the Russian rulers are seriously interested in disarmament other than as a propaganda issue. This is indicated by their professed willingness to conclude treaties with entirely inadequate inspection provisions, which is quite inconsistent with their extreme distrust of capitalist societies on other issues.

The lack of serious interest in disarmament negotiations up to this point does not, however, necessarily imply that the Russians may not become seriously—and perhaps suddenly—interested in the subject. The example of the Austrian Treaty negotiations shows that a long period of pseudo-negotiations may be followed by rapid progress once all parties have made up their minds that they really want an agreement.

Why *might* the USSR come to take disarmament seriously? Essentially because the possible payoff of continuing the arms race may come to seem trivial in comparison with its dangers, although originally the pay-offs must have seemed very high, in terms of gaining international prestige, protecting the regime, and shielding expansionist probes. The Russians are intelligent enough to realize the increasing gravity of the risks, and also to appreciate the improved standard of living which disarmament would make possible.

The United States defense effort absorbs about a tenth of the national output of goods and services, and provides employment, either directly or indirectly, for about six million people. Any major degree of disarmament would obviously create some problems of adjustment. One would expect the government to recognize the need for studying economic adjustments to the kind of disarmed order which is the stated object of disarmament negotiations. There has been considerable resistance to making such studies, based on the notion that disarmament is impossible to attain, and that such studies may create overoptimism and lead to a relaxation of vigilance or increased resistance to bearing the heavy tax burden of Big Defense.

Such fears are fortunately lessening and the new administration in Washington is showing increased willingness to examine all aspects of disarmament in a more serious and intensive way, including economic aspects. It is also encouraging that the United Nations has indicated its interest in economic aspects of disarmament by undertaking a substantial study of the subject.

While in the United States there is still considerable emphasis upon preparing a disarmament position which will create a favorable impression upon world opinion, there is also an increased interest in considering seriously how far this nation might reasonably go toward disarmament if Russian agreement could be obtained.

On the Russian side, there is indication that at least a number of the top scientists and strategists are quite serious about wanting disarmament and being willing to accept comprehensive inspection. However, it is not at all clear that any significant body of Russian opinion is even vaguely aware of the need for a supranational peace-keeping authority to prevent direct and indirect aggression, as well as to implement the arms agreement.

The official Russian position has firmly supported studies on the economic aspects of disarmament, apparently in the hope of demonstrating that the economic difficulties are negligible or illusory, even in capitalist countries. This is somewhat at variance with the position which Communist propaganda has frequently upheld in the past, and would appear to indicate a growing desire to influence the non-Communist countries to disarm, whether because of a sincere desire for disarmament in itself, or for some other reason.

In the United States, the aspect of economic adjustment which has been of greatest public concern is the problem of avoiding a pronounced depression or period of slow growth when government purchases for defense suddenly cease. This is frequently confused with the question of the direct impact of defense cutbacks in particular industries or localities. Actually, these two problems are by no means identical. The immediate impacts, even though severe, would be unlikely to create a depression, providing there were *adequate over-all demand* to provide re-employment opportunities for the displaced workers and reinvestment opportunities for those whose capital and enterprise could no longer find a use in defense production. Hence it would be worthwhile to consider, first, the likely magnitude of the initial impact, and second, the problem of maintaining a high enough level of demand to prevent a major reduction or slowing down of economic activity, with serious and continuing unemployment.

The Initial Impact of Defense Cutbacks

In appraising the potential impact of defense cutbacks, it may be helpful first to look at the total amount of employment and production which is now directly or indirectly created or sustained by defense expenditures. An example of the indirect effect would be the amount of employment going into the production of steel which is used to make the delivery trucks which are used to deliver munitions from the manufacturer to the military base. This kind of estimate can be made by means of an "input-output" or interindustry study showing the sales of every industry to every other industry and to every category of final buyer. Such a study has been prepared in conjunction with the Research Program on Economic Adjustments to Disarmament.[1]

On the basis of this study, it appears that in 1958 military spending led to the employment of 700,000 workers in the aircraft and parts industry. In the making of radio and other communications equipment it employed over 200,000. Five fields, each of which employed in defense work over 100,000 workers, were: (1) ships and boats, (2) ordnance, (3) transportation, (4) trade, and (5) the professional and service occupations. Five additional fields, which employed on defense work more than 50,000 each, were: (1) business services, (2) iron and steel, (3) construction, (4) petroleum and its products, and (5) chemicals and chemical products. Farther down the list were copper with 16,000 workers and aluminum with 13,000. Some industries, while not particularly defense-oriented, had nevertheless a substantial number of workers dependent on defense purchases—running from 36,000 to 38,000. Included in this range were paper and allied products, lumber and wood products, and apparel and textile mill products.

These are absolute figures. A better gauge of the potential shock of a sizable cut in defense spending on specific industries may be the percentage of the total employment in each industry which is devoted to defense orders. Still using 1958 figures, we find that the four industries with the heaviest absolute dependence also had the heaviest relative dependence: ordnance, with obviously 100 percent; aircraft and parts, with approximately 94 percent; ships and boats, with 61 percent; and radio and other communications equipment, with 38 percent. Only 1 percent of employment in trade was created by defense demand. The comparable percentage for transportation was 6, for professional and service 2, for construction 2. In a number of other industries dependence ranged between 10 and 20 percent—for example, iron and steel, petroleum and its products, metal stamping and machine-shop products, motors and generators, cutlery, tools and hardware, machine tools and metal-working equipment, copper and aluminum.

It should perhaps be noted that all the preceding discussion of defense-related employment has not included either the armed forces or civilian employees of the government. The number of civilian employees alone working on defense matters—822,000—exceeded even the number in the aircraft industry and was close to 20 percent of all government workers. And the number of people in the armed forces dwarfed any of the other figures—2.6 million.

The number of jobs that would be eliminated by a defense cutback, and the extent to which individual industries would be hit, depends of course on the composition of the military budget at the time it is cut and the size and composition—and speed—of the cuts. In the absence of arms control or reduction, with present trends, defense expenditures in 1965, including the National Aeronautics and Space Administration, may be about 60 billion dollars.

Even if there is intensive and successful work in the next few years on getting a disarmament agreement, we could hardly be ready to implement it before 1965. We may take that year, therefore, as an assumed cutoff date—which appears to be the most optimistic assumption politically possible.

The actual extent and timing of the defense cutbacks will depend upon the kind of disarmament agreement which it proves possible to negotiate. If, as is here assumed, a practical and secure disarmament agreement will require the creation of a world authority with a substantial inspectorate, police force, and strategic deterrent force, it is clear that at least a part of United States defense expenditures will be diverted to the equipment, provisioning, and maintenance of these supranational forces. Indeed, a part of the United States military, scientific, and engineering manpower, along with that of other countries, might also be contributed to this effort. In addition, even comprehensive disarmament will presumably permit the maintenance of some minimal forces of a strictly national character for the preservation of internal order and possibly also to provide an element of additional national protection against attack. Such remaining national forces will presumably create no danger if they are armed only with light and essentially defensive weapons, and if an international police and deterrent force is at hand to help protect all nations against external aggression.

Because of uncertainty as to the nature of the disarmament agreement that might be accepted, it is not possible to foresee the exact extent and pace of reduction in defense expenditures that might result. To provide an example, however, we shall simply assume here that we might see a total reduction of about 35 billion dollars within a twelve-year period between 1965 and 1977. While additional cuts might be made thereafter, it would be the initial major cutbacks of defense production, along with the paring down of military forces, that would create the major impact problem.

By applying input-output analysis to this disarmament model, we can get a rough idea of potential disemployment by industry in the event of a disarmament program of this magnitude. So far we have not gone beyond the first stage of assuming that the industrial input patterns, both in 1965 at the start of the program, and in 1977 at the end of the program, will be the same as in 1958. On this admittedly not too realistic assumption, an input-output estimate shows an employment impact of almost 450,000 in aircraft; nearly 200,000 for radio and communications; around 225,000 each for shipbuilding and ordnance; over 58,000 for iron and steel; 42,000 for petroleum and its products.

It must be emphasized that the above figures are *not* estimates of postdefense *unemployment*. *Potential* disemployment need never be translated into actual unemployment. Some end-products not highly specialized for defense may readily be absorbed into nondefense end-uses, and many raw materials and intermediate products could readily be utilized by nondefense industries. Even where reconversion of specialized defense facilities is necessary, the time interval may be brief, and in some cases skilled and high-quality workers may be kept on the payroll in the interim to assure their availability after reconversion. In other cases disemployed defense workers and demobilized members of the armed forces may find other jobs without delay, or may take vacations which keep them for a time out of the ranks of the unemployed since statistically they have withdrawn temporarily from the labor force. How fast the residual labor transfers occur will depend primarily on how rapidly other nondefense activities expand, which itself depends chiefly on how well over-all demand is sustained. Secondarily it will depend on how well the reconversion or transfer function is planned and executed—including physical reconversion of defense facilities, retraining, relocation, and rehiring of personnel, and in some cases the direction of additional production facilities to labor surplus areas.

Obviously, if demand remains adequate, the solution of transfer problems is greatly facilitated. If demand is *not* maintained at an adequate level, not only are transfer problems harder to solve, but it makes less difference *whether* they are solved, since a successful transfer simply results in putting or keeping some *other* man out of a job.

A sense of proportion is restored in this matter when one realizes that our economy is now capable of 22 billion dollars a year of regular growth, and that by 1965 the corresponding figure may be 27 billion dollars. An economy of this magnitude is capable of junking two to three billion dollars a year of defense goods and services, or leaving unutilized the facilities that produced them, and still making substantial progress, provided this can be done without shrinking over-all demand.

It is here, though, that the difficulty lies. For in our market economy, unutilized facilities and unemployed workers earn no incomes.[2] Unless they are enabled one way or another to earn incomes, the initial deflationary impact of their income losses may be multiplied up to two or three times by the indirect effects of the cutbacks in expenditures by workers who become unemployed, and the reductions in new investment by companies which become alarmed at the shrinkage of their markets and their inability to operate their existing facilities to a reasonable extent of capacity at a profit, leading often to further lay-offs, and so on.

We turn now to the sort of measures which might be helpful in coping with this type of problem. The suggestions that follow are not intended as definitive; they are based on research which is still incomplete, and no attempt has been made to consider their political acceptability.

Stabilization Measures

1. *Measures to stabilize the public sector.* Within certain tolerable limits, the simplest way to offset economic difficulties connected with

disarmament is by a rapid expansion of nondefense public programs. This principle cannot be carried too far because of widespread Congressional and public opposition to rapid expansion of public activity other than in the defense field. However, it might be possible to get acceptance of the general principle that cuts in defense expenditure of up to a given scale (for example, 5 percent) would be immediately offset by an expansion of public nondefense programs. Thus, the objective would be to stabilize, within acceptable limits, the total size of the public sector.

In implementing such a principle it would be necessary to prepare a shelf of public projects widely diffused throughout the country. If the commitment were fully to offset any decline in the defense program of up to 5 percent in any one year, the backlog of ready-to-go public projects should be of the value of perhaps three billion dollars. Such projects should not only have been authorized by the Congress, but the funds should already have been appropriated on a stand-by basis.

The matter of timing here is crucial. For such a commitment and program to exercise full beneficial effects, the President would need to be empowered to sign contracts for the new projects at the very time the defense contracts were being canceled or not renewed. Only in this way could the powerful deflationary effects of defense-contract cancellation be offset or mitigated.

2. *Measures to avoid a budget surplus.* Particularly during a period of reduced government expenditures, there is serious deflationary danger in attempting to achieve a budget surplus. If cuts in the defense program are of a magnitude too great to be offset by the public-sector stabilization commitment described above, then it is of fundamental importance to avoid the temptation to aim for a budget surplus by maintaining existing high tax rates while expenditures are falling. Most economists now realize the serious deflationary impact of attempting to reduce the national debt during a period of declining government expenditures. A second principle, therefore, that should be embodied in the disarmament adjustment program is that tax reductions be applied quickly enough, and be of sufficient size, fully to offset any net shrinkage in total federal expenditure. To obtain such full offset it would ideally be necessary to have tax cuts that somewhat exceed the size of the net reduction in public expenditures. This may, however, be a counsel of perfection. At the least, tax cuts should be no less than the decline in public expenditure, and should be announced and put into effect quickly enough to restore disposable income as quickly as it is being reduced by declining government expenditures.

The practical application of this principle involves serious political problems because of the strong predisposition of Congress and the public to seek the attainment of a budget surplus for reduction of the national debt when the defense burden is reduced. Such attempts are largely self-frustrating, but are likely to have quite depressive effects.[3]

3. *Stabilizing the private sector.* The foregoing measures should do a great deal to stabilize the public sector, and to offset any net reductions in it by means of increases in private disposable income through tax reduction. In a private enterprise economy, however, it is not easily possible directly to stabilize the *private investment sector.* The most practical method to attain a reasonable degree of such stability is again through stabilizing the public sector, and also *personal consumption,* which accounts for approximately two-thirds of final demand. Assuming that all feasible measures have been taken to stabilize the public sector, what measures can be taken with respect to the stabilization of personal consumption?

The measure proposed here—the "tax holiday"—is based chiefly on the relative stability of the consumption function, or the percentage of consumer expenditure out of personal disposable income. A tax holiday, with respect to personal income tax, would be declared for a period of at least one month, but renewable thereafter whenever the data indicated that consumer expenditure was failing to rise at a satisfactory rate. A satisfactory rate might be defined as 1 percent a quarter, or slightly less, after seasonal adjustment. (The norm might be reduced whenever an exceptionally high rate of capital formation or export surplus was adjudged necessary for public policy reasons.) Current indicators might be prepared on the basis of monthly personal income estimates supplemented by retail sales data, and new current estimates of consumer purchasing based on budget analysis of a sample of consumers, developed along lines similar to the Commerce Department's unemployment estimates.

In essence, the tax holiday would be a simple across-the-board rescinding of income tax obligations of all income tax payers for a period of one or more months, renewable whenever the data indicated. It could function for most taxpayers through a simple suspension of the withholding tax for the period in question, and all taxpayers would have their end-of-the-year tax obligations reduced by the appropriate percentage (i.e., 8½ percent or a multiplier thereof, depending on the number of months the tax holiday lasted). The crucial objective here should be to make the tax holiday as different as possible from ordinary tax reductions so as to avoid the protracted Congressional battles (with respect to equity, favoritism, loopholes, rich versus poor, etc.) which always arise when major tax changes are in question. In sharp contrast to usual tax reductions, tax holidays would be recognized from the beginning to be impermanent and to have no redistributionist intentions.

Growth Problems

Defense cuts which depressed postdefense growth rates could have grave long-term effects on our international position in the extended period of intensified economic and political rivalry which would probably follow upon a disarmament agreement. Because of the large "fallout effect" on the civilian economy of defense expenditures on science, research, education, new product development, training of skills, and public construction and other investment-like activities supported by the defense program, it would be important to find substitute programs which could be financed within a nondefense context and which would provide comparable or greater benefits for the civilian economy.

The most obvious and politically palatable measures of this sort would be similar to certain programs now financed under the defense program whose contributions are not exclusively to national defense. For example, the work of the Atomic Energy Commission and the Military Space Program makes a major contribution to basic research and to the development of resources, knowledge, and skills useful for the growth of the civilian economy.

A disarmament adjustment program should include measures to identify such expenditures, and to arrange for their rapid transfer to nondefense budget categories as soon as a disarmament program started. In order to prevent disorganization and loss of momentum within these programs, it would even be desirable, if possible, to arrange for advance authorization and appropriations by Congress to continue such programs for one full year after the shift to the new budget category, with the right of the President to modify the character of these programs as required to comply with our international obligations or with a change in the government defense programs.

A similar approach might have application to the financing of research and education in the universities. A substantial contribution to higher education is now being made by Defense Department support of university research of potential defense usefulness. It would be helpful to have legislation which would authorize the continuance of such subsidies to universities without restriction on their research or educational content, in the event of a disarmament agreement or a change in the character of defense requirements. In this connection there might be great benefit from the creation of a new government Department of Higher Education, Research and Development, which might administer a large new program devoted to the following purposes:

1. Strengthening the United States system of higher education and administering an enlarged fellowship program.

2. Coordinating all of the various types of public research now being undertaken for nondefense purposes.

3. Reviewing the United States patent system from the point of view of encouraging pure as well as applied research. For example, serious consideration should be given to the possibility of providing patent protection to ideas as well as processes and models, and giving the right to discoverers of key scientific concepts and hypotheses to benefit at least to a small extent from profitable applications of such ideas.[4]

4. Giving corporate charters to, and supervising, public corporations specifically devoted to a rapid development of promising new processes and products including new pilot plants, where private financing proved unattainable owing to the long-term nature of the probable payoff. Such public corporations might be empowered to borrow on the capital market and to float issues of their own securities to the general public; and they might be empowered not only to engage in research development and product-testing activities under their own direction, but also to subscribe to convertible debentures or even limited quantities of common stock of private companies fulfilling similar objectives.

5. Establishing other public corporations as "productivity centers," comparable to those established in Europe under the Marshall Plan, devoted to the rapid diffusion throughout industry of advanced techniques and methods, as well as promising new processes and products.

Substantial benefits might also be achieved by reducing the tax burdens on innovation, risk bearing, and extra work. For example, companies and individuals could be permitted the privilege of averaging their incomes for tax purposes over an indefinite period of years so as to avoid penalizing the type of enterprise which brings in a high level of income in a relatively brief period of time.[5] Reductions of very high progressive taxes would also help. (Some beneficial reductions would occur automatically to the extent that across-the-board percentage reductions were permitted under the short-term tax reduction provisions for stabilization purposes sketched above.) This would permit progress on closing various loopholes which now permit upper-income taxpayers to pay substantially less average taxes on the top income brackets than would be anticipated on the basis of the income tax schedules. Accelerated depreciation and special tax benefits for new investments, such as proposed in the Kennedy tax message, might also be beneficial.

At the other end of the income scale, substantial growth effects might be derived from measures which would permit and indeed encourage older persons to avoid premature retirement, and which would encourage women to pursue gainful employment and careers. Such measures would probably include elimination of present restrictions on employment and income received from employment of persons otherwise entitled to OASI benefits, and improved tax deduction allowances for married women who are gainfully employed, especially when this requires the employment of others in housekeeping functions. Another such measure might involve the subjecting of overtime pay and earnings on secondary and occasional jobs to a lower rate than applies to basic income.

None of the proposed measures would be of much benefit, however, unless accompanied by a policy and program for sustained high levels of employment and rapid growth. In the absence of economic policies promoting adequate over-all demand, there is little gain to be derived by increasing the effective labor force, lengthening the work week, or encouraging people to undertake additional work responsibilities. Indeed, all such notions will appear unnecessary and impractical until we have achieved a situation of relatively full employment and full utilization of industrial capacity, when the shortage of manpower, skill, and enterprise may again become visible as a primary ceiling on achievable growth.

The Transfer or Reconversion Problem

This is the aspect of the problem that is most apparent to the general public but, under most foreseeable conditions, it would be of lesser total importance than the stabilization or growth problems already discussed. From the point of view of economic analysis, the problem is essentially that defense expenditures pay for a rather highly specialized bill of goods and services, whether in the armed forces, defense industry, or specialized defense research and development. This specialization is geographic as well as industrial, and relates also to the skills and attitudes of personnel employed. Thus, the shift over to nondefense economic activities may require complex redeployment of people, changes in the pattern of industrial output, and abandonment of certain skills and attitudes and the learning of new ones, with the attendant possibilities of loss of salary, status, and perquisites.

Many of the specific measures required are obvious and well known. These include provision for prompt and liberal settlement of canceled contracts; liberal allowances for termination pay to disemployed workers as an includable cost of defense contracts; low-interest loans to defense contractors to help finance reconversion and diversification measures; liberal educational retraining and relocation benefits or loans to disemployed defense workers and military personnel; loans to assist in securing housing, purchasing small businesses, and the like for those who find it necessary to relocate or make other major readjustments.

More controversial, perhaps, are the various measures which might be taken to bring new industry into areas and communities suffering major disemployment and loss of business as a result of disarmament measures. Useful experience should be gained in the next few years in the administration of the depressed areas legislation recently passed by the Congress. Extensive foreign experience, especially in the United Kingdom and in the administration of the Coal and Steel Community and the Common Market social funds may also prove applicable. There is a growing realization that the rising costs of providing new housing, schools, roads, and other social infrastructure, relative to the cost of providing industrial facilities, may now make it more economic to bring new industry into an area with well-developed basic structure, rather than to insist, along conventional economic lines, on moving an existing labor force to areas where industrial facilities already exist. Other factors pointing in this direction are the improved facilities for rapid retraining of personnel (such as teaching machines and educational TV) and the possibility of expanding the use of automation to take care of those parts of the industrial processes formerly requiring prolonged training in special manual skills. The development in advance of a complex of techniques for rapid retraining would be an important contribution to the solution of the reconversion problem.

A more fundamental difficulty arises in the case of highly specialized defense contractors peculiarly well adapted to large-scale research development programs and programs for the development of new kinds of end-items. Such firms, typical of the new "armaments industry" and concentrated particularly in aeronautics, space work, missiles, and electronics, are particularly adjusted to preparing bids for large government contracts and negotiating such contracts, but have shown relatively less ability to engage successfully in ordinary commercial enterprises selling in competitive markets. In a number of cases, the attempts they have already made toward diversification, as insurance against the loss of government contracts, have not worked out too successfully. Not only might there be substantial costs involved in forcing such firms to make the transition, but grave losses to society would result if they were broken up. These considerations point to the desirability of a permanent acceptance by government—even in a private enterprise economy—of considerably larger responsibilities of a broad, developmental nature.

Particularly useful in absorbing the specific types of resources and talents released from defense production would be an enlarged space program. The existing nonmilitary space program has undoubtedly been pushed and supported in part because of its indirect benefits to defense. Disarmament might diminish the motivation for such a large space program. On the other hand, the *economic* benefits of retaining the existing program, and even considerably enlarging it, might be very great.

The nature of these benefits is not widely understood. It in no way involves a pay-off in the traditional sense of the direct return from the end-product—successful space exploration. The benefits are rather of an indirect character. Basically they arise from the very large scale organization of research and development and associated industrial effort which can proceed without concern for the commercial salability of the product. Among the indirect benefits already achieved or likely to be achieved in this connection are greatly improved electronic equipment of all sorts, improved methods of water purification and desalting, greatly improved and cheapened metals and alloys, and many other unexpected and useful side-products.[6] The long-term benefits from side-effects of an enlarged space program may greatly transcend any practical benefits ever achieved for humanity by actual space exploration. Yet there is a good reason to believe that these side-benefits could not readily be obtained by any direct attempt to achieve more limited profit-making goals. What may be essential about such an effort as the space program is precisely that it transcends any rational and ordinary commercial relation of means to ends, and infuses a quality of imagination, daring, and pursuit of large national objectives without too closely counting the costs. It may well be that the most rapid development, even in a private-enterprise economy, requires a large publicly directed sector outside the normal range of private enterprise motivations.

The past development of the American economy has included large elements of governmental stimulus, even though they have not been generally stressed in the folklore about our economic history. They include such measures as governmental involvement in and subsidies to canals and railroads, government support of the vast elementary school system, government contribution to road building—which made the automobile industry and the development of truck transportation possible—and, most recently, the enormous contributions of the Department of Agriculture and the land-grant agricultural colleges to improved agricultural methods—resulting in recent gains in agricultural productivity far transcending those in industry. It would thus not be entirely outside the American historic tradition to have a large government program indirectly benefiting industry but directly aimed at the achievement of some wider national purpose. Exploring the universe fits rather well into the tradition of exploration and expansion as a vital interest of government.

If such a program were to make the maximum contribution to the problem of adjustment to disarmament, there would need to be a firm purpose in the national government, not only to maintain but vigorously to expand the space program when the military benefits of such a program were no longer desired. A large supplementary grant for such a program, on a contingent basis, would admirably fulfill this purpose, since it would reassure those in the missile and defense space projects that congenial work would be available after disarmament.

Another significant area for absorbing the specific talents and facilities of existing defense contractors lies in the "hardware" requirements of the disarmament inspection itself. While the opportunities in this area are sometimes overestimated—through overlooking the multipurpose inspection possibilities of a given set of inspection tools and personnel—yet undoubtedly large opportunities will be created, particularly for the electronics, space, aeronautics, and photographic industries.

There are also potential opportunities for some of the great research and development firms and procurement industries in a coordinated international program, supported by governments and international agencies, devoted to accelerating the development of the less industrialized countries. One can imagine, for example, the dynamic effects that might be achieved by widespread production and utilization of teaching machines, the mass production of simple housing, basic water supply and sewage systems, simple road-making machinery, and even the setting up of a large number of river-valley developments and industrial plants on a systematic basis. Such large-scale enterprises might offer adequate challenges and opportunity for the kinds of talent and productive capacity available within the present defense complex.

Similarly challenging opportunities are conceivable for the utilization of the directive ability of some released military personnel who were strong leaders, willing to live and work in difficult environments, and highly motivated toward public service. Advance planning and the use of defense forces for international development objectives, while no panacea, might nevertheless contribute substantially to easing the transition. The field of oceanography and the industrial development of ocean resources might in turn offer challenges for the specialized knowledge and abilities of the world's naval forces and naval research personnel.

To grasp opportunities, a substantial amount of advance planning would be necessary. For this purpose, the following measures are proposed:

1. Defense contractors should now be encouraged to budget, as a deductible cost, expenses up to 2 percent of the value of defense contracts for undertaking or subsidizing studies of their own reconversion problems, their potential civilian markets, their diversification capabilities and opportunities, and their possible contributions to a nondefense research and development program, including space exploration, oceanography, and other practical applications.
2. The armed forces themselves, in conjunction with civilian consultants, should establish planning units to make comparable studies of just how they might usefully fit into a world with only vestigial national military forces. They should also study the types of benefits which would aid many of them to revert to civilian life without undue hardship. Such studies would be highly motivated and far more accurate and valuable than those which any outside agency could produce. The Congress should include in the defense budget a substantial additional sum for financing such studies.
3. The Congress should also appropriate for the United States Arms Control and Disarmament Agency adequate sums to prepare a general government research and planning study on the whole problem of economic adjustments to disarmament.[7]

The Problem of Equity

A preliminary decision needs to be made whether and to what extent it is desirable public policy to spread the costs of the needed adjustments widely—over the general taxpaying public—rather than leaving the burden to be borne entirely or disproportionately by the persons, firms, and communities particularly involved in the reconversion effort. Public policy in this regard might appropriately consider not only the purely ethical issues involved, but the positive advantage of weakening the probable resistance to disarmament of those whose economic interests might otherwise be severely damaged by it. The nation would gain objectivity in its approach to disarmament, and its policies would gain respect from other countries if pains were taken to remove the opposition to disarmament which the existence of a politically potent bloc with a large interest in the defense program tends to create.

The implementation of such a policy would pose problems. Many of the measures proposed for facilitating reconversion would serve also to reduce its burden on the persons, communities, and companies adversely affected. Perhaps it would be possible, by further liberalizing these benefits, to offer more adequate compensation to the parties involved. Just how far such measures could appropriately be carried is not easy to say.

For example, the government might not only extend unemployment compensation over a longer period—say, for two years—for disemployed defense workers and military personnel, but also liberalize the benefits—say, up to 80 percent of previous wage levels. Moreover, one might even allow the former defense workers and military personnel to continue collecting, during the two years, a portion of the unemployment compensation—perhaps up to 120 percent of the shortfall in current wages below those previously attained and including, in the case of former military personnel, a fair allowance for living expenses and other perquisites of their former occupation. While such provisions may seem overgenerous, they would certainly cost the government much less than continuing the military program at present levels; and they would not, in all likelihood, fully compensate for the sacrifices which those making post-defense job shifts would actually incur.

Similarly, it would be possible to allow to defense industries, and to communities especially dependent on defense facilities, particularly generous tax privileges with respect to losses—such as double or triple deductions from the income-tax base.

One group that would be particularly hard to protect is that of investors in the securities of defense firms or of companies importantly benefiting from defense contracts. The price of such securities is often, obviously, very high, capitalizing for a long period ahead the anticipated earnings from defense contracts. A serious stock market break would be hard to avoid in the event of any significant move toward disarmament. One device that might conceivably be studied in this field would be a liberalization of tax regulations, permitting investors in such firms to take double or triple deductions from their income bases for losses suffered from the sale of the securities of these firms after the beginning of a disarmament program if these securities were purchased before a given date, say six months before the passage of the new legislation. This would avoid giving support to further inflation of security prices, but would reduce the likely losses of those who had contributed their capital in good faith to the financing of companies in the defense effort.

Summary

Among conclusions that emerge from this brief survey of the economic problems of disarmament are, first, that while these problems should not be underestimated, they are by no means insoluble; second, that they can be solved with a minimum of social dislocation and personal hardship if given careful study and well-considered advance planning, leading to appropriate action by government and community agencies, industrial firms, and employee groups. Certain basic legislative action is to be desired.

The main lines of optimal economic planning and action for a comfortable transition to disarmament are beginning to appear. They may run counter to certain venerable prejudices and habits. Yet no system or habit of thought is ordained for all time, least of all economic thought. In this field, as in other areas of modern science and technology, today's crisis presents a decisive challenge to human ingenuity, boldness, and perseverance.

NOTES

1. See Wassily W. Leontief and Marvin Hoffenberg, "The Economic Effects of Disarmament," *Scientific American* 204 (April, 1961), pp. 47–55.

2. Unemployed workers may for short periods draw unemployment compensation payments of less than half of their regular wages, and businesses establishing losses may under some circumstances recoup 52 percent of them by using them as profit offsets, but these are only transitory and partial offsets.

3. See Emile Benoit, "The Propensity to Reduce the National Debt Out of Defense Savings," *American Economic Review,* LI, No. 2 (May, 1961), pp. 455–9.

4. This might well require the development of new administrative agencies with judicial or quasi-judicial functions, possessing more scientific expertise than ordinary courts. The judgment of such agencies would be subject, of course, to review by the courts, but primarily with respect to procedural matters and without reviewing the adequacy of the judgments.

5. Many devices which would improve either the equity of the tax system or its favorable influence on enterprise and productivity are increasingly being made possible by new computers which permit, for example, the reaveraging of a large number of figures with great ease. There is a real lag in our recognition of the potentialities of new techniques in this respect.

6. Perhaps the most startling is the discovery of a medicine made from a component of missile fuels which provides one of the best existing antidepressants for the treatment of certain mental diseases and emotional problems.

7. A panel report of experts, under the chairmanship of Emile Benoit, has now been published. See *Economic Impacts of Disarmament,* United States Arms Control and Disarmament Agency, Publication 2, January 1962.

PART II

REDUCING INTERNATIONAL TENSIONS

INTRODUCTION

THE DIFFERENCES that divide East and West are political, economic, and ideological in nature. Conflicts arising out of these differences are therefore intrinsically difficult to resolve. The difficulties of resolving such conflicts are compounded by the absence of mutually-agreed adjudicative procedures and a mechanism for enforcing the decisions of an accepted tribunal. As a consequence, these unresolved conflicts have led to an ever-increasing and dangerous arms race; in turn, the arms race has generated a rising level of international tensions.

In the case of nations, as in the case of individuals, we do not know with any precision what is the optimum level of tension. To strive to eliminate tensions entirely may not only be impossible but also undesirable for nations as well as individuals. We do know, however, that a high level of tension in individuals, as in nations, impairs the capacity for rational behavior.

The cold war, though fraught with many dangers, is a substitute for a hot war. But there is a danger inherent in a high level of international tension, the danger that it may lead to accidental, preemptive, or preventive nuclear war. Consequently, it is of critical importance for world peace to reduce the level of international tension and thereby increase the chances for a type of conflict to develop which does not involve the risk of nuclear war.

Since the immediate cause of international tension, as we have seen in Part I, is the arms race, progress in the direction of stopping the arms race would decrease the level of international tension. However, the dilemma that East and West have been faced with for approximately fifteen years is that the arms race and international tensions are part of a vicious circle: reducing the level of international tensions appears to be impossible because of the mutual distrust and fear generated by the arms race; and stopping the arms race seems to be impossible because of the high level of tensions in great measure due to the existence of nuclear arsenals in the East and the West. To break this vicious circle, new strategies are urgently needed. It is this spirit which pervades all the essays in Part II.

There appear to be as many strategies proposed for reducing international tensions as the number of authors of proposals in Part II. However, at least two general types of strategies underlie all these proposals: One is a strategy of unilateral action and the other is a strategy of mutilateral action. By a unilateral strategy in this context is meant a course of action initiated by any nation designed to promote peace rather than to threaten it. Customarily, unilateral action connotes aggressive or hostile action by any party in a dispute to further its interests or advantages vis-à-vis its adversary. In the present context, the focus is on unilateral actions for peace. Similarly, bilateral or multilateral strategies can be designed in the service of peace or war and here, again, the focus is on such courses of action which might contribute to the reduction of the level of international tension and, in turn, to the reduction of the chances of war.

Unilateral Proposals

All but four of the papers in Part II advocate unilateral actions to break the arms race-international tensions spiral. Osgood, after presenting a psychological analysis of the dynamics of the cold war, sets forth a proposal for a program of "graduated reciprocation in tension-reduction." The actions envisioned in this proposal could be very diverse, e.g., sharing of scientific information, reducing trade barriers, elimination of military bases, etc. Actions selected would not endanger the security of the nation undertaking them, nor would they be based on any promise of reciprocation by the other party. If such actions were reciprocated, they would be followed by still other unilateral actions calculated to break the current stalemate in international relations. In his emphasis on the potentialities of graduated unilateral actions in stopping the arms race and in creating patterns of peaceful relations among nations, Osgood's analysis converges with some elements of Fisher's proposal, in Part III, on strategies of constructing rules which can regulate the actions of governments.

Unlike Osgood's *graduated* approach to unilateralism, Fromm presents the case for *unconditional* and *complete* unilateral disarmament. Although he does not believe that unconditional unilateral disarmament is a feasible policy in the near future for the major powers, he believes the arguments in behalf of this position can contribute to "breaking through the thought barrier which prevents us now from getting out of the dangerous circle of seeking peace by means of threat and counterthreat." Daiches does advocate the position of unconditional unilateral disarmament and argues for the need for launching an educational campaign (a) on the arts of nonviolent resistance to any potential conqueror who seeks to exploit the unilateral disarmament of his enemy, and (b) on the superiority of the cultural values of the West as against the East. Similarly, Frank, in the course of his psychological analysis of a warless world, espouses nonviolent resistance to a potential enemy who attempts to take advantage of a unilaterally disarmed opponent and considers the problem of developing new methods of nonviolent resistance to an opponent possessing superior force.

Riesman in his "Nylon War" seeks to dramatize, by means of satire, the potential value of unilateral actions as "moral equivalents of war." In this case, the use of consumer goods as a focus for competition between East and West is only a vehicle for Riesman's advocacy of an imaginative and unilateral approach to peaceful international conflict.

In the spirit of Riesman's and Osgood's plea for inventive unilateral initiatives for peace is Etzioni's proposal that the United States abandon the competition for prestige in outer space, with its attendant dangers of engendering war. Etzioni proposes that the United States disengage itself from this outer-space contest which he, along with others, contends has largely prestige rather than military value. Instead, he proposes that the United States embark on a "development race" and use its vast resources in areas where there is an urgent need for spectacular achievements, namely in the rapid industrialization of underdeveloped countries.

Multilateral Proposals

The remaining papers in Part II presuppose a bilateral or multilateral strategy. Rapoport analyzes three modes of conflict—"fights," "games," and "debates"—and argues for the need for converting fights and games into debates. Debates between representatives from East and West, according to Rapoport, require new ground rules, e.g., that each party state the position of the adversary in a manner satisfactory to the adversary before being permitted to argue his own case. The proposed rules for debates, Rapoport suggests, would insure proper communication as to one another's objectives and would make debates more fruitful, thus increasing the chances of consensus emerging among the parties.

In a similar vein, Russell believes in the potential value of deliberations by a conciliation committee appointed by the United Nations. Eminent representatives of East and West and of neutral countries would associate with one another on the proposed committee, for a protracted period of time. During this time, Russell hopes they would become impressed with each other's humanity and come to share a body of values transcending the ideologies of their respective societies, thereby increasing the chances of discovering new areas of agreement. The conciliation committee would have only an advisory capacity, recommending to their governments solutions to problems endangering world peace.

Establishing what human beings want and the nature of their resources is the subject of Churchman's essay. He proposes that an inventory be made of the values and resources of various societies of the world to ascertain not only whether human beings want peace, but also how the world's resources can be allocated to maximize the chances for peace. Underlying Churchman's proposal is the premise that the more we know about the values and resources of human beings, the more rational and effective our actions might be in an effort to build a peaceful world.

The final essay in Part II, by Pokrovsky, proposes the establishment of a world-wide weather and solar service as one possible field for international cooperation. Pokrovsky contends that such a joint venture by all nations, using a variety of technological innovations, including rockets and communication satellites, would not only increase our knowledge of weather forecasting but would also prove highly profitable. He thinks that such forms of international cooperation could have important consequences for improving the world "as a dwelling place for man" as well as for preserving peace.

If proposals such as those presented in Part II were implemented, they would probably transform the arms race and the consequent international tensions into a "peace race," namely, a contest between the great powers to build a better world with the awesome resources of science and technology instead of using these resources to destroy the world.

W. M. E.

GRADUATED UNILATERAL INITIATIVES FOR PEACE

By CHARLES E. OSGOOD

THERE ARE MANY PARADOXES about the nuclear age in which we live. I shall delineate four of them which provide a framework for this paper.

PARADOX I. *The greater the destructive capacity of the weapons in our hands, the less concern most people seem to have about the problem.* I have heard it estimated that if all of the energy in weapons now stockpiled were to be transformed into its measuring unit—that is, every ten-megaton bomb into ten million tons of TNT and so forth—and then spread evenly over the area of our country, we would be wading around in TNT well above our ankles! Be that as it may, it is certainly true that never before in human history have so few been able to destroy so many and so much in so short a time. Yet how many intellectuals have fully committed themselves to working on this problem? How much attention have our mass media given to the search for fresh alternatives? How much success have we had in disarmament negotiations?

PARADOX II. *While feverishly engaged in a nuclear arms race, all sides express peaceful intentions and fervent hopes that these weapons never will be used.* I believe these hopes and intentions are sincere, yet roughly half the national budgets of the two polar powers go into military preparations. Surely, future generations will look back upon these years as the Age of Unreason.

PARADOX III. *The more nations spend for what they call "defense," the less real security they seem to have.* The basic reason for this is that, in terms of military technology, offensive capability has far outstripped defensive capability. Policy-makers are fond of talking about great defensive "shields" or "umbrellas," but these defenses are more in men's minds than in their weapons.

PARADOX IV. *The greater a nation's military power, the less rather than greater seems to be its freedom of initiative in foreign policy.* Witness the squashing of the Suez situation, the attempts on all sides to neutralize Laos, or the actions of the United States with respect to little Cuba. Quite apart from fears of retaliation, the mere possession of nuclear weapons has a sobering, restraining effect. For rational men, at least, possession of power brings with it a sense of responsibility. And so we find the nuclear age characterized by a Great Freeze on initiative along traditional lines.

If a psychologist or psychiatrist were faced with an individual human being so full of irrational paradoxes in his thinking, he would probably recommend that he be institutionalized. Unfortunately, there are no institutions for nations. However, the psychologist or psychiatrist would also realize that this individual's behavior seems paradoxical only because the dynamics of his case are not understood. Therefore *the first purpose of this paper will be to explore the dynamics of the cold war mentality.* We will be looking for psychological sources of the sense of inevitability which most people feel about war and which blocks serious consideration of other alternatives.

But, you may object, the fact is that we are concerned with the behavior of nations, not individuals, so of what relevance is a psychological analysis? By way of answer I would say, first, that the problems we face are primarily matters of human nature and human relationships; there is nothing about nuclear science that automatically produces bombs and nothing about space science that automatically produces missiles; it takes human decisions based upon human fears and aggressions to produce these things. Second, I would say that, in the absence of any real science of international relations, what we do know about the principles of individual behavior may provide a model and at least a set of hypotheses about the behavior of nations. And finally I would point out that the extraordinary development of the media of mass communication during this century has done much to bridge the gap between publics and elites. The greater the communality of stimuli, the greater the communality of responses.

This poses the second problem for this paper. Novel situations usually demand novel solutions. As the paradoxes of our time indicate, we certainly face a novel situation today. Yet relations among nations are still being governed by traditional policies that are felt to be realistic primarily because they are habitual. Recent technological developments in communications, transportation, and other forms of human interdependence—to say nothing of weaponry—have not merely made some kind of world government feasible, they have made it essential if our civilization is to survive. But the problem is to get from here to there, to somehow bridge the great cultural lag between our technology and our form of political organization. We find ourselves at the crest of nationalism at a time when our technology requires one world under common law. *The second purpose of this paper will be to suggest a kind of international behavior, based on behavioral science considerations, that may be more appropriate to this nuclear age.* But first we must look into some of the dynamics of the cold war mentality.

Dynamics of the Cold War Mentality

Denial. When faced with overwhelming danger, but having no acceptable way of handling it, the typical human reaction is to deny its existence, that is, repress it. This mechanism underlies public apathy about civilian defense. It leads people to avoid exposing themselves to information which revives the danger and to seek out information which promises security, however illusory. Once unconscious acceptance of the danger has been repressed, the unconscious anxiety is free to produce symptoms. A typical symptom is what Edgar Allan Poe has called "the Imp of the Perverse." This is the irrational compulsion to flirt with the threatening situation—to play with fire, to lean out over the edge of a cliff, or to press that critical button. The more one denies the seriousness of the danger intellectually, the less the restraint on the compulsion. The way out of this dilemma is to have some acceptable solution which will channel the fear into constructive action. One of the troubles with pacifist approaches to this problem has been that they frighten the living daylights out of people with threats of nuclear fire and brimstone without providing any acceptable solution—acceptable, that is, under present conditions of competing national sovereignties.

The meaninglessness of abstract terms. Most of the words we use to talk about nuclear war are abstract terms that get their meanings indirectly through association with other words rather than directly through association with real objects and events. Words like "intercontinental ballistic missiles," "megatons," and "thirty million casualties" just simply do not have the emotional, gut meanings of words like "blood," "bread," and "mother." Furthermore, one cannot directly sense the potential danger of a nuclear missile five thousand miles away as he can the danger in a man seen holding a gun or knife; we require special gadgets to tell us that we are exposed to even lethal doses of radiation, and it takes a truly magnificent feat of imagination to comprehend the significance of "thirty million casualties." I am told that most Russians seem more concerned about the dangers of a "hot" nuclear war than most Americans. Perhaps it is because they have lost many millions under conditions of ordinary war well within the memory of present adults.

Psycho-logic. Over the past two decades a great deal of social psychological research has been converging on a conclusion about human thinking that common sense had already isolated as "the consistency of little minds." Whenever cognitively inconsistent elements are brought together in assertions, stress toward mental consistency is produced; psycho-logic resolves this stress along the lines of least resistance, in such a way as to retain the simplest possible cognitive structure. Thus if Our Revered Leader praises some obscure diplomat, it is cognitively consistent for us to feel more favorably inclined toward this man ourselves; but if The Enemy says this same diplomat's ideas are sound, we find ourselves suspecting him.

Psycho-logic is the lowest common denominator of human thinking. It contributes to the oversimplified "two-valued orientation" stressed by the general semanticists. It runs rampant into the area of international relations, where the usual corrective process of reality-testing is difficult to apply, and it forces all shades of gray toward absolute blacks and whites. Psycho-logic has made bogeymen of the opponents in every human conflict: If WE are *good, kind, fair,* and so on—as most of us are in everyday relationships—then psycho-logic dictates that THEY (the enemy) must be equally *bad, cruel, unfair,* and so on throughout the opposites of all traits we attribute to ourselves.

Once this fundamental evaluative polarity has been established, psycho-logic operates subtly but continuously on the interpretation of all subsequent incoming information. One effect is to push both sides in a conflict down opposite paths of *self-delusion.* Observe the alacrity and near-universality with which American media people jumped on the "Blame It All on Khrushchev" bandwagon even before the dust of the Paris Summit fiasco had settled—at the expense of some healthy self-criticism. Another effect is the setting up of *double standards of national morality.* Exactly the same behavior is moral if the WEs do it but immoral if the THEYs do it. Why? Because different motives are attributed to WE and to THEY in keeping with psycho-logic. Witness the debate in the United Nations over the U-2 spy-plane incident: Americans, knowing themselves to be peaceful in intent but being afraid of treacherous surprise attack, viewed this as a legitimate defensive operation; Russians, knowing themselves to be peace-loving, not treacherous, but suspecting treachery from the other side, viewed this as an illegitimate aggressive operation.

Many American travelers to Russia, including statesmen, scientists, and scholars, have been impressed by the "mirror image" of their own attitudes they find there. I have no information about it, but I strongly suspect that the same observation has been made by Russians visiting the United States. Each group blames the other for the mutually aggressive relation. Each sees the other as untrustworthy and not sincerely desirous of peace; each sees the other as warlike, but itself as peace-loving. If—as is certainly true—each can recognize the falsity of the other's image of him, can he not admit the probability of bias in his own image of the other? The mutual bogeyman images certainly can be cut down to more realistic size and shape. By so doing, we open the doors to mutually acceptable alternatives; by taking the bogeyman images at their face value, we close the doors to anything other than mutual annihilation.

The relativity of human judgment. "Man is the measure of all things," it has been said—but surely this is true only to the extent that his science is primitive. One can trace in the development of science a progressive freeing of man's measurements from the arbitrary platform of his own senses. Social judgments are also made relative to one's own position as observer. What a person perceives as "neutral" or "normal" on any dimension of judgment depends upon the particular range of relevant objects or events to which he happens to have been exposed. These norms, taken together, constitute his "frame of reference" for judging subsequent objects and events. Consistent shifts in the range of stimuli produce a gradual drift in one's norms. Stimuli which deviate only slightly from a norm tend to assimilate with it, and real differences are minimized; stimuli which deviate a great deal produce a contrast effect, and real differences are exaggerated.

We are seldom aware of our own norms. They are projected outward as the natural design of the universe. When Ego unconsciously assumes that Alter shares his frame of reference, it is natural for him to think of Alter as somehow dishonest, evil, or at least abnormal in some way when he calls "straight" what to Ego is obviously crooked and calls "tasty" what to Ego is obviously distasteful. It is a quite sophisticated Ego who recognizes the relativity of Alter's frame of reference; this produces a more humane approach, a "forgive *them* for they know not what they do" kind of attitude. But it is the unusually sophisticated—or civilized, if you will—Ego who realizes the equally relativistic nature of his own norms, who will accept his own judgments on the tasty-distasteful or even moral-immoral scales as being as arbitrary as those of the Mexican or Hindu. Social relativity does *not* mean that there are no external criteria for distinguishing good from evil; quite the reverse, it means that we must search for dependable external criteria just because social judgments are so liable to bias.

To fully appreciate the arbitrariness of one's own norms it helps to get outside the pervasive frame of reference provided by one's own culture, including its mass media. Foreign travel is a great help, particularly if you can escape from the protective "bubble" of your own culture. During the past few years I have spent considerable time outside the United States, in connection with some cross-cultural research on the generality of meaning systems. I read foreign newspapers as avidly as my linguistic talents would permit me, and I found them full of refreshing heresy—at least as far as East-West relations were concerned—to the extent that I was moved to wish with Robert Burns:

> O wad some Pow'r the giftie gi'e us
> To see oursels as ithers see us!

The admonition of many religious teachers to "Know Thyself" seems *a propos* here; only to the extent that we understand the dynamics of our own minds can we hope to understand others.

Possibilistic decision-making. The tendency to make decisions in terms of mere possibilities rather than in terms of estimated probabilities is seen most clearly in paranoid schizophrenics, but it also colors the judgments of normal people under stress. The fact that there is a general correlation between what people wish (or fear) would happen and how strongly they believe it actually will happen is well known to psychologists—but I think I should also mention, somewhat ruefully, that in one study this correlation turned out to be highest for professional gamblers and social scientists! If the paranoid knows it is *possible* that his doctor belongs to the secret society that is persecuting him, he leaps to the conclusion that he *does* belong and acts accordingly. Similarly in the international arena, if the WEs know that the THEYs *could* be cheating, lying, or planning a surprise attack, it is easy for the WEs to conclude that the THEYs *are* doing these immoral things—and then, driven by psycho-logic, the WEs are liable to do the same immoral things *first* in order to protect themselves, firmly proclaiming their motives benign.

Cognitive stereotypy. The basic psychological notion here is that, beyond some optimal level, increasing emotion serves not only to further energize the organism but also to reduce its capacity to select among alternatives. The multiplicative relation between drive and habit strength means that the most probable responses become even more so relatively while the less probable become even less so. Since the behavioral system seems to be organized throughout in hierarchies of alternatives, heightened motivation or emotion serves to produce stereotypy in perceiving, in associating, and in interpreting as well as in overt behavior.

One effect of drive-produced stereotopy is that *it reduces capacity to solve problems.* Problem situations are more or less defined by the fact that the dominant, habitual responses don't work—if they did, there obviously wouldn't be any problem. The raccoon is a pretty intelligent little animal; in a situation where it must discover which of several doors to food is open, it will flexibly try one after the other; but if we then put it under a stinging shower it will persistently bang its head against a locked door that *used to be open,* completely ignoring free passageways to left and right. In analogous fashion, nations today are lumbering down the one habitual path to "security"—bigger and better weapons—gathering as they go tensions which make it less and less possible to conceive of any other alternatives. Being the habitual response to external threat, this course is felt to be "realistic." Unfortunately, anthropologists are familiar with cultures that, through blind adherence to practices that once were realistic, have gradually committed suicide. I think that we are in exactly the same spot: We are continuing to practice rites and rituals of international relations that were developed in and appropriate to the past—firmly believing them to be realistic—in a nuclear present that renders them suicidal.

Another effect of heightened motivation is *foreshortening of perspective.* In general, as we trace the course of evolution and particularly the development of the cortex, we find higher species capable of maintaining longer delays, employing more extended foresight, and striving for more remote goals. But emotion has the effect of primitivizing this capacity. The motivational conditions of controversy, e.g., our present tensions/arms-race dilemma, are precisely those designed to restrict perspective. Thus we find that the truly magnificent achievements of human science—achievements that soon may free us from earthly bondage and catapult us toward the stars—seem to have significance only within the petty framework of the cold war; the only question we ask is, who's ahead? We seem fixated on the immediate goal of passing our opponent in total military power—without asking whether being able to annihilate an enemy ten or a hundred times over deters him much more than being able to annihilate him just once. And no one in the mad scramble pauses to even consider the obvious next question: *when and how does this end?* Surely a policy of nuclear deterrence that, at best, can offer us nothing more than a world continually poised for mutual destruction, held together by nothing more than fragile psychological needs of mutual fear, must not be the last word.

Arms Control and Tension Control

The combination of nationalism, cold-war thinking, and the paradoxes of the nuclear age—particularly the imbalance between offensive and defensive capabilities—is forcing nations inexorably toward the policy of mutual nuclear deterrence. This combination of factors has simultaneously been forcing policy-makers toward serious consideration of the stability of such deterrence. Just because we have a phrase, "stabilized deterrence," which seems to imply that there must be some solid, protective technological system, does not mean that such a referent really exists.

Deterrence is more a psychological question than a technological answer. An opponent is assumed to be deterred from initiating a nuclear attack by his expectation of unacceptable retaliation. But if the opponent is not deterred, if he makes a wrong decision—whether due to fear, to overconfidence, to misinformation, or even to some accident—then the invulnerability of one's retaliatory capacity and the certainty of its delivery does nothing whatsoever to defend one's own civilian population. This is why discussions of stabilized deterrence inevitably involve matters like the "credibility" of retaliation and the "rationality" of human decisions, which are also psychological problems. So let us now confront some of the assumptions of stabilized deterrence with some of the facts of human decision-making under stress that we have just been analyzing.

The credibility of deterrence assumes full appreciation of the dangers of nuclear war on all sides; but the mechanism of denial, the perverse attractiveness of denied dangers, and the essential meaninglessness of the words with which we talk about it all prevent such full appreciation. Stability of deterrence assumes objective evaluation of the intentions of an opponent and objective interpretation of world events; but both psycho-logic and the relativity of social judgment hinder such objectivity and transform the complexities of international relations into an oversimplified contest between the Good Guys and the Bad Guys. Stability requires that decisions be based on accurate determination of probabilities rather than emotional reaction to mere possibilities; but the wishful-fearful thinking characteristic of schizophrenics also affects the decisions of normals under stress, and they become prone to deciding in terms of their wishes (overconfidence) or their fears (underconfidence). Maintaining stable deterrence in a world where situations change with bewildering speed and complexity demands great flexibility of means yet consistency of ends; but cognitive stereotypy both restricts the range of alternatives and shortens perspective, substituting blind reactions to immediate pressures for long-range persistence toward ultimate goals.

It is true that men can be rational, and often are, but it is also true that they can be nonrational, and these are merely some of the mechanisms of nonrationality. These are some of the ways in which humans reach decisions without the benefit of logic and without even maximizing their own self-interest in the game-theoretic sense, and yet these ways of thinking are lawful in that they conform to and are predictable from the principles of human behavior. In a situation where the consequences of wrong decisions are so awesome, where a single bit of irrationality can set a whole chain of traumatic events in motion, I do not think that we can be satisfied with the assurance that "most people behave rationally most of the time."

What are the conditions that strengthen and exaggerate these nonrational mechanisms in human decision-making? What conditions make normal people appear irrational? And we must add, what conditions make truly irrational people appear normal, because under analysis it seems that the same conditions which make normals seem irrational make irrationals seem normal: To a population driven into nonrationality, a fanatic may seem not only normal but ideal. There are two general sets of conditions that magnify nonrationality: The first concerns *information*—its availability, bias, and overload in the human decision system; the second, and the one I wish to emphasize here, is *tension-level.*

We have already seen that, beyond some optimal level, further increases in tension serve to restrict the range of perceived alternatives, thereby limiting the flexibility and creativity of human problem-solving. It is also certainly true that increases in tension, beyond some optimal level, serve to magnify the ratio of nonrational to rational alternatives. Under stress men are more likely to act irrationally, to strike out blindly or even to freeze into stupid immobility. In other words, both flexibility and rationality "ride on the back" of tension-level.

World events may have either a tension-increasing or a tension-decreasing impact upon the international system. *The real stability of the system depends upon its capacity to absorb such event-shocks, and this in turn depends upon the absolute level of tension.* If the system is at a relatively low level of tension, it can absorb a succession of event-shocks, such as a revolution in Latin America, the demonstration of a new weapon, or the accidental explosion of an old one, without being moved far from an optimum level of flexibility and rationality. But if the system is already functioning at a relatively high level of tension, then the same set of event-shocks may push it over into the region of rigidity and irrationality.

It is important to realize that while tension cumulates across various sources, its effect upon flexibility and rationality is independent of source. Equally important for the remainder of my argument is the fact that reduction in tension-level is independent of its sources. In other words, tension is something like money in a bank account; its amount can be increased by "deposits" from a variety of sources and decreased by "withdrawals" for a variety of uses.

If my analysis of the relation between what is called "stability of the military environment" and tension-level is valid, then it puts a premium on the development and application of *techniques of tension control.* Stability is a dynamic concept, not a static one, and we need to create and maintain a dynamic, shock-absorbing "cushion" for the international system. But tension control cannot be entirely a unilateral affair, so we must look for techniques which are likely to induce reciprocation.

The traditional, if seldom successful, method of reducing international tensions is through mutual-disarmament negotiations. We have behind us a long and dismal history of unsuccessful negotiations. It is perhaps another paradox that the greater the need for negotiated agreements, the more difficult they are to obtain. It is easy for each side to blame these failures on the intractability and insincerity of the other, but the same mechanisms operate on both sides. One is what I call *biased perception of the equable:* Given their quite different national life-histories, both sides approach negotiations with different sets of meanings; "inspection" means espionage for one but elimination of secrecy for the other, "The United Nations" means a biased tool to one but an unbiased international body to the other, "overseas bases" mean aggressive intent to one but defensive intent to the other, and so on. Another mechanism is *the self-fulfilling prophecy:* Prior to any negotiation, the press on each side predicts that the other is insincere and merely using the discussions for propaganda purposes; each side then behaves in such a way as to counteract what it expects of the other; nothing is accomplished, and both sides go away saying, "I told you so!" And then there is the plain, ordinary matter of *mutual distrust:* Under the impetus of psycho-logic, each side expects the other to cheat, and one even hears it said that treaties with THEM are not worth the paper they're written on.

The conclusion we seem driven to is this: *Negotiated agreements require commitment prior to action, and under the conditions of the cold war mentality commitments of any significance are difficult to obtain; thus neither side is able to take the initiative as long as it remains chained to the requirement of prior commitment by the other.* Clearly, some other approach is needed if we are ever to break out of this impasse.

Initiative Through Unilateral Action

In the remainder of this paper I would like to explore with you the possibilities that may lie in unilateral action of a particular type. For several years I have been trying to develop and justify an approach to international relations which I call *Graduated Reciprocation in Tension-Reduction.* The essence of the idea is that the tensions/arms-race spiral may provide the model for its own reversal. As a type of international behavior, *the arms race is a case of graduated and reciprocated unilateral action.* It is unilateral in that the nation developing a new weapon, increasing its stockpile, or setting up a new military base does not make its action contingent upon any prior agreement with the other side. It is reciprocal, however, because each increment in military power by one side provides the stimulus for the other to try to catch up and get ahead. It is necessarily graduated, first by the irregular and somewhat unpredictable occurrences of technological break-through and second by the oscillating nature of the threat stimulus itself.

But the arms race is obviously a *tension-increasing* system. One can readily conceive of a graduated and reciprocated, unilaterally initiated system that is *tension-reducing* in nature. The question is whether or not it is feasible under present conditions. I will try to demonstrate that, given anything like the dedication and energy now being thrown into the arms race, it would be feasible, even though by no means magically simple.

This approach must be sharply distinguished from the kind of abject and complete unilateral disarmament sponsored by pacifist groups. To the contrary, what I am proposing is a flexible, self-regulating procedure in which the participants continually monitor their own actions on the basis of their evaluation of the reciprocating actions taken by the other side. It involves some risk, to be sure, but the risk is limited; merely going on doing what we are now doing involves infinitely greater risk! It is broader than disarmament, or even disengagement as usually conceived, since it would include programs of graduated unilateral actions of a tension-reducing nature in the areas of science and secrecy, social, economic, and cultural exchange, Communist China and the United Nations, controls and inspection, and so forth, as well as actual military and disarmament steps. It may be viewed as a kind of international (rather than interpersonal) communicating and learning situation, where the communication is more by deeds than by words and where what is learned is mutual understanding and trust.

However, being both unconventional and conciliatory in nature, this procedure is liable to suspicion abroad and resistance at home, particularly under conditions of the cold war mentality. Therefore it needs to be spelled out in detail, critically evaluated, and even tried out under both laboratory and field conditions. Specifically, it is necessary to indicate the characteristics that unilateral actions in such a program should have in order to maintain adequate felt security while nevertheless inducing reciprocation from an opponent; furthermore, we need to clarify the criteria for both determining the substance of unilateral initiatives and evaluating the bonafideness and significance of unilateral reciprocations. In other words, while admittedly idealistic in purpose, this rather novel approach must be shown to be realistic and feasible within the existing situation of competing sovereign states.

In the following analysis I will be speaking from the viewpoint of a nation which initiates such a policy of graduated reciprocation in tension-reduction. This is necessary to maintain a consistent orientation. But I want it understood that I have no particular nation in mind as the initiator—it could be either of the two polar nuclear powers, the United States or the USSR, or it could very well be some other nation or group of nations, present or future. Furthermore, just as with an arms race, once this kind of international behavior were underway, the distinction between initiation and reciprocation would become as meaningless as the distinction between stimulus and response within the central nervous system.

Maintaining Security

1. *Unilateral actions should not reduce a nation's capacity to inflict unacceptable nuclear retaliation on an opponent should it be attacked.* I would be the first to agree that nuclear deterrence does not provide any real security over the long haul, but on the other hand, highly invulnerable second-strike forces will exist in the near future, if not already, and under present levels of tension they are not likely to be given up. Particularly if their retaliatory nature is made explicit, and moral prohibition against their first use is accepted by all sides, nuclear weapons can be viewed not only as a deterrent *but also as a security base from which limited risks can be taken.* I am assuming that since there is no necessary correlation between the tension-

reducing impacts of actions and their military significance, a program of graduated reciprocation in tension-reduction could produce an atmosphere of mutual trust in which the nuclear deterrents themselves could ultimately be eliminated by negotiated agreement.

2. *Unilateral actions should be graduated in risk potential according to the degree of reciprocation obtained.* This is the essential self-regulating characteristic of the proposal. The magnitude of a unilateral step taken at a particular time would depend upon that nation's evaluation of the reciprocative behavior of the other. The process can be slowed down or speeded up, as conditions require, but it should be kept going.

3. *Unilateral actions should be diversified in nature so as not to weaken a nation progressively in any one sphere.* Diversity in areas of action both provides an essential flexibility of approach and prevents the unstabilizing effect of too large steps in a single sphere. The only common property of the actions envisaged in this proposal is their tension-reducing nature. This, as I pointed out earlier, can be cumulative over a highly diversified range of actions, e.g., student exchanges, sharing of scientific information, reducing trade barriers, diplomatic recognition, elimination of bases, and so on.

4. *Prior to announcement, unilateral actions should be unpredictable by an opponent as to their nature, locus, and time of execution.* This is to minimize the likelihood of encroachment. I submit that, psychologically, an opponent is much less likely to encroach aggressively in an area after public announcement of intent by another than prior to it, and he is certainly less likely to gain world support if he does. However, if encroachments do occur they must be resisted just as firmly as if this policy were not in operation. Yet, this resistance should be pinpointed to the area of encroachment and the program of tension-reducing moves continued flexibly in other areas. This is clearly a different approach than the traditional, monolithic reaction of nations to tension-increasing events, but it is an approach that seems necessary in a nuclear age. Under conditions of nuclear deterrence, encroachments are likely to be tentative and probing in nature, and therefore can constitute a learning experience on all sides—learning that graduated reciprocation in reducing tensions is not synonymous with surrender.

Inducing Reciprocation

1. *Unilateral actions should be announced publicly at some reasonable interval prior to their execution and identified as part of a deliberate policy of reducing tensions.* Announcement prior to action

is suggested as a means of augmenting pressure toward reciprocation, of avoiding the unstabilizing effect of unexpected moves, of providing time for preparing reciprocation, and, particularly, of influencing the interpretation of the action when it comes. Public announcement makes it possible to enlist pressures of world opinion toward reciprocation, and identification of each act as part of a deliberate policy is designed to make the pressures toward reciprocation cumulative.

2. *In their announcement, unilateral actions should include explicit invitation to reciprocation in some form.* Initiation and reciprocation need not be the same in kind nor even equal in quantity. There are some unilateral actions that could not be reciprocated in kind (e.g., if the United States were to denuclearize some Pacific base, the Chinese Communists could not reciprocate in kind) and the burden of the same rule may be quite different in two countries (e.g., absolute amounts of inspection permitted). On the other hand, the fact that reciprocation in some form is expected must be made explicit. The isolated unilateral gestures that have occasionally been made in the past have been largely abortive, in part because they did not call for reciprocation.

3. *Unilateral actions that have been announced must be executed on schedule regardless of prior commitment by the opponent to reciprocate.* This is the characteristic that distinguishes this policy from traditional bargaining and negotiating procedures; it is the characteristic that provides an increased degree of freedom on all sides for taking the initiative. Of course, if no reciprocation is forthcoming, or attempts are made to take advantage of the initiator, then the process slows down or stops. In this sense, reciprocation can be viewed as a kind of postcommitment that enables the policy to continue.

4. *Unilateral actions should be planned in graded series and continued over a considerable period regardless of immediate reciprocation or police action elsewhere.* Given the tense atmosphere in which such a strategy must begin, it is likely that initial actions would be greeted by cries of "cold war trick!"; but the bonafideness of the intent becomes more and more difficult to deny and rationalize as action follows announced action. Furthermore, the pressure toward reciprocation should cumulate over such a period of continued action. Here again we have a kind of international learning situation—in this case, unlearning the bogeyman image of the opponent, since the psycho-logic expectations and prophesies being made about him are being repeatedly denied.

5. *As far as possible, unilateral actions should be overt deeds rather than either positive or negative sanctions and should be as*

unambiguous and as susceptible to verification as possible. Overt acts have the obvious advantage of bonafideness, particularly if the announced action includes invitation to observe and inspect. Sanctions, on the other hand, have no visible execution or test until their failure —the unilaterally imposed bans on nuclear testing are a case in point. This emphasizes another difference between this kind of policy and ordinary negotiations, a difference well expressed by the homely saying, "actions speak louder than words."

What about the problem of *evaluating reciprocations* (and, for that matter, the problem an opponent has in evaluating one's unilateral initiations)? There are two rather different questions here: One concerns the bonafideness of actions, which seems to come down to the adequacy of intelligence in the military sense; the other concerns the significance of actions, and this seems to be a matter for strategic analysis. To enhance *bonafideness,* both the initiator's unilateral acts and the reciprocations requested should be as unambiguous and susceptible to verification as possible; provisions for adequate inspection may be included in both initiations and requested reciprocations. As a matter of fact, it might be possible to get around the apparent deadlock on inspection by introducing it in small, manageable and perhaps palatable packages under such a program as this; if one side accepts an invitation to unilaterally inspect some specific action of the other, it becomes psychologically difficult to deny him the same privilege. As to the *significance* of reciprocations, two criteria would have to be kept in mind: first, that the risk potential in the unilateral actions by one party should be roughly balanced by the increased security gained through the reciprocations of the other party; second, that tension-decreasing steps in one area must be balanced against the total level of tension-increasing and tension-decreasing events in all areas. I realize that these estimations are not easy, but they involve the sort of strategic analysis that is going on all the time anyhow.

Finally, there are some additional criteria for selecting actions that should be mentioned. First, it is probably wisest to begin such a program with actions in areas other than the critical military and disarmament spheres, moving in toward these matters only when the general level of tension has been sufficiently reduced. Second, particularly in the early phases, unilateral initiatives should involve areas in which both parties in the conflict are known to be ready to move, in which restraints may already have been reciprocally self-imposed, and in which both are likely to see issues of human welfare rather than national security. Again, we have here a kind of learning situation on all sides, and it is important that the probabilities of reinforcement be high at first. And since we would wish the substance of our actions to be consistent with our long-term goals as well as our immediate needs to control tensions, they should be designed to gradually shape the world of tomorrow; therefore, unilateral initiatives and reciprocations should involve gradual transfer of sovereignty from national to international auspices, gradual lessening of the imbalance between "have" and "have not" countries, and gradual shifting of scientific research onto an international basis on the model of the IGY, particularly research having military implications where scientific breakthroughs have an unstabilizing impact.

Despite the unilateral initiative which characterizes this proposal, it should be apparent that the two parties in conflict are really dependent on each other for its success. This is because on each side there are competing factions spread over the spectrum of policy alternatives. If President Kennedy, exercising administrative initiative, were to announce and execute a carefully planned series of tension-reducing moves, opposition groups in the United States government, in its mass media, and in its public would become increasingly critical. The only way to quiet this opposition and keep the policy moving, in the long run, would be to receive reciprocation from the opponent. I am sure that much the same situation would hold in the case of Soviet initiation. Now it is true that the leadership of a nation would be risking its position by initiating such a policy and that an opponent might assist in the demise by withholding reciprocation—*but in doing so the opponent should be fully aware of the fact that he is strengthening forces more violently antagonistic to him and more likely to act inflexibly and irrationally in future relations.* Thus it would be to the advantage of both sides to be on the alert for tension-reducing probes from the other and to be prepared for reciprocations that will allow the process to continue.

Could the initiator of such a policy expect to obtain bonafide and significant reciprocation under present conditions? I cannot give an unqualified "yes" to this question. Here, obviously, lies the risk—but as I pointed out earlier, merely going on as we are involves even greater risk. And surely it would be cause for cosmic irony if two human groups in conflict were to bring their world down in destruction because of their threatening images of each other without ever testing the validity of these images. Despite the differences between us, there are many things we share; we share common modes of thinking and feeling, we share a common technology that is rapidly transforming us into one world whether we like it or not, and above all we share a common desire to get out of this dangerous situation and go on living. If my basic assumption about the contemporary motivation of international behavior is right—that it is based more on fear and insecurity than on any urge toward national aggrandizement—then I think reciprocation would be forthcoming, if not for reasons of good will then for reasons of good sense. And here another psychological principle applies: If two people are forced to keep on behaving *as if* they trusted each other, their beliefs and attitudes tend to fall in line with their behaviors. I think the same applies to nations.

Conclusion

The preservation of peace is the biggest problem of our time, and I have no illusions about my own capacity to comprehend it all. Although the problem has important psychological components, much more than psychology is involved—political science, economics, international law, communications, nuclear and space technology, diplomacy, and the military, to call only part of the roll. And no one as aware as I am of the strength of the contrary forces, of the deeply ingrained mechanisms of the cold war mentality, could be very sanguine about our chances of escaping from this situation unscathed.

On the other hand, I have convinced myself, at least, that such a policy of graduated reciprocation in tension control is feasible for our time. True, it would require extraordinary sensitivity, flexibility, and restraint from leadership on all sides, as well as high-level strategic planning and execution, but this could be viewed as a challenge rather than a flaw. If it were successfully initiated, such a policy could, over the short term, increase the stability of the military environment and perhaps create an atmosphere in which more significant steps toward disarmament could be taken; over the long term, it might offer a model for international relations that is more appropriate to this age of nuclear technology. I can do no better than close with a quotation from Albert Einstein that might have been written today: "The unleashed power of the atom has changed everything except our ways of thinking. Thus we are drifting toward a catastrophe beyond comparison. We shall require a substantially new manner of thinking if mankind is to survive."

THE CASE FOR UNILATERAL DISARMAMENT

By ERICH FROMM

THERE IS LITTLE DOUBT that the proposal for a unilateral disarmament—in the broad sense of the unconditional dismantling of a country's military establishment—will be acceptable neither to the United States nor to the Soviet Union in the immediate future. Hence, inasmuch as this paper is concerned with *practical* suggestions for arms control, it proposes another and very limited concept of unilateral disarmament, one which has been called by Charles Osgood "*graduated unilateral action (or disengagement)*" or which might be called *unilateral initiative in taking practical steps toward disarmament.* The basic idea underlying this concept is that of a radical change of our method of negotiating multilateral disarmament. This change implies that we give up the present method of bargaining in which every concession we make is dependent on a corresponding and guaranteed concession on the part of the Russians; that, instead, we take, unilaterally, gradual steps toward disarmament in the expectation that the Russians will reciprocate and that, thus, the present deadlock in the negotiations for universal disarmament can be broken through.

In order to describe the nature of this policy of unilateral steps, I cannot improve on the following description by Osgood, who as far as I know was the first one to express this idea, in two brilliant and profound articles.[1] "To be maximally effective," he writes, "in inducing the enemy to reciprocate, a unilateral act (1) should, in terms of *military aggression,* be clearly disadvantageous to the side making it, yet not cripplingly so; (2) should be such as to be clearly perceived by the enemy as reducing his external threat; (3) should not increase the enemy's threat to our heartland;[2] (4) should be such that reciprocal action by the enemy is clearly available and clearly indicated; (5) should be announced in advance and widely publicized to ally, neutral, and enemy countries—as regards the nature of the act, its purpose as part of a consistent policy, and the expected reciprocation; but (6) should not demand prior commitment to reciprocation by the enemy as a condition for its commission."[3]

As to the specific steps which should be taken in this fashion, it would require a great deal of further thought, aided by competent specialists. But in order to give at least an idea of the concrete steps this policy would envisage, I want to mention the following (some of them in agreement with Osgood): sharing of scientific information; stopping of atomic tests; troop reductions; evacuation of one or more military bases; discontinuation of German rearmament; etc. The expectation is that the Russians are as willing as we are to avoid war, hence that they will begin to reciprocate and that once the course of mutual suspicion has been reversed, bigger steps can be taken which may lead to complete bilateral disarmament. Furthermore, I believe that disarmament negotiations should be paralleled by *political* negotiations, which aim essentially at mutual noninterference on the basis of the recognition of the *status quo*. Here, too (and again in essential agreement with Osgood's position), unilateral steps such as the recognition of the Oder-Neisse line and admission of China to the United Nations would be taken in the expectation of reciprocation by the Russians (i.e., curbing of Chinese aggression, noninterference in the Middle and Far East).

What are the premises underlying the proposition for unilateral steps toward disarmament? (At this point I shall mention only some fundamental ones, while others will be discussed in the second part of this paper which presents the argument for total unilateral disarmament.) They are briefly: (1) that, as indicated before, the present method of negotiations does not seem to lead to the goal of bilateral disarmament because of the deeply ingrained mutual suspicions and fears; (2) that without achieving *complete* disarmament, the armament race will continue and lead to the destruction of our civilization as well as that of the Russians or, even without the outbreak of a war, will slowly undermine and eventually destroy the values in defense of which we are risking our physical existence; (3) that while unilateral steps constitute a definite risk (and must do so by the very nature of the idea), the risk at every step is not a crippling one and is infinitely smaller than the danger we run by the continuation of the arms race.

Even though the broader concept of complete—rather than graduated—unilateral disarmament is, as stated before, not a practical possibility in the near future, as far as the United States and the USSR are concerned, I believe it worth while to present the arguments for this position, not primarily because the editors of this volume asked me to present this position nor even because I share it with a small minority of others who believe that the risks in the continuation of the armament race are far greater than the very serious risks of unilateral disarmament. While both reasons might not be sufficient to justify the following presentation, I do believe that it is not only justified but important for another reason: Thinking through the arguments for a radical—even though practically unacceptable—position contributes to breaking through the thought barrier which prevents us now from getting out of the dangerous circle of seeking peace by means of threat and counterthreat. Taking seriously the reasoning which supports the unpopular position of complete unilateral disarmament can open up new approaches and viewpoints which are important even if our practical aim is that of graduated unilateral action or even only that of negotiated bilateral disarmament. I believe that the difficulty of arriving at complete disarmament lies to a large extent in the frozen stereotypes of feelings and thought habits on both sides and that any attempt at unfreezing these patterns and of rethinking the whole problem can be of importance in finding a way out of the present dangerous impasse.

The proposal for complete unilateral disarmament has been advocated from a religious, moral, or pacifist position by such men as Victor Gollancz, Lewis Mumford, and some Quakers. It has also been supported by men like Bertrand Russell, Stephen King-Hall, and C. W. Mills, who are not opposed to the use of force under all or any circumstances, yet who are uncompromisingly opposed both to thermonuclear war and to all and any preparation for it. This writer finds himself somewhat between the position of the strict pacifists and men like Bertrand Russell and Stephen King-Hall.[4]

The difference between these two groups, however, is not as fundamental as it may seem. They are united by their critical attitude toward the irrational aspects of international politics and by their deep reverence for life. They share the conviction of the oneness of the human race and faith in the spiritual and intellectual potentialities of man. They follow the dictates of their conscience in refusing to have any "part in making millions of women and children and noncombatants hostages for the behavior of their own governments."[5] Whether they think in theistic terms or in those of nontheistic humanism (in the sense of the philosophic continuum from Stoic to eighteenth-century Enlightenment philosophy), they all are rooted in the same spiritual tradition and are unwilling to compromise with its principles. They are united by their uncompromising opposition to any kind of idolatry, including the idolatry of the state. While their opposition to the Soviet system is rooted precisely in this attitude against idolatry, they are critical of idolatry whenever it appears in the Western world whether it is in the name of God or of democracy.

While there is no proponent of unilateral disarmament who does not believe that the individual must be willing to give his life for the sake of his supreme values, if such an ultimate necessity arises, they are all equally convinced that to risk the life of the human race, or even the results of its best efforts in the last five thousand years, is immoral and irresponsible. As warfare becomes at once more senseless and more devastating, the convergence between religious pacifist, humanist, and pragmatic opponents to nuclear armament grows.

From the standpoint of the proponents of unilateral disarmament, to continue the armament race is catastrophic, *whether the deterrent works or not.* In the first place, they have little faith that the deterrent will prevent the outbreak of a thermonuclear war.[6] They believe that the results of a thermonuclear war would be such that in the very "best" case they completely belie the idea that we ought to fight such a war in order to save our democratic way of life. There is no need to enter the guessing game as to whether one-third or two-thirds of the population of the two opponents and what proportion of the neutral world (depending on how the wind blows) will be destroyed. This is a guessing game that verges on madness; for to consider the possibility of the destruction of 30 percent, 60 percent, or 90 percent of one's own and the enemy's population as an acceptable (although, of course, most undesirable) result of one's policy is indeed approaching pathology. The increasing split between intellect and affect, which is so characteristic of our Western development in the last centuries, has reached its dangerous, schizoid peak in the calm and allegedly rational way in which we can discuss possible world destruction as a result of our own action. It does not take much imagination to visualize that sudden destruction and the threat of slow death to a large part of the American population, or the Russian population, or large parts of the world, will create such a panic, fury, and despair as could only be compared with the mass psychosis resulting from the Black Death in the Middle Ages. The traumatic effects of such a catastrophe would lead to a new form of primitive barbarism, to the resurgence of the most archaic elements, which are still potentialities in every man and of which we have had ample evidence in the terror systems of Hitler and Stalin. It would sound most unlikely to many students of human nature and psychopathology that human beings could cherish freedom, respect for life, or love after having witnessed and participated in the unlimited cruelty of man against man which thermonuclear war would mean. It is a psychological fact that acts of brutality have a brutalizing effect on the participants and lead to more brutality.

But What If the Deterrent Works?

What is the likely future of the social character of man in a bilateral or multilateral armed world, where, no matter how complex the problems or how full the satisfactions of any particular society,[7] the biggest and most pervasive reality in any man's life is the poised missile, the humming data processor connected to it, the waiting radiation counters and seismographs, the over-all technocratic perfection (overlying the nagging but impotent fear of its imperfection) of the mechanism of holocaust? To live for any length of time under the constant threat of destruction creates certain psychological effects in most human beings—fright, hostility, callousness, a hardening of the heart, and a resulting indifference to all the values we cherish. Such conditions will transform us into barbarians—though barbarians equipped with the most complicated machines. If we are serious in claiming that our aim is to preserve freedom (that is, to prevent the subordination of the individual under an all-powerful state), we must admit that this freedom will be lost, whether the deterrent works or does not work.

Aside from these psychological facts, the continuation of the arms race constitutes a particular threat to Western culture. In the process of conquering nature, producing and consuming have become Western man's main preoccupation—the goal of his life. We have transformed means into ends. We manufacture machines which are like men, and we produce men who are like machines. In his work, the individual is managed as a part of a production team. During his leisure time, he is manipulated as a consumer who likes what he is told to like and yet has the illusion that he follows his own taste. In centering his life around the production of things, man himself is in danger of becoming a thing, worshiping the idols of the production machine and the state while he is under the illusion of worshiping God. "Things are in the saddle and ride mankind," as Emerson has put it. Circumstances which we created have consolidated themselves into powers which rule over us. The technical and bureaucratic system we have built tells us what to do; it decides for us. We may not be in danger of becoming slaves, but we are in danger of becoming robots, and the human values of our tradition are threatened—integrity, individuality, responsibility, reason, and love. Talking about these values more and more becomes an empty ritual.

This trend toward a world of impotent men directed by virile machines (both in the United States and in the Soviet Union)—

brought about by technological and demographic factors, and by the increasing centralization and bureaucracy in big corporations and government—will reach the point of no return if we continue the arms race. Dangerous as our present situation is, we still have a chance to put man back into the saddle, to effect a renaissance of the spiritual values of the great humanistic tradition. Unless such a renaissance occurs, unless we can achieve a radical revitalization of the spirit on which our culture is founded, we shall lose the vitality necessary for survival and we shall decay, just as many other great powers have decayed in history. The real threat to our existence is not Communist ideology, it is not even the Communist military power —it is the hollowness of our beliefs, the fact that freedom, individuality, and faith have become empty formulas, that God has become an idol, that our vitality is sapped because we have no vision except that of having more of the same. It seems that a great deal of the hatred of Communism is, in the last analysis, based on a deep disbelief in the spiritual values of democracy. Hence, instead of experiencing love of what we are *for,* we experience hate of what we are *against.* If we continue to live in fear of extinction and to plan mass destruction of others, the last chance for a revival of our humanist-spiritual tradition will be lost.

Benefits and Dangers of Unilateral Disarmament

If these are the dangers of the policy of the deterrent, what do the proponents of unilateral disarmament consider to be the benefits—and the dangers—of their policy?

The most likely result of unilateral disarmament—whether it be undertaken by the United States or by the Soviet Union—is that it would prevent war. The main reason which could impel either the Soviet Union or the United States to atomic war is the constant fear of being attacked and pulverized by the opponent. This position is succinctly expressed by Herman Kahn, who is in no way a proponent of unilateral disarmament. Kahn states that, "aside from the ideological differences and the problem of security itself, there does not seem to be any objective quarrel between the United States and Russia that justifies the risks and costs that we subject each other to. The big thing that the Soviet Union and the United States have to fear from each other is fear itself."[8] If, indeed, the main cause of war lies in mutual fear, then the disarmament of either the Soviet Union or the United States would most likely do away with this major cause and, thus, with the probability of war.

But are there motives other than fear which could prompt the Soviet Union to try for world conquest? One such motive could be economic interest in expansion, which was a basic motivation for the initiation of war in the nineteenth century and also for the first two World Wars. Exactly here we see the difference between the nature of the conflicts in 1914 or 1939 and the present situation. In World War I, Germany threatened British markets and the French sources of coal and iron; in 1939, Hitler needed territorial conquest for the economic expansion he wanted. Today, neither the Soviet Union nor the United States has overriding economic interests in the conquest of markets and supplies, since a 2 or 3 percent rise in the level of national productivity would bring a greater advantage than would any military conquest, and, moreover, each has the capital, raw material, supplies, and population for a constant increase in its general productivity.[9]

The more serious possible motive is found in the fear, widely held in the United States, that the Soviet Union is out to conquer the world for Communism and that, if the United States disarmed, Russia would be all the more eager to achieve her wish for world domination. This idea of Russian intentions is based on an erroneous appreciation of the nature of the present-day Soviet Union. It is true that under Lenin and Trotzky the Russian Revolution was aimed at conquering the capitalistic world (or at least, Europe) for Communism, partly because the Communist leaders were convinced that there was no possibility of success for Communist Russia unless the highly industrialized states of Europe (or at least Germany) joined their system, and partly because they were prompted by the belief that the victory of the Communist revolution in the world would bring about the fulfillment of their secular-messianic hopes.

The failure of these hopes and the ensuing victory of Stalin brought about a complete change in the nature of Soviet Communism. The annihilation of almost all the old Bolsheviks was only a symbolic act for the destruction of the old revolutionary idea. Stalin's slogan of "socialism in one country" covered one simple aim—the rapid industrialization of Russia, which the Czarist system had not accomplished. Russia repeated the same process of accumulating capital which Western capitalism had gone through in the eighteenth and nineteenth centuries. The essential difference is that, while in these centuries in the West the sanctions were purely economic, the Stalinist system now developed political sanctions of direct terror; in addition, it employed socialist ideology to sugar-coat the exploitation of the masses. The Stalinist system was neither a socialist nor a revolutionary system, but a state capitalism based on ruthless methods of planning and economic centralization.

The period of Khrushchevism is characterized by the fact that capital accumulation has succeeded to a point where the population can enjoy a great deal more consumption and is less forced to make sacrifices; as a result, the political terror can be greatly reduced.

But Khrushchevism has by no means changed the basic character of Soviet society in one essential respect: it is not a revolutionary nor a socialist regime, but one of the most conservative, class-ridden regimes anywhere in the Western world, humanly coercive, economically effective. While the aim of democratic socialism was the emancipation of man, the overcoming of his alienation, and the eventual abolition of the state, the "socialist" slogans used in Soviet Russia reflect empty ideologies, and the social reality is the very opposite of true socialism. The ruling class of the Soviet Union is no more revolutionary than the Renaissance popes were followers of the teachings of Christ. To try to explain Khrushchev by quoting Marx, Lenin, or Trotzky shows an utter failure to understand the historical development which has taken place in the Soviet Union and an incapacity to appreciate the difference between facts and ideologies. It should be added that our attitude is the best propaganda service the Russians could wish for. Against the facts, they try to convince the workers of Western Europe and the peasants in Asia that they represent the ideas of socialism, of a classless society, etc. The Western attitude, of falling for this propaganda, does exactly what the Russians want: to confirm these claims. (Unfortunately, very few people except democratic socialists have sufficient knowledge of the difference between socialism and its distorted and corrupt form which calls itself Soviet socialism.)

The role of Russia is still more emphasized by the fact that Russia feels threatened by a potentially expansionist China. Russia one day might be in the same position with regard to China as we believe we are in relation to Russia. If the threat to Russia from the United States were to disappear, Russia could devote her energy to coping with the threat from China, unless by universal disarmament this threat would cease to exist.

The above-mentioned considerations indicate that the dangers which might arise if the Soviet Union were not to give up its armaments are more remote than they seem to many. Would the Soviet Union use her military superiority to try to occupy the United States or Western Europe? Aside from the fact that it would be exceedingly difficult, to say the least, for the Soviet Union's agents to run the economic and political machines of the United States or Western Europe, and aside from the fact that there is no vital need for Russia to conquer these territories, it would be most inconvenient to try to do so—and for a reason which is generally not sufficiently appreciated. Even the pro-Communist workers in the West have no idea of the degree of coercion to which they would have to submit under a Soviet system. They, as well as non-Communist workers, would oppose the new authorities, who would be forced to use tanks and machine guns against the protesting workers. This would encourage revolutionary tendencies in the satellite states, or even within the Soviet Union, and be most undesirable to the Soviet rulers; it would especially endanger Khrushchev's policy of liberalization, and hence his whole political position.

Eventually the Soviet Union might try to exploit its military superiority for the penetration of Asia and Africa. This is possible, but, with our present policy of the deterrent, it is doubtful whether the United States would really be willing to start a thermonuclear war in order to prevent the Russians from gaining certain advantages in the world outside of Europe and the Americas.

All these assumptions may be wrong. The position of the proponents of unilateral disarmament is that the chance that they are wrong is much smaller than the chance that the continuation of the arms race will finish civilization as we cherish it.

Some Psychological Considerations

One cannot discuss the question of what might happen as a result of unilateral disarmament—or, for that matter, of any mutual disarmament—without examining some psychological arguments. The most popular one is that "the Russians cannot be trusted." If "trust" is meant in a moral sense, it is unfortunately true that political leaders can rarely be trusted. The reason lies in the split between private and public morals: the state, having become an idol, justifies any immorality if committed in its interest, while the very same political leaders would not commit the same acts if they were acting in behalf of their own private interests. However, there is another meaning to "trust in people," a meaning which is much more relevant to the problem of politics: the trust that they are sane and rational beings, and that they will act accordingly. If I deal with an opponent in whose sanity I trust, I can appreciate his motivations and to some extent predict them, because there are certain rules and aims, like that of survival or that of commensurateness between aims and means, which are common to all sane people. Hitler could not be trusted because he was lacking in sanity, and this very lack destroyed both him and his regime. It seems quite clear that the Russian leaders of today are sane and rational people; therefore it is important not only to know what they are capable of, but also to predict what they might be motivated to do.[10]

This question of the leaders' and the people's sanity leads to another consideration which affects us as much as it does the Russians. In the current discussion on armament control, many arguments are based on the question of what is *possible,* rather than on what is *probable.* The difference between these two modes of thinking is precisely the difference between *paranoid* and *sane* thinking. The paranoiac's unshakable conviction in the validity of his delusion rests upon the fact that it is logically possible, and, so, unassailable. It is logically possible that his wife, children, and colleagues hate him and are conspiring to kill him. The patient cannot be convinced that his delusion is *impossible;* he can only be told that it is exceedingly *unlikely.* While the latter position requires an examination and evaluation of the facts and also a certain amount of faith in life, the paranoid position can satisfy itself with the possibility alone. I submit that our political thinking suffers from such paranoid trends. We should be concerned, not with the possibilities, but rather with the probabilities. This is the only sane and realistic way of conducting the affairs of national as well as of individual life.

Again on the psychological plane, there are certain misunderstandings of the radical disarmament position which occur in many of the discussions. First of all, the position of unilateral disarmament has been understood as one of submission and resignation. On the contrary, the pacifists as well as the humanist pragmatists believe that unilateral disarmament is possible only as an expression of a deep spiritual and moral change within ourselves: it is an act of courage and resistance—not one of cowardice or surrender. Forms of resistance differ in accordance with the respective viewpoints. On the other hand, Gandhists and men like King-Hall advocate nonviolent resistance, which undoubtedly requires the maximum of courage and faith; they refer to the example of Indian resistance against Britain or Norwegian resistance against the Nazis. This point of view is succinctly expressed in *Speak Truth to Power:*

> Thus, we dissociate ourselves from the basically selfish attitude that has been miscalled pacifism, but that might be more accurately described as a kind of irresponsible antimilitarism. We dissociate ourselves also from utopianism. Though the choice of nonviolence involves a radical change in men, it does not require perfection. . . . We have tried to make it clear that readiness to accept suffering—rather than inflict it on others—is the essence of the nonviolent life, and that we must be prepared if called upon to pay the ultimate price.

> Obviously, if men are willing to spend billions of treasure and countless lives in war, they cannot dismiss the case for nonviolence by saying that in a nonviolent struggle people might be killed! It is equally clear that where commitment and the readiness to sacrifice are lacking, nonviolent resistance cannot be effective. On the contrary, it demands greater discipline, more arduous training, and more courage than its violent counterpart.[11]

Some think of armed resistance, of men and women defending their lives and their freedom with rifles, pistols, or knives. It is not unrealistic to think that both forms of resistance, nonviolent or violent, might deter an aggressor from attacking. At least, it is more realistic than to think that the use of thermonuclear weapons could lead to a "victory for democracy."

The proponents of "security by armament" sometimes accuse us of having an unrealistic, flatly optimistic picture of the nature of man. They remind us that this "perverse human being has a dark, illogical, irrational side."[12] They even go so far as to say that "the paradox of nuclear deterrence is a variant of the fundamental Christian paradox. In order to *live,* we must express our willingness to kill and to die."[13] Apart from this crude falsification of Christian teaching, we are by no means oblivious of the potential evil within man and of the tragic aspect of life. Indeed, there are situations in which man must be willing to die in order to live. In the sacrifices necessary for violent or nonviolent resistance, I can see an expression of the acceptance of tragedy and sacrifice. But, there is no tragedy or sacrifice in irresponsibility and carelessness: there is no meaning or dignity in the idea of the destruction of mankind and of civilization. Man has in himself a potential for evil; his whole existence is beset by dichotomies rooted in the very conditions of his existence. But these truly tragic aspects must not be confused with the results of stupidity and lack of imagination, with the willingness to stake the future of mankind on a gamble.

Finally, to take up one last criticism, directed against the position of unilateral disarmament: that it is "soft" on Communism. Our position is precisely based on the negation of the Soviet principle of the omnipotence of the state. Just because the spokesmen for unilateral disarmament are drastically opposed to the supremacy of the state, they do not want to grant the state the ever-increasing power which is unavoidable in the arms race, and they deny the right of the state to make decisions which can lead to the destruction of a great part of humanity and can doom future generations. If the basic conflict between the Soviet system and the democratic world is the question of the defense of the individual against the encroachment of an omnipotent state, then, indeed, the position for unilateral disarmament is the one which is most radically opposed to the Soviet principle.

Having discussed the case for unilateral disarmament (in the broad sense), I want to return to the practical proposition of unilateral steps toward disarmament. I do not deny that there are risks involved in this limited form of unilateral action but, considering the fact that the present method of negotiations has produced no results and that the chances that they will in the future are rather slim, considering furthermore the grave risk involved in the continuation of the arms race, I believe that it is practically and morally justified to take this risk. At present we are caught in a position with little chance for survival, unless we want to take refuge in hopes. *If* we have enough shelters, *if* there is enough time for a warning and strategic evacuation of cities, *if* the "United States' active offenses and active defenses can gain control of the military situation after only a few exchanges,"[14] we might have only five, or twenty-five, or seventy million killed. However, if these conditions do not materialize, "an enemy could, by repeated strikes, reach almost any level of death and destruction he wished."[15] (And, I assume, the same threat exists for the Soviet Union.) In such a situation, "when nations are poised at the last moment when an agreement appears possible to end the risk of horrifying war, unleashed by fanatics, lunatics or men of ambition,"[16] it is imperative to shake off the inertia of our accustomed thinking, to seek for new approaches to the problem, and above all, to see new alternatives to the present choices that confront us.

NOTES

1. Charles E. Osgood, "Suggestions for Winning the Real War with Communism," *Conflict Resolution,* III, No. 4 (December 1959), p. 131, and also "A Case for Graduated Unilateral Disarmament," *Bulletin of the Atomic Scientists,* XVI, No. 4, pp. 127 ff.

2. This condition is in my opinion to be taken only as an optimal *desideratum,* since any weakening of one power's aggressive potential means strategically some increase in the opponent's aggressive potential.

3. Osgood, "Suggestions for Winning the Real War with Communism," p. 316.

4. See Bertrand Russell, *Common Sense and Nuclear Warfare,* (London: Allen & Unwin, 1959); Stephen King-Hall, *Defense in the Nuclear Age* (Nyack, N.Y.: Fellowship Publications, 1959); Jerome

Davis and General H. B. Hester, *On the Brink* (New York: Lyle Stuart, 1959); Lewis Mumford, *The Human Way Out* (Pendell Hill Pamphlet No. 97, 1958); C. W. Mills, *The Causes of World War Three* (New York: Simon and Schuster, 1959); George F. Kennan, "Foreign Policy and Christian Conscience," *The Atlantic Monthly,* (May, 1959); Richard B. Gregg, *The Power of Nonviolence* (Nyack, N.Y.: Fellowship Publications, 1959); and American Friends Service Committee, *Speak Truth to Power, Quaker Search for an Alternative to Balance* (Philadelphia, Pa.: American Friends Service Committee, 1955).

5. George F. Kennan, *op. cit.,* pp. 44 ff.

6. This premise is shared by the report of the National Planning Association of America: *1970 Without Arms Control; Implications of Modern Weapons Technology* (by NPA Special Project Committee on Security through Arms Control; Planning Pamphlet No. 104, May 1958, Washington, D.C.), which states: "Not only does the danger of war remain a possibility, but the probability totalled over time increases, becoming a certainty if sufficient time elapses without succeeding in finding alternatives." Or, E. Finley Carter, president of the Stanford Research Institute, writes: "In the search for security through the application of technology to weapons for destruction, the Soviet bloc and the Western allies have created a mortal common enemy—the threat of accidental nuclear war" (*SRI Journal,* Stanford Research Institute, Fourth Quarter, III (1959), p. 198). Herman Kahn also concludes, "It is most unlikely that the world can live with an uncontrolled arms race lasting for several decades" (*ibid.,* p. 139). He emphasizes that it is unrealistic to believe that war has become impossible because of its extremely destructive character.

   The advisor on Science and Technology of the Democratic Advisory Council on 27 December 1959 declared: "All-out nuclear war seems not only possible but probable as long as we pursue our present military policies and fail to achieve international agreements of broad scope designed to alleviate this unstable situation. The triggering of a nuclear war by mistake, by misadventure or by miscalculation is a constant danger." It must be stressed that the danger lies not only in technical errors, but equally in the blundering decision-making by political and military leaders. If one remembers the political and military blunders committed by many of the leaders in the conduct of the wars of 1914 and 1939, it is not difficult to visualize that, given present-day weapons, the same type of leaders will blow the world to pieces, in spite of good intentions.

7. For a detailed analysis of modern society see my *The Sane Society* (New York: Rinehart, 1955).

8. Kahn, *SRI Journal,* III (1959), 140.

9. For the very same reasons, there is a real chance for the future abolition of war, a chance which never existed in the past. In most

of man's history, the improvement of his material situation required an increase in human energy (slaves), additional land for cattle-raising or agriculture, or new sources of raw materials. The techniques of the present and of the future will permit an increase in material wealth by an increased industrial and—indirectly—an agricultural productivity, without the need of enslaving or robbing others. At present and in the future, war would have as its only "rationale" the irrationality of human desire for power and conquest.

10. Whether or not political leaders are sane is not a matter of historical accident. Any government which has set out to do the impossible—for instance, to achieve equality and justice when the requisite material conditions are lacking—will produce fanatical and irrational leaders. This was the case with Robespierre, as it was with Stalin. Or, a government which tries to reconcile the interests of the most backward social class (the lower middle class) with those of the economically progressive classes (workers and businessmen) as the Nazi government did, again will produce fanatical and irrational leaders. The Soviet Union today is on the road toward solving its economic problems successfully; hence it is not surprising that her leaders are realistic men of common sense.

11. American Friends Service Committee, *op. cit.,* pp. 52 and 65.

12. Peter B. Young, "The Renunciationists," *Airpower,* Air Force Historical Foundation, VII, No. 1, p. 33.

13. *Ibid.*

14. Herman Kahn, *Report on a Study of Non-Military Defense* (New York: Rand Corporation, 1958), p. 13.

15. *Ibid.*

16. General de Gaulle, in a speech in April, 1960.

HUMAN NATURE AND NONVIOLENT RESISTANCE

By JEROME D. FRANK

THIS BOOK CONTAINS many ingenious and hopeful proposals for postponing World War III or creating conditions which reduce the probability of its occurrence. Such measures are necessary if Western civilization is to survive in the immediate future, but they do not come to grips with the central problem. For there will always be occasions for conflict which will tempt protagonists to resort to force. Since the knowledge of how to construct weapons of mass destruction will never be lost, the temptation to re-create them as a means of winning a conflict by their use will always exist.

It is generally agreed that any prolonged war, even if it starts with conventional weapons, is very likely to escalate into a nuclear war, and that the prospects of limiting a nuclear war are very small indeed. Unlimited nuclear war cannot possibly bring victory to any participant in the sense of achieving the aims for which it is fighting. The best each side can hope for is that it will destroy the other more completely than it is itself destroyed. Since from now on any war may lead to this type of mutual catastrophe, the long-term security and progress of mankind requires the elimination of war itself as an instrument of national policy.

Hitherto the elimination of war has been viewed as a utopian ideal fit only for the contemplation of philosophers and saints, rather than a concern of practical men, much less an actual requirement for survival. Therefore, before much progress can be made toward attaining this goal, leaders of opinion and action must be shown that it lies within the realm of the possible. To this end, the purpose of this essay is to consider some of the major motivational obstacles to the elimination of war and to adduce evidence that they are not necessarily insuperable.[1] It is recognized that the ultimate conquest of war involves problems not only of group and individual psychology but also of economic, political, and other aspects of human functioning. Consideration of these other kinds of problems lies beyond my competence, but it seems likely that if the psychological problems can be solved, the others will also be manageable.

The "Inevitability" of War

WAR IS INEVITABLE

Before proceeding further, it may be well to consider two powerful arguments against the possibility of the elimination of war—its prevalence throughout human history, and the inevitability of conflict between individuals and groups.

There is no doubt that war has been the constant companion of man, but some hope may be gained from the realization that humanity has been able to relinquish patterns of behavior which were equally widespread and deeply entrenched. One example is slavery, which has diminished enormously in the past century. Human sacrifice in religious rites is another deeply engrained pattern which has virtually vanished. Perhaps even more striking is Gandhi's success in thoroughly undermining, in the short space of one lifetime, the age-old institution of untouchability so deeply anchored in Hindu religious beliefs and folkways.

It is also undoubtedly true that humans will always get into conflict situations. Human existence without conflict is unthinkable. Conflict gives life much of its meaning, so that its elimination, even if attainable, would not be desirable. The task is rather to strengthen the existing institutionalized methods for nonviolent resolution of conflict and to devise means for nonviolent coercion of an adversary who possesses and is prepared to use superior destructive power.

Aggressive Tendencies

These goals, as will be seen, may not be beyond the realm of possibility. Their attainment requires the development of means of satisfying certain aspects of human nature which have contributed to the occurrence of war or have been stimulated by it. The most obvious of these is pugnacity. Humans are aggressive creatures who readily resort to violence, especially when they or their loved ones are threatened. This propensity, it is claimed, makes the elimination of war impossible. Fortunately, matters are not quite this simple. Man is an ambiguous conglomeration of self-aggrandizing, aggressive drives on the one hand and altruistic ones on the other. His tendency to aggrandize himself and his group has been responsible for his conquest of his environment and so is basic to civilization. When these and other drives are thwarted, humans tend to try to destroy the persons or things perceived as responsible for their frustration. Thus the urge to destroy a person or group perceived as an enemy is strengthened by the universal perception of the enemy as somehow blocking the legitimate aspirations of oneself or one's group. From this standpoint, war is both a consequence of and a means of attempting to satisfy self-aggrandizing, destructive impulses.

These impulses are counterbalanced, however, by equally strong and deeply rooted altruistic drives,[2] without which civilization would be impossible. Paradoxically, these drives, too, are stimulated and gratified by war. Its hardships and dangers powerfully enhance the sense of group solidarity, leading otherwise selfish persons freely to make great sacrifices, including that of life itself, for the welfare of their fellows. The problem of satisfying man's altruistic propensities in a world without war does not appear too formidable. There are plenty of opportunities for self-sacrifice in civilian life, and any situation in which a group faces a common danger affords stimuli and outlets for altruism. However, it would be important through training and example to strengthen altruistic tendencies to help counterbalance the aggressive ones.

The aggressive tendencies are more difficult to deal with. Any reduction in frustration—as occasioned, for example, by a rising standard of living—probably weakens destructive tendencies, but it is highly unlikely that efforts in this direction alone would suffice. As considered below, mere reduction of frustrations, if not accompanied by new types of challenge, may increase tension rather than reduce it. The greatest hope lies in the enormous modifiability of human behavior. It probably is not possible to eliminate basic drives such as aggressiveness, but it may be entirely possible to redirect them. The human capacity to symbolize permits an enormous variation of the means used for satisfying the same physiological need in different societies. Foods which deliciously satisfy hunger in one society are regarded as inedible by the members of another, depending on the connotations and symbolic meanings assigned to the foods. The development of alternative means for need-satisfaction is facilitated by the capacity for vicarious experience, which also depends largely on the mind's symbolic power. Reading descriptions of erotic activities, for example, under some circumstances may be almost as satisfying as performing them. The same holds for aggressive actions. To be sure, it remains unclear under which conditions watching boxing matches or gangster movies will afford a harmless release for aggressive impulses rather than stimulating violent behavior. However, the fact that humans do discharge considerable aggressiveness vicariously suggests that this mode of release could be further expanded. At present the chief mass channel for this mode of release is spectator sports, at both national and international levels. With sufficient ingenuity it should be possible to create similar international contests in the arts, perhaps on the model of the original Olympic Games, and in the sciences as well. The germ of this expansion already exists in the Russian-American competition in space exploration.

Love of Excitement

War also gains psychological support from the craving for excitement and novelty, which seems to spring from innate characteristics of the nervous system. The prospect of war is a wonderful antidote to the boredom of humdrum everyday existence. The more comfortable and free of challenge life becomes, the more restless human beings seem to be. The rise in delinquency in modern societies may be partly attributable to this source. The ultimate excitement is the risk of one's life, and, as we know, this is not infrequent, especially in young males. Witness the game of "chicken" or, in a less antisocial vein, the sport of mountain-climbing.[3] Fortunately, the advance of modern technology is supplying ample means for satisfying the craving for excitement, including aid missions to faraway corners of the earth, space travel, exploration of the oceans, speleology, and so on.

Wars are fed by the dislike of the stranger, which man shares with all gregarious creatures. The deep-seated, automatic tendency to distrust and derogate members of groups who look and behave differently from members of one's own group and subscribe to different values is perhaps the basic source of the "bogeyman concept of the enemy" which so potently contributes to the outbreak of war.[4] Fortunately, the rapid shrinkage of the world produced by improved transportation and communication means that soon no men will be strangers to each other. If modern civilization can survive long enough for this process to reach its end, this particular problem will disappear. In the meantime, it is extremely important to exploit every possible means of communication between different groups that serve to increase mutual understanding. To consider the characteristics of communication which diminish mutual hostility and those which simply serve to increase unfavorable stereotypes would lead too far afield.[5] It has already been demonstrated that cultural and scientific interchanges are particularly helpful, and that cooperative activities are perhaps the most useful of all. When members of different groups cooperate toward achievement of goals both groups desire, and discover that each group can facilitate the progress of the other toward that goal, there develop habits of cooperation which counteract antagonism.[6] An excellent example is the recent successful International Geophysical Year which made possible the subsequent signing of a treaty for peaceful exploitation of the Antarctic which almost certainly would not otherwise have come to pass.

It is relatively easy to conceive ways other than war to overcome the fear of the stranger and to satisfy aggressiveness, altruism, and the craving for excitement, especially with the aid of modern technology. More difficult to deal with are two human characteristics which tend to push quarrels toward violent solutions and to prolong them, once the violence begins, to the bitter end. One is the remarkable tendency of humans to value certain abstractions more than life itself, leading to a willingness to sacrifice one's life in their defense. The other is that in conflict situations any sign of weakness or fear in one antagonist stimulates the other to attack.

Sacrifice for Ideals

The destructiveness of wars rests in part on the fact that once a person or group of persons has become firmly committed to an ideal, there is no limit to the lengths to which he or they will go to defend it, and the more abstract the goal the more intense the commitment seems to be. Wars fought for food or territory have probably been less bitter and inexorable, on the whole, than those fought over ideological differences. Whether in the long run the propensity of humans to commit themselves absolutely to certain ideals is good or bad, is debatable. Certainly the world would be a poorer place today were it not for religious, national, and intellectual heroes who sacrifice their lives for their convictions. On the other hand, this propensity has led to endless catastrophic conflicts over differences in world-views which seemed vital at the time but now seem trivial or meaningless, as for example the dispute as to whether God is unitarian or trinitarian.

Modern weapons of mass destruction have changed the context of dying for one's ideals in two respects. First, one cannot die for one's beliefs in a nuclear war without sacrificing millions of bystanders who may be quite indifferent to the beliefs in question. Secondly, death in nuclear war cannot preserve the ideals for which the martyr sacrifices his life, since the war would destroy the social organization necessary for their fulfillment. The task of a modern world is to devise forms of waging conflict in which it will still be possible for people to fight for their ideals to the death, but without destroying the uninvolved and also with some hope that the sacrifice may actually help to achieve its aim.

Mutual Threat Perception

Wars gain ferocity, finally, from the recognition that it is dangerous to be afraid in the face of an adversary, and even more dangerous to show one's fear. Human behavior tends to be reciprocal; that is, the behavior of one person tends either to stimulate or to dampen the behavior of the other. In a situation of mutual antagonism the display of fear by one contestant demoralizes his allies and himself and encourages his foe. Hence, the automatic way of responding to the threats of an adversary is to threaten him in return and back up the threat by increasing one's military might. At the same time one proclaims one's willingness to die if necessary for one's point of view. This attitude sustains the morale of each side by demonstrating to itself and the other that it has not allowed itself to be intimidated. Unfortunately, it simultaneously intensifies the mutual threat perception which increases the likelihood of war.

A recent example may illustrate this point. After the U-2 incident, the House Appropriations Committee restored a large appropriation for the development of a nuclear airplane, which was admittedly a dubious undertaking, on the grounds that it would be a psychological mistake not to do so. In one sense, of course, to restore the appropriation was a gross psychological mistake in that its effect would be to stimulate Russia to intensify its own armament efforts. What apparently was meant was that not to restore the appropriation might be viewed by ourselves and the Russians as a sign that we were intimidated by her threats.

From the standpoint of individual psychology, then, a world without war becomes conceivable only if it contains adequate means for nonviolent waging of conflict that can be successfully employed by normal, aggressive humans, that permit antagonists to die for their ideals if necessary, and that contain convincing means for demonstrating fearlessness and steadfastness of purpose without recourse to the threat of violence. On the face of it, these stipulations may seem impossible to meet. Fortunately, there have been examples of conflicts between groups in recent years in which they have been fulfilled.

Mention of these examples, which will be considered presently, calls attention to a major omission in the analysis to this point. By focusing primarily on the psychology of individuals it has neglected a crucial consideration, namely that war is a group phenomenon, and that cultural and group factors probably play a greater part in its cause and cure than do individual ones.

Group Behavior

War is a socially learned pattern of group behavior; its techniques, as well as the values and standards supporting it, must be transmitted afresh to each generation. There have been occasional societies which have never developed war patterns,[7] and some which were warlike at one period of their existence and completely pacifist at another.[8] This suggests that group standards interdicting organized violence can be developed without necessarily requiring the elimination of force in certain situations of personal conflict. Members of societies without war patterns presumably defend themselves and their families against personal assaults.

In this connection it may be worth recalling that there has been a progressive diminution in individual and group violence within societies, without any evidence that this has been due to any equally drastic reduction in aggressiveness of individuals. Americans readily get into fights, but they no longer indulge in duels, and they accept shattering defeats in lawsuits without attempting to shoot their adversaries. At a group level, the last major steel strike was certainly as bitter as many which have resulted in violence in the past, yet neither side resorted to violence. It is doubtful that the individual strikers and factory managers were any less aggressive than their forebears. The reason that strikes several decades ago characteristically involved violence, while many of those today do not, lies in the fact that institutions of arbitration and adjudication have been developed, along with powerful expectations on the part of the society as a whole that they will be used. This creates a situation in which resort to force by either side stands to cost them more than they can hope to gain by it.

It will at once be objected that examples of nonviolent solutions of conflict within societies are irrelevant to conflicts between societies since many of the conditions which facilitate peaceful solution of the former do not exist in the latter. For example, contending groups within a society tend to share the same ideology, at least in large measure, and they are in constant, close personal contact. The first of these conditions often does not hold for international conflicts; the second never does.

But while some of the conditions for peaceful resolution are indeed lacking in inter-society conflict, others are present in greater measure. Nations may have more powerful nonviolent means of influencing each other through their control of methods of mass communication, economic forces, and so on, than do groups within societies. The United States, for example, possesses ample destructive power to blow Cuba, or for that matter all of Latin America, off the map. Yet it has been effectively inhibited so far from overthrowing Castro by force, not primarily by the faint threat of Russian retaliation, but by the adverse effects of such a move on world public opinion and its probable political and economic repercussions.

The Dangers of Disarmament

But these considerations, it may be argued, are remote from the dangers which would face a disarmed America. Four assertions are commonly offered as conclusive arguments against disarmament. The first is that in a truly disarmed world the Communists would win because their system is more successful in appealing to the underprivileged nations; the Communists probably genuinely desire disarmament, not out of idealist or altruistic motives but because they believe that they have a superior socioeconomic system which would eventually prevail in a disarmed world. Unfortunately, many Americans seem to have accepted the image of Communism created by Communist propaganda. Actually many Communist claims of superiority are extremely shaky. It may be true, as they maintain, that a free-market economy cannot compel inhabitants of undeveloped countries to make the sacrifices needed to accumulate the capital necessary to start industrialization. But it would be cheaper, and far less dangerous, for the Free World to supply this pump-priming capital rather than to squander the money on arms. The Communist system appears to have no advantages over ours other than this dubious one. Their farm problem is worse than ours and they have made less progress in solving it.[9] While they may have a more efficient political system in some respects, they are saddled with a massive bureaucracy which, like all bureaucracy, bogs down in its own red tape. Abroad they have made real headway only in adjacent countries, or in those which had suffered under extremely repressive and exploitative dictatorships, such as Cuba. They have failed recently in both Burma and the Congo, where these conditions did not obtain. It seems likely that with some increase in effort and ingenuity the democracies could make a case for their way of life that would capture the imagination of the peoples of the world, who want freedom as well as bread, much more effectively than could Communism.

The second objection, essentially a variant of the first, is that unless we are able to defend our standard of living by arms, it will sink to the level of the Chinese. There is ample reason to believe, however, that standards of living throughout the world could be rapidly raised. Mankind now has access to limitless supplies of energy for the production of goods. Practical methods of changing salt water into fresh are on the verge of achievement. This will make the desert areas arable and solve the world's food problems for many years. Finally, cheap, reliable, simple contraceptive methods will make it possible to halt the population explosion. A nuclear war, to be sure, would solve the problem of surplus population for a long time to come; fortunately, there are better solutions.

If resources now squandered on armaments and creative minds now absorbed with weapons development could be diverted to the solution of these problems, it seems entirely reasonable to hope that the standard of living of the underprivileged areas of the world would approach ours, rather than the reverse.

A third presumably conclusive objection to the hope of achieving a warless world is that in such a world nothing could prevent one country from secretly rebuilding a few nuclear weapons and gaining its end through blackmail. The temptation to do this would be particularly strong when all nations were disarmed, because only a few weapons would afford a crushing supremacy. This line of argument presupposes that the world would be the same as it is today, with the exception that the nations would be disarmed. Actually, as already indicated, a disarmed world would be different in essential respects, and any national leaders who contemplated nuclear blackmail would have to consider the likelihood of certain very unpleasant consequences.

The sudden unveiling of concealed nuclear weapons would be very demoralizing to the country that made such a move, for it would destroy its own image of itself as peaceful. Disarmament could not have been achieved without massive "peace offensives" within each country, so that popular opinion against war would be strong. If any leaders tried clandestinely to accumulate arms, they would probably be betrayed by members of their own society. Even if they should succeed, they would still have to cope with a disillusioned populace. Even a dictatorship cannot reverse its policies overnight.

Furthermore, the effect of this disclosure would be to shatter the structure for the peaceful solution of disputes which had been developed and to impel all countries to rush to the manufacture of arms. The common enemy of all would be the one nation which attempted nuclear blackmail. Since many types of weapons of mass deadliness can be quickly, cheaply, and secretly created, this would pose a severe threat to the blackmailers. They could not hope successfully to embark on such a venture unless they were prepared to subdue and police the entire world. It seems reasonable that these considerations would act as powerful deterrents against an attempt at secret rearmament.

The possibility must be reckoned with, however, that these deterrents would not suffice and that, under threat of superior arms, the Communists would attempt a military occupation of the United States. The prospect of an occupation by hordes of hungry Orientals is generally regarded as the final refutation of the possibility of achieving a disarmed world. For, it is argued, the only protection against this eventuality is to defend our borders by force.

In reply it may be pointed out, first, that once the Chinese have nuclear arms, they can only be stopped by force at the cost of our own suicide. With or without arms, our main defense will have to be reducing the temptation to invade by working toward the reduction of inequalities in population densities and living standards through such measures as those outlined above.

To assemble the necessary transportation and to persuade members of a country enjoying a rising standard of living to emigrate en masse would be no small undertaking. The response at best would be unlikely to be enthusiastic, especially since the threatened country would be using all possible means of mobilizing world opinion against such a move, and would inform the invaders through mass communication media of the difficulties awaiting them. In short, many deterrents of both positive and negative nature could be mobilized to discourage such an attempt.

Nonviolent Resistance

Nevertheless, the remote possibility of an attempted military occupation of the United States must be included in any calculation of risks. Such an occupation would, to be sure, force upon us the necessity of defeating it through nonviolent means. Evidence that this is not necessarily impossible is afforded by the success of two planned nonviolent campaigns in different societies and under totally different circumstances—Gandhi's for Indian independence and Martin Luther King's for desegregation of public transportation in Montgomery, Alabama.

After the fact it is easy to point out many special conditions which contributed to the success of these campaigns, and indeed one cannot generalize widely from them. Yet they do require a re-examination of some widely held convictions about human nature and conduct. In particular, they showed that nonviolent campaigners need not all be saints. Gandhi and King were able to mold ordinary Indians and Negroes into effective nonviolent fighting forces by creating powerful group standards that held despair and violence in check despite extreme provocations. These standards required of their members the same intense dedication to an ideal as does the successful conduct of war, up to the point of sacrifice of life itself, but afforded opportunities to die without endangering the lives of others and in such a way as to help achieve the goal for which the sacrifice was made.

A remarkable feature of these campaigns was that they made refusal to use violence a manifestation of strength and resort to violence an admission of weakness. A main incentive for the steady increase of armaments today is the justified fear that appearing weak or irresolute to an enemy will tempt him to attack. Gandhi and King have shown that one can convince an adversary of one's strength by abjuring violence. When the implications of this astonishing achievement are fully grasped, it may open up entirely new avenues to the achievement of disarmament.

It is claimed that nonviolent campaigns would certainly fail against a ruthless dictatorship conducted by persons with less regard for human life than Americans and Englishmen. Perhaps so; yet it must not be forgotten that the English, when faced with violence in Kenya, resorted to very savage countermeasures.

The endless historical examples of the crushing of resistance by armies of occupation do not conclusively dispose of the possibility of successful nonviolent resistance against an occupying power. In all, the winning power at the peak of its morale occupied a country demoralized by defeat in war and without training in resistance methods. Even under these conditions it is difficult to maintain the morale of an army of occupation. Nor has a consistent, thoroughly planned program of nonviolent resistance against an occupying force ever been tested. It is worth recalling that even the spontaneous nonviolent resistance campaigns in Denmark and Norway demoralized the Nazi troops so badly that they had to be frequently rotated, and that in the East German uprising some Russian soldiers refused to fire on unarmed Germans at the cost of their own lives. Since an occupation requires continual face-to-face contact with the subject peoples, and the henchmen of dictators are human, it seems conceivable that they, too, would eventually respond to types of behavior that inhibit the use of violence and demoralize its possessors.

A nonviolent campaign against a Communist occupation would,

of course, have to be conducted on lines quite different from Gandhi's against the English or King's against white Americans. It would require a tight, highly disciplined organization with diffusion of leadership, carefully worked-out clandestine methods of communication, and other measures very similar to those which would be required to survive a nuclear attack.[10] In fact, if a country ever committed itself to an exclusive policy of nonviolence, it would probably have to rely on the military, as the only group with sufficient knowledge of organization and discipline, to train and lead the civilian population in this type of combat. Such a struggle would undoubtedly cost a great many lives and might fail, as can any form of defense. But at worst it could not result in as great a slaughter as a nuclear war or reduce the level of civilization as drastically.

A crying need at present is for detailed, sophisticated, hard-headed analyses of possible methods of nonviolent struggle analogous to current studies of methods of war. In the present state of ignorance, one can say no more than that a nonviolent campaign conducted at a level of sophistication and determination equal to that of the occupying power need not inevitably fail of its aim.

Conversion to Nonviolence

It would be difficult to persuade a nation like America, which has grown great through wars, to put its faith in nonviolent methods of combat. So far, nonviolence has appealed only to underprivileged groups without hope of achieving superior arms, for whom it offers enhanced self-respect and a new means of achieving their aims. Acceptance of nonviolence by Western nations would require changes in attitudes and values of the magnitude of the religious conversion of an individual or of a major revolution inside a country such as that which took place in Russia with the overthrow of czarism.

We do not know much about the conditions fostering either individual or group conversions. Individual conversions may be the result of a long, gradual process of education and indoctrination, or they may be precipitated suddenly by a catastrophic psychic experience. Sudden religious conversions occur typically in persons who have undergone a long period of desperation, hopelessness, or panic. To use a phrase of which alcoholics are fond, they have "hit bottom." Even less is known about forces making for conversion of groups. There are some hints that it may be easier to change group standards than to change those of individuals. Witness the fact that Germany and Japan have changed in our eyes from diabolical enemies to trusted allies in about a decade.

Conversion to nonviolence might conceivably be brought about through either education or catastrophe or a combination of the two. The longer one contemplates present and future weapons of mass destruction, the more hopeless reliance on superior force appears, while active exploration and development of methods for nonviolent combat resolution should gradually increase their acceptability. This process would be greatly accelerated by a nuclear accident sufficiently grave to bring home the horrors of modern war, an unpleasant but unfortunately not improbable contingency.

The achievement of a world without a war system would require the invention of many new institutions and devices for peaceful resolution of conflicts and the rechanneling of certain human drives which have hitherto found their chief satisfaction in armed combat. The purpose of this essay has been to indicate that although the obstacles to achieving these goals are formidable, they are not necessarily insurmountable. It should be relatively easy to find alternative outlets for pugnacity and the craving for excitement. The fear of the stranger can be expected to wither as increased communication and transportation knit the peoples of the world ever more closely together. The creation of nonviolent means—for coercing an opponent possessing superior force—that convey strength and courage and allow the sacrifice of life for one's ideals might seem impossible, were it not that such methods have already been devised and effectively used in special circumstances. The task is to develop further methods of nonviolent resistance which have a reasonable chance of success against a ruthless occupying power. If this can be achieved, it will remove the threat of occupation of a disarmed power by an armed one. This will eliminate the greatest psychological block to the general disarmament which is a prerequisite for the abolition of war.

Though difficult to initiate, progress in this direction should become progressively easier as the rewards of cooperative efforts to use the world's human and physical resources for the betterment of mankind become increasingly obvious and the inequalities and tensions which lead to a resort to violence correspondingly diminish.

NOTES

1. For a fuller exposition of some of the points in this article, see Jerome D. Frank, "Breaking the Thought Barrier: Psychological Challenges of the Nuclear Age," *Psychiatry,* XXIII (1960), pp. 245–66.

2. D. O. Hebb and W. R. Thompson adduce interesting evidence that genuinely altruistic behavior increases as one ascends the phylogenetic scale, and is already prominent in the chimpanzee. See "The

Social Significance of Animal Studies," pp. 532–61 in *Handbook of Social Psychology,* I, ed. by Gardner Lindzey (Cambridge: Addison Wesley, 1954).

3. See, for example, William O. Douglas, *Of Men and Mountains* (New York: Harper, 1950).
4. Charles E. Osgood, "Suggestions for Winning the Real War with Communism," *Journal of Conflict Resolution,* III (1959), pp. 295–325.
5. Jeanne Watson and Ronald Lippitt, *Learning Across Cultures* (Ann Arbor: Research Center for Group Dynamics, series No. 4, University of Michigan, 1955).
6. Musafer Sherif, *et al., Intergroup Conflict and Cooperation: The Robbers' Cave Experiment* (Norman, Okla.: University of Oklahoma, 1961).
7. For example, the Hopi. See Dorothy Eggan, "The General Problem of Hopi Adjustment," *American Anthropologist,* XLV (1943), pp. 357–73.
8. For example, the Comanche. See Abram Kardiner *et al., The Psychological Frontiers of Society* (New York: Columbia University Press, 1945).
9. Walt W. Rostow, "Marx Was a City Boy," *Harpers* (February, 1955), pp. 25–30.
10. Herman Kahn, *On Thermonuclear War* (Princeton: Princeton University Press, 1960).

RENOUNCING NUCLEAR WEAPONS

By DAVID DAICHES

I AM NEITHER A POLITICIAN nor a military strategist, but there seems to be little chance that either politicians or military strategists are going to be of much help in getting the world out of its present frightful dilemma. We all know how two ways of life confront each other and how the tension between the two great powers, the United States and the USSR, is a practical consequence of that confrontation; we all know, too, that each side is armed with nuclear weapons which, if used, can virtually destroy humanity or at the very least severely prejudice the future of the human race on this planet. Is there any way of thinking or of acting that would help to avoid the disaster that threatens?

We can at least be clear about what is involved. In the past, war has been an instrument of policy, a last-resort means adopted by national governments against other national governments. There have always been people who have deplored war, and even those who precipitated it have often professed regret at having to use this ultimate weapon. I think myself that on certain occasions, as a last-resort weapon when all else failed, it could be justified. (The war against Hitler, though I do not think it would have been necessary if politicians had acted wisely and destroyed Hitler's power by political and economic means at an earlier stage in his career, was by 1939 inevitable and, I should maintain, just, in spite of the horrors that it inevitably brought about.) This is because war was a means to ends that could not be realized in any other way. A minority of adventurers or lunatics have enjoyed war for its own sake; but generally it has been employed as a means to a specific end, or in order to prevent another nation from gaining an end which seemed detrimental or in some way undesirable. (I am not speaking of the remote past, but of modern European history.) It was necessary to try to gain these ends by war because sovereign nation states had no common authority over them and they were, in fact, so far as their relations with each other were concerned, in precisely the "state of nature" described by Hobbes in his *Leviathan:* "Where there is no common Power, there is no Law: where no Law, no Injustice. Force and Fraud are in warre the two Cardinall vertues." If there were an international government, with real authority, this situation of course would not prevail; and the setting up of an international government with real authority has often been thought of as a way out of war. But a stream can rise no higher than its source, and an international government can never acquire more authority than its member governments are willing to yield to it. There seems no likelihood at present of the major powers' being willing to yield any serious part of their sovereignty to a common authority in which members of the rival world bloc will participate. This is certainly not the immediate way out of the predicament involved in the constant threat of nuclear war.

In the past, war has been a means to an end—a drastic and last-resort means, but still a means which could actually achieve the proposed end; while it may have been cruel it was not necessarily absurd. But modern nuclear weapons alter this situation *radically*. Nuclear war cannot be a means to any end; it can only bring about the destruction of both sides. And since today any war may develop into nuclear war, then it is clear that war on any large international scale cannot be a way of achieving any rational objective. It follows also that the threat of starting such a war involves self-delusion on the part of the threatener. We all know that in a major modern war there can be no victor; all will be vanquished, and the future of the human race jeopardized. Most thinking people recognize this. They see that nuclear war would mean the destruction of *all* sides, but some nevertheless argue either (a) that such destruction would be better than life under a Communist regime, or (b) we can prevent the Communists from attacking us by *threatening* to retaliate immediately if they start anything.

Now argument (a) can easily be disposed of: it is dishonest, selfish, and arrogant. Even where it does not mean (as I am afraid that it often does) simply "If I can't continue to make my profits in a free-enterprise economy which provides a suitable context for my personal ambitions, then I should prefer humanity to come to an end in an appalling and agonizing disaster"—even where it does not mean this, it involves making a decision for the whole human race which no generation, and even more certainly no individual, has any right to make. Whatever we think of life under a Communist regime, where there is life there is hope; the future remains problematical; and to be prepared to risk extinguishing all human life on this planet rather than relinquish some personal comfort and satisfaction is criminally egotistical. But relatively few people, so far as I am aware, take this position. Many more take position (b), that we can prevent Russia from attacking us if we threaten immediate nuclear retaliation and maintain constant readiness to carry out that retaliation. But this way of thinking is based on a complete fallacy. A deterrent can only function if one is prepared to use it and if by using it one still achieves a better result than by not using it. "If you do this, I will punish you," a loving parent may say to a child, hoping that the child will not do what is thus forbidden and not liking the idea of punishing him, but still prepared to punish him, for his own good, if he does the forbidden thing. "If you commit murder, you will be put to death," society may say to its members, and this law would be meant as a deterrent, to prevent people from committing murder. But if a man does commit murder, he pays the penalty. The deterrent has not worked in his case, but society survives and presumably other people will be less likely to commit murder because of what happened to this murderer. (I myself do not believe in capital punishment; I use this argument only as an illustration.) But if the law were to say to a potential criminal, "If you steal or murder or commit some other grave crime the law will destroy you with an apparatus so dangerous that every other member of society will run the risk of appalling suffering and of destruction when it is employed on you," then the law will be talking dangerous nonsense and no potential criminal in his senses would pay any attention to it. One must be able to use a deterrent, if pushed, and still achieve a better result than if the deterrent had not been used. This, clearly, cannot be done with nuclear weapons. Thus all talk of the "nuclear deterrent" seems to me to be arrant nonsense. Both sides in the cold war talk such nonsense, and each is afraid that the other, regardless of the logic of the situation, will use its nuclear weapon. The result is mounting fear on each side, and mounting fear produces irrationality.

How do we get out of such a situation? I think the first step is for us to state categorically that we shall not in any circumstances use this obscene weapon which if used would launch a nuclear war that would threaten the continuance of human life on this planet. But if we do that, it will at once be objected, won't the Russians immediately take over? Isn't it only the fear of our nuclear retaliation that prevents them from taking over as it is? Nobody knows whether this would occur or not; nobody can say to what extent the immense lowering of tension that would result from a renunciation of nuclear weapons would produce a totally new international situation. But certainly the

Russians would not use nuclear weapons unless they had to, and even if the repudiation of the "deterrent" by our side led to a rush of Russian conquest, it would not destroy all human future.

The real issue is whether we have sufficient conviction in the inherent superiority of our way of life that we can envisage techniques of passive resistance to enable our people to stand out against any successful physical attack on them. This attack, if we first repudiate nuclear weapons, is in any case problematical; but if it did come it would, as I have tried to prove, be non-nuclear. (Would the Russians willingly risk contaminating the atmosphere when they could gain their ends without it? Nuclear war, as I have shown, is not a realistic means to any given end.) Why are we so afraid of Communist aggression? Why are we so distrustful of the morale of our own people? How far do we trust our own people to defend *by inward knowledge and conviction* their own way of life? Surely our immediate and most urgent task is to improve our way of life so as to make it invulnerable to the obvious attacks of Communist propaganda (it is not now invulnerable: to take only one example, we often talk of Communist atheist materialism, but a study of the advertising in any slick-paper magazine in the West suggests a crude materialism much more than the study of Communist writings or behavior does). The trouble with Communism is not its materialism but its areas of inhumanity, deriving from the fact that its leaders are dedicated—are, in a sense, religious. If Communism were not a religion it would be less dangerous. We must improve our techniques of education so that people take it as a matter of course that if the worst happens and they are subjected to an alien regime their protests will be continuous and in the long run effective. That, after all, is the way Christianity won.

It seems to me that both sides in the cold war are too shrill in protesting the superiority of their way of life; and certainly in the West it simply is not true that the ordinary citizen really understands what is involved in this contest of civilizations. If we really understand *why* our way of life is better than any challenging way, and if we improve it to eliminate peripheral doubts about it, and if at the same time we make it absolutely clear that we shall in no circumstances use a nuclear weapon since it would mean the destruction of both sides and of all hope for the future, then the other side will have both to concentrate on eliminating the vulnerable points from *its* way of life and it will not feel the fear that leads it to maintain *its* deterrent. A deterrent that can never be used without destroying deterrer and deterred is not a deterrent but a perpetual threat which increases terror and so decreases reason in international affairs. The deadlock must be broken somehow. I suggest that *we* break it, because I am writing in English for my own side, as it were: I wish I were in a position to give similar advice to the Russians.

Any action involves a balancing of risks, but the worst risk of all is to take no action and let the present nuclear-backed cold war proceed. A renunciation on our part of nuclear weapons, backed by an intensive educational campaign of the kind I have indicated, *might* invite the Russians to move in (non-nuclearly). In case they should do so, we must see to it that our people have the intellectual and spiritual resources to resist passively and effectively. This can be done only if we truly *believe* in our civilization and do not simply rant about its superiority. The risk is there, and I do not wish to minimize the unpleasantness of having to engage in passive resistance to a cruel regime. (But think of the extent and variety of America alone, and the impossibility of holding down its people permanently, when they have no tradition—as the Russians have—of that kind of subjugation.) I myself feel more optimistic about the consequences of our acting in the way I suggest; I do not think the risk of immediate Russian aggression is really great. But I concede that there is an element of risk. Compared to the alternative, however, the risk is small and *involves a chance that it is possible to take.* The alternative is nuclear war, and that is *not* a chance which it is possible to take.

I think also that a renunciation of the kind I have suggested would appeal to the so-called "uncommitted" nations as an act of tremendous humanity and generosity and swing them behind us with such emotional force that no country, least of all one which claims to embody the hopes of oppressed humanity as Russia does, could afford to fight against it. That is one reason why I believe that the risk involved is slight. To conventional thinkers and nonthinkers who might protest that my solution is cowardly or treacherous or unrealistic, I can only reply that conventional attitudes seem to be leading us straight to irrevocable disaster and it is time that somebody looked at the situation from a quite different point of view. If such a policy does involve us in some kind of subjugation to Russia (and, as I say, I think the risk of this is extremely slight), then the true heroism of passive resistance to such subjugation made by people who know what they value and really believe in it would be something much more splendid than the pushing of buttons by top military men in order to set off the most destructive war in history. The long-term hope for humanity lies in more and more people's recognizing the good life with such a deep force of inward conviction that neither physical nor psychological weapons can make them feel wrong.

It must be remembered that a society that has the dynamic of a revolution behind it can claim a much more dedicated loyalty from its members than a society that merely fears change as subversive or unthinkingly regards any alternative way of life to its own as automatically evil. A loyalty that can withstand hardship and brainwashing, a loyalty that can compete with the fanatical loyalty of the trained Communist, must be based on a deep positive understanding of the nature, meaning, and values of the civilization it serves. The fanaticism of the Communist, produced by careful education and stimulated by success, can afford to manifest itself in slogans and catchwords. But mere slogans and catchwords will not do for our side, because we do not have the monolithic educational system of a totalitarian state to support them. We believe in diversity, in tolerance, in cultural pluralism; but unless such a belief is held with proper knowledge and thoughtfulness it can become a belief in moral relativism, in the proposition that "anything goes," and that kind of belief is extremely vulnerable to hardship. If Communism could demonstrate that it could provide us with even more washing machines and television sets than we now have (and it is not impossible that it may some day be able to), this demonstration *should* be totally irrelevant to the reasons why we disapprove of it. But would it be, for many of us? Is there not a widespread confusion in the West between the belief that our way of life is better because it provides us with more material comforts and the belief that it is better because it is based on a respect for human personality and human diversity? If everybody in the West were so educated that he really understood why the Communist way of life impoverished the human spirit *and would still impoverish the human spirit even if it provided more material comforts than our own way of life does,* then we should be in a position to resist Communism by conviction rather than by force. It is its drably mechanistic view of human personality, not its incapacity to produce large quantities of consumer goods, that provides the true case against the Communist way of life as now practiced behind the iron curtain. The problem is an ethical not an economic one. Passive resistance to a Communist aggressor is possible to a large nation occupying a vast area such as the United States; but it would only be successful if its ethical basis is understood and profoundly felt by the people as a whole. Of course, in a poor country with a low standard of living, any invaders who made it possible for the masses of the people to eat more would in the long run be successful; but that is not the position in the United States.

The analysis of Soviet novels, with their intolerably drab ideal of the good life, of Soviet political speeches, with their iterated slogans and ready-made formulas, of Soviet history with its cruelties and cynical tergiversations, would be an important part of the education

I have in mind, though less important than the positive investigation of the sources of our own moral strength. Such a program would only risk encouraging subversion if our own statesmen were to talk in empty slogans and invite the same destructive analysis as had been applied to Communist propaganda. Politicians as well as teachers—indeed, all elements in society—would have to join in the new educational effort. It may be argued that the whole idea is utopian, but this is really to plead disbelief in the moral resources of our civilization. Perhaps this disbelief is justified: if it is, I cannot see why we want to try to resist Communism at all, except on the simplest materialist grounds, and they provide no true basis for resistance.

I should emphasize that I do not believe that the chances of its ever coming to a test of passive resistance against a Soviet invader are more than extremely remote. The appeal of international Communism to the uncommitted nations and to the undeveloped countries of Africa and Asia in particular is a moral one: it emphasizes anti-colonialism, freedom, humanity, progress. Any Soviet government would think more than twice before once and for all destroying this image of what it stands for in the neutral world, for on the continuance of this image its hopes of success depend. (The Hungarian affair does not disprove this. Subsequent accounts show that the Soviet government *did* think more than twice before intervening and that it was very sensitive to neutral opinion on the matter. The risk had to be taken because this was a case of a country already within the Soviet orbit trying to get out, and success in this would have been an irreparable blow to Soviet prestige. Even so, there were special circumstances, such as the moral vulnerability of Britain and France over Suez.) I think that if our side renounced nuclear weapons first, the Soviet Union would be compelled by its need to preserve its international image to do the same, and immediate relaxation in tension would ensue. An element of risk, however, does remain.

May I say in conclusion that I am not a pacifist; I think that in the past there have been some (very few) just and necessary wars. But the existence of nuclear weapons poses a radically new situation, and this demands a radically new way of looking at the problem of resisting what we do not like.

THE NYLON WAR

By DAVID RIESMAN

Prologue

"THE NYLON WAR" was a serious attempt, couched as satire, to suggest ways of channeling American energies "short of war"; in one aspect it can be considered a foray in Keynesian economics in reverse. I conceived the idea originally as something of a heuristic device to sharpen discussion among a group of social scientists meeting in 1947 to discuss "the world community." Two points of view had been vocal at the meeting. There were the self-proclaimed "realists," some of them geopolitically oriented, who thought in terms of the bipolar "big powers" and exchanged strategic details about Iranian oil or Skoda's output or de Gasperi's majority. Opposed to them was a smaller group who occasionally also sought the prestige of "realism" but did so in terms of psychology and culture rather than of steel plants or armored divisions. This latter group's theme song was, "The Russians have a culture, too, and on this basis we can and must understand them." Although less patently nationalistic, this second group was no less devoted to the cause of the Western powers in the cold war, but it did conceive of cross-cultural communication as a realistic possibility, once American ethnocentrism could be overcome. Some of them, to my mind, appeared to scant the fact that "the" Russians were not in charge, but had been conquered by a dictatorship, whereas some of the geopolitically minded were preparing to fight World War I over again with better military weapons—they assumed an enemy as rationalistic as they thought they themselves were; they missed the wild irrationality of a "people's imperialism" and underestimated the rational appeal of ideals to the West.

I recur to these events because the attitudes expressed at this conference are still so dominant, and especially the mood and method of realism. One limitation of this mood is that it robs academic life of one of its principal pleasures and functions, that of serving as a counterpoise to the life of statesmen and executives. My fellow conferees tended to gravitate toward immediate policy questions—and to bind themselves to the alternatives the State Department might be willing or able to accept at the moment. Since we were a bunch of professors, and not the State Department, since we lacked its channels of information and misinformation, but also had less of an emergency mandate, I felt we should liberate ourselves from the conventions of thought which pass as realism. The notion of the Nylon War was intended to confront us with the very excess of realism in American domestic policy, as well as with the fact the anthropologists sometimes understressed, namely that we Americans also have a culture, and one not capable of perennial patience or inaction. As the reader will see, my satire sought to highlight some of the more amiable qualities of the United States—industrial energy and romanticism, activism, ingenuity—as well as some of the salient qualities of the Stalin regime, such as the use of the United States as a model, great but disguised inefficiency, and in their case even more than in our own, "projective" interpretations of the enemy. Perhaps, also, the essay can be read as a backhanded defense of "materialism" as against more honorific and to my way of thinking inhuman attitudes; it is striking that no country has ever been called materialistic for its war matériel, but only for its consumer goods.

The Nylon War

Today—August 1, 1951—the Nylon War enters upon the third month since the United States began all-out bombing of the Soviet Union with consumer's goods, and it seems time to take a retrospective look. Behind the initial raid of June 1 were years of secret and complex preparations, and an idea of disarming simplicity: that if allowed to sample the riches of America, the Russian people would not long tolerate masters who gave them tanks and spies instead of vacuum cleaners and beauty parlors. The Russian rulers would thereupon be forced to turn out consumers' goods, or face mass discontent on an increasing scale.

The Nylon War was conceived by an army colonel—we shall call him "Y"— whose name cannot yet be revealed. Working with secret funds which the Central Intelligence Agency had found itself unable to spend, Y organized shortly after World War II the so-called "Bar Harbor Project," the nucleus of what, some five years later, became

"Operation Abundance," or, as the press soon dubbed it, the "Nylon War." After experiments with rockets and balloons, it was concluded that only cargo planes—navigating, it was hoped, above the range of Russian radar—could successfully deliver the many billion dollars' worth of consumer goods it was planned to send. Nevertheless, when Y and his group first broached their plans to a few selected Congressional leaders in the winter of 1948 they were dismissed as hopelessly academic. America had neither the goods nor the planes nor the politics to begin such an undertaking. But in the fall of 1950, with the country bogged down in a seemingly endless small-scale war in Korea, Y's hopes revived. For one thing, the cargo planes needed for the job were beginning to become available. Moreover, a certain amount of overordering by the armed services, panicky over Korea, had created a stockpile of consumer goods. More important, the administration, having locked up all known and many suspected Communists in one of the old camps for Japanese aliens, had still not convinced the country that it was sufficiently anti-Soviet, though at the same time many Americans wanted peace but did not dare admit it. A plan which, in fact and in presentation, took attention away from alleged Far-Eastern bungling, and which was both violently anti-Soviet and pro-peace, appeared to offer the possibility of restoring the administration's tottering position in the country.

This is not the place to recount the political maneuverings that preceded Truman's success in securing a two-billion-dollar initial appropriation from Congress, nor the Potomac maneuverings that led to the recruitment of top-flight production and merchandising talent from civilian life. Our story begins with Truman going before Congress to secure authority to "bring the benefits of American technology to less fortunate nations" by round-the-clock bombing, the day after the news of the first raids hit the American public.

The planners of the Bar Harbor Project had staked American prestige, their professional futures, and the lives of six thousand airmen on the belief that the Soviets would not know of these first flights nor meet them with armed resistance. When the opening missions were accomplished without incident, permitting Truman to make his appeal, Washington was immensely relieved; but when the second wave of planes met with no resistance either, Washington was baffled. It was at first assumed that the Soviet radar network had again simply failed to spot the high-flying planes—cruising at 48,000 feet and self-protected from radar by some still presumably secret device. We now know that what actually happened was a division of opinion in the Kremlin—we can piece the story together from intelligence reports and from clues in *Pravda*. A faction, led by foreign trade chief

Mikoyan, maintained that the scheme was a huge hoax, designed to stampede Russia into a crusade against a fairy tale—and so to make her the laughing stock of the world. He counseled, wait and see. And, indeed, it *was* a fairy tale for secret-police boss Beria, who argued that the raids had never taken place, but that reports of them had been faked by some Social Democratic East Germans who had somehow gotten access to the communications networks. When this idea was exploded, Beria counseled shooting the planes down, on the ground that they were simply a screen spying out plants for an atomic attack. Stalin himself believed with repentant economist Varga that American capitalism had reached so critical a point that only through forcible gifts overseas could the Wall Street ruling clique hope to maintain its profits and dominance. Coupled with these divisions of opinion, which stalemated action, was the fear in some quarters that America might welcome attacks on its errand-of-mercy planes as a pretext for the war of extermination openly preached by some only mildly rebuked American leaders.

At any rate, the confusion in the Politburo was more than mirrored by the confusion in the target cities caused by the baptismal raids. Over 600 C-54's streamed high over Rostov, and another 200 over Vladivostok, dropped their cargoes, and headed back to their bases in the Middle East and Japan. By today's standard these initial forays were small-scale—200,000 pairs of nylon hose, 4,000,000 packs of cigarettes, 35,000 Toni-wave kits, 20,000 yo-yos, 10,000 wrist watches, and a number of odds and ends from P-X overstock. Yet this was more than enough to provoke frenzied rioting as the inhabitants scrambled for a share. Within a few hours after the first parcels had fallen, the roads into the target cities were jammed. Roadblocks had to be thrown up around the cities, and communications with the outside were severed. The fast-spreading rumors of largesse from above were branded "criminally insane," and their source traced to machinations of the recently purged "homeless cosmopolitan Simeon Osnavitch (Rosenblum)."

But the propaganda of the deed proved stronger than the propaganda of the word. As Odessa, Yakutsk, Smolensk, and other cities became targets of aggressive generosity, as Soviet housewives saw with their own eyes American stoves, refrigerators, clothing, and toys, the Kremlin was forced to change its line and, ignoring earlier denials, to give the raids full but negative publicity. David Zaslavsky's article in the June 10 *Izvestia* heralded the new approach. Entitled "The Mad Dogs of Imperialism Foam at the Mouth," he saw the airlift as harbinger of America's economic collapse. "Unable because of the valiant resistance of the peace-loving democracies to conquer foreign markets, America's Fascist plutocracy is now reduced to giving away goods. . . ." Taking another line, *Red Star* argued that to accept American consumer goods would make stalwart Russians as decadent as rich New Yorkers.

However, the Russian people who could get access, either directly or through the black market that soon arose, to American goods seemed not to fear decadence. Again, there was a change of line. Falling back on a trick learned during Lend-Lease, it was claimed that the goods were Russian-made, and *Pravda* on June 14 stated that the Toni-wave kit had been invented by Pavlov before World War I. However, Colonel Y's staff had anticipated this altogether routine reaction. On June 17, the target cities of that day—Kiev, Stalingrad, Magnitogorsk—received their wares wrapped in large cartoons of Stalin bending over, in a somewhat undignified pose, to pick up a dropped Ansco camera. This forced still another switch of line. On June 20, Beria went on the air to announce that the Americans were sending over goods poisoned by atomic radiation, and all papers and broadcasts carried scare stories about people who had died from using Revlon or Schick shavers. And indeed booby traps (planted by the MVD) succeeded in killing a number of overeager citizens. For a while, this permitted specially recruited Party members to gather up the goods and take them to headquarters for alleged deradiation.

But here something unexpected occurred. We know from a few people who managed to escape to the West that a number of Party elements themselves became disaffected. Asked to turn in all American goods, they held on to some possessions secretly—there was a brisk underground trade in fake Russian labels. Sometimes wives, having gotten used to the comforts of Tampax and other disappearing items, would hide them from their more ascetic husbands; children of Party members cached pogo sticks and even tricycles. Thus it came about that when Party members were ordered to join "decontamination" squads the depots were re-entered at night and portable items taken. By the beginning of July, all attempts to deceive the people had only made matters worse; things were getting out of hand.

Faring badly in the "War," the Kremlin turned to diplomacy. On July 5 at Lake Success, Malik described the airlift as "an outrage remindful of Hitlerite aggression" and, invoking Article 39 of the U.N. Charter, he called on the Security Council to halt the "shameful depredations of the American warmongers." Austin replied that "these gifts are no more or less than a new-fashioned application of ancient principles," and the Russian resolution was defeated, 9–2. The next step occurred in Washington, when Ambassador Panyushkin handed Secretary Acheson a sharply worded note warning that "should these present outrages continue, the USSR will have no recourse but to reply in kind."

Seattle was the first American city to learn the meaning of the Soviet warning as on July 15 a hundred Russian heavy bombers (presumably from bases in the Kuriles) left behind them 15,000 tins of caviar, 500 fur coats, and 80,000 copies of Stalin's speeches on the minorities question. When the Russian planes came, followed in by American jets, many were apprehensive, but as the counterattack had been anticipated it proved possible to prevent incidents in the air and panic on the ground. Since then, Butte, Minneapolis, Buffalo, and Moscow, Idaho, have been added to the list of America's front-line cities. But in quantity and quality the counteroffensive has been unimpressive. Searing vodka, badly styled mink coats (the only really selling item), undependable cigarette lighters—these betray a sad lack of know-how in production and merchandising. In an editorial, "Worse than Lend-Lease," the N.Y. *Daily News* has charged that the Nylon War gives the Soviets free lessons in the secrets of America's success, but truly conservative papers like the *Herald-Tribune* see the comparative showing of Americans and Russians as a world demonstration of the superiority of free enterprise.

It is clear, at any rate, that free enterprise has not suffered much of a jolt—nor, indeed, has the mounting inflation been much reduced—by the Russian campaign. To be sure, the massive air-borne shipments of caviar have made luxury grocers fear inventory losses and Portugal, heavily dependent on the American anchovy market, has been worried. But these pin-pricks are nothing to what is now becoming evident on the Russian side—namely the imminent collapse of the economy. For the homeland of centralized economic planning is experiencing its own form of want in the midst of plenty. Soviet consumers, given a free choice between shoddy domestic merchandise and airlift items, want nothing to do with the former and in a score of fields Russians goods go unwanted as the potential buyer dreams of soon owning an American version. Soviet housewives, eager to keep up with American-supplied "Joneses," pester their local stores, often to the point of creating local shortages—indeed, the American refrigerators have created demands, not only for electricity, but also for many foods which can now be stored (and hoarded).

Much of this disruption is the result of careful planning by the Bar Harbor Project's Division of Economic Dislocation. The Division, for example, early began studies of Russian power distribution, and saw to the landing of 60-cycle radios, shavers, toasters, milking machines, in 60-cycle areas; 25-cycle appliances in 25-cycle areas, and so on, especially with an eye to areas of power-shortage or competition with critical industries. In cooperation with G.E., methods were worked out by which the Russian donees could plug their appliances, with appropriate transformers, directly into high-voltage or street power lines; thus simply shutting off house current could not save the Russian utilities from overload. Similarly, drawing on the American monopolistic practice of tie-in sales, goods were dropped whose use demanded other items in short supply—oil ranges, for instance, were dropped throughout the Baku fields. Of course, mistakes were made and in one or two cases bottlenecks in the Russian economy were relieved, as when some containers were salvaged to repair a tin shortage of which the planners had not been advised.

But it is not only on the production end that the raids have been disruptive. Last Friday's raid on Moscow—when 22,000 tons of goods were dropped—may be taken as an illustration. For the first time General Vandenburg's airmen tackled—and successfully solved—the knotty engineering problem of dropping jeeps (complete with 150 gallons of gasoline and directions in simple Russian). So skillfully was the job done that half the three hundred vehicles parachuted down landed directly on the Kremlin's doorstep—in the center of Red Square. The raid was given wide advance publicity through the Voice and leaflets and when the great day came Moscow's factories were deserted as people fought for roof-top perches; in addition, an estimated 250,000 collective farmers swarmed into the city. In fact, as people drift from place to place hoping that their ship may fly in, the phrase "rootless cosmopolite" at last assumes real meaning. Economists, talking learnedly of "multipliers," calculate that Russian output is dropping 3 percent a month.

The Kremlin has reacted in the only way it knows, by a series of purges. Serge Churnik, erstwhile head of the cigarette trust, is on trial for "deliberate wrecking and economic treason." Bureaucrats live in terror lest their region or their industry be next disrupted by the American bombardment, and they waver between inactivity and frantic Stakhanovite shows of activity. These human tragedies testify to the growing fear in the Politburo concerning the long-run consequences of the American offensive. The tangible proofs of American prosperity, ingenuity, and generosity can no longer be gainsaid; and the new official line that Wall Street is bleeding America white in order to create scarcity and raise prices at home, while "believed," has little impact against the ever-mounting volume, and fascinating variety, of goods and rumors of goods. Can the capitalistic gluttons of privilege be such bad fellows if we, the Russians, are aided by them to enjoy luxuries previously reserved for the dachas of novelists and plant managers? In an article in the *New Statesman and Nation,*

Geoffrey Gorer has recently contended that the airlift serves to revive primitive Russian "orality," and that the image of America can no longer be that of a leering Uncle Sam or top-hatted banker but must soon become amiably matronly. It is thoughts along this line that most worry the Politburo although, of course, the MVD sees to it that only a tiny fraction of the mounting skepticism expresses itself openly or even in whispered jokes. But what is the MVD to do about a resolution of the All-Workers Congress of Tiflis that "Marxist-Leninist-Stalinist democracy demands that party cadres install officials who can cope with the mounting crisis"?

Translated into plain talk, this means that the Russian people, without saying so in as many words, are now putting a price on their collaboration with the regime. The price—"goods instead of guns." For Russia's industrial plant, harassed by the rapidly growing impact of Operation Abundance, cannot supply both, let alone carry on the counteroffensive against America. Intelligence reports speak of scheduled production cutbacks varying from 25 percent on tanks to 75 percent on artillery; it is symptomatic that washing machines, designed to compete with the American Bendixes which are being dropped in ever-increasing numbers, will soon start rolling off the assembly lines of the great Red October Tank Works—after its former manager had been shot for asserting that conversion to peacetime production could not be achieved in less than two years.

Meanwhile, diplomatic moves are under way—so, at least, the Alsop brothers report—to liquidate the Nylon War. It is obvious why the Russian leaders are prepared to make very considerable concessions in the satellite countries, in China, and in Indo-China in order to regain the strategic initiative in their domestic affairs. But on the American side the willingness of many to listen to Russian overtures is based on the success, rather than the failure, of the campaign. One sees a repetition of 1940 as the Washington *Times-Herald* and the *Daily Compass* join hands in attacking Operation Abundance, the former calling it "an international WPA," the latter arguing "you can't fight ideas with goods." Addressing the Stanford Alumni Club of Los Angeles, Herbert Hoover spoke for millions in observing that the monthly cost of the airlift has already exceeded the entire Federal budget for the year 1839. Still another tack has been taken by Senators who want the airlift to continue, but with different targets; some, insisting that charity begins at home, have wanted free goods landed on their districts; others have supported the claims of Japan, the Philippines, or Franco. Still others fear that many of the air-lift items could be reconverted in some way for use by the Russian war machine; they are especially opposed to the jeep delivery program, despite reports it is wreaking havoc with the Russian road system as well as with the gasoline supply. And the House Un-American Affairs Committee has charged that trade secrets are being delivered to Russian spies by Red homosexual officials and professors disguised as plane pilots.

These are the obvious enemies, and against them stand some obvious friends of the Nylon War. Both AFL and CIO, now in their eighth round of wage increases, vigorously support the program, though it is rumored that the Railroad Brotherhoods have done so only in return for a fact-finding board's support of a fourteen-hour week. Farmers have become reconciled by the promise that bulk agricultural products will soon move over the aerial transmission belt—in part to encourage the wanderings of Russian farmers. The business community is divided, with the CED, Juan Trippe, and Baruch leading the supporters of the airlift.[1] But it would be a mistake to assume that support of Operation Abundance springs only from hopes of material gain. The renewed fight against oppression and want, the excitement of following the raids in maps and betting pools, the ridiculousness of the Russian response—all these things have made many millions of Americans less anxious than they have been since the days in October 1950 when it seemed as if the Korean War would be quickly concluded.

Indeed, it is just this loss of tension which has given rise to much of the covert opposition to the Nylon War, as distinguished from the overt opposition already discussed. On the one hand, certain leaders are frightened that the Russian dictatorship may indeed be overthrown—as Colonel Y in his more optimistic moments had ventured to hope. This is thought to raise the possibility of all sorts of chaotic movements developing in Central and Eastern Europe, and even further west—Franco, for instance, feels threatened at the loss of his "enemy," and has offered to act as mediator in the Nylon War. On the other hand, it has become increasingly difficult for American politicians to frighten the American public about Russia: the once-feared monolith now appears as almost a joke, with its crude poster-and-caviar reprisals, its riots over stockings, soap, Ronsons, and other gadgets which Americans regard in matter-of-fact fashion. The sharp drop in war sentiment in the United States has resulted in psychological and even actual unemployment for a number of people.

What do the coming months hold? It is significant that this depends almost entirely on the outcome of the American domestic struggle: the Nylon War has altered the whole power-complex which, as the Korean War dragged on, still heavily favored Russia. It is now Russia, not America, whose resources are overcommitted, whose alliances are overstrained. In fact, Mao's visit to Moscow at the end of July seems to have been attended with apprehension lest he ask America to cut Red China in on Operation Abundance—at a price, of course. The possibility that this may redound to the credit of the Truman Administration in the 1952 campaign is not the least of the nightmares haunting many Americans, and at this writing it is impossible to predict whether the opponents of the program will win out.

Meanwhile, Operation Abundance marches on, solving technical problems of incredible complexity. The latest move is the perfection of an ordering system whereby Russians can "vote" for the commodities they most want, according to a point system, by the use of radio-sending equipment, battery-run, with which we have provided them. The commodities available will be described over the Voice of America—now for the first time having something to "sell"—by Sears Roebuck-type catalogues, and by dropped samples in the case of soft goods. The method making it impossible for the Russian government effectively to jam this two-way communication of distributor and consumer is still the great secret of the Nylon War.

Epilogue

The merely extrapolative and unfictional character of much science fiction (though the genre as a whole has become the repository of a good deal of genuinely satiric or utopian thought) is one of many indications of the disorientation from which many people suffer, the terrible bewilderment about what is going on in the modern world. When *The Nylon War* was first published, I began to get letters and telephone calls asking me if the "war" (whose fictitious date had then been passed) had actually gotten under way! People have asked for references to *The New York Times* or periodical literature where they could catch up on these events. I was reminded of the "Invasion from Mars" broadcast analyzed in the book of that name by Hadley Cantril and of the still unresolved disquiet about flying saucers. That my tale could be taken for literal fact was a sign of the remoteness of the inquirers from the current of what was probably so. The mass media that, like the typical newsreel, parade events without historical or other context, give them a discreteness and lack of structure that make it easier to picture the enemy of the moment as devoid of human qualities. Indeed, I have had a letter from a man in Sydney, New South Wales, asking me for further references on the Nylon War on the assumption that it has occurred and also asking whether *Common Cause* (where the article first appeared) is not (as charged by a local representative of the United States Information Service), a "Commie magazine" in which case presumably the article itself, if not the "war," would be "Commie propaganda." So humorless and fearful an American representative abroad is, I would hope, not characteristic. But it seems clear that satire is too playful and perhaps too snobbish a mode, save in cartoon form, to combat the combination of fright and self-righteousness of many Americans, who would accept the *fait accompli* of a Nylon War if the authorities ordered it, but who could not otherwise possibly grasp a world they never made.

Both in England and in the United States several movie makers have been interested in making a film of "The Nylon War." A few years ago one British effort got bogged down, apparently because they had shifted the locale to Yugoslavia and this ran afoul both of recent events and of British foreign policy. More recently an American producer bought the rights to the idea—but then discovered to his dismay that the Russians were no longer so short of consumer goods but were themselves sending out technical-aid missions to far poorer countries.

Since "The Nylon War" was written, my interest—nay, preoccupation—with the interrelation of disarmament, foreign policy, and domestic policy has become still more intense. I have attended many conferences, and have read and written many memoranda on these matters. But I still haven't encountered many fruitful discussions which simultaneously analyze both American and Soviet (and now also Chinese) social character and social structure as these affect the possibilities of a *modus vivendi*. People who understand the Soviet Union tend to believe that in a disarmed world Communism would indeed win out, as the Communists themselves profess to believe. Not only does this give the Communists too much credit and America and other Western countries too little, but it assumes that "tomorrow is already here" not only in the quite evident fact that one country can destroy the world unilaterally, but also in the not yet evident idea that one country can rule the world from one place unilaterally (George Kennan, a sober student at once of American and Soviet bureaucracy, doesn't think this can be done). In this state of barely avowed defeatism, the covert American fear that the cold war will come to an end has, if anything, increased since the period in 1948–1949 when I was working on "The Nylon War." At the same time, it is far more widely recognized now than it was before Stalin's death that in many ways the Soviet Union has become, like the United States, a *status quo* power, with a strong residual dynamism whose strengths and weaknesses are hidden by ideological cant and dogma. The importance of Marxist-Leninist ideology in the minds of Soviet leaders is less, it would seem, in turning them into driving fanatics out to conquer the world than in distorting their perceptions of day-to-day events and their image of the future.[2]

Whatever its crudities as morality and satire, there is still one viable lesson in "The Nylon War," namely one concerning the possibilities of unilateralism. In trying to mitigate the cold war, we need not always either negotiate explicitly nor respond at those points of obvious tension where both adversaries are locked in domestically irresolvable conflict. We can break out of the stalemate by seeking fresh ground, whether by withdrawing from West German rearmament and bases, or by some of the steps that Charles Osgood has suggested in a companion paper to this one (see pp. 161–177).

The release of energies in areas other than the arms race could serve to give Americans a sense of vitality and flexibility of our society, and thus make it less difficult to negotiate an agreement with the Soviet Union which, for domestic reasons, we would have to dress up as not weakening our posture—that word that expresses the *rigor mortis* of the mindlessly energetic—in any way. Let us suppose that the United States and the Soviet Union were competitively—or, even more improbably, jointly—engaged in intensive efforts to assist at once Chinese and Indian industrialization—would we not then feel less passive, less worried, and as a total society, less disarmed? And would we not then be better able to give up the false and delusive security of our deterrents without falling back either on the Maginot Line of the budget or on the Maginot Line of military sufficiency?

Clearly enough, the Chinese now are obdurate, and overtures that might once have moderated their fanaticism will no longer suffice. My point here, however, does not depend on the political feasibility, either domestically or internationally, of one or another particular proposal, but rather I aim to emphasize more generally that steps toward disarmament need not be taken in the field of disarmament itself. If I am right that articulate Americans suffer from a sense of doom about our own society which leads in turn to frozen thinking about alternatives, then it follows that a wise administration would not go before a suspicious Congress with only a test ban in hand, but would at the same time present other measures which would make our country stronger internationally, and still others that would make clear to Soviet leaders that we were really intending by the test ban to reduce tension, and not simply to save money or to hold our lead in weaponry—we would simultaneously announce, for instance, that we were halting all cooperation by American firms in the rearmament of Western Germany, and make clear our disapproval of such rearmament by whatever measures of economic and political pressure we can bring to bear; in that case, the violent protests of Adenauer, Strauss, and other German leaders would help convince the Soviet Union, the Germans, the Poles, and our own citizens that we really meant business. This is the kind of creative many-sided policy that I associate on the one hand with unilateralism, for the policy could be pursued even in the face of a frozen foe, in the hope of unfreezing him, and on the other hand with the possibility of negotiating particular steps that might then give rise to other steps.

While there are millions of doggedly defeatist Americans who hang on desperately to what they have got, though this is a sure way to lose both it and themselves, there are, I hope, others whose imagination and generosity and historical understanding can in cooperation with like-minded men everywhere discover not only moral equivalents for war but also economic equivalents for the arms race and political equivalents for the use and threat of force in the drive to implement one's ideals and protect one's other interests at home and abroad.

NOTES

1. It goes without saying that there are many fights within pressure groups as to *what* the airlift shall carry—and ideological considerations are not confined to the Soviet side. Thus, the Committee Against Juvenile Delinquency has registered strong protests against sending comic books. More serious issues revolve around the Planned Parenthood League's campaign to get contraceptives included in the airlift items. In addition to humanitarian arguments, the claim is made that this will reverse the demographic trend now so favorable to Russia; the League's slogan is "Give them the tools and they will do the job." Walter Lippmann predicts a Rome-Moscow axis if the League should win out.
2. I do not say this dogmatically, for Soviet policy is unstable as indeed is America's, and of course not entirely unaffected by our own actions and those of other powers and would-be powers. The matters discussed here, and others of the same order of difficulty, are among the preoccupations of a small informal group, the Council for Correspondence (P.O. Box 536, Cooper Station, New York 3, New York), devoted to discussion and research and the publication of a Newsletter on just such topics.

INTERNATIONAL PRESTIGE AND PEACEFUL COMPETITION

By AMITAI ETZIONI

UNILATERAL INITIATIVE can improve international relations in areas other than nuclear test bans, the cessation of bomb production, or general disarmament. One such area—the subject of this article—concerns the effects of international competition for prestige on peaceful coexistence.

The significance of unilateral action is that it does not require the international cooperation presupposed by many other proposals aimed at improving these international relations. Multilateral action is blocked by a vicious circle: inter-bloc cooperation is not forthcoming unless tension is somewhat reduced; tension cannot be reduced till a higher degree of cooperation is attained. Hence the special significance of unilateral initiative: in addition to whatever improvement it produces in itself, it also opens the way for multilateral action.

Objection to most unilateral programs is based on the belief that they engender a sacrifice to the initiator which will not be matched by the other side. The nature of the unilateral action to be suggested here is such that if it is carried out adequately it will not only give the party which initiates it an advantage but it will also improve the state of international affairs. The other party can reduce the advantage of the initiator only by joining the activity, and thus adding to the improvement of international relations.

This is not to imply that a magic key to the solution of international problems has been found. The present analysis focuses on one and only one factor: *the effect of international competition for prestige on the probability of war*. Many other factors affect this probability; some are more important or more immediate in their effect than the nature of the international prestige. I choose to focus on prestige, both because it seems to be a factor which can be tackled by unilateral action without risk, and because it is rarely examined in this context. The determinants of international prestige are considered first; then the character of the prestige contest itself is examined from the viewpoint of its effects on international tension; finally I discuss the ways in which this contest can be modified, both to reduce its present inflammatory nature and to enable it to enhance peaceful coexistence.

The Determinants of International Prestige

Citizens see in the state more than an agency to which they pay taxes and which supplies them with security, welfare, and other services; they identify with it and its fate. Most citizens derive symbolic gratifications and deprivations from changes in the international status of their nation. But it is easy to exaggerate grossly the emotional significance of prestige, of the relative standing a person, group, or nation has in the eyes of others. It is chiefly under two conditions that national prestige does become a major factor: when loss of prestige adds to a severe crisis brought about by other things; and when national leaders fan the limited concern citizens normally feel for the standing of their nation abroad into a prestige-obsession.

Loss of prestige, like other frustrations, might generate a large variety of responses, from withdrawal to enhanced efforts. But it seems that when a *large* and *rapid* loss of prestige is added to economic insecurity (generated by a sharp depression or wild inflation) and to deprivations of emotional satisfaction resulting from loss of family and community ties (e.g., long bombardments; husbands in combat), intensive and widespread feelings of aggression are likely to be aroused. Thus, the humiliation of Germany in World War I is frequently cited as a contributory factor in the 1917 revolution and the foundation of the Weimar Republic; the prestige-deprivation inflicted by the Versailles treaty is commonly seen as a factor contributing to the emergence of Nazism, a movement obsessed with national status. The 1905 and 1917 defeats of Tsarist Russia, which augmented the alienation of the rigidly oppressed industrial classes, triggering the Soviet revolution. In periods of peace, stable economies, and integrated social relations, frustrations of national prestige rarely lead to aggressive behavior—except for student demonstrations before the embassies of the countries which inflict the prestige loss. Britain lost much of its empire, the United States its post-World War II position as the superior power, without any marked increase in internal or external aggression.

A decline in prestige which does not lead to aggressive behavior of the masses may nevertheless lead to popular demand for a more aggressive foreign policy. The attitudes of Americans toward Cuba and toward the Communist bloc in general are cases in point. But so long as no agitation occurs, the aggressive tone of the public tends to decline with time; other events attract its attention.

There is one way, though, in which even in stable societies international prestige can become a permanent salient factor in determining the public attitudes: if the leadership of a country itself consistently makes the national standing of the country a central political issue. While we agree with Schumpeter that the political elites—even in democracies—shape the public opinion more than public opinion shapes the politicians' course (a 1957 study by Samuel Lubell showed that American citizens viewed the missile race just the way President Eisenhower viewed it), still it should be pointed out that once public feeling has been aroused—let us say national prestige has been staked on two small forsaken islands—even skilled politicians find it difficult to change the country's stand.[1] The American attitude toward Communist China is probably the best recent illustration of this tendency.

It is hence crucial to realize that building up excessive public concern with the prestige of a country may be detrimental to the improvement of international relations. For once, the analogue to individual behavior seems justified. A certain amount of concern with the image one creates in the eyes of others is both unavoidable and desirable. It makes for responsiveness to the public opinion of other countries, and, in a sense, to world public opinion. But *excessive* concern with one's standing in the eyes of others heightens frustration generated by minute prestige fluctuations. This frustration might be expressed in various irrational responses including aggression. Countries which constantly brood over their prestige, which change the allocation of their labor force, public budget, and educational system in part to improve their "international status," are as irrational as individuals who keep rearranging their lives to suit the latest pattern advocated by the proverbial Joneses. In short, one has to distinguish between a normal responsiveness to others and a prestige-obsession.

Prestige Constants and Prestige Variables

The danger of excessive concern with prestige is rather obvious; what is less evident, to judge from the amount of investment in prestige-building activities, is the limited effect of many of these activities. The prestige of a person, a social group, or a nation is a product of (a) basic characteristics; (b) the values of the others who grant prestige; (c) short-run activities partly governed by prestige considerations; and (d) activities chiefly governed by such considerations. Only the latter two are subject to manipulation.

The prestige of a country rests first of all on its basic characteristics, including the nature of its political structure (democratic or authoritarian), its economy (rich or poor), its "culture" (how many great writers, poets, and painters has it given the world in the course of history?), the general level of its technology, its basic military potential, and the like. The essential quality of these assets is that they have accumulated over generations, or are a basic element of the structure of the society. They change slowly and gradually; they cannot be adjusted to affect the contemporary international prestige contest. It is these constants which limit the fluctuations of prestige. Whatever, for instance, the United States does, it still is a democratic, rich, highly industrialized, technologically advanced country. It is still the country of Washington, Jefferson, and Lincoln. Much of its international standing is based on that. People may add an ounce for a successful space program, deduct half an ounce for a U-2, but the basic stock is hardly affected. To truly affect the prestige of a country requires an accumulation of such short-run activities and incidents much longer and larger than is often realized.

Not less crucial are the values of the persons, groups, or nations which grant prestige. Prestige is a judgment about the relative standing of one party made by other parties. This judgment depends not only on what a country is, but also on the standards by which the country is evaluated. Thus, for example, the question is not only, does the United States have a more effective technology than Soviet Russia or the other way around, but, how much prestige does India grant technological achievements?

A country anxious to improve its prestige may wish to affect these values so that its existing assets will be more highly regarded. Hence countries whose per capita income is high stress the value of a high standard of living. Countries whose per capital income is low but rapidly increasing emphasize the value of economic growth. But the fact is that the values and beliefs of nations change slowly; and the degree to which another nation can affect these values, despite all the modern means of mass communication and persuasion, appears to be quite limited. We know from studies of advertising and other uses of mass communication that they are most effective when the information supplied fits into an existing cognitive and normative frame of reference; conversely, the greater the cultural differences, the less effective cross-cultural communication becomes. Hence cross-cultural propaganda and related efforts seem to have considerably less effect on the standing of a country than is often believed. Thus, in addition to limits imposed on prestige-variability by basic characteristics there are limits imposed by the basic values of the prestige-granting societies.

It is only within the limits established by the characteristics of the society which is evaluated and the values of those doing the evaluating that action can be undertaken to affect the international prestige of a country. This may be attained either by introducing prestige as *one* consideration in directing short-run, manipulable activities, or by allowing prestige considerations to be the chief determinant of a course of action. To illustrate the distinction on a personal level, when a person considers buying a car, one factor which might affect his decision is that owning a car has a prestige value; but many other factors, such as the availability of convenient and inexpensive transportation, are to be considered. Whether to buy a Ford or a Cadillac is, on the other hand, predominantly a question of prestige. Similarly, while building missiles and developing their guidance systems has a clear, "real" military value, the frequency with which they are fired into outer space (where they are difficult to observe) and the dates at which they are fired (on the eve of Khrushchev's visit to the United States; on the eve of Eisenhower's planned visit to Japan) are governed by prestige considerations. In particular, sending a man to the moon is chiefly a prestige-oriented activity. It is extremely expensive; it would cost at least thirty billion dollars (*New York Times,* February 5, 1961), but at the same time has little value in any area other than prestige. Dr. Vannevar Bush, a leading figure among natural scientists, termed this endeavor a "stunt" in his 1960 testimony before the House Committee on Science and Astronautics. Many other scientists have expressed a similar position. From the military and scientific viewpoint, a robot will do as well as, and from many viewpoints considerably better than, an astronaut. A robot's life is not endangered by radiation; he does not have to be retrieved; he does not become unconscious, nervous, or homesick. Dr. Harlow Shapley, director of the Harvard Observatory, is reported to have stated that a "man up there would be a hindrance." Similar statements have been made by Alvin M. Weinberg (director of the Oak Ridge National Laboratory for nuclear research) and a number of other outstanding and responsible scholars (quoted in an article by Stuart H. Loory in *The Reporter,* April 27, 1961). But from a public relations viewpoint, a man is more effective; his flight is more appealing to the imagination of the masses.

We have already pointed out the limited degree to which a nation's prestige can be affected by any short-run, deliberate activity. What has to be added is that the international political consequences of changes in prestige are even smaller. Columnists and politicians constantly allude to the effect a country's international prestige has on its international standings in matters other than prestige, let us say its power position. But actually the power and international strategy of any one country, like that of its allies or of "uncommitted" countries, is to a very large degree determined by its geopolitical position, its basic military might, its economic structure, its manpower, and by the positions of other countries. Thus the same factors which limit the fluctuation of prestige limit the effects of these fluctuations; therefore not only is prestige hard to change, its variability does not count for much.

In summary, the problem is not to abolish concern with international prestige. Some such concern makes for responsiveness to world public opinion; it is sometimes even credited with being one of the reasons nations avoid a preventive nuclear war.[2] The problem is to limit involvement in the prestige contest, to realize the limits in which changes in prestige can be induced, and to keep in mind the limited effect of prestige on international politics. Not only is obsession with prestige costly; it might lead to rigidity, to an unaccommodating international policy.

We turn now to examine the intrinsic characteristics of the international prestige contest, to see under what conditions it is likely to cause a prestige obsession and thus be one factor contributing to a worsening of international relations. The examination suggests action which would change the contest so that it can support rather than undermine peaceful coexistence.

The Prestige Contest and Peaceful Coexistence

Two factors are invariably listed as conditions for nonviolent competition: (a) shared values between the competing parties, especially values which forbid the use of violence (though other shared values are also significant because they tend to support the norms which directly limit the conflict); (b) the existence of a superior force, which neutrally imposes restricting norms on the contending parties. Thus, boxing matches are controlled not only by sports regulations and belief in fair play, but also by referees (and by the police); and competition among democratic parties is regulated not only by parliamentary procedures and belief in the constitution, but also by the police (and by military forces).

While these two conditions for peaceful competition are of the first importance, they are more helpful to planners of international utopias than to students of international relations and to those concerned with their improvement in the near future. There is hardly a better way to characterize East-West relations than to state that they lack precisely these two conditions: the sharing of ultimate values and the existence of a superior neutral force. Suggestions to improve international relations by creating these conditions, by forming a global community of shared values, to enact a universal law and a world government with an international army to enforce it, is to beg the question. The issue is how to get them, not to show that once you have them the likelihood of violent international conflict is greatly reduced.

And so long as we do not have world-wide shared beliefs and an effective international police force, the pertinent question is, what other factors reduce the probability of international conflict? What less stringent but more attainable conditions will have containing effects?

In particular, under what conditions does the "peaceful" prestige contest build up tensions which might help set off a war, and under what conditions does prestige-seeking have a harmless character?

A Gang Model

The following analysis, like many studies of conflict, draws on a model which serves both as an analogue—allowing the illustration of somewhat abstract ideas—and as a small-scale case in which generalizations can be readily examined and tested. Like many students of conflict I use games as the source of this model. But this sociological-psychological analysis differs from much game theory in that it assumes neither that the opponents act rationally nor that they observe the rules of the game, both conditions often lacking in international relations. Actually, what many studies assume is exactly what this analysis is intended to establish: under what conditions are conflicts contained within the limits set by the rules of the games, and under what conditions are the limits violated? In particular, what role does prestige play in turning contests into lawless violence?

I have chosen a sports festival in a slum area as a model suitable for the purposes of both illustration and testing. Assume that a sports festival is being conducted in the slum area of any metropolitan district, in which several teen-age gangs are competing. These gangs have in the past been involved in violent fights, they share few values, and the police, for one reason or another, are not available. The question is, what pattern of organization of the sports contest will make it least likely that the contest will "escalate" into a fight?

Single Event Vs. Multievent Contests

Probably the most elementary question is, is the competition limited to *one* type of sport, let us say football, or are there several kinds of competitions going on simultaneously? Drawing on our sociological and psychological knowledge, it seems that *providing a larger number of contests rather than focusing on one will be less predisposing to violence.* In such sports festivals each team's prestige in the gang world is at stake. Having only one sphere of competition channels all the involvement of each group's members into one race. All the spectators watch one game; losing the one race means losing all. On the other hand, having many concomitant matches makes for a distribution of ego-involvement; it reduces the emotional investment and prestige stake in each competition. The lower the emotional stake, the less the temptation to resort to violence when the game seems sure to be lost, or when one contender is close to victory and suddenly the other is improving his score and seems likely to win.

Ranking of Contests

The success of a multievent contest requires that *no one contest be considered crucial and all others marginal.* If the outcome of football is considered all important, and nobody—even on the losing team—cares who wins in any one of the various field and track races, the situation approaches that of a single-event contest. A feeling that the team's standing in several contests is significant is hence another factor contributing to the observation of the rules.

The nature of the international competition has changed from these two viewpoints over recent years. Since 1957 it has become more and more exclusively focused on space achievements. Other spheres have not disappeared; countries still compare their standards of living (or per capita income), their rate of economic growth, rate of literacy, aid given to developing countries, success in combating disease, number of Nobel prize winners, Olympic medals, and so on. But these areas have lost a good part of their prestige-bestowing power; space has taken the center of the stage.

Since gangs, to return to our analogue, usually differ from each other at least in terms of some skills and capacities, most teams will have some "relative advantages" in one game or another. Hence, a multievent competition—especially when there are many games and variability is high—is likely to lead to *some victories for each gang.* This makes the loss of other events much more tolerable. No longer is there one winner and one loser; there is a winner in games a, b, and c, and a winner in games d and e. Moreover, since findings of various psychological and sociological studies suggest that each party will tend to consider the games it wins the most important ones, the total amount of prestige-ambitions frustrated will be comparatively small. Such face-saving can hardly be attained when there is only one event, or when only one event is considered important.

Consensus on Ranking

A contest in which *one side sets the criteria for evaluation of the relative import of various events* is more likely to become violent than one in which there are no agreed criteria. Each side tends, of course, to favor a monolithic evaluation of the events based on those in which it has an advantage. To the degree that one team is successful in imposing its criteria on the spectators and on other teams, the value of multievent competition is greatly reduced. It follows that while communication among the teams about procedures and the rules of the game, including of course those concerning scoring, contribute to peaceful competition, too much communication and increasing consensus over the comparative *evaluation* of the scores is not conducive to nonviolent competition, in particular as long as one side succeeds in making the spheres in which it is most likely to excel the most valued ones.

In recent years there seems to have been a rapid increase in consensus over the evaluation of the outcome of international races. Earlier differences of evaluation have not completely disappeared; the West still emphasizes its higher standards of living, the East its greater economic growth, though the tendency has been to accept economic growth as more "relevant." The amount of support given to developing countries and the extent to which atomic power is converted to peaceful uses were stressed not long ago. But since the first Soviet satellite broadcast its dramatic beeps, projects such as that of ploughing Alaska or watering the Sahara have hardly been heard of. Outer space, a Russian specialty, has become the contest which commands the center of attention and an ever-increasing amount of resources. To a considerable degree the West has accepted the East's evaluations of the relative import of various races, evaluations which are closely associated with the relative advantages of the East.[3] This is not only to the disadvantage of the West, but reduces the chances that the competition over prestige will continue without major frustrations and in peace.

When the nature of the games and the pressures of the spectators are such that one game, let us say football, is considered far more important than the others, and all efforts for a more even distribution of attention and prestige-staking are unsuccessful, it is still possible to realize that there is *more than one criterion by which to judge the standing and outcome of this one race.* There is not only the score, but also the questions of who showed best teamwork, had the best individual player, and so forth. It is possible that a team which lost on score did well by any one of the other standards. While doing well on these secondary criteria is rarely if ever a substitute for victory by score, obviously the more highly these secondary criteria are valued, the more soothing the effect of doing well by them.

Of special import are cases in which the observance of the non-violent character of the game is in itself a criterion (e.g., which team had fewer fouls), because this makes the inhibition of violence a source of prestige in itself.

As these lines are written, the competition in space is undoubtedly the "football" of the international prestige contest. At least at present there are too many prestige stakes in this area for the two superpowers to give it up completely. But it should be noted that while the Russians have succeeded in shooting heavier objects deeper into space, the Americans have shot considerably more objects into orbit (at least eight times as many), have had a larger payload of instruments per satellite, and per pound, were the first to have reconnaissance satellites, and have been the first and only ones to shoot rockets from under water. The tendency to focus on distance and weight instead of number and payload has little objective foundation on either scientific or military grounds. It has consequences similar to those of focusing on one race and to letting one party determine the criteria for evaluating the competition.[4]

Scope of Victory

Even when the contest includes many events and when prestige stakes are not concentrated in a single contest, *an intensive quest for total victory, of victory in each and every race,* is similarly detrimental to non-violent competition. It makes the games almost as monolithic as if there were only one race, one score.

Pursuit of total victory seems to be not uncommon in the West. It explains in part the acceptance of each and every challenge of the East. When the Russians do better in any significant Olympic game, the West feels deeply embarrassed. When the Russians orbited a satellite in October 1957, the Americans orbited one in 1958. When the Russians shot a capsule to the vicinity of the moon, the Americans did, too. When the Russians shot two dogs into orbit, the Americans followed with a monkey. A few days after the space trip of Gagarin, came the space jump of Shepard. As in the popular song, "anything you can do, I can do better"; the Americans have tried to match the Russians in every single act and activity initiated by the Russians, from space weight lifting to lunar target shooting.

The roots of this tendency are worth exploring. After World War II there was one major power on the global scene, one international might never defeated, its country undamaged, its military power intact, the only possessor of atomic bombs. In the subsequent fifteen years a second power has gained first rank. This requires the acceptance of another bloc as a full-fledged contender, one who is likely to win some races. The effort for victory in every single match and in all of them, the striving for a total prestige advantage, reflects and expresses a rejection of the existence of other first-class powers and in a way that of peaceful coexistence. That the other side both has a right to exist and is "big" implies that in some activities it is going to excel. Acceptance of peaceful coexistence and the desire for total superiority are contradictory positions. A contestant who seeks total victory undermines the continuation of the games.

Means of Competition

The *means used* in the sports festival are crucial to our problem. "Instruments" used by the contenders differ in the degree to which they can be turned into means of violence. Obviously swimming, running, and jumping matches are safer than boxing, hockey, or target shooting.

Space constitutes a shooting gallery where the two contestants, using high-thrust missiles, play an old game: I hit the mark, your turn next. The game has one big virtue, that instead of using each other's cities as targets to demonstrate might, the contenders use stars or marks. But everybody who reads his Robin Hood knows that the contestants might easily turn their arrows on each other, in particular when one continuously hits the target and the other consistently misses, or thinks he does. It has been suggested that the space race constitutes the "moral equivalent of war," that it supplies a peaceful way for the two sides to demonstrate their relative power. It is hence essential to realize what frame of reference is applied when one evaluates the space race. Since peace is preferred to war and space exploration is a peaceful activity, it is obviously preferable to international violence; but so are many other peaceful activities.[5] The problem is to compare various nonviolent lines of action with regard to the likelihood that they will lead to war. From this viewpoint a contest which is conducted with missiles is less "safe" than one conducted by most other means. Competition over the sums granted to underdeveloped countries, the number of bona fide teachers or technicians or doctors supplied, the schools or roads or dams built, are all considerably more conducive to peace than is space exploration. Most activities have some indirect military significance. Schools improve the army of an ally; dams increase his economic potential. But activities differ in the degree to which means used or produced can be directly turned into weapons. In contrast to missiles, schools and dams, I dare say, are quite safe.

Number of Contenders

The number of gangs which participate in a sports festival is also relevant to the probability that the peaceful character of the competition will be maintained. If participation is limited to two gangs, tension will be highest; it is in a way like having only one event. Participation of many gangs reduces the psychological investment in any single event, even if there are only two major contenders for first place.

When the nature of the contest requires that only two gangs compete at one time, as in basketball, the presence of other gangs as spectators contributes to the observation of the nonviolent character of the contest so long as the spectators grant or withdraw prestige on this ground. In a contest in which many teams play concomitantly, let us say a relay match, the larger number allows a mitigation of prestige problems. There is only one "absolute" winner and one "absolute" loser; all the others are in between. Victory or loss becomes a question of degree, not a dichotomous state.

This is not to imply that the largest possible number of gangs is the best one. When the number is very large, let us say a hundred teams, it becomes rather hard to observe the behavior of the various parties, to assure conformity to the rules, and even more important, it becomes rather difficult to reach an agreement on anything, from allocation of the fields to scoring procedures, from the timing of inspection of the contenders to the timing of intervals. Obviously, the ideal contest avoids both extremes.

In the international competition the number of the teams is in part dependent on the two superpowers' tolerance of all kinds of neutrals: neutrals close to one side, neutrals close to the other side, and neutral-neutrals. In general, neutral countries put a premium on moderate behavior of the two leading contenders. A contender who takes extreme positions is likely to lose the support of neutral-neutrals, endanger the commitment of "his" neutrals, and build up the commitment of the other side's neutrals to its bloc. The neutral countries have the same function that the floating vote has in intranational political systems. If there is no floating vote, the smaller party feels it has no chance of ever gaining power in a legitimate way. On the other hand, if there is a bonus for moderation in terms of gains from the floating vote, there is greater incentive to limit the competition to legitimate means.

Neutrals shift their support in the United Nations and other international organizations according to the merit of the positions each bloc presents. Alger points out that countries' votes in the seven U.N. committees split differentially according to the committee and the issue:

> In the political committee the United States and the Soviet Union are the main protagonists, with their political allies aligning on the appropriate side and primarily some Afro-Asian nations playing a mediating role. . . . But in the economic committee it is the haves against the havenots, with the Latin Americans joining the Afro-Asians in a drive for an increase in multi-lateral economic programs. . . . On the trusteeship and non-self-governing territories committee the colonial nations and the newly independent countries are the main protagonists. On matters before the legal committee related to ocean shipping, the maritime nations are lined up against non-maritime members. Finally, on the budgetary committee the lines of conflict are sometimes drawn with virtually all member nations on one side and the Secretariat on the other.[6]

The flexibility of the neutral vote thus compels, at least occasionally, the major blocs to take relevant and flexible rather than ideological and totalistic positions and makes mutual concessions and compromises more likely.

That neutrals' flexibility has beneficial effects does not mean, however, that blocs and alliances have only negative effects, that a system of a hundred isolated nations would be the most peaceful one. The same points which hold for consensus-formation on the national level may apply on the international level, even if we are concerned only with working consensus and not with consensus over ultimate values. As long as each major interest group is represented on the top level of decision-making, a state approached by the French Fourth Republic, the ability to reach a compromise and an agreed-upon course of action is severely limited. Too many different positions have to be reconciled at once. Effective political systems have two, frequently more, consensus-formation levels. First, various interest groups work out a compromise policy on the party level; then the parties arrive at their compromise on the national level.[7] International alliances, especially supranational communities, work as such first-order consensus-formation bodies of a small group of nations.[8] Then, in the U.N. or G.A.T.T. or O.C.E.D. or other intergovernmental bodies, bloc (and sometimes global) consensus is worked out.

Time Perspective

Every captain concerned with sustaining a peaceful competition will emphasize to his team that whatever the outcome of the present round of games, *there is always another year, another round, another occasion to excel,* as long as the institutions of peaceful competition are not undermined. Political parties are much more likely to become violent when they feel that if a certain election is lost, their cause is lost forever (as when the vote concerns the independence or position of a country like Algeria or the Cameroons, or constitutional matters which have or seem to have only one "round"), than when a defeat in a particular election can be turned into a victory in the next. Similarly, full recognition that international contests continue in the space, economic, cultural, and many other spheres every day, keeping the following rounds in mind, can reduce the psychological investment in the outcome of each round. It may often seem that the success of the one side in a particular round threatens the very existence of the other side. History shows that this is rarely the case. For most nations there is always another day.

Unilateral Action in the Prestige Contest

The conclusion suggested by the two preceding parts of this discussion is that it is in the interest of both the United States and the USSR and of continued peaceful coexistence to reduce the emotional investments in international prestige contests, both by realizing the limited significance of success in this area and the large costs and dangers involved in obsessive efforts to maximize international prestige, and by remaking the nature of the international competition.

The question arises, can one party change the nature of the international prestige contest, or is the cooperation of both sides required? Can the captain of a team change the nature of the contest? The answer is a resounding yes, though the various steps actually to be taken depend to a large degree on the responses of the other captains to each step taken. In the following paragraphs we focus on the Western team as the initiator of such a change. This focus is chosen both because most of the readers of this volume are likely to be members of Western nations, and because it seems that the West has suffered in recent years from overinvolvement in the prestige contest and can gain considerably from some disengagement. The following simple example illustrates how such a modification of the international status-seeking can be obtained. There are probably many other, possibly more effective ways to apply the principles suggested above, to make the international contest less predisposed to prestige obsession and hence to rigidity, frustration, and possibly violence. The major concern here is to illustrate ways in which the contest can be remodeled, not to develop detailed programs.

A change in administration, a new inauguration of a re-elected president, or a change of a secretary of state supplies a legitimation for a change of policy and hence reduces the usual accusations about "succumbing to pressure" or "weakness" which follow changes of policy in the present rigid state of the contest. Assume that a new policy-maker were to issue a declaration to the effect that the United States and its allies were pulling out of the "man to the moon" race. No more government funds would be spent on it. Other activities in outer space would also be sharply curtailed. Sums earlier allocated to such programs would be diverted to increase aid to underdeveloped countries.

The declaration would place heavy emphasis on the difference between outer and inner space. It is widely agreed that outer space has little if any military or economic value.[9] The great gains to be realized by various space activities, such as weather forecast and control, surveillance, and communication, are all best served not by moonshots or trips to Venus but by activities in inner space, where distances are measured in hundreds of miles rather than in light-years. Now the prestige element of outer space activities is high, their "real" value low; hence these activities rather than the less prestigeful but more valuable inner-space explorations would be the natural candidate for termination.

The financial basis for the change of policy would also be clearly stated. Extensive expenditure on exploration of outer space is justified in terms of human curiosity and man's limitless desire to know.[10] But man's curiosity is not confined to outer space; there are numerous subjects which can and do arouse his explorative urge. Why focus on a high expense, low-yield area? Why not satisfy first our "curiosity" about the causes of cancer, mental illness, or the common cold? Or the sources of sociological and psychological resistance to social progress, and the ways to overcome it? Surely the much more promising exploration of the oceans or the depths of the earth is not less intriguing than new maps of the moon. Stress would be laid on a point often neglected in this context: among the numerous subjects of man's interest and exploration there are only a few which taxpayers subsidize to any extensive degree. If private foundations or some university professors wish to continue to satisfy their own and the common human desire to know about outer space, fine. But can the public spend thirty billion dollars—the amount required to send one man to the moon—to answer some questions about the shape of the moon? Are we that curious, when the same amount of money would serve to develop the whole of India?[11]

It would be freely admitted that the Russians are ahead in the outer-space contest, at least when it comes to weight lifting. They might well be invited to provide heavy rockets for a United Nations scientific program of outer-space exploration (the United States would contribute its already developed high-yield payloads). On the other hand, the United States would announce that it sees the major contest in a development race; that is, in "hard" contributions to backward countries, such as investment funds, and providing of bona fide experts and teachers to accelerate development. To underscore the peaceful nature of the race, each bloc might choose one or more countries clearly in its sphere of influence, to demonstrate its superior ability to construct dams, water deserts, drain swamps, and more important, to develop an economy to a state where it can go on developing itself without continued outside aid. It would be stated from the outset that in this new contest no empty gestures, no prestige stunts, would be matched.

If the Russians should choose to invest comparatively less but in big conspicuous projects such as oversized steel mills or dams, the United States would not try to match them. It would patiently point out to the developing countries that the amount of the aid and the rationality of its distribution are what count, not its visibility.

Shifting from the man-to-the-moon race to the development race could be undertaken unilaterally without causing a loss. It would quite likely render a gain to the initiator of such a shift and to international relations, *whatever* the other did in response. One way this can be demonstrated is by applying the seven criteria suggested above for evaluation of the potential predisposition to violence of such contests.

If the East were to continue to insist that prestige should be derived chiefly from success in outer space, the United States' change in policy would result in a more *diversified* international prestige contest, even if only part of the world public were to validate her claim for prestige to be based on aid to developing countries rather than on shooting objects into outer space. The dangerous situation in which one side monopolistically sets the criteria for the evaluation of the outcome of the international prestige contest would be broken. The sense that *victory* in *all* spheres is necessary would be changed by the free and deliberate admission that in one sphere the Soviets are ahead.

If, on the other hand, the Russians were to accept the challenge and see in contributions to underdeveloped countries the chief yardstick of international competition, a shift to "*safer*" *means* of competing would be obtained. True, shooting cameras, Geiger counters, and mice around the moon is a harmless activity compared to shooting anything at the other camp. But since obviously all non-war contests are "safer" than international violence this can hardly be seen as a virtue of the space contest. When the relative safety of space exploration and of development is considered from this viewpoint, it is evidently much easier to directly convert means of space exploration to means of warfare than make investments in development into weapons. While in the long run development increases the military potential of a country, space exploration requires an immediate and constant improvement of the most dangerous modern firearms, long-range missiles. Comparatively speaking, the value of dams, plowed deserts, and schools to military might lies in the distant future and is highly indirect. In addition, nobody ever argued that space trips could as much as approach the increase in human happiness generated by development. As emotional as it may sound, this is truly a question of investment in feeding starving children as against improving the maps of Van Allen belts, of suppressing ignorance and disease on earth as against finding new moons in the skies.

A major advantage of a development race over an outer-space contest is that the comparative success of development—especially of different countries, in particular when not only economic but also cultural and social development are pursued—is much more difficult to determine. There are so many undetermined criteria by which to judge development that a clear-cut scoring is impossible, a sharp failure or victory inconceivable.

Following the criteria derived from our gang model and common sense, development should be supported in all backward countries according to the degree of their need for help, not their willingness to join various bloc alliances, especially military ones. Recognizing and legitimizing neutrality, among other things by maintaining, not cutting, economic and technological aid, will make for more contenders and keeping or increasing the international "floating vote." This supplies an essential reward for peaceful competition and moderate contenders, that of winning the respect—possibly the valuable voluntary support—of uncommitted nations.

As a long-range process, development allows for practically endless future "rounds"; no failure can be interpreted as ultimate or as hopelessly undermining the status of an aid-granting power. Next year's development budget and administration might well not only make up for past failures, but surpass last year's and the present year's achievements of the other side.

It is often suggested that it is more difficult to secure psychological investment in a development race because its outcome is less visible, harder to score, and takes longer to develop than that of a space race, and the race itself is less dramatic. Following the general line of our analysis, we would suggest that this is to the better; some reduction in involvement is highly desirable. But it should be pointed out that development might well steal the limelight from space since (a) there is a place for rather dramatic and visible operations in development, such as using one big atomic blast to divert rivers into arid deserts, opening warm-water harbors for ice-bound countries, and opening huge mines for surface exploitation; and (b) while space exploration appeals to man's curiosity, his desire to know, that is, to relatively "cool" values, economic development appeals to values which are much more emotionally laden, such as international equality, help to the poor, hungry, and ignorant—in short, to humanitarianism.

The suggested unilateral activity illustrates that one side can initiate a change in the international prestige contest so as to reduce involvement in it, to break the prestige-obsession, and thus contribute to peaceful coexistence. A development race is preferable to a space race since, while both supply a nonviolent contest area, the development race contributes more to central human values and is inherently less volatile than the space race.

NOTES

I am indebted to my colleagues, especially to Samuel P. Huntington, of the Institute of War and Peace Studies, at Columbia University, for comments on an earlier version of this article. For a more intensive discussion see my *The Hard Way to Peace: A New Strategy* (New York: Collier Books, 1962), Ch. 4.

1. "Dulles made it his first order of business to secure for his person and policies the support of the Congress and of public opinion at large; in this endeavor, he was eminently successful. But as a result something happened to him that had never happened to Mr. Acheson:

He became the prisoner of a public opinion—in good measure created by his own words and deeds—which limited his freedom of action. . . ." Hans J. Morgenthau, "Prospects for a New Foreign Policy," *Commentary,* February, 1961, p. 107.

2. John Herz, *International Politics in the Atomic Age* (New York: Columbia University Press, 1959).

3. This in part is the case because the two camps had some shared values to begin with, such as the stress on technological and scientific achievement. But this does not necessitate or explain the acceptance of *specific* evaluations of the other, e.g., which particular technological achievement is "higher."

4. The same point holds in intrapolitical systems. The most stable coalition governments are composed of parties which attach *different* significance to various policy spheres—for instance, religious and secular parties. This allows each party to make concessions in matters which are less important to it and of much importance to the other party, and to demand in exchange concessions in those matters of greater import to it than to the other coalition partners. When there is consensus on the saliency of the various policy spheres such concessions are impossible. This point is spelled out in my "Kulturkampf or Coalition: The Case of Israel," *Revue Française de Science Politique,* VII, No. 2 (June, 1958), pp. 311–31.

5. Not all nonviolent activities enhance peace. For instance, a disarmament competition is not necessarily a highly desirable one. Russia and the United States "competed" for a while over size of cuts of military manpower, but this led only to a greater reliance on nuclear bombs in war plans.

6. Chadwich F. Alger, "Non-Resolution Consequences of the United Nations and Their Effect on International Conflict," forthcoming, p. 15.

7. This is attained in bipartisan foreign policy in cases in which the legislature is controlled by a party other than that which holds the executive power; through coalition governments; and through the very change of the party in office.

8. In particular, in case they have a shared or coordinated representation such as E.E.C. has in the Western Union, the Nordic Council in G.A.T.T., or the West often has in the General Assembly or political committees of the United Nations.

9. The editor of the *Bulletin of the Atomic Scientists,* summarizing the opinions of eighteen scientists participating in a special issue on space explorations (April, 1961) stated: "The talk of 'dominating Earth by dominating space,' of military moon bases, of the strategic importance of Mars and Venus, not to speak of the colonization of other planets . . . has little or no relation to the realities of military balance of power in the foreseeable future. . . . The Soviet spaceships as

well as the great variety of miniaturized American satellites should be looked upon *entirely* as feats of scientific exploration whose only non-scientific implications lie in accretions to national prestige" (p. 170).

10. Ralph E. Lapp suggests that a moon trip will yield a pinch of moon-dust which would be an "astronomical rosetta stone"; evidence of life in space would have philosophical repercussions as profound as those which followed Copernicus' and Galileo's conclusions that the earth was not the center of the universe. See *Man and Space* (New York: Harper, 1961), pp. 81–82.

11. "It would be insane for Britain to devote any considerable part of her limited resources to such an adventure, while our people remain so largely uneducated, our slums so great a national disgrace and our contribution to the welfare of the underdeveloped nations so miserably inadequate," states Kingsley Martin in "Reflections on Outer Space," *New Statesman,* LX (August 27, 1960), p. 265.

RULES FOR DEBATE

By ANATOL RAPOPORT

THE TERM "COLD WAR" suggests that in the minds of men World War II was never ended. Instead there was a realignment of forces and a transformation from an acute stage to a chronic stage of a vast struggle engulfing all of humanity. The problem of preventing another, possibly fatal, outbreak of the acute stage of the struggle is, therefore, inseparable from the problems associated with the chronic stage. Reasonable prognoses and prudent policies can be formed only on the basis of some knowledge about the laws (if such exist) governing such large-scale events. Of such knowledge we have next to nothing. We can, however, attempt a preliminary analysis of the general dynamics of conflict. What follows is offered as an example of such analysis.

Fights

It is possible to distinguish three levels of conflict. One level can be exemplified by a "fight," i.e., a combat motivated only by mutual animosity or mutual fear. In a fight, the opponent is just a noxious stimulus. The actions of the combatants are dominated by an urge to destroy or to drive away this noxious stimulus. The aggressive acts of each of the opponents stimulate aggressive counter-acts of the other. This process, then, is mostly self-perpetuating and automatic. Such are the combats one finds in the subhuman world, combats between enemy species, between rivals for a mate, between competitors for food or living space.

Human conflicts are often determined by semantic reactions, among which the so-called self-predictive assumptions play an important role. Having assumed animosity in the Other, we often evoke that very animosity by reacting to our own preconceived notions and thus by furnishing the Other with "proof" that his own suspicions regarding us have been justified, which in turn triggers behavior on his part, which confirms our original assumptions.

Although these semantic reactions are characteristically human, the conflicts so engendered are of the same basic type as the conflicts characteristic of the subhuman world, namely fights. Fights are compounded of automatic actions and reactions, jabs and counterjabs, snarls, growls, gnashings of teeth, shaking of fists, thrusting of weapons physical and symbolic. All these acts are more or less determined by preceding chains of events, not by rational choice.

Once rational choice enters as a component of conflict, we have left the level of the "fight" and have reached a level of conflict no more to be found among subhumans. This level is exemplified by games of strategy.

Games

In a game, each player foresees a number of possible outcomes resulting from choices of action which he and his opponent may make. Further, the player of a game is able to assign relative strengths of preference to the outcomes. Further, he knows that although the outcome of the conflict depends to some extent on acts which he himself controls, it also depends on acts which his opponent controls, and his opponent has potentially just as much foresight and strategic skill as he himself has. In other words, the participant in a gamelike conflict ascribes rationality equal to his own to his opponent.

Games of strategy have long intrigued the imagination of thinkers. Some such games—for example, chess—have developed into fine arts. One of the great chess masters glorified chess as a form of conflict truly worthy of man, a contest in which not body weight nor brute force but rather clear thinking and creative imagination are the decisive factors.

There is no doubt that conflicts of intellect, such as the intricate games of strategy, are noteworthy challenges to human creativity. One can also, perhaps, extol the virtue of such games as particularly happy outlets for aggressive urges. In chess, for example, one may be cunning, ruthless, vicious, and merciless without risking the trauma associated with receiving or inflicting injury. Even possible injury to the ego can be discounted among mature players; for a mature player is one who values the artistry involved in the contest more than his personal vanity.

There was a time when war too came in this category. A "continuation of diplomacy by other means," as Clausewitz once defined it, the gamelike war was once fought according to rules. Not hatred but decorum dominated choices and decisions. Professional pride underlay considerations of strategy, and professional pride dictated surrender when positions became untenable in much the same way as self-respect compels a competent chess player to concede the hopeless game. War was then a gentleman's game rather than organized butchery; its victims were regrettable casualties rather than objects of deliberate extermination.

Recently the idea of limited war has been revived and seriously discussed—an attempt, I suspect, to restore war to its traditional respectable position as a normal human activity. Much could be said on the feasibility of this proposal and on the possible motivations of its authors. However, our interest is not the proposed restoration of decorum and sportsmanship in war. I would prefer to examine the views of those who hope to avoid war altogether by casting the present conflict between East and West entirely within the framework of political and economic maneuvers. Those are the people who realize the inadequacy of the purely military posture, the ineffectiveness of self-righteous recriminations, which both Soviet and American leaders have engaged in throughout the cold war. These people advocate coolheadedness and detachment in the present conflict, realizing the danger that otherwise the conflict may get out of hand. Nevertheless they assume as self-evident that the conflict will be pursued to the end, and that in the end "victory" will crown the efforts of the more clever opponent. The advocates of bloodless war are essentially trying to lift the present world conflict from the level of the fight to the level of the game. The object of any game, of course, is to win it at least possible cost, which means, in this case, to get your own way without war if possible.

Those clever men are saying, in effect, "Let's play it smart. Let's not be blinded by hatred for the enemy. Hatred or any passion is a liability in a game of strategy. Let's use all the tools and weapons at our disposal, but let's see that they are used effectively. We should talk softly if soft talk will get results, and we should talk tough if toughness is likely to make the right impression. Our actions and our attitudes should be thought out, not spontaneously evoked by whatever the enemy does."

This is sound advice when given in the context of a game, in which the opponent is clearly the enemy. In such games there can be no doubt about preferences of outcomes. What I win, the opponent loses; what he wins, I lose. In the recently developed mathematical theory of games, such games are called two-person zero-sum games, because no matter what the outcome the sum of the pay-offs of the two players is always zero.

The two-person zero-sum game is the simplest to understand. For this reason, a complete mathematical theory of such games was the first to be worked out. It is a definitive theory in the sense that the conclusions rest on a fundamental theorem, the so-called Minimax Theorem of John von Neumann, the ingenious founder of the mathematical theory of games. This theorem states: In every two-person zero-sum game there exists a "best" strategy for each opponent which guarantees that (at least in the long run) the user of this strategy will win for himself as much as it is possible to win under the rules of the game. This theorem reduces the practical aspect of gamesmanship to the straightforward problem of finding this "best" strategy.

This result is so much in accord with common sense that it is difficult to conceive a conflict to which it would not apply, where it would be impossible to find the "best" strategy by rational considerations alone. Yet examples of such conflicts, represented as games, can be given. Such are some non-zero-sum games, i.e., games in which the winnings of one player are not necessarily the losses of the other.

As an example of a two-person non-zero-sum game, consider the following situation, by now well known. Each player must write on a piece of paper either "Red" or "Green." Neither knows what the other will write. The papers are given to a third party who pays out or collects money from the players but does not otherwise participate in the game. If both words written down are "Green," the third party pays each of the players $1.00. If both words are "Red," he collects $1.00 from each. But if one of the words is "Green," and the other "Red," then the player who wrote "Red" gets $2.00, while the one who wrote "Green" pays $2.00.

Theoretical difficulties in games of this sort stem from the fact that in situations they depict, the concept of self-interest (which is clear-cut in zero-sum games) becomes hazy. For example, in the game just described each player can argue that it is *clearly* in his interest to write "Red." Should the other player write "Green," "Red" wins $2.00, while "Green" wins only $1.00. Should the other write "Red," then "Red" loses $1.00, while "Green" loses $2.00. In other words, *whatever* the other does, "Red" seems the prudent choice. But since *both* players think so (and each supposes the other thinks so), they are both likely to write "Red" and so lose $1.00 each, whereas if they both wrote "Green," they would both win $1.00.

The lesson to be learned from games which are not zero-sum games is that the sort of gamesmanship which is natural in zero-sum games with two players may lead to disaster in other types of games. Those other types may involve considerations entirely different from the usual considerations of gamesmanship. In particular "solidarity based on collective interest" may have to be given preference to calculations based on self-interest, even though this may involve solidarity with a potential opponent. These sorts of considerations were largely absent in the original formulations of game theory which revolved largely around the zero-sum game.

Understandably, the hard-headed decision theorists, whose backgrounds were usually in mathematics, statistics, or economics, not infrequently acquired in the atmosphere of business schools, tended to shy away from questions involving vague psychological notions akin to conscience, faith, altruism, etc. The military also soon began to take an active interest in the theory of games, and the military atmosphere was equally unsuited for the development of notions which cannot be discussed without embarrassment in business and military circles, namely the role in human affairs of solidarity, integrity, and trust. Nevertheless, the notions could not be dismissed, since they did not originate with soft-headed hecklers but were shown to be by-products of the "hard-headed" theory itself. That is to say, strictly rigorous game theory when extrapolated to cover other than two-person zero-sum games led *perforce* to those extra-game theoretic notions. Von Neumann himself recognized but did not pursue this direction. In his treatment of some types of games, he concedes that the final outcome will be mainly determined by a "social norm," i.e., what is considered "fair" by the players, rather than by the "winning strategy" which invariably forces the outcome of the two-person zero-sum game.

We see, then, that a rigorous examination of gamelike conflicts leads inevitably to considerations of conflicts of still another sort—conflicts of conviction. For "what is fair" cannot be discovered by empirical evidence nor decided by the outcome of a game but is a matter of conviction. For example, taking group interest as a point of departure in calculating self-interest depends on a conviction—namely, that the same point of departure will be taken by others. Usually a person acts in a socially acceptable manner only if he is convinced that others, too, normally act that way. Therefore, to make an individual social-minded instead of egocentric, we must convince him that others are social-minded too.

Debates

The problem of convincing another—that is, the problem of changing another's outlook—is the central aspect of the third category of conflict, the debate.

To summarize, in a fight the urge is to eliminate the opponent; in a game the problem is to outwit the opponent; in the debate, the goal is to convince the opponent. My thesis is that these levels form a hierarchy. It is indeed true that generally speaking strategic conflict is more worthy of the human mind than the blind type of struggle motivated and determined by hatred alone. However, the limitations of purely strategic conflict are still severe in the sense that the *mixed character* of most human conflicts is often overlooked in an analysis of struggle based on strategic considerations alone. A human opponent in real life (as opposed to parlor games) is rarely all enemy. Usually he is part friend, part foe. Mutual recognition of the common area of interest is a problem of communication, not of strategy. And so is the problem of modifying the outlook of the other.

A rational debate is one which is truly aimed at modifying the outlook of the Other. In this sense, the conventional arguments going on in legislative bodies, in courtrooms, and in the forums of the international arena are not rational debates, for clearly they are not conducted to convince the opponents. At most, these arguments are calculated to influence uncommitted third parties; usually they are simply aimed at assuring the people *already* sold on a set of prejudices that their vociferous representatives are on the job, chastising the infidels by verbal drumfire.

To change the Other's outlook, the first thing you must do is to get him to listen to you. How do you get someone to listen to you? How do you get someone to do anything? It is sometimes easy to *prevent* the Other from doing something, if you can make it physically impossible. You can put a man in jail and so prevent his running around. Or you can put yourself in jail by building a wall around yourself, and so keep others from reaching you with their alien ideas, at least for a time. But all these are negative constraints—aimed, sometimes successfully, at *preventing* specific actions of others. To *induce* an action by physical means, however, is virtually impossible. The most you can do is offer a choice between alternatives—for example, "Sign this or die." We call such an offer intimidation by the use of force, but in the last analysis, it is the Other who makes the choice. If he chooses not to sign, he cannot be forced to do so, because his nervous system and his muscles cannot be controlled by another in coordinated fashion.

It is true, of course, that people can be induced to do certain things, and this is done usually in one of two ways: (1) we can take advantage of people's propensity to imitate other people, and (2) we can make it appear to people that it is to their advantage to do what we wish them to do. In other words, we can induce behavior in others by setting an example or by appealing to the Other's self-interest.

Hayakawa has proposed that we listen to the Russians in order to get them to listen: if we listen long enough and earnestly enough, they may begin to imitate us.[1] It has been proposed by Carl Rogers that in a rational debate each opponent, before he is allowed to state his own case, should be required to state the case of the other to the other's satisfaction, in order to convince the other that he has been understood. If this proposal is ever adopted, it will be of advantage to each opponent to listen carefully to the other, because only in this way can he hope to be able to present the other's case to the latter's satisfaction and so to get on to his own case.

The ingenuity of this proposal is that it allows each opponent in a debate to score a "victory" without arousing the animosity of the opponent. The "victory" is gaining the admission by the opponent that one has successfully presented his side. Of course this admission is likely to improve the opponent's disposition to listen to you, because he will want to do as well.

Playing "Chicken"

In addition to these proposals, to try to induce listening by example and by making listening advantageous in a debate, I submit two further principles of rational debate. One of them I call the delineation of the validity of the opponent's position; the other I call the assumption of similarity. To delineate the validity of a position means to state the conditions under which the position is justified. Practically every opinion, even seemingly absurd ones, can be partly justified. If someone maintains that black is white, we can always say, "Yes, that is true, if you are interpreting a photographic negative." If someone maintains that freedom is slavery, we can recognize the grain of truth by recalling that to some people freedom means the absence of responsibility, and that frequently such people become slaves to their whims or to their insatiable ambitions.

In so delineating the region of validity of your opponent's position, you indicate, of course, the limits beyond which the position is false. But you do so indirectly by pointing inside rather than outside the limits. The absence of No Smoking signs at the university where I work is based on the same principle. Instead of the authoritarian prohibition, one reads, "Smoking permitted in offices, seminar rooms, and other designated areas."

The assumption of similarity is more difficult to define. It is not enough to say that you must ascribe to the opponent a psyche similar to your own. You must do so *all the way,* not just part of the way. A homely example may serve as illustration.

There is a game called Chicken, which is said to be played by spirited youngsters in the United States. Two teams pile into two jalopies and rush headlong at each other, keeping the left wheels on the center line of the road. The team whose driver swerves away first gets the unsavory epithet "chicken." As the distance between the two cars diminishes, the driver of one of the cars could be thinking as follows. "Since I would rather be called chicken than be killed, I assume the other driver feels the same. Therefore, he will swerve away in time. Therefore, I will not give in, and be safe in doing so."

The driver who thinks in this way is making the assumption of similarity, but he has not pursued it far enough. If he had, he would have concluded that the other driver *also* had decided to stick it out, convinced that the first driver will swerve at the last moment. With both drivers equally convinced of the good sense of the other, the results are easily imaginable but not pretty.

The relevance to the present international situation hardly needs to be emphasized. The *objective* meaning of the assumption of similarity is readily admitted. Hardly anyone doubts that if they perish in a holocaust, so do we. The fates of the two worlds are thus clearly seen to be linked. However, the *subjective* implication of the assumption still escapes the strategists. Because of the very nature of strategic thinking, they still tacitly divide the psyche of mankind into "us" and "them," thus perpetuating the impasse. Only when this dichotomy is transcended (the greatest spiritual leaders of humanity have urged just this sort of transcendence), when the schism between "us" and "them" actually appears as an illusion, will the present game of chicken played by the powers appear unthinkably absurd.

The Need for Debate

If the present conflict between the Communist and the non-Communist worlds is to be lifted above the level of a fight and above the level of a game of maneuver, to the level of debate where the issues can be squarely faced, we must first learn to listen; second, we need to find out and to admit the extent to which the opponent's position has merit; third, we need to probe deeply within ourselves to discover the profound similarities *between us and them.*

It seems to me that we must face these issues. The fight mentality can lead only to disaster. The game mentality offers somewhat more hope, since it at least enables the participants to take stock of existing states of affairs and necessitates at least a partial consideration of possible consequences of actions. But in the long run, the game mentality is profoundly demoralizing. Its formulations demand the reduction of value decisions to the calculation of tangibles. Granted that calculation of tangibles may be the only justifiable basis for rational decision, it is nevertheless disturbing that the game mentality tends to take the meaning of rationality for granted and a set of values as given. Values which are not constantly re-examined and probed into tend to deteriorate into operating procedures.

We all feel that it is better that fewer people die than that more people die. Therefore, a civil defense project which can be expected to reduce fatalities of the first day of nuclear war from sixty million to forty million ought to appear to us as a problem worthy of our concern. Who would object to saving twenty million lives? I insist, however, that this sort of reasoning is demoralizing, because as we get used to such calculations, we tend to regard them in the same way as calculations with dollars and horsepower. Thinking of human lives in the language of arithmetic may well lead to a conclusion that if we can be sure of killing more of the Russians than they can kill of us, the outcome will be to our advantage. We lose sight of the fact that as war becomes imminent, even more frightening than the impending loss of life is the matter-of-factness with which words like megaton and overkill have established themselves in the vocabulary of men entrusted with the conduct of public affairs. We lose sight of the fact that sacrificing lives and even saving lives is meaningless unless life itself has some meaning—that is, unless we are truly cognizant of our values, not through pronouncing reassuring clichés but through probing within. There is no better incentive for such probing than the presence of a rival, seemingly opposing set of values in another civilization which we can no longer ignore.

An engagement in a debate requires courage of a very special kind. I believe that the well-known law of action and reaction in mechanics has a counterpart in a genuine debate, in the sense that a shift in the outlook of the Other can take place only together with a shift in one's own outlook. This is because a shift in the Other's outlook can occur only if he has re-examined it, and he will re-examine it only if he listens to someone else, and he will listen only if he is listened to. But if we really are ready to listen, then we are ready to re-examine our *own* outlook. The courage needed to become genuinely engaged in a genuine debate is the courage to be prepared to accept a change in one's own outlook.

The object of a fruitful debate is not victory; and its conduct does not involve the adroit use of force, as in a fight, nor of technical skill, as in a game. The object of debate, I repeat, is to modify the opponent's image of himself and of the world. This can be done by inducing new insights; and new insights can be induced only if the self-image is not seriously threatened. New insights can also be induced in the Other if in the process of debate one gets them oneself.

If somehow such conditions could be brought about, what could we and the Communists say to each other in a real, not a sham debate?

The Communist Case for Democracy

In a real debate, the Communist spokesman, aware of his responsibility to present first the opposing view, could begin by outlining the basic assumptions of what we in the United States call democracy. He should first tell us what we already know, namely that we justify the existence of governments only to the extent that they safeguard the liberties of the people; that the existence of natural rights of the single biological unit—the individual—is the cornerstone of our social faith and that consequently the restriction of individual liberty is regarded by us as at best a necessary evil.

He should next remind us of our dedication to the idea of "pursuit of happiness" as the foundation of the good social order and how this idea was constantly reinforced during the last century by the ever-present frontier: at first the geographical frontier, later the frontier of industrial expansion made possible by abundant resources, by the Puritan habit of equating enterprise with virtue, and by security from invasion.

The Communist should make clear to us that our clinging to the free enterprise idea is entirely understandable in the light of our historical experience, now encrusted in a nostalgia for the days of vigorous adventure and growth. He should probe and fathom and communicate to us the meanings concealed in our great national epics, the epic of Captain Ahab, the hunter, and the epic of Huckleberry Finn, the hunted, and how these meanings relate to the Protestant ethos and to the Promethean cult of the Individual, the foundations of the traditional American outlook.

If he says these things to us sympathetically and eloquently, we shall listen to him. Once he gets our attention, he can begin to hint at things which we ordinarily try to shut out of our awareness, but which are all too known to the enlightened among us. He would go on as follows.

"The world as a whole is not prosperous, and there is hardly any freedom or justice in it. Only in the United States can any reasonable claim be made for the theory that an economy controlled by the market rather than by a rational plan can lift the common people from the abject poverty in which they have always lived. Most of the human race continues to live in abject poverty, not because modern technology cannot provide a decent standard of living but because there is no concerted plan of improving the lot of man. Corporate control of economics, especially control by foreign or absentee ownership, results in a total alienation between those who are responsible for economic decisions and those whose very lives depend on those decisions. Thus corporate control, which reduces "labor" to an item on the balance sheet, insures continued poverty and degradation of the majority of the human race.

"The usual justification of free enterprise is based on the idea of the freedom of contract. But freedom of contract can also be a sham freedom. If the worker must sell his labor or starve, his bargaining power is seriously limited. He is *not* really free to refuse to sell his labor for whatever the market price of labor happens to be."

This is, of course, the classical Marxist picture of private-enterprise economics. Anticipating our arguments that this picture does not apply in the United States, because of the dynamics of mass production, trade unionism, etc., the Communist might point out that the picture is still largely true on the world scale; that the United States and other progressive capitalist countries are only islands in a vast sea of poverty, rich suburbs surrounded by slums.

"But you do not see yourselves as the rest of the world sees you," the Communist might go on. "Forgetting that you appear to the poverty-stricken as privileged, pampered, and overfed, you solemnly keep proclaiming yourselves as the defenders of 'the Free World,' and confer this title on anyone who flatters you. You count among your allies the king of Saudi Arabia, who pockets one half the income of his country, in which the standard of living is among the lowest in the world. You give military aid to regimes which would not last a day without such aid. In other words, in the ongoing struggle between the common people and their oppressors, you have by and large taken the side of the oppressors. You have taken on the role of the world gendarme, contrary to the social philosophy upon which your society had been founded, and this you have done not because you have turned evil, but because you have become obsessed with fear, the fear that grips those who are growing old without having become mature.

"What is this future that you are afraid of? Is it the next step in man's development, the step toward the elimination of exploitation of man by man, the step toward greater cooperation among men?

"The fundamental social philosophy of Communism rests on the assumption that the individual has intrinsic worth by simply being a member of his society. And so society is obliged not simply to pay its members at going rates whenever they are needed on specific jobs but to provide for the needs of its members. In order to do so, society must change the motivational basis of production. As long as the primary motive for production is wages, salaries, or profits, decisions governing production are made as results of conflicting interests. At best these decisions are compromises; mostly they are determined by the interests of those to whom profits accrue. Communists maintain that such decisions should be made by the whole society, just as political decisions are presumably made in democracies. Hence Communism is no more than the extension of the democratic ideal to the productive process, which can be implemented only if private groups surrender their control of the means of production to society at large."

Aware of our abhorrence of violence as an instrument of social change and of our emphasis on economic opportunity and social mobility as the mainstays of freedom, the spokesman for Communism might conclude as follows.

"Admirable as social mobility and individual self-reliance have seemed against the historical background of caste-ridden societies, they are not truly expressive of man's freedom. A truly free man is not a self-seeker. He is free to fulfill himself, and this means in human terms to transcend himself and his purely selfish interests. Such a man seeks to rise not above his neighbors but *with* his neighbors. He has learned the meaning of freedom for the mature human being—to be able to cooperate with others to achieve common goals. It is this experience which Communism offers to man. The impoverished and the disinherited will eagerly grasp this idea. This is what we Communists mean when we insist that Communism will be victorious. Everything else that you think we mean is only what you imagine or what may happen if you persist in fighting the normal development of human history. If you tell the peoples of the world that their aspirations toward a cooperative society are wicked, they will reject you rather than their aspirations. If you try to prevent overdue social changes by force or intrigue, violent struggles will surely ensue. It is these derivative struggles which have occurred and may occur and which the Communists are always expecting, that cause people to link Communism with violence, ruthlessness, and dictatorship. Violent, ruthless, and dictatorial methods are not Communist inventions; nor are they more terrible than the methods of anti-Communists. They only appear more terrible when one is on the receiving instead of on the giving end.

"Freedom is the recognition of necessity. Face the future instead of the past, and you will see that there is nothing to fear. Not slavery but freedom awaits man as he discards the bonds of narrow self-interest and transcends his individual consciousness to merge with the entire human race."

So might a dedicated Communist present the case for Communism to an American audience.

Now the first thing that occurs to one well acquainted with the tone and content of Communist propaganda is that a real Communist could not present his case in this way. In all likelihood he would not be allowed to do so by his superiors. They would insist on the usual clichés and invectives, on the usual tone of finality, to which no reply can be made except in the same spirit of invective and rejection. If such a reply is made, the debate will degenerate into a fight.

There is only one way of breaking out of the vicious circle. We must not imitate the Communist if he presents his case poorly. On the contrary, if he fails in his task, we *must present the case for him* and present it in such a way that he will say to himself, "I wish I were allowed to say it as well."

Our Case for Communism

But this is only half of our job. We must also make a reply. Our reply should contain a careful delineation of the conditions under which the Communist's case may have validity. An examination of recent history may be enlightening. Contrary to Marx's predictions, successful Communist revolutions occurred not in highly industrialized countries but in underdeveloped ones, namely Russia and China. No satisfactory Marxist explanation of these facts has ever been given. Therefore, on the basis of evidence we are forced to the conclusion that impoverished masses do indeed tend to embrace Communism, but the would-be proletariats, that is, the working classes of highly industrialized countries, do not. Why is this so? Can it be that the classical proletariat, that is, the population with no stake in the social order in which it lives, is a product of primitive, not of advanced capitalism? Can it be that the mass misery which was concomitant to the early decades of European industrialization was simply a product of early industrialization, not of the specific mechanisms of social control which have effected the industrialization? Were not the early years of industrialization in Russia also accompanied by mass misery, even though they were carried out under entirely different mechanisms of social control?

Let us see what happens if we view the history of the Western world of the last two hundred years in terms of changing forms of social control. We know that industrialization involves a diversion of effort to produce capital goods. We also know (in retrospect) that in the long run these capital goods insure a higher standard of living for every one in a highly industrialized society, though admittedly not in equal degree. But at the time when these capital goods are being created, the standard of living of the majority of the population remains low and may even be depressed, because a part of production is diverted into goods which cannot be consumed. Under capitalism this diversion is enforced by those who control the allocation of capital. By virtue of this control, the allocation can be made without overt coercion by the state. But where no large and powerful capitalist class exists, this diversion can be enforced only by the state with all the concomitant overt forms of coercion that state control involves.

It follows that in the absence of a large capitalist class, industrialization must either wait until this class appears or the state must assume the prerogatives of economic control. Now we know that in Europe the capitalist class emerged from the mercantile system—that is, capital was finally accumulated through trade. This process took about two hundred and fifty years. This would seem too long to a starving population, especially since recent history has shown that under strong state control, as in the Soviet Union, sufficient accumulation of capital has been accomplished in about forty years despite a terribly devastating war. It is therefore not surprising that the coercive measures associated with Communism are viewed by large impoverished populations as necessary and are accordingly tolerated or rationalized. But this is not the view of the well-fed populations of the United States and other prosperous industrialized countries. Where surplus of income is distributed over broad strata of population, capital investment appears as a voluntary act, and the population gets the impression that it lives in freedom. Coercive measures of whatever nature by the state appear to such a population as manifestations of tyranny.

Marx's great achievement has been to show how ideologies and political convictions develop as rationalizations of existing economic arrangements. But the same general method can be used to get alternative theories of social evolution and can be pushed further to apply to an analysis of social relations in newly emerging social systems. Moreover, the notion of power, which in Marxist analysis is a derivative of *ownership,* can be generalized so as to appear as a derivative of *control.* Not who owns but who controls is the essential question in deciding whether power is concentrated and if so where. Nor is power confined to decisions regarding the allocation of merchandise. In conditions of scarcity, the allocation of wealth is of overwhelming importance, and it is natural to view power as identical with economic power. But in conditions of abundance, or in other situations where the allocation of goods is not the main issue, the struggles for power take on very different forms. We need to go no further than to examine the power struggles in some of our civic organizations or in affluent but highly neurotic families. Here the focus of the struggle becomes usually the vantage position of psychological control: who will get his way. Psychology, not economics, asks the appropriate questions relevant to the study of such power struggles. There is no reason why psychological power struggles cannot also become central in a society, particularly in a society like the Soviet Union, in which considerable consensus has been achieved on the methods of economic control and the allocation of goods. By no stretch of the imagination can the bloody Soviet purges of the 1930's be rationalized in terms of an economic class struggle.

As long as the analysis offered by Marx was new and fresh and unorthodox, it provided a leverage for re-examining the nature of social relations. Thus the Marxist method conferred freedom on progressive social thinkers and activists to expose entrenched prejudices in social thought. In due time, however, the Marxist ideas have themselves become dogmatized. Orthodox Marxism now represents the entrenched, conservative point of view in Communist countries. Our debate, therefore, must be directed at the potential progressives in the Communist countries. A progressive in a Communist country, like the progressive anywhere, looks forward, not backward. Hence a Communist progressive is not one who longs for the return of the good old days of free enterprise, which incidentally never even existed in his country, but one who is looking forward to the emergence of the next phase of collective endeavor.

The Chance for Debate

Indications show that the time is ripe for a re-examination. The recent loosening of thought control in some Communist countries has released a respectable trickle of ideas from abroad, particularly in science. Russians have always been hungry for science, both for its technological potential and as a result of profound intellectual curiosity. The attempts of the Communist Party to draw a line of demarcation between bourgeois and socialist science have largely failed. One by one the new scientific directions originating in the West have broken through the intellectual quarantine.

Once scientific methods of investigation break through to the examination of behavior, particularly social behavior, the Soviet intellectual cannot but see that he has been deprived of opportunities of pursuing knowledge in a vastly important and fertile field. This discovery will be of immense social importance, because the Soviet intellectual stands in a position of leadership perhaps enjoyed by no other intellectual, least of all by the intellectuals of our own country.

I believe, therefore, that the Communist intellectual can be engaged in a fruitful debate, provided it is conducted in a spirit acceptable to him. This means that we must avoid any suggestion that Communism was established by imposing a tyranny on his people. This sounds as absurd to his ears as the familiar slogans of the Communists about the capitalist bloodsuckers sound to our ears. Rather, appeal must be made to the Soviet intellectual's mission as an intellectual, the mission that he believes he is already performing, that of examining, criticizing, and analyzing all aspects of reality, including social relations, according to objective (he calls them "materialistic") criteria of truth.

We must realize that for the Soviet man there can be no going back. There is only the future to look to. The people of Communist states, like all other peoples, want to improve their lot. Like any other people, they also want to cling to certain values. The big problem facing any people anywhere is how to improve one's lot without betraying the values to which one is emotionally committed. Ideas are branded alien if they are seen as threats to emotionally anchored values. That is why alien ideas are feared, hated, dismissed, and ridiculed. It is silly for us to sing the glories of free enterprise to a people who view the efforts of an individual to enrich himself personally regardless of what happens to his neighbors as a betrayal of a firmly established notion of social solidarity. It is equally silly for the Russians to preach proletarian dictatorship to us because most of us see any sort of overt dictatorship as a betrayal of our fundamental values derived from the natural-rights doctrine of Rousseau, Jefferson, and Paine.

On the other hand, it does make sense for the Russian to induce us to ask ourselves whether our democratic ideal has not been in part perverted by extending the dogma of individual initiative beyond its proper sphere. And it does make sense to suggest to the Russians that their ideal of achieving the dignity of the individual through collective solidarity has been in part perverted by Stalinism, with its cynicism, institutionalized paranoia, and terror.

I believe that an ethically conducted debate between sincere proponents of the two systems would attack the present dilemma of humanity at its very source. Moreover, such a debate, if it does engender new insights in us and in the Russians, will enable both us and them to attack the dilemma jointly. The outcome depends on the occurrence of one crucial insight: We are all in the same boat.

NOTES

1. S. I. Hayakawa, "On Communication with the Soviet Union," *ETC*, XVII (1960), pp. 389–400.

CONCILIATING EAST AND WEST

By BERTRAND RUSSELL

THE HOSTILITY BETWEEN EAST AND WEST, as it exists at the present day, is a cause of the gravest anxiety to all sane men. It involves the catastrophic possibility of an all-out nuclear war and, short of that, demands continually increasing expenditure upon continually more deadly and more expensive weapons of war, to which no end can be seen except reducing both East and West to subsistence level. In view of these obvious facts, a great many people perceive the desirability of producing more friendly relations, especially between Russia and America. But efforts in this direction have hitherto proved fruitless, and their failure has, if anything, augmented the general danger. It seems, therefore, that, if peaceful coexistence is to be successfully promoted, some fresh diagnosis must be found and other methods must be sought.

It is my belief that the source of the trouble lies in the minds of men and not in any nonmental facts. I think that the place where conciliation ought to begin is in the beliefs of statesmen and plain men as to the true character of the conflict. I think that, if these beliefs were changed, the difficulties which at present make disarmament congresses abortive would melt away. At present, each side is firmly persuaded of the other's wickedness, so firmly as to believe that any concession by one's own side, however slight, has the character of surrender to Absolute Evil. While this mood persists, it is obvious that no negotiations can succeed.

In analyzing the present troubles, there are two kinds of facts to be borne in mind. There are what might be called hard facts, concerned with armaments, risks of unintended war, Western obligations to West Berlin, Russian tyranny in Hungary, and so on. There are also what, in comparison, may be called soft facts. These consist of the hopes and fears that have inspired actions which have increased hostility. There is a continual interaction between these two sets of facts, and to debate which set should come first may seem like the old problem of the hen and the egg. I think, however, that a smaller effort is needed to change the soft facts than to change the hard ones, and that the easiest way to change the hard facts is to tackle the soft facts first.

Let us, for the moment, consider the matter from the point of view of human welfare rather than from that of the victory of either side. It is obvious that, if the feelings of East and West toward each other were friendly and neither had any wish to exterminate the other, both sides would perceive the futility of immense expenditure on weapons of mass destruction. Both sides would emerge from the cloud of fear which now darkens every moment in the life of every thinking person. Both sides could combine to lessen the load of poverty and malnutrition which still weighs down the majority of the population of the globe. All the immense and truly remarkable skill which is now employed in the technical business of new armaments could be employed instead in inventions that would make human life happier and more prosperous. What is needed to bring about this change? Only that both East and West should have friendly, instead of hostile, feelings toward each other.

"But," both sides will say, "how is it possible to have any friendly feeling toward people so abysmally wicked as the other side?" The rest of this speech, from our side, is sadly familiar. "Do you not know," we shall be told, "that the Soviets are atheistical materialists? Do you not know that they permit no individual freedom in any country that they dominate? Have you not heard of their brutal tyranny in Hungary and Eastern Germany? Were you unaware of their barbarous expulsion of Germans from formerly German territory in 1945? Can you ask us to tolerate the monsters who put in Arctic concentration camps every man and woman throughout Communist territory who showed one spark of independence?" So much for the Western case. But the East, also, believes that it has a case, which is the only one that its subjects are allowed to hear. The East maintains that the West is incurably imperialistic and that, while it prates of individual liberty, it suppresses national liberty wherever it can in Asia, Africa, or Latin America. Communists, we are assured, stand for world peace, which the imperialistic West is continually threatening. And as for the supposed love of freedom in the West, how about its ally Franco, who established a brutal military tyranny by the help of Hitler and Mussolini, and to this day enforces a censorship against all the beliefs by which the West pretends that it is inspired. Moreover, they assure each other that American wage-earners to this day are as badly off as the British wage-earners of 1844 whose plight was so eloquently depicted by Engels.

Each of these speeches is a mixture of truth and falsehood. Each produces furious vituperative retorts from the other side. Both speeches are made by eminent statesmen at meetings of the United Nations, but, to everybody's astonishment, they do not generate friendly feelings between East and West.

Propaganda, however, is seldom a prime cause of the emotions which it is intended to stimulate. At the beginning of the First World War, stories of German atrocities, however untrue, were eagerly absorbed and repeated throughout Britain. At the end of the Second World War, far worse atrocity stories about German concentration camps, though completely authenticated, were shrugged off by the British public as unrealistic propaganda. The difference lay solely in the popular mood. In 1914, the great majority of the British public felt warlike and was glad of reasons to justify its feelings. In 1945, with victory assured, war-weariness caused an exactly opposite reaction. The moral of these two sets of facts is that what is believed about an opposing group depends upon prevailing fashions much more than upon what is happening.

It would be idle to deny that both East and West have had reasons for mutual hostility such as, in an earlier state of armaments, might, without complete insanity, have been thought to justify a war. In 1917 and 1918, the new Bolshevik government did several things that annoyed the West: it made a separate peace treaty with Germany; it repudiated the czarist national debt; and it confiscated the Lena gold fields. As a consequence of these acts, Britain, France, Japan, and Czechoslovakia joined in an attack on Russia. Unfortunately for the governments which ordered this attack, the soldiers felt no hostility to the Bolsheviks and mutinied so vigorously that they had to be withdrawn. The baffled governments tried to sway public opinion by inventing stories of the nationalization of women and similar fables, but they did not at that time succeed in rousing hostility to Russia among wage-earners. They did succeed, however, in rousing a deep-seated and passionate hostility to Western governing classes in most politically conscious Russians.

All this might have simmered down in time if it had not been for nuclear weapons. These produced, first in Russia and then in the Western world, a new feeling of terror and a new conviction of each other's wickedness. This was, of course, the sort of reaction that psychiatrists study in mentally afflicted patients, who, when they are in danger, are apt to do everything possible to increase the danger. Governments have always acted in this way. When I was a boy, the

British government was afraid that Russia, advancing through central Asia, would be in a position to invade British India. It was feared that Afghanistan might help them in this project, and the British therefore made two wars on Afghanistan under the impression that this would cause Afghans to love the British. This was a folly, but a little one. The present folly is psychologically very similar, but on a global scale, and may well bring disaster to the whole world.

The present trouble is caused by the vast mass emotions of fear, hate, and suspicion which each side feels toward the other. I do not deny that on each side there are grounds for these feelings. What I do deny is that acts which they inspire are such as to diminish danger. They are, on both sides, essentially insane reactions in the sense that they make the danger immensely greater than it would otherwise be. If both sides were capable of thinking rationally about the danger, they would minimize the ground of conflict instead of using all the arts of propaganda to inflame it.

Take, as a very noteworthy part of the conflict, the difference of ideologies between East and West. We are told that the Russians are atheists, and that it is our religious duty to oppose them in every possible way. In our time this accusation has an old-fashioned sound. Socrates was accused of atheism, and this was one of the grounds on which he was put to death. The early Christians were accused of atheism because they did not believe in the Olympic gods. As Gibbon states it: "Malice and prejudice concurred in representing the Christians as a society of atheists, who, by the most daring attack on the religious constitution of the Empire, had merited the severest animadversion of the civil magistrate" (*Decline and Fall,* Chapter XVI). But in later times atheism, like other kinds of unorthodox theology, has come to be tolerated. The Chinese became atheists in the eleventh century, and remained so until Chiang Kai-shek came to power, but this was never alleged as a ground for fighting the Chinese, even at times when we were at war with them. The ideological differences between Christianity and Islam were thought, for many centuries, to make peace between the two impossible. When it was found that neither side could win, it was realized at last that adherents of the two ideologies could live together without any difficulty. Britain had the same hostility to Russia as it has now from 1854 to 1907, although at that time the Russian government was earnestly Christian and a wholehearted supporter of capitalism. When I was a boy, hostility to Russia was taken for granted in England until Gladstone excited the country against the Turks. One of my amusements in those days consisted of demolishing nettles, which I, and all other English boys, called "Russians." But in 1907 it was decided by the British Government that we were to hate the Germans and not the Russians. All the disputes that caused a half-century of enmity between Russia and Britain were solved by a month or two of negotiation, and from then until 1917 any criticism of the czarist government was frowned upon. At the present day, if China increases in power and becomes a threat to Russia, the ideological conflict between Russia and the West will be quickly forgotten.

Another of the grounds alleged for hostility to Russia is the question of freedom versus dictatorship. There is one curious fact about this, which is that those who profess the greatest eagerness to defend Western freedom against the Communist menace are the very men who are doing the most to diminish Western freedom and produce an approximation to the Soviet system, whereas those in the West who have a genuine love of freedom are, for the most part, those who are most firmly persuaded that peaceful coexistence with Communism is both possible and desirable. The spectacle of McCarthyism in defense of freedom is so ludicrous that, if a fiction writer had invented it, he would have been thought unpardonably fantastic. To anyone not deafened by slogans, it should be obvious that the lack of freedom in the East and the grave threat to freedom in the West are both products of fear, and that the first step toward increase of freedom must be diminution of fear. Perhaps, without being accused of paradox, one might add that freedom is not very useful to corpses, and that any defense of freedom conducted by means of a nuclear war can only be supported by those who deserve to be patients in psychiatric wards. To an impartial observer, it must, therefore, be obvious that the professed love of freedom in the West is a pretext, usually unconscious, to cover up aims which are not avowed.

Militarists, in the past, have often been able to achieve their aims. History, in fact, may be viewed as a long series of imperialistic conquests. The Persians subdued the Ionian Greeks, the Romans subdued everybody who lived near the Mediterranean. When Rome fell, hordes of barbarians established new kingdoms and in many cases—for example, in Britain—exterminated most of the former inhabitants. For a time, imperialist leadership was acquired by the Mohammedans, but, with Columbus and Vasco da Gama, it returned to the West. There was no shadow of legal justification for white dominion over Indians, either in the Western hemisphere or in India. The pursuit of world dominion inspired successively the Spaniards, the French, the British, and the Germans. This long history, from the time of Cyrus to the time of Hitler, has become deeply imbedded in the unconscious aspirations of militarists and statesmen both in the East and in the West—and not only of militarists and statesmen, but of a very large part of the general population.

It is difficult, especially for those accustomed to power at home, to realize that the happy days of successful slaughter have been brought to an end. What has brought them to an end is the deadly character of modern weapons of war. The influence of weapons of war on social structure is no new thing. It begins at the dawn of history with the conflict between the horse and the ass, in which, as was to be expected, the horse was victorious. The age of chivalry, as the word implies, was the age of the horse. It was gunpowder that put an end to this age. Throughout the Middle Ages, barons in their castles were able to maintain freedom against the central governments of their countries. When gunpowder was able to demolish their castles, the barons, though they made all the speeches in defense of freedom which are being repeated in our own day, were compelled to submit to the newly strengthened monarchies of Spain, France, and England. All this is familiar. What is new is the impossibility of victory. This new fact is so unpalatable that those in whom history has inspired a belief that the defeat of enemies is noble and splendid are totally unable to adapt themselves to the modern world. Fabre describes a collection of insects which had the habit of following their leader. He placed them on a circular disc which their leader did not know to be circular. They marched round and round until they dropped dead of fatigue. Modern statesmen and their admirers are guilty of equal and very similar folly.

There are those in the Western world, and presumably also in the East, who carry folly a step further than it was carried by Fabre's insects. When forced to acknowledge that victory in a general war is no longer possible, they take refuge in applauding the heroism of those who die fighting, and they almost invariably conclude their rhetoric by quoting Patrick Henry. It does not occur to them that Patrick Henry, if he should die in the struggle, expected to leave behind him others who would enjoy the fruits of his heroism. His modern would-be imitators profess to think that one should fight for the Right even if assured that the only outcome will be a world without life. Although many of the people who take this extreme view profess to be democrats, they nevertheless consider that a small percentage of fanatics have a right to inflict the death penalty upon all the rest of mankind. This morbid view involves an extreme of religious persecution surpassing all that previous ages have known. I do not doubt that it would have horrified Torquemada almost as much as it horrifies me. It is scarcely possible to doubt that there is an element of unconscious insincerity in those who would prefer the end of Man to the victory of a faction which they dislike. It seems probable that they find the impossibility of victory through war so intolerably painful that in a corner of their minds they reject it and continue to believe that in a nuclear war some miracle will give the victory to what they consider the Right. This is a common delusion of fanatics. But it is a pity when such men control the policy of a great state.

The first step toward the recovery of sanity in our mad world should be the public and solemn recognition by both sides that the worst thing that can possibly happen is a general nuclear war. I should like to see the statesmen of East and West declare that the success of their opponents would be a smaller misfortune than war. If this were acknowledged sincerely and after due study, it would become possible for the two sides to come together and examine how peaceful co-existence could be secured without sacrifice of the vital interests of either. But it seems hardly worth while to prolong the tedious process of negotiations while each side hopes that negotiations will continue to end in failure and secretly cherishes the belief that, against all the evidence, its own side would, in war, achieve a victory in the old-fashioned sense. I am credibly informed that the young men who undergo military training in the United States are instructed as to what to do *when* war comes, not *if* war comes. I have little doubt that the same is true in Russia. This means that young men at an impressionable age are encouraged by the authorities of their country to expect, if not to desire, a course of events which must be utterly catastrophic, although all imaginable pains are taken to prevent the young men from becoming aware of the magnitude of the disaster toward which they are told to march. This sort of thing will have to be changed if the danger of war is to be diminished.

How can such a change be brought about? I think it will have to begin at the summit. Publicity and propaganda have now such influence that the majority in any powerful country is pretty sure to believe whatever its government wishes it to believe. It is unlikely that what the government wishes us to believe will be what the government believes to be the truth, and it is still more unlikely that it will be what, in fact, is the truth. Power impulses in great states have such a hold upon men's desires and instincts that it is very difficult to secure acknowledgment of facts when such acknowledgment thwarts the impulse to dominion. This is the psychological truth which underlies the warlike preparations of East and West. The mutual talk about each other's wickedness is merely a smoke-screen behind which conscience can hide. I do not mean that either East or West is impeccable. On the contrary, I think the governments of both are deeply criminal. But I do not think that this fact, if it be a fact, is a reason for desiring the extermination of the populations of both and also of neutral countries. Propaganda which promotes mutual hate serves no useful purpose, and those who indulge in it are encouraging mass murder.

I believe, I repeat, that conciliation will have to begin at the top. Camp David might have been a beginning, but was sabotaged by the militarists of West and East who continued the U-2 flights and their interception during the preparations for the summit meeting which consequently proved abortive. What I should like to see is the establishment of a very small body, which might be called the Conciliation Committee, consisting of eminent men from East and West and, also, certain eminent neutrals, who should spend some time in each other's company until they had become accustomed to thinking of each other as individuals and not as emissaries of Satan. This committee could be appointed by the United Nations, given the previous admission of China. I should wish these men, in the early stages of their association, to make no attempt at concrete and definite proposals. I should wish them, at first, only to arrive at a state of mind in which agreement seemed possible and the necessity of reaching agreement had become evident. After the mellowing influence of propinquity had produced this state of mind, it would then become possible to proceed to the tackling of questions as to which agreement is difficult.

It may be thought that nothing would come of such a procedure except renewed quarrels and increased bitterness. There is, however, some evidence to the contrary. The Pugwash Conferences in which scientists, Eastern and Western and neutral, all meet, have found it possible to preserve good personal relations and to arrive at unanimous resolutions. The melodramatic picture of each other which East and West have created through the years does not easily survive close personal contact. In the course of such contact, people become aware of each other's common humanity. They share sensations of heat and cold, of hunger and thirst, and even, at long last, an appreciation of each other's jokes, and it comes gradually to be felt that the political part of each of us is only a small part, and that the common humanity which we share covers a larger area than the abstract creeds in which we differ. Such a group of men as I have in mind, if encouraged by their governments, could gradually become a source of sanity, and accustom East and West alike to admit the limitations of their power which have resulted from the modern possibility of mass destruction and have made victory in the old-fashioned sense impossible for either side.

Perhaps the first work which such a body should recommend to governments would be the spread of truthful knowledge about each other. At present such knowledge is regarded on both sides as dangerous. In America, books giving truthful information about Russia are banned from some public libraries. In Russia, there is almost complete prohibition of accurate knowledge about the West. At the end of the

Second World War, Russian soldiers who had been prisoners in the West were all suspect to the Russian government because they knew that the West is not what Russian propaganda presents it as being. The governments of East and West should do what lies in their power to moderate the virulence and untruthfulness of the press and to use the press to refute such popular misconceptions as are calculated to inflame suspicion.

The primary motive in any attempt at conciliation should be the prevention of war, and correct information about what a war would mean should be widely disseminated. It should be made clear to the nations of both East and West that survival is not to be secured by multiplying weapons of war or by exacerbating hatred and suspicion.

The world at present, not only that of Communists and anti-Communists, but also that of uncommitted nations, is living in daily and hourly peril of complete extinction. If this peril is to be lessened, it will be necessary to diminish the autonomy of those who control the major weapons of war. The present state of tension has made it seem necessary to both sides to be prepared for instant retaliation, since each side believes the other to be capable of an unprovoked attack and has devised fallible methods of detection which may cause a false belief that such an attack has been perpetrated. The life of each one of us is at the mercy of those who control technical inventions of marvelous ingenuity. These men, as is humanly inevitable, tend to regard the modern triumphs of technique as ends in themselves and to deplore anything that would divert technical skill into less dangerous channels. While the tension between East and West persists, those who have technical control are thought to be the guardians of our safety, whereas, in fact, they are the exact reverse. They will not be felt to be a danger until the feelings of East and West toward each other have grown less suspicious and less filled with fear. The dangerous state of the world is caused, I repeat, by the dangerous passions of ordinary men and women which have been inflamed by unwise propaganda on both sides. It is these widespread passions that must be assuaged if we are to be no longer exposed to the imminent risk of total annihilation.

If the governments of East and West were at last persuaded that the safety of each demands successful negotiations, many things would quickly become possible. I should put first the total abolition of nuclear weapons under a system of inspection conducted by neutrals, for, until this is achieved, the present state of popular terror on both sides is difficult to mitigate. If this had been achieved, I should invite the Conciliation Committee to approach both sides with a view to finding acceptable solutions of difficult problems such as that of Germany and Berlin. Such solutions should not alter the balance of power between East and West, and should be such as each side could accept without loss of face, for, if these conditions are not fulfilled, there will be little hope of both sides' accepting the suggested solutions. The Conciliation Committee should have only an advisory capacity, but it may be hoped that it would in time acquire such moral authority as would make resistance to its proposed solutions difficult. If it achieved success and had been appointed by the United Nations, the United Nations should take up its work and might lead the way to the creation of a real world government endowed with the only powerful armed forces in the world. In any case, only a world government affords a long-term hope of the survival of the human race. In the present temper of the great powers, world government is not possible, but for all friends of Man it must remain the goal toward which our efforts should tend.

AN INVENTORY OF VALUES AND RESOURCES

By C. WEST CHURCHMAN

CONTRIBUTORS TO A VOLUME SUCH AS THIS must inevitably suffer from a lack of information. A well-designed proposal for world peace must show that in fact the world ought to want peace and the sacrifices it ought to be willing to make to attain it. Such a proposal must also display a list of alternatives and prove that in terms of forecastable consequences, the proposed alternative is optimal. Since few of us are fortunate enough to know enough to possess the evidence for either of these tasks, we must resort instead to making suggestions that we believe would have to be considered if a well-designed proposal were to be constructed.

Since in back of every proposal for peace there is a moral assumption that men ought to be peaceful, or ought to strive to survive, the intellectually wary scientist may want to question whether there is any ultimate evidence for or against a specific proposal. The answer to this question may be negative, but no answer can be given with a clear conscience until the relevant facts are collected. Our heritage of objective inquiry does not permit us to make a facile and unsupported judgment as to whether men deserve peace and ought to strive for it. One major area of our ignorance is concerned with man's needs, wants, and values. We cannot know what men ought to do until we know a great deal more about what they really want to do. Whether a better knowledge of man as a purposeful animal will indicate man's morality is a question that can only be pursued in sufficient depth once we have come to understand the animal's purposes.

This paper, therefore, is an outline of a suggestion for learning about human values. It intentionally has a long-run tone, but its application could occur in a very short time. The short-run benefit may be that when men become collectively active in ascertaining what kind of a world man wants, they may be less active in destroying that world. Of course, no scientist believes any longer that knowledge alone will save mankind. But he ought not to give up his faith that knowledge is essential. If as a scientist I try to help an organization pursue its objectives, I believe that a major part of my research effort should be put into discovering what these objectives really are. And if I try to help man to arrive at a safer world, I must try to discover what kind of safety men want.

The outline of the proposed inquiry is based on a series of steps that at the present time seem to be ranked in terms of difficulty. When investigation begins, it may very well turn out that this assumed hierarchy of difficulty is illusionary. But then all research proceeds by a systematic redesign of the research procedures.

Briefly, the simplest inquiry seems to be one that assumes men want to survive; such inquiry tries to define survival, and to identify the resources of survival. Where these resources are poorly allocated, it tries to devise plans for proper reallocation. The second inquiry assumes that men require some standard of living in terms of their physical environment, without committing itself to any universal standard. This inquiry tries to identify the appropriate environmental standards, and to study the problem of allocation of relevant resources. The third inquiry assumes that man is an expressive animal, and tries to identify the potentials of these expressions, as well as the resources that will permit their actualization. The fourth inquiry tries to understand the direction, pattern, or evolution of man's needs and wants, with the aim of better preparing coming generations for the problems they will face. It scarcely needs saying, but I recognize that phases of each of these inquiries are already being carried out in certain parts of the world.

The First Inquiry

The aim of the first inquiry is to attain a world map of human survival. The measure of survival need is simply the measure of the relationship between survival potential if the best available resources were present, and the actual survival patterns of a people.

Such a world map should be paired with a survival-resources map which would show those parts of the world that have excess capacity for producing survival. The next step of this inquiry would be a listing of the hypotheses that explain why excess capacity is not utilized for survival-deficient societies.

The last stage of this inquiry would consist of a gigantic allocation problem. But recent investigations into allocation planning, and the expected advent of very high-speed computers with giant memories, lend credence to the hypothesis that a world allocation problem could be investigated in a realistic manner, even though the estimate of a true "optimal" might have to be postponed for several decades.

The Second Inquiry

The weaknesses of the first inquiry are obvious enough. For one thing, we can ask whether people want to survive if survival means drudgery or pain, or pleasure and leisure. Hence, I think the second inquiry, although intellectually much vaguer and more challenging, is also essential. This should be an assessment of how the world's peoples want to live; that is, the environment of living they find most desirable. I am not naïvely suggesting that the United States concept of a standard of living would be the best basis for measurement in this level of inquiry. Frankly, I don't know how this second inquiry should be conducted, but I am fairly sure it should not consist merely of asking people. As everyone knows, it is impossible for a person to say what he wants if he is ignorant of the consequences of his choices. But I am willing to assume that the aim of this inquiry is to estimate what kind of environment men would choose, if they were aware of the full scope of their choices.

Since we are here making proposals and not designing their implementation, I will simply assert that I believe the second inquiry would require a development period in which men learn a lot more about how to determine what people really want. I might add that we spend very little of our intellectual time on this concern, and a large part of the little effort we put into it is the work of people who want to sell products. Perhaps if value research could hope to engage the attention of 10 percent of those who are trying to find a way to get men into space, it would take a significant leap forward. (But then it might turn up the sad fact that lots of people don't want to go into space.)

Again, if this level of research were successful, it would also try to develop a resource excess and deficiency map of the world with respect to living wants, a set of hypotheses that explain the disparities, and an allocation model for standards of living.

The Third Inquiry

Supposing that we could acquire some evidence about living wants, I think then we should turn attention to the third inquiry: the determination of man's needs for self-expression. Do we live in a world where only a relatively few people have interest in science, the arts, sports, and other forms of the activity of creation and discovery? Or is intellectual curiosity and creative expression an essential need of everyone? If the need is general, what are our resources for satisfying it?

Here again, I know of no method that would produce reliable evidence of man's expressive needs. Whereas in the case of survival and living needs, the alternatives are fairly clear, the possibilities of self-expression are only vaguely ascertained. The arts and sciences are limitless in kind. I also think that we need to understand how much our world hampers creativity. How many murders of creative lives are committed each year by various forms of suppression?

The Fourth Inquiry

Finally, we require something more than a static inventory of wants and resources. The fourth inquiry asks how men's wants and needs move with time and environmental change. Are our want patterns developmental, random, or decadent? The fourth inquiry is the most important of all, because very likely this generation is not going to solve the problems of world peace. It may, however, be able to hand on to the next generation enough of a beginning to learning so that they can find the way. An essential part of this learning is the understanding of what men really want and how these wants change.

Implementation

What are the realistic possibilities of the suggestion contained in this paper? These are the steps of implementation that have occurred to me.

1. The establishment of Wants and Resources Agencies in national governments. These agencies would collect and classify information about national resources, and spot and analyze need centers. Hopefully, such agencies would be able to forecast survival and living needs long before events turned these needs into disaster. They would also try to forecast technological change. Finally, the agencies would also have the responsibility of recommending reallocation of resources to meet the needs.

2. A world research organization that would do much the same thing for the world population.

3. Inquiry without communication is blind; therefore, the na-

tional and international agencies would be responsible for public education on world needs, in articles, lectures, courses, editorials, etc.

4. A continuing "Geneva Conference" of scientists and civil servants from all nations concerned with human needs and resources.

Biases and Benefits

There remains to discuss two questions: (1) how to eliminate bias in the study of human needs, and (2) whether the proposal if carried out could do any good.

As for the existence of bias, the answer is obvious. Of course the East will show that the people of the West are unhappy and vice versa. This proposal does not show how the conflict can be directly solved by a means that is bound to succeed. Rather, the suggestion is to broaden the conflict as widely as possible, so that the issues are not merely political ones, but also matters of fact. There is some hope that when conflict turns into disagreement over what is or will be, there may be a basis for pushing the disagreement to a higher level of sophistication. Hence, there will be bias—yes. But the bias may be a good one.

Will a world inventory of wants and resources do any good? It certainly has a reactionary, Benthamite tone to it: reasonable man will be driven to seek policies that serve the greatest good of the greatest number. Of course I don't know that even a reasonable man would do anything of the kind. But our politicians and political experts make their decisions largely on an intuitive basis. This is the reason they can be so positive they are right. Many will look on reason and evidence as too slow-working a method to solve pressing problems of today. But those who still believe in reason and evidence will seek to find the means of confronting the decision-makers. The trouble with many plans for world peace is that they don't confront anybody with anything. They simply say that *if* men could be persuaded to do thus-and-so, then such-and-such desirable events would occur. But this is no confrontation, because probably man cannot be persuaded. I want to know enough about men so that I know they can be persuaded, and that the consequences will be desirable.

It is about time we knew what man wants without our being informed solely by conflicting and unsupported expert testimony. It is about time we understood what the problem of world peace really is: What do men want of their world anyway?

IMPROVING THE WORLD: THE BASIS FOR PEACEFUL COEXISTENCE

By G. I. POKROVSKY

THERE CAN BE NO DOUBT that a great part of humanity today realizes the catastrophic consequences of a war involving the use of modern means of mass extermination, nuclear, chemical, bacteriological, and so on. There are, however, a certain number of people who set out to prove the possibility of waging local small-scale wars in which destruction and killing could be limited and would not threaten humanity as a whole. There is no point in dwelling here upon the immorality and lack of integrity involved in this conception of destroying people, gradually, as it were, in small doses. But merely to point out the immorality and cynical nature of local and limited wars is not enough to prevent such wars from breaking out or to keep them from spreading into a global war that would threaten the whole of mankind with annihilation.

History teaches us that wars have always been determined by the material interests of the participants. It follows, then, that the struggle against war cannot be organized solely on an awareness of its disastrous consequences. What is needed is a firm material basis, involving the participation of all peoples in an undeniably practical and useful project that would demand peaceful cooperation between states, and would bring them and also individual firms and businessmen in the capitalist world more real and more reliable advantages than an unchecked and criminal arms race.

The task of contemporary science today is to find such a project and to prove to the world at large, including the business circles of the capitalist countries, that not only is this project profitable, but the profit to be gained from it far exceeds any that may accrue from the arms race and the fanning of war hysteria.

It is thus extremely important at the present time to establish which of the scientific and technical problems presented by modern science as a whole could prove to be the soundest and most realistic basis for international cooperation. In the present article an attempt is made to examine this task in some detail and to offer a possible solution.

Science and the World Economy

The rapid increase of man's power over nature and his ability to subject various forms of the movement of matter to mathematical analysis that has been a typical feature of the past century has resulted in the creation of technical undertakings embracing the whole world.

One can cite such obvious examples as the world systems of rail, road, sea, and air transport, the world cable and wireless system, which is rapidly outgrowing the frontiers of separate states, the electrical power transmission system, the systems of oil and gas pipelines, and many others.

The course of historical development of these forms of technology has followed an irresistible logical sequence. Each form of technology, originating and developing first within the framework of one state, has grown out of this framework, encompassed several different states, and subsequently developed into a system embracing whole continents and, finally, the whole of our planet.

The various forms of technology pass through this evolution in different ways according to their physical nature. Some forms, the railways, for example, or electric transmission lines, can at first be developed and brought to a considerable degree of perfection within the isolated territory of one state or a limited group of states. At any rate, a limit to the scale of such forms of technology can in principle be set and does not block the path to progress, although it does, of course, hinder progress to a certain degree.

There are, however, other forms of technology that from the very outset of their development cannot be strictly confined to a definite territory. Ordinary radio communication and broadcasting is a well-known example. The same is true of certain forms of space flight that are at present developing, particularly the putting into orbit around the earth of artificial satellites performing scientific and practical tasks concerning navigation, geodesy and cartography, radio communication and television.

It may thus be assumed that with the development of the scientific foundations of technology, the scale of its practical results constantly increases and to an ever greater extent embraces the whole world.

Science, Scale of Enterprise, and Profitability

The whole development of the world economy for centuries past indicates that an increase in the scale of technical and organizational undertakings leads to an increase in the profits deriving from them. Moreover, increase of scale should be understood in its widest sense. It involves not only the growth of capacities and resources, but also scientific planning for long periods ahead. In addition, the degree of scientific research into the physical processes on which the technology is based is of decisive importance. The bigger the scale of the project, the further ahead it is planned and the greater the resources and capacities involved, the deeper and more extensive this research must be. Maximum objectivity in the work of research and invention is also of importance. This requirement is best ensured by the organized, creative interaction of several organizations assisting each other, checking each other, and thus producing a reliable solution to the problem based on the objective laws of nature and human society.

It would seem that this means of tackling complex technical and organizational problems can be best implemented on a basis of co-operation between a few or even many states uniting their efforts on voluntary principles and carrying out the work in a spirit of maximum good will and mutual assistance.

The International Geophysical Year (1957–58) and also the well-known agreement of a number of countries on the study of Antarctica may be considered typical examples of such projects. These projects, however, cannot be regarded as a full-scale development of the idea under consideration. To obtain real, maximum benefit in the shortest possible time from a broad common effort, a far greater development in a practical direction is needed. It is most essential to satisfy this last condition so that proof of the usefulness of the project should stimulate the further development of common effort.

Long-Term Weather Forecasts

When considering technical and organizational problems that require international cooperation and that could produce considerable benefits for all peoples and states, one is primarily attracted to agriculture.

We know that agriculture in a number of countries is extremely dependent on unexpected changes in the weather. These changes prevent the planning of agricultural work or the carrying out of plans that are drawn up. In this respect agriculture differs considerably from manufacturing and mining, where planned processes can be brought to a high degree of perfection. Regions with low rainfall and artificial irrigation systems are to some extent an exception to the great dependence of agriculture on the weather.

In these regions human planning has for many centuries brought considerable success to agriculture. As we know, it was on this foundation that the culture of the ancient peoples inhabiting the valleys of the Nile, the Tigris, the Euphrates, and the Indus was built. But this exception only confirms the general rule that agriculture is extremely dependent on the vagaries of the weather.

This dependence is particularly evident in the less developed countries, which are primarily agrarian and where drought, floods, frosts, and hurricanes quite often bring national disaster that is subsequently intensified by terrible epidemics and a sharp aggravation of social contradictions. Agricultural damage and losses are multiplied by these consequences.

Assistance to underdeveloped countries guaranteeing them more regular participation in world trade could be ensured by providing for the whole world exact and reliable weather forecasts over a period of not less than one vegetative season, that is, four to six months.

One must stress at once the international, world-wide nature of this problem: phenomena determining the weather affect the atmosphere of the earth as a whole and are in no respect confined to the territory of separate states.

An International Space Weather Service

It must be admitted that consideration of this problem as a matter of first priority could arouse serious doubts and even objections as to its practicality. For a long time meteorology has been trying to provide long-term and short-term weather forecasts. So far, however, these forecasts have not been exact enough to satisfy the agricultural needs of many countries and areas of the globe.

The question therefore arises of how one can guarantee success of an attempt to improve weather forecasts on the basis of international cooperation. Unless this is clear from the start, the problem becomes pointless.

To provide a sufficiently convincing answer to this question we must refer to the data available on research into the upper atmosphere and the so-called geocorona that surrounds our planet.

On the basis of considerable information obtained with the aid of artificial satellites and space rockets by American and Soviet scientists, it has been established that the earth is surrounded by several radiation belts, currents of high-energy particles influenced by the earth's magnetic field. These belts girdle the earth, attaining their maximum thickness on the plane of the earth's equator. The earth's outer radiation belt, discovered quite recently by Soviet scientists, has a diameter of about 200,000 kilometers. The adjoining belt, which in the USSR has been studied by a research team under the leadership of Professor S. N. Vernov and in the United States by a group of scientists led by Van Allen, has an outer diameter of approximately 100,000 kilometers. The innermost belt is located comparatively close to the earth's surface. Over Europe its altitude is about 500 kilometers; over Australia it has an altitude of about 1,500 kilometers. This belt is strongly influenced by solar activity and apparently by other cosmic factors as well. The totality of these belts is known as the earth's corona or the geocorona. The geocorona cuts into the upper layer of the earth's atmosphere, which reaches, as has now been established, to an altitude of 3,000 kilometers.

The whole of this enormous system, enveloping the globe and moving with it in outer space, is also integrated with the lower layers of the atmosphere directly adjoining the surface of the earth. It is, as it were, a single organism and lives a single unified life. To study this system adequately it must be kept under constant observation not only near the earth but also at distances of up to 100,000 kilometers away from it. In addition, all streams of particles and irradiation entering the geocorona and the outer atmosphere from the sun and from outer space must be kept under constant observation from outer space.

Up to the present this has not been done and could not be done by meteorologists. Their instruments have regularly penetrated the atmosphere only to a distance of a few dozen kilometers, and even these penetrations have not been sufficiently regular and have not been effected in all areas of the globe. It is quite obvious that under such circumstances it cannot be considered that the system of the earth's atmosphere has been adequately studied. For the same reason there should be no surprise at the unsatisfactory state of weather forecasting.

From what has been said it follows that a satisfactory solution of the problem of long-term weather forecasting demands the organization of an international weather service which utilizes a sufficiently powerful system of artificial earth satellites with automatic radio apparatus for recording and transmitting to the earth characteristics of the upper atmosphere and likewise observations of the sun, radiation, and streams of particles entering the region of the earth from the cosmos. These satellites should move in orbits of from 13,000 kilometers to 200,000 kilometers in diameter. In addition, space rockets will evidently be needed to make ascents of up to 100,000 kilometers. It is most probable that for the further development of this project, manned space ships will also be needed to conduct research and deal with various complex and unexpected problems on the spot, as it were, without loss of time in preparing programs for automatic space apparatus and in analyzing their findings on earth.

Such a "space meteorological service" and a "space solar service" could be the subject of combined international effort. The most highly developed countries could produce and operate the powerful carrier-rockets. Countries less extensively equipped but possessing highly skilled instrument-making industries could produce and operate the automatic devices and radio apparatus. The underdeveloped countries could maintain observation posts on their territory and carry out other functions.

Profitability of Weather and Solar Services

Any attempt to calculate exactly what benefits would arise from the proposed improvement of weather forecasting would at the moment be rather unconvincing. However, this does not exclude the possibility of making some general estimate that could act as a guide. If we assume that the expected increase in precision in weather forecasting can reduce the losses in agriculture by approximately a third compared with the losses suffered today, and also take into account the additional losses suffered by the population through bad harvests, as well as from various natural disasters caused by unexpected changes in the weather, we may estimate the probable gains at approximately 200 billion dollars a year.

If we calculate that the space meteorological service would cost about 10 billion dollars a year, and the space solar service 5 billion dollars a year, and also leave 5 billion dollars in reserve in view of the novelty and probable rapid development of this branch of technology, the clear profit would amount to an annual figure of approximately 180 billion dollars. This sum is considerably larger than the total superprofits earned at present by firms producing military equipment and weapons in all the capitalist countries of the world. Part of this sum could be allotted to provide adequate profits for the firms producing space apparatus for peaceful purposes and thus create an economic situation in which the shareholders in firms producing armaments would simply change their shares for those of firms producing peaceful space apparatus. The basic stimulus of the arms race and the fanning of war hysteria required to keep it up would thus disappear.

This happy state of affairs cannot, of course, be achieved as simply as it might appear. The difficulty lies in directing the actual economic gains into the right channels and keeping them under the control of progressive world opinion. To achieve this there must be competent consideration of the problem by financial experts and statesmen with the necessary experience and initiative to solve complex international financial problems. However, given the conditions described here, we have indicated a physical and technical basis for solving the problem. As experience shows, the existence of such a basis is usually sufficient guarantee of the success of the economic and financial side of the matter.

Other Peaceful Uses of Weather and Solar Services

The question of space weather and solar services examined in the previous sections should not be regarded either as the only or as unquestionably the best way of developing peaceful cooperation between states. It is only one example, perhaps rather arbitrarily chosen. If the attention of the most active scientists, inventors, and organizers of all countries could be focused on finding new ways of developing scientific and technical cooperation among all states, it could undoubtedly yield an amazing wealth of ideas, proposals, and inventions.

Much else besides what has already been suggested could be proposed in the field of space rocketry. Take, for instance, the following problem: We know that a characteristic feature of the distribution and movement of population in our age is that large cities whose inhabitants can reach each other in the course of about one hour tend to grow particularly rapidly. Apparently this requirement is so essential that we have come to recognize a definite connection between the size of a populated area and the means of transport it possesses: the faster the transport, the wider the dispersion of population.

These conditions give rise to the following proposal. Is it not possible to provide mankind with the opportunity of communicating with one another, at any rate for essential purposes, in the same way as if they were all living in one city? Perhaps this, too, would help to relieve contradictions and tensions in the relations between states?

To solve this problem it would be necessary to have superfast transport, and this could be constructed on the basis of modern rocket techniques. Measures for reducing acceleration and deceleration strains are already quite a practical possibility; we therefore have good reason to believe that in a comparatively short time rocket transport will become comfortable enough not only for trained spacemen but also for ordinary passengers. It would be even easier to adapt intercontinental rockets for high-speed freighting of such peaceful cargoes as newspaper matrices or urgently needed medical supplies.

It is beyond the scope of this article to deal with the economic aspects of such projects. It should be remembered, however, that from the physical point of view a rationally constructed long-distance transport rocket (operating between New York and Antarctica, for example) would require less power than a high-speed aircraft, which would travel considerably slower.

Many other examples of the peaceful and progressive application of space rockets have been cited in the press. Taking all this into account, we may assume that modern science offers an almost unlimited number of projects for peaceful and profitable cooperation between states. Today it is not a matter of ideas, of science and technology. What is now needed is the good will to use the rich resources of modern science and technology for joint action by all states in the service of peace and progress for all people.

World-Wide Technology and Disarmament

It is generally realized that the problem of disarmament is a matter of great urgency. It would seem to be an undeniable conclusion of economic history that an enlargement of the scale of output and volume of trade on the basis of application of the latest achievements in technology always provides in the last analysis far greater advantages than the artificial maintenance of antagonism and disunity. In such circumstances disarmament sooner or later becomes not so much the result of special organizational measures as the natural consequence of the demise of war industries as insufficiently profitable forms of production.

At the same time it is obvious that the solution of many of the latest problems of science, technology, and culture can be achieved only when correspondingly large funds are available. At present even the biggest states cannot even mount a project for improving the climate of the whole or even parts of the globe. Such a project could be carried out only by mobilizing the great resources possessed by humanity as a whole. Even now there are prospects of changing the climate by transporting great masses of water, directing ocean currents, and also by modifying the reflective properties of the earth's surface (particularly of ice and snow) by spraying them with dyes, and so on. This can only yield practical results if the projects are conducted on a large scale involving the joint effort of all the nations of our planet.

It can be taken as an undisputed axiom that a considerable portion of the modern scientific potential remains unused and is even wasted merely because of the lack of ways of realizing it on an international scale through cooperation between states. Thus it may be said that the great achievements of human reason are coming into ever sharper and more intolerable conflict with the disjointed efforts of states and with an artificially boosted antagonism between peoples that is quite out of keeping with our epoch. Indisputably the course of history will sooner or later overcome this conflict; this, however, can be brought about only on the basis of consciously developed and strengthened friendship among the peoples of the earth.

Conclusion

The ideas suggested here make no claim to be a complete and exhaustive plan of action. They are merely a series of examples chosen rather subjectively and arbitrarily in the hope of stimulating creative thought and discussion concerning fields for international cooperation.

Though the problem has been only vaguely outlined, it should be considered absolutely clear that the solution of the problem of international cooperation cannot be postponed or reduced to an extremely small scale. Half-measures are not enough and delay must be eliminated. International cooperation for the joint solution of vital scientific and technical problems, as well as problems of a general cultural nature, should be considered one of the primary behests of the contemporary international policy of all countries of the world.

PART III

BUILDING A WORLD SOCIETY

INTRODUCTION

All of the papers in Part III are based on the assumption that a world society capable of settling international disputes and preventing war is possible, and that without such a society the maintenance of peace in the shrinking world will be increasingly difficult. The basic problem in preventing World War III is, therefore, the building of such a society. Observation of the history of groups merging into supersocieties indicates that such a development normally proceeds through four stages which may considerably overlap. They are (1) the establishment of *communication* and trade among independent groups; (2) the process of *acculturation* through mutual borrowing of technologies and syntheses of values; (3) the emergence of common cultural standards and techniques, inducing *cooperation* to maintain norms, achieve goals, and promote common interests in the developing culture; and (4) the increase of the efficiency of such cooperation by the establishment of a central *organization* with authority to recommend, guide, or even compel appropriate action, at first by the component groups and eventually by individuals.

This process may be reversed, as in the history of empires. Organization may come first through conquest compelling cooperation and gradually establishing a uniform culture and regular communication, but this effort to force the natural evolution of a supersociety has not often been successful in the long run. The component groups resent compulsion and resist cultural incorporation. Empires usually break up as national movements develop in the component parts.

The process of federation has elements of both peaceful union and compulsory unification. Federations have never been voluntarily established unless the processes of communication and acculturation have developed a considerable measure of cultural uniformity and voluntary cooperation among the federating states. Furthermore, resort to central compulsion by the federal authority has often led to resistance and sometimes secession and war, as in the Swiss Sonderbund War and the American Civil War.

In the essays in Part III the writers explore the possibility that an effective world society will develop naturally from the present situation of general communication, general vulnerability, and emerging general organization coupled with great ideological, cultural, and political divergencies. Each suggests steps which might be taken by governments or international organizations to forward this process. These suggestions can be classified according to the stages set forth above as proposals for improved communication of information and understanding, improved cultural and social integration, improved norms of cooperation, or improved organization with powers of compulsion.

Development of International Communication

The Yugoslav physicist, Ivan Supek, emphasizes the role of free communication, especially among scientists of all nations, who with the common language of nuclear science can reach common understanding of the possibility of human creativity. "With the dissolution of classical determinism scientific man has regained his freedom. We are no longer driven to observational passivity by the automatism of a mechanical cosmos . . . Now, in proceeding from human activity, we are immediately oriented toward the future—which we create, more or less consciously" (p. 295).

Supek does not call for a party of scientists but states that the universal spirit of science is "what we most need in the national parliaments and in the halls of the United Nations" (p. 298). "Until recently 'secrecy' could be justified in the interest of national defense; today, it is quite obvious where the 'defense' of the West and the East has brought us. Universal science has been given a new start, and the increased influence of scientists will help break the wall raised between the world powers" (p. 297).

Zellig S. Harris views the possibility of creating an auxiliary world language with considerable optimism and discusses some technical problems of constructing such a language, but emphasizes that: "Neither in social nor in international conflicts can peace or understanding be reached by overcoming semantic confusions. For the conflicts are due not to semantic differences, but to real clashes of interest —between employer and employed, between ruler and ruled, between competing economic and governmental groups" (p. 307). Semantics, he explains, is used in international controversy as a rationalization of positions taken for economic or political reasons, not to develop mutual understanding. He believes that language in politics is the handmaid of interests, thus differing from the scientists who perceive in the common language of science a means of modifying interests. Harris does not deny the value of easy communication among travelers, merchants, and scientists (as distinct from translator-equipped governments), though its influence on international affairs is problematic. "The creation of an auxiliary language may therefore be worth attempting, even if we can only guess at the pressures and chains of circumstances that might bring it into use or at its possible consequences for the development of actions and attitudes transcending national lines" (p. 302).

The Growth of Universal Culture

The problem of whether freer communication can generate better understanding and common values is discussed in sociological terms by Talcott Parsons. (For a discussion in political terms, see the essay by the present writer, pp. 410–441).

Parsons sees in the bipolarization of the world, dangerous as it is, an opportunity for building a world society: "For the first time in history, we must acknowledge the existence of a *world* political community, at least in a relative sense. Through the development of mass media of communication, the nations of the world have become increasingly aware of their interdependence. Inevitably important events in any major country will have rapid repercussions in all others. Indeed, any attempt to isolate a subsystem, unless that system is one of minor intrinsic significance, must rely on special insulating mechanisms which impose rather rigid controls. With rapidly diminishing exceptions, we are all members of the world political community—for better or worse" (p. 310).

This situation, he thinks, makes possible a dialectic by which the thesis of free democracy and the antithesis of Communism can develop a synthesis in values, norms, interests, and ideologies. He proposes policies of states and international organizations by which divergent ideologies, like parties in a constitutional system, may react upon each other peacefully and constructively to effect this synthesis p. 317). He finds that there are a wealth of common values and norms in the two systems and a pluralism of interests which may gradually disintegrate the apparent monolithic character of the Communist system—so as to reveal that apparent ideological differences are protectionist devices permitting different social systems to develop their potentialities without too rapid disintegration under the influence of other systems.

International Cooperation and the Rule of Law

Two papers emphasize the role of law in providing the necessary basis for peaceful cooperation among states. Arthur Larson indicates the extent to which legal issues are involved in current international disputes and suggests as building blocks of the law structure of peace a body of law and tribunals for applying it that are accessible, up-to-date and capable of settling the disputes that cause tension; such acceptance of that law that peoples in all the civilizations of the world will regard it as their law; and compliance with the decisions of the tribunals. The last condition he finds least difficult, although many people worry about it. The first two conditions are in a measure satisfied by the existence of general international law, a network of bilateral and multilateral treaties, and the International Court of Justice. Improvements in both the rules and the accessibility of law are needed, and a major difficulty exists in the limited acceptance of the compulsory jurisdiction of the Court. The article should correct some widespread misconceptions of the nature and functions of law in building a world society.

Roger Fisher's contribution is similar, elaborating on Larson's first and third points. Fisher assumes that a world legislature to enact formal law by majority vote and a world executive with enough power to enforce it are not likely among sovereign states in the immediate future; but he believes this need not prevent either the development of international law or its general observance. He examines realistically the sanctions of that law provided by reactions of the state injured by a violation, and also by other states and world public opinion. Furthermore, the sentiment within governments that law ought to be observed and the inertia of the national decision-making authorities—making it easier to follow custom and precedent than to depart from them—support observance of international law. He also indicates that, apart from the often difficult treaty-making process, rules of international law may evolve through conduct or articulation of a rule by a single government, or through resolutions of international bodies, such as the United Nations General Assembly, engendering tacit agreement or custom. His analysis points to practical ways for moving toward rules for arms regulation if formal agreement fails. In some cases, he believes informal or tacit agreement, less susceptible of evasion by verbal argument, may be even more effective than written instruments.

The Organization of World Security

Ever since the founding of the United Nations much thought has been given to the strengthening of this international organization as an agency for preserving world peace. The demand for international organization with coercive power was widespread after World War II. Accordingly, provisions for enforcing commitments to refrain from aggression and to observe decisions of the International Court of Justice are to be found in the United Nations Charter. But their applicability has been seriously restricted by the great-power veto.

Louis Sohn sees hope of strengthening the United Nations through the action of the smaller states that now abound in the organization. Realizing their dependence on the United Nations and reflecting a world opinion that atomic war must be prevented, they favor adequate safeguards of peace, tend to assume a neutralist position between the great power blocs, and recognize the strength they gain from the anxiety of both power blocs lest this third of the world's population and resources be driven to the other side. Sohn proposes devices for assuring the "positive neutralism" of these states in the General Assembly and of the Secretary-General supported by them. By skillful leadership of this pro-United Nations neutralism of the lesser states, which he hopes may include all except actual members of the NATO and Warsaw alliances, he believes that the United Nations may inspire confidence that its decisions are fair to all and that its legislative, judicial, and executive powers may be gradually extended.

While these essays on building the world society give different and in some cases conflicting emphases, they are in the main complementary and justify a certain confidence that with the present atomic stalemate, unstable as it is, a world society capable of maintaining peace may emerge before the cold war degenerates into a hot war.

Q.W.

THE UNIVERSALITY OF SCIENCE: OUR LAST HOPE

By IVAN SUPEK

Translated from the German by Marianne Cowan

BEFORE WE CONDEMN SCIENCE, which under its various political tutors has led the world to the brink of disaster, we had better ask whether it does not offer us hope after all, perhaps the last hope we have in the suicidal race for armaments. Despite the decline of militant internationalism and the continued existence of an ideologically supercharged atmosphere out of which the Babel of diplomatic conferences emerges, the universal spirit of science has been preserved. "Atomic policing" and narrow-hearted national demands have not destroyed it. It is the common bridge which leads across the river of death to the shores of peace. Nonpartisan truth and its revolutionary applications are creating a common ground which extends on both sides of the red boundary-stone. Even though the disputing parties may seem to be caught fast in their ancient differences, their evolutionary development is nonetheless approaching similar goals.

What most impedes mutual understanding today is our inability to think anew when faced with new reality, or rather, with a new reality potential. All our old words are dirtied and loaded, more often banners of war than means of communication. And so the first demand of the moment is to avoid all provocative slogans that plunge us into the abyss of hatred. In addition to our ideological name-calling, a number of ancient philosophies serve to intensify the prevailing cold war. Fortunately all parties concerned do have a common language, the language of science. We need to tackle our problems with the sincerity and lack of prejudice that scientists bring to theirs. By all means let us honor tradition. But our noblest tradition rests in ever-increasing cultural advance, not in sacred terminologies.

Modern atomic physics has overcome many older views which had irreconcilably split the philosophical schools. Thus it has opened the door to new syntheses. Einstein's theory of relativity and (even more decisively) the quantum theory interpretations by Bohr and Heisenberg have brought to the fore the innate oneness of man and nature. The metaphysical segregation of subject and object, of spirit and matter, has thus lost its seeming scientific support. To quote a slightly altered Faust: "In the beginning was activity." In today's science, which leans more toward experimentation and less toward passive observation, this dialectic is strongly felt. What seemed to us to be purely objective now turns out to have subjective features; what long appeared to be a structure of the abstract imagination now proves to be the most adequate form for new laws. The world understood as activity in history is much more complex and much more meaningful than the world reflected by simple mirror images, and classical determinism is replaced by statistical prognoses.

With the dissolution of classical determinism scientific man has regained his freedom. We are no longer driven to observational passivity by the automatism of a mechanical cosmos. This change is decisive so far as insight and creativity are concerned, for the world without human intervention is an empty concept. Now, in proceeding from human activity, we are immediately oriented toward the future—which we create, more or less consciously. Our will had been lulled to sleep by the belief that science had a predetermined object. Instead, science is found to be continuously creative. Like the world itself, it permits continuous discovery. Our actions and our insight go beyond ourselves. The products of human activity exist in relationship to each other as well—a dialectic which clears all existentialist irresponsibility out of the way. Absolute freedom, on the other hand, could only originate from nothingness and dissolve into nothingness—an empty verbal specter.

Science in the form of creative research has more and more enriched our reality. Its progress—whose rate of increase is proportional to its magnitude—has surged forward with exponential rapidity. After a certain stage (roughly during the first decades of our century), this exponential growth gained the upper hand. Newly discovered processes are being included in social production with steadily increasing impetus. Scientific applications have completely altered classical industry with its manually-skilled proletariat. The increasing number of laboratories with their armies of scientific workers are orienting all our industrial practices in undreamed-of directions and displacing the old-fashioned entrepreneur. The fact that the economy of the West does not succumb to wretchedness is not a miracle wrought by the concepts of liberalism. It is science that has enriched men's labor to such an extent, and produced such effective forms of organization, that a number of developmental features have been completely altered. The undreamed-of increase in efficiency has benefited the masses in the West as well as the East. The resulting creation of a richer domestic market has frequently prevented trade cycles from running wild. The fact that (either involuntarily or through enlightenment) a number of ancient imperialist powers are relinquishing their colonies is at least in part due to their realization that the most valuable raw materials and the most abundant working force can be found in their own scientific laboratories. Despite ideological shots in the arm, the old free-enterprise economy lies dying, and new organizational forms are pushing up on both sides of the Iron Curtain. Alongside the old ringleaders, science too is now acquiring the guiding hand—an epoch-making development!

As a result of the tremendous increase in power, especially that due to nuclear energy, science has given the means for total destruction into the hands of the military staffs of East and West. So far political negotiations have run up against a stone wall and one cannot visualize how they might be finally settled. And yet, if this co-existence founded on rocket bases is to extend indefinitely, the end will dawn in a technical failure or a political or human eclipse.

In the desperation of a world so divided, where can there be any hope? The answer is: just exactly at the point of greatest danger. If science has forged the hellish sword, it has also provided the salvation. In spite of all enslavements and all misuses, the universal spirit of science cannot be throttled without throttling science itself. An international homeland has risen above and beyond all national boundaries, a nonpartisan mother who brings up all her children in equal truth. The universal atmosphere surrounds the battlefields of all the earth; beneath its peaceful winds a similar social development is taking place. And this will be our common platform toward ultimate mutual understanding.

Though history from its very beginnings has been impelled onward by economic necessity and personal ambition, our highly organized society with its effective technology today makes consciously purposeful action the decisive factor. We may no longer regard the future as a product of the old historical forces. The immense power of modern science enables us to "produce our future" in all its essentials ourselves, always keeping in view, of course, our reality potentials. The creation of developmental perspectives has become the highest duty of science, and the creation of the necessary tools the highest task of society. The world is still ruled by stereotypes. The transition from the old power-pyramid to a scientific organization is one of the essential features of today's crisis.

Scientific development requires means of increasing magnitude; consequently, their adequate application is feasible only on a world-wide scale. The repetition of effort in our currently split and isolated world encampments and the ever-increasing gap between highly developed and underdeveloped countries show our crass irrationality. The alliance of nations is not only a necessity in the face of atomic death, it is the imperative of our whole development.

At the crossroads of total destruction and undreamed-of advances, science has a fateful mission. After political inertia has driven the world into the forecourts of hell, it would be a mistake to try to found a political party of scientists. Pasteur once said that science has no fatherland but the scientist does. International cooperation has, however, offered a "home" to many scientists. Real patriotism, especially under present conditions, can by no means hinder universal humanism. Though three internationals have failed, the community of human culture has not been destroyed by political action, in spite of "atomic" policy and in spite of ideological declarations. Until recently, "secrecy" could be justified in the interest of national defense; today, it is quite obvious where the "defense" of the West and the East has brought us. Universal science has been given a new start, and the increased influence of scientists will help break the wall between the world powers. It is of utmost importance that the scientific-technical and educational organizations of the United Nations obtain more authority in solving international problems and thus, beside the diplomatic corps, form a new element in building up the world union. In exile, Albert Einstein often dreamed of the existence of a single state on our planet. Instead of merely visualizing the final image, we should rather find the way to peace amidst the jungle of prejudice and hatred.

The whole world—now stiffened in its historical controversies—is horror-stricken at the vision of meeting its death. Should the co-existence of nuclear-electronic automata continue in this ideologically overcharged atmosphere, one finger might—in a fit of terror and madness—push the whole planet into oblivion. Neither classes nor principles are at stake any longer. The whole human race, with the prospect of beauty and goodness before it, nevertheless stands on a political scaffold. Whether an amnesty will be granted at the last moment depends upon the effectiveness of the philosophy of reconciliation.

Science must continue to be universal. Its development must continue to undermine the fortified walls. By pledging ourselves to follow the guidance of scientific progress we can best aid all society everywhere. The universities, academies, institutes, and scientific societies must step forth from their helpless isolation and act as the "hand of destiny" to put a stop to blind desperation. What we most need in the national parliaments and in the halls of the United Nations is the universal spirit of science. It would be wise if the General Assembly of the United Nations were to fortify itself with a Science Council; the same is true for the national parliaments. A decisive peace factor would be introduced into world politics by such scientific councils and conferences, and many a now hopeless-seeming gap might be bridged. The engagement of science in the creation of a new world of peace is the burning need of our time.

The future can be what we want it to be. In this lies our freedom and our necessity. Gone forever are those comfortable points of view from which we used calmly to contemplate a cosmic order. Modern science has taught us that the world is our business. Our reality, erected at the edge of the abyss, is seeking its leaders. And universal science cannot dodge this duty. May man's good will drive the demons of chaos and terror out of the way of the future!

A LANGUAGE FOR INTERNATIONAL COOPERATION

By ZELLIG S. HARRIS

PROPOSALS FOR AN INTERNATIONAL AUXILIARY LANGUAGE were relatively widespread in the decades around the turn of the century, when hopes for a more decent and reasonable world society were common and perhaps a bit innocent. The proposals, too, were too simple to be viable. The languages were constructed with some arbitrariness; and there was not enough knowledge of how a language could be constructed so as to be more adequate for carrying particular kinds of information and discussion, or so as to be more easily used by the speakers of the existing major languages. And little thought was given to the question of what conditions, and what chains of social events, might lead to the actual use of such an auxiliary language. It is possible now to consider these questions somewhat more carefully.

Potential Uses of a World-Wide Auxiliary Language

The failure of past proposals does not mean that languages for communication across linguistic boundaries are impossible. Occurrences of an auxiliary lingua franca are known in various places in the world: pidgin English in the South Sea Islands, Swahili in eastern Africa. Such auxiliary tongues enable speakers of different languages to converse with each other. And the mere learning of a second language is not a difficult matter. In border areas (e.g., at the German-French border) and in countries in which different languages are spoken (e.g., Morocco, with Arabic and Berber) large parts of the population can speak a second language. The failure of the proposed international languages has been due not to the impossibility of maintaining a second or auxiliary language but to lack of a social basis, of real occasion for its use. There is also no need to fear that an international language would soon break up into local dialects. Modern communication operates against dialect formation. And an auxiliary language would have little regional life, and is not likely to be increasingly swallowed up by the local language.

It is not easy to see what pressing and continuing uses such a language could have in the world of today, and for what groups of people. One use might be a lingua franca for scientists, and for other occupational groups which deal with their colleagues in other countries. But the language could hardly be kept up if its only use was in occasional conversations. If a Japanese learns English in order to read scientific articles, he will hardly use an international language in speaking to an English scientist. A lingua franca for science could perhaps be maintained if scientific works for international use (excluding those textbooks or research and discussions which are used only locally) were all translated into a common auxiliary language, so that scientists would not have to learn foreign languages (aside from the auxiliary) in order to read the works of foreign scientists or in order to talk with them.

At present, few scientific articles are translated (except, for war reasons, between Russian and English), and only the major scientific books get translated into a few other languages, usually only after several years. Many scientists acquire some knowledge of the major languages of science (and of politics); in effect, Russian-satellite scientists can read Russian, and scientists in the rest of the world often learn English. In the smaller or less technological countries, scientists often write their major articles in English. However, for most people, reading the foreign language is harder and slower, with the result that in the major countries working scientists, after their school days are over, read little except what is written in their own language. In some fields, like physics, the problem is reduced because the great bulk of major articles is published in English or Russian; in mathematics, chemistry, and biology, the concentration is far less. This whole situation fosters certain insularities and delays in the scientific work of various countries—though this is not to say that different schools of work in a science are not desirable, and inevitable, even within a single country, on the basis of close personal communication.

Translating scientific, technical, and practical writing in a routine manner, perhaps even mechanically, into a specially constructed common language would be easier than translation of all writing between arbitrary languages, because of the greater explicitness and simplicity of the grammar of scientific writing, and because these grammatical features can be reflected in the constructed language. We here distinguish science writing from the language arts, and from writing in the fields of values, opinion, and persuasion (criticism and comment, philosophy, politics, propaganda), where translation is more a matter of judgment, and where a constructed language, necessarily poor in connotations, ranges of meaning, grammatical allusion, and the like, may prove an inadequate vehicle. The translation problem is less important here, because it is precisely in the language arts and value fields (which are less technical and have wider audiences) that books are widely translated at present.

It thus appears that a real social use exists for something which is technically possible: a common language for translation, and for talking with foreigners, in scientific and practical matters. This may be too limited a use, involving too restricted an audience, to constitute by itself the occasion for the rise of such a language. Other realistic uses are possible, for example in the growing international travel, and in technological activities requiring direct, even if brief, communication among people of different parts of the world. There are also uses related to linguistic theory and application. For example, we will see, when we discuss some technical problems of constructing the language, that a well-constructed detailed auxiliary would be of great value to linguistic research, and would have some of the properties useful for an intermediate translation language (for translating from one language to the auxiliary and from it to the second language).

It is of course possible that if a sensible, promising, and not too difficult language is devised, those who wish to establish contact with people in other countries might learn and use this language. Although such plans have failed in the past, this kind of use might possibly develop in the shadow of the bomb. The fact that man has never had an auxiliary language in the sense considered here is not in itself an argument against the possibilities of the future, just as the absence of a complex decent social structure in the past is no argument against the possibility of one in the future. Under the new conditions and dangers that are developing, men may be led to do what they have not needed or been able to do in the past.

The presence of possible social uses, however, and even of social needs, is no guarantee that a particular solution, or any solution, will arise. Every social institution and behavior has been adjusted to by the people involved, and the process of changing is usually more difficult and costly to them than going on with the existing ways, no matter how inefficient or harmful these may be. Gradual changes go on all the time, but these rarely make a major difference, and in any case can hardly bring about such a specific thing as an international language. Sharp changes and overturns also pepper human history;

but these appear in special and extreme circumstances, of a kind not foreseeable for such an incidental as an auxiliary language. When extreme circumstances do come, they can in general make use only of already developed alternatives, rather than suddenly create new social forms (though the new use of existing social alternatives may look like a new social form). In this sense, social preparation in a direction which seems to us possible and desirable may not be wasted, even if we cannot foresee the need or opportunity which may bring it into real life. The creation of an auxiliary language may therefore be worth attempting, even if we can only guess at the pressures and chains of circumstances that might bring it into use or at its possible consequences for the development of actions and attitudes transcending national lines.

However, our present interest in an auxiliary language is not as a tool for such specific needs, but as a social instrument which might facilitate the cooperation of individuals in spite of national conflicts, and which might have some effect toward counteracting the divisive national languages and cultures. Naturally, one cannot expect too much. The opinion-molding institutions and the instruments of social control enable the ruling social elements in each nation to affect the opinions and actions of their population in the direction of international hatreds and conflicts, far more than such supranational considerations as the common human destiny and emotions, the increasingly world-wide sciences and arts, and the direct communication made possible by a general human language, could affect people toward world peace and cooperation. Nevertheless, we cannot doubt that people could feel themselves more a part of an interrelated world population if they had a common language which they could use with other human beings of whatever land. And aside from how people feel and see themselves, there is also the matter of practical possibilities of behavior.

If people were able to talk to each other across national boundaries, it would be easier for people (as distinct from translator-equipped governments) to exchange opinions on their common problems, and to act jointly. Such communication is more possible today, with the increased international travel and with the possibility of world-wide immediate conversation through communication satellites. Finally, if we are to face reality, rather than just hope that the interests of ruling groups and the inability to act of ruled populations will somehow run their course without nuclear war, we may have to think of a situation in which the governments have destroyed themselves together with much of their populations, and in which the remaining people will have to find direct ways of dealing with each other.

Structure of a World-Wide Language

We have seen that an auxiliary language may be more likely to come into use if it is technically superior for various purposes, and much easier to learn, than the existing major languages of the world. While it might seem impossible to construct a language easily learnable for the people of many different countries, modern linguistics gives considerable information on how this can be attempted. And we must realize that whereas Esperanto was merely based on Latin, with elements from current European languages, today's language would have to suit not only the Germanic-Romance-Slavic languages, but also Chinese and Japanese, some of the major languages of Southeast Asia, Indic and Dravidian, Arabic, and perhaps the main Finno-Ugric and African languages.

Before we consider the structure of an auxiliary language and how it should relate to the existing ones, it should be mentioned that no language can be constructed directly on the basis of general laws of thought, or any fixed system of concepts and relations. No laws of thought adequate to language, and no sets of terms and operations sufficient or necessary for science, are yet known. What is known today about the processes of thought, or about the universe of discourse and the methods of statement for science as a whole, is uncertain, vague, episodic, and lacking in definitive frame of reference. The systems of logic and mathematics are explicit and powerful, but apply only to truth-value and to a few kinds of relations, most of them ultimately set-theoretic. They are not sufficient for science, for practical affairs, or for the value-judgmental fields. Natural language, however, has been sufficient for man; or rather, man has only been able to express explicitly that which he could put into language, with the addition of such special tools as mathematics, representational methods like graphs, and the apparatus of gesture. For the part handled by language, the only method available now is not to find out semantically what the speaker really means and express this in some new system natural to all people, but to follow whatever way natural language has developed for expressing things in an open, inadequate but adjustable, system—in effect, simply to translate what the speaker says into an intermediate common language which the hearer or reader can understand. An auxiliary language would therefore be based not on some theory of thought and knowledge but on the existing languages.

The learnability and intertranslatability of the auxiliary can be best considered under three heads: sounds (and writing), vocabulary, grammar.

Sounds. The sounds of a language are arbitrary. The only thing that can be asked is that the auxiliary should not contain any sounds or sound-combinations which speakers of any major language cannot discern or pronounce, and above all should not contain any sound-distinctions which are automatic sound-replacements in any major language (whose speakers have learned to disregard these particular sound-differences). Furthermore, since the sounds of the auxiliary will be pronounced by each person in a manner related to his own language, the auxiliary should avoid such sounds or letters as would be pronounced in unrecognizably different ways by different people. Beyond this, the only consideration is that the sounds be simple and clearly distinguishable. Finally, the auxiliary would have to contain some approximation to the sounds used in the present scientific terms and international words, since they would be incorporated into the language. All these requirements restrict the advisable complement of sounds, and some compromises will have to be made; but the cautions indicated here can be followed in practice to a considerable extent.

There is also the matter of the writing system—undoubtedly alphabetic, and most likely based on the very widespread Latin letters. But problems would arise in assigning letters to the sounds in such a way as to minimize confusions and difficulties.

Vocabulary. Vocabulary presents more complicated problems. The many international words—scientific, cultural, political—would undoubtedly be retained, and in a form which most speakers can recognize on the basis of their own pronunciation or spelling of the word. For the mass of remaining vocabulary, the burden of learning should presumably be spread among the major languages in some way. That is, some words would be taken from each major language, so that the speakers of that language would at least not have to learn those particular words. Various considerations can be used in deciding which words should be taken from which language—depending, for example, on the semantic adequacy of the word, on the amount of help that this word is likely to give to those who know it in remembering or guessing the meaning of other words which occur with it in a sentence of the auxiliary language.

In addition to this question about the stock of words—what sound-sequences shall be taken for the various meanings—there are two more complicated problems with respect to vocabulary.

One is the ranges of meaning for each word. The way in which range of meaning is cut up for assignment to words differs in different languages: in English, *floor* means flooring and house-level, while *plane* means flat surface; but in Italian, *pavimento* means flooring, while *piano* means house-level and flat surface. As a result, the translation of *floor* is sometimes *pavimento* and sometimes *piano,* while the translation of *piano* is sometimes *floor* and sometimes *plane.* Since people who use the auxiliary language will be translating from their own (more, even, than people who just learn a foreign language), they will tend to use the words of the auxiliary with the meaning-ranges of their own language. In making the dictionary of the auxiliary, in stating what meaning-ranges each word has and what its translation is in each language (for each of its meanings), it will be necessary to seek such an assignment of meaning-ranges to words as will be easiest to translate for each major language, and at the same time will offer least misunderstanding between speakers of different languages. And this without greatly increasing the number of words in the vocabulary; for one costly direction of solution is simply to reduce the range of meaning of each word by introducing separate words for each discernible meaning. All this is a very cumbersome problem. However, investigations in this area may be useful for current activity about translation; and it is therefore possible that they may be carried out.

Grammar. The other problem leads from vocabulary to grammar. It is the question of how the vocabulary shall be divided as between independent and derived words. In German, *Grundlage* contains the word *Grund,* "ground"; its translation in English, *foundation,* is just a noun-form of the independent verb *found,* "establish." Thus a word *W* in one language may contain ("be derived from") certain other words, *Y, Z* of that language; whereas its translation *W′* in another language may not contain the corresponding words (translations) *Y′, Z′* of the other language; *W′* may be an independent word, or it may contain words other than *Y′, Z′*. Since the stock of words in a language is one of the hardest things to learn, being arbitrary and large, it is desirable to have a relatively small stock of independent words and prefixes and suffixes, and to have the great bulk of the words of the language built up out of these independent words and affixes. However, it is necessary that the way in which words are built up (the "rules" by which words are "derived" from other words) should be as simple as possible, as consistent as possible with the way people think and speak, and describable in a general way, so that if anyone forms a word—new or just unknown to him—out of parts, people anywhere can understand its meaning fairly accurately from the component elements and the rules of combination—plus the environment in which the word is used. And it is desirable that the methods and meanings of these combining operations be translatable into, or understandable on the basis of, those of the major languages.

Finally, we have to consider the way in which words are arranged so as to form a sentence. Here certain linguistic results are particularly useful. In all languages, speaking and writing consists of a series of word-strings, each string being what we may call a sentence. It appears that in all languages there are certain simple sentence structures, with all of the more complicated or longer sentences being built up out of these (either by combining two sentences—themselves simple or combined—or by altering the shape of a simple or combined or already altered sentence). To a large extent, and perhaps to as complete an extent as the language is analyzed, these operations of combining and altering sentences depend not on the meaning or individuality of the sentences, but only on their structure and word-classes. This means that, for each language separately, a method can be found for breaking down each sentence into its component sentences and the operations used on them, or for applying the operations to simple sentences so as to obtain complex ones. Furthermore, the substantive meaning (though not the stylistic effect) of each sentence is not changed by this reduction; it is equivalent to the meaning of the component sentences and operations (especially the combining operations). Finally, while the operations of one language may differ appreciably from those of another, the simple sentence structures are rather similar, much more similar than the complex sentences of the two languages.

As a result of all this, if for each major language we find the method of decomposing its complex sentences into its simple ones, we would have a simpler ("basic") version of that language: namely, its simple sentence structures plus its operations (chiefly the combining ones). If the auxiliary is constructed so as to be as similar as possible, or rather as translatable as possible, to the simple versions of each major language, we would have a very effective auxiliary. In order to learn the auxiliary, each person would have to learn how to reduce the sentences of his own language, and then how to translate between his reduced sentences and the auxiliary. Learning how to decompose the sentences of one's own language is tantamount to learning the grammar of one's language in this form. And translation from the reduced sentences is related to the general method of a proceduralized translation, for translation between the reduced versions of two languages, directly or through an intermediate like the auxiliary, is much easier and more orderly than translation from the complex sentences of one language to those of another.

Semantic Confusions vs. Conflicting Interests

Any discussion about the possibilities of a world-wide language for cooperation among people must first clear away the common misconception that semantics is a key to mutual understanding. Neither in social nor in international conflicts can peace or understanding be reached by overcoming semantic confusions. For the conflicts are due not to semantic differences, but to real clashes of interest—between employer and employed, between ruler and ruled, between competing economic and governmental groups.

Not only are semantic confusions not causes of class and national conflicts; they do not even deepen these conflicts to any appreciable degree. The chief effect they have on the conflicting sides is to diffuse the conscious scope of conflict, so that each group doesn't even understand the opponents' arguments, and pays them little heed, where if it did understand them it would merely oppose them more explicitly. If workers talk about their customary practices and pace in carrying out the work they do, while the boss talks about management prerogatives in allocating or in timing their work, no conflict will be reduced by bringing these terms to a common denominator. If the American government speaks about freedom (or about the occupation of Eastern Europe), and the Russian government about bread (or about colonialism), no lessening of the cold war can be expected from clarifying the arguments. As always, the attack on the opponent will contain much truth, the defense of oneself will be mealy-mouthed and dishonest. If one makes a critique of the meaning of "free" for the victims of all the employers, institutions, and courts that cooperated with McCarthyism, if one asks what is the meaning of "workers' state" for the Russian regime, one may find hoary techniques of propaganda, but no key to peace. And with the social and international differences inherent in the structure of the human world today, it is certain that crucial conflicts will occur which no semantics can mitigate.

Even the more powerful critique by the sociology of knowledge can only show what economic and political conditions motivate each opponent, partly expressed and partly camouflaged by what he says; it cannot in general lead to a resolution of the conflict. The function that the semantic camouflages have, indeed, is to square the actions of governments and economic or political groups with the values which they, or those whose support they need, maintain at least overtly. A semantic clarification therefore will often have the effect not of removing error or of bringing people's understandings together, but of unmasking this camouflage. The unmasking, however, does not free the actor to act differently, nor the supporter to remove his support, because the direction of action and support is limited by the possibilities and needs of each group: the interests of the Russian government in controlling Eastern Europe remain even after the meaning of "people's democracy" for Hungary or wherever is unmasked; the interests of American business and government in Guatemala and Cuba remain, independently of the way the question is treated in public statements; the employer has to get as much as he can from his workers, even if the "agitators" whom he blames are semantically clarified as being the dissatisfactions and needs of the employees; and the workers have to find employment under some employer even if they understand that employment means not just work but the control of others over their work.

The chief case where something like verbal camouflage has a deep effect, making people accept and support situations which they might otherwise oppose, is in systems of outlook and belief, for example religious or national, which the members of a population find around them from childhood on. By the same token, however, no semantic analysis can by itself free the people from the concepts and attitudes which are inculcated by these long-term formulations and which are integrated with the existing institutions of control, social intercourse, and production.

All this is not to say that clarification of meanings, in the popular sense of "semantics," and unmasking of social sources in the sense of the sociology of knowledge, are not valuable. But these critiques can affect the world which they describe only in certain social constellations, those same ones in which positive ideals (such as freedom of belief, rationalism, civil liberty and equality, socialism) can be moving forces—that is when ideas, critical or positive, can be weapons: when the social groups to whom the ideas are addressed have alternatives actually available to them—in terms of the organization of work, of different international alliances and military possibilities, etc.—which the ideas can help them use.

We have stressed here the limitations of popular semantics, in order to remove any expectation that an international language would lead to common understanding (most social conflicts and not a few wars are fought within a common language), or that it can be so constructed as to have explicit and fixed meanings which would deter intentional or unintentional falsification. Every language (excluding formal systems, such as mathematics) has to be open to new meanings and extensions of meaning and to new understandings; no language can be structurally protected from containing false or confusing statements. Methods of checking and criticizing may be developed, based both on logic and on the structure of scientific writing, which would be useful in recognizing or correcting falsehoods, ignorance, or points of view. But such methods would be ex post facto tests of what has been said; they cannot (except in restricted conditions) be built in as a priori structure of the language in order to limit what can be said.

Conclusion

We have seen that a world-wide auxiliary language is not impossible in principle, but would fill certain present needs, and could come into use if an adequate language were formed, and if a chain of social events favored it. We have also seen that while an international language will not eliminate conflict, it can help people see themselves as part of the whole of humanity rather than as members of particular nations, and can help understanding and cooperation among people (if not among governments). The excellence of the construction of the language is itself a factor that would affect its spread; a rough picture already exists of how to construct an effective auxiliary language, or of what has to be investigated in order to know how to construct one. Such a language would require the collaboration of linguists and other scientists from different countries. The necessary research could be initiated by individual scientists of different countries, by scientific societies, or possibly even by UNESCO or some other agency of the United Nations.

There is reason to think that such a language will be simpler and easier to learn than the present utilization of foreign languages, and that it (and the investigations toward it) may find many uses in addition to those of peace and social cooperation. If effort is being expended in searching the skies for signals transmitted by intelligent beings on other planets, it makes far more sense to expend effort on the construction of a world-wide language to facilitate communication among the peoples of the earth.

POLARIZATION OF THE WORLD AND INTERNATIONAL ORDER

By TALCOTT PARSONS

THE GREATEST AND MOST IMMEDIATE DANGER to world peace stems from the bipolarization of the world community. It is wholly understandable, therefore, that this situation has been subjected to the most intensive discussion in this volume and elsewhere, and that, moreover, its threatening aspects have stood overwhelmingly at the center of attention. In this brief paper, I should like to explore the other side of this coin. For it is my contention that in certain respects these "most threatening" aspects may present an opportunity, however tenuous, to achieve a more stable system of international order.

The most obvious point of reference for the elaboration of this view is the fact that for the first time in history, we must acknowledge the existence of a world political community, at least in a relative sense. Through the development of mass media of communication, the nations of the world have become increasingly aware of their interdependence. Inevitably, important events in any major country will have rapid repercussions in all others. Indeed, any attempt to isolate a subsystem, unless that system is of minor intrinsic significance, must rely on special insulating mechanisms which impose rather rigid controls. With rapidly diminishing exceptions, we are all members of the world political community—for better or worse. In the United States, there has been a growing recognition of this phenomenon during the last three decades. Interestingly, "isolationism," which was formerly a major area of debate, was not even an issue in the recent Presidential campaign; American "involvement" was taken for granted by both parties.

I am aware, of course, that the very propriety of my use of the term "world community" may be questioned, since it implies at least a rudimentary element of order. However, I maintain that polarization, in itself, implies the existence of such an element of order. While it is conceivable, of course, that this element of order is inherent in certain geopolitical constellations which have been wholly independent of the main trends in social development, the enormous diversity of societies and cultures would seem to argue against this view. "East" and "West" may merely be geographical symbols, but these symbols refer to an emergent patterning of sociocultural organization, rather than an inevitable geographically or even ideologically based conflict of interest. Indeed the ideological "battle for men's minds" constitutes a crucial factor in this argument, for an ideological conflict presupposes a common frame of reference in terms of which the ideological differences make sense.

Insofar as a conflict of orientation can be defined as "political," and insofar as it occurs within a pattern of order rather than a Hobbesian state of nature, polarization bears some similarity to the intranational two-party system. This is not to imply that such a party system now exists in the world political community. However, it does not seem beyond the realm of possibility to suggest that some of the ingredients for such a system are present.

Some Basic Components of International Order

Certain major clues emerge as to the nature of those components of international order which are currently most significant. These concern, first, the position which the Western countries have occupied in relation to the rest of the world, particularly since the eighteenth century; and second, the designation of "modernization" as the primary goal of the non-Western sector, along with various subgoals, such as industrialization, economic development, political independence and autonomy, and the like. These developments stem from a crucial historic event, namely, the emergence in the Western world of what is known today as "industrial society" ("capitalism" is clearly too narrow a term)—in Great Britain, the United States, and Germany in the main—which came almost to full flower in the latter half of the last century, although there have been very important further developments during this century as well. Apart from the powerful "material" influence which industrialism exerts on society (whether this influence is regarded as "exploitative" or not), the concept of industrialism and its implications have been accepted almost universally.

The Implementation of a Common Set of Values

From the point of view of values, economic productivity would appear to be at the core of this pattern. Productivity has been evaluated in a variety of contexts, but a few themes have been particularly prominent. For one, economic productivity enables an improvement in living standards, along with certain concomitant benefits, in the form of higher levels of consumption, greater economic security, better health, and the like. Secondly, economic productivity has been related to autonomy, to emancipation. At this level, it has appealed to "dependent" groups; and it is in this context that it is connected with nationalism. A third and similar theme focuses on equality. As might be expected, this has involved a general challenge to the superior status of traditional elites. On the one hand, this theme has had an "internal" frame of reference, in that it pertains to territorial societies; on the other, it pertains to a demand for equal status as societies, with its bearing on political independence. The fourth important theme has been concerned with education, more specifically, its instrumental function, with respect to productivity as well as its intrinsic value.

Clearly, this broad value complex is common to both of the ideologies which today are engaged in a bitter struggle for ascendancy. Marxism grew out of Western culture during the era of emancipation from the traditionalism and "legitimism" of the European Old Regime. Its concepts stem largely from utilitarian liberalism, especially in the economic sphere; they include the political heritage of the French Revolution. The basic differences between Marxist ideology and that of the "free world" center on two points. The first, of course, involves the concept of socialism as distinguished from capitalism or free enterprise, namely, the relationship between productive organization and public authority. The second involves the interpretation of the concept of democracy, namely, the "liberal" principle of political enfranchisement and open electoral alternatives in the choice of political leadership, as opposed to guidance by a single party which assumes the trusteeship of the interests of the people. Obviously, there are other basic differences as well, such as the hostility of Communism to traditional religion, at least in principle, but important elements in the liberal world may be similarly characterized. However, on the whole, we are impressed by the fact that both of these widely divergent ideologies which, presumably, gave rise to polarization, emerged during various stages of development in the process of industrialization.

It is widely acknowledged that the recent history of the Communist movement constitutes a drastic invalidation of Marx's prediction that the revolution would originate within the most highly industrialized societies (clearly, he had England and Germany in mind). Indeed, evidence has been accumulating which would appear to indicate that the appeal of the radical left in a given society bears an inverse relation to the degree of industrialization of that society.[1] In general, the more successful industrial economies have been able to integrate their working classes into the society—with varying degrees of success, of course, and with many residual strains. In any event, this integration carries with it the legitimation of the appropriate role and status of organizational leadership and responsibility, and the recognition and reward of technical competence. The development of the Soviet Union has been in accord with these fundamental trends. On the other hand, the leftist appeal has been most effective in those instances where the structured inferiority of status, with its concomitant resentment against discrimination, exploitation, imperialism, etc., involves not classes in the Marxian sense, but societies in the territorial-political sense.

In one sense, this phenomenon is in accord with the character and significance of Marxism, although it may not conform to its original intentions. Viewed in the perspective of later developments, I consider the most important feature of Marxism to be its assertion of the inherent fusion of economic and political factors in human societies; from the perspective of our Western society, this might be interpreted as the doctrine of politization of the economy. A process of differentiation has in fact been in progress, in more highly industrialized societies, which has decreased the relative importance of the area of such fusion. The fact that such a large proportion of the working-class vote in the United States is split between the major parties is very much a case in point. It is interesting to speculate as to what might be expected in this connection in an industrially "mature" Soviet Union, if a system of plural parties were permitted there.

As mentioned earlier, the strong interest in economic development in underdeveloped societies can be linked directly to the powerful force of nationalism. There is no question, of course, that the working classes in Western societies were more "underdeveloped" economically in Marx's time than they are at present. But the economic interests of these groups were said to cut across the main, nationally defined lines, which denoted the cleavage of political interests, whereas in present so-called underdeveloped countries, economic and political interests more nearly coincide.

Theoretically, then, economics and politics comprise the two major categories of "interests." We have yet to consider their relation to systems of normative order, however. For it is a fundamental proposition of social science that no system of the "play of interests" can be considered stable, unless these interests are pursued within an institutionalized normative system—a common framework of values, of generalized norms, and of the structuring of the interests themselves.

As suggested above, there is a certain plausibility in the view that the primary achievement of modern industrial societies has been the resolution of the class conflict (as defined by Marx), in the sense that, insofar as they may be said to operate, internal political polarizations do not simply follow the lines of cleavage dictated by the economic interests of particular classes. Indeed, there is no clear-cut dichotomization of economic interest itself. Our problem, then, may be stated as follows: First, in the newly emergent world community, is it inevitable that the cleavage between "have" and "have-not" nations must lead to polarization? Second, is this phenomenon susceptible to those integrative processes which have, in fact, operated within successfully industrialized societies? Since the earlier Marxist assumption that integration was impossible without violent revolution has proved invalid, is it not reasonable to discount the neo-Marxist assumption that "war"—whether military or economic—between the "imperialist" nations and the "people's democracies" is equally inevitable? If we accept this view, we must then attempt to identify the mechanisms which may facilitate this integrative process.

From a sociological point of view, the process of industrialization within national societies can be interpreted as most essentially one of structural differentiation. This concept, in turn, presupposes a common normative framework, primarily at the level of values. Our first concern, then, is whether there is a common value system which at least to some extent extends across the line which separates the contemporary antagonists. Despite the older ideal of a generalized cultural relativity, and an attendant ideological conflict, if the problem is defined with sufficient care there seems to be little question of the validity of this hypothesis. In each case, economic productivity on the one hand and political power (including autonomy) on the other, are the foci of concern. In societies where the status of these value components cannot be based on historical tradition, something approaching their Western evaluation has emerged, in terms of a very general set of commitments, very broadly conceived. Clearly this is historically intimately related to the overwhelmingly predominant position of the West in the areas of productivity, power, and prestige, precisely during the "imperialist" era. In other words, even in those societies where hostility toward the West has been particularly prominent, the social equivalent of a process of identification has taken place, which might be likened to "identification with the aggressor" or what Rostow has termed the "demonstration effect."[2]

In addition, there have been varying kinds and degrees of reinforcement of the existing components of other value systems.[3]

Obviously, this can hardly be said to constitute a consensus on the valuation of basic goals or meanings. Rather, it represents an instrumental consensus on the valuation of capacities, at various levels of the organization of the society, to undertake whatever activities may be deemed most important to the welfare of that society. It involves the recognition that the economic productivity of the community and its political integration—the capacity to mobilize community resources for the pursuit of collective goals without external constraints—enable new levels of possible achievement in a variety of directions. There is a hierarchical element involved here as well, in that economic "opportunity" depends on political order in a more immediate sense than political order depends on the economic status of a society. Therefore, the normative ordering of the political sphere takes a certain precedence over the regulation of its economy. I consider this the primary reason for the fact that present major conflicts are conceptualized in political terms, in spite of the ideological prominence of economic considerations.

The achievement of autonomy is clearly central to this issue. Autonomy at the national level obviously removes certain constraints which are inherent in the status of colonial dependency. However, it also creates new problems, since the potentialities of "autarchic" self-sufficiency are clearly limited. Moreover, the smaller the unit, relative to the potential system of which it may be a part, the more limited are its potentialities. These limitations can be diminished only if relevant values are institutionalized in a community which is wider than the autonomous unit. In other words, parochial interests must be subordinated to those of a more extensive (and more efficient) system. Once this subordination has been institutionalized, it enables a higher level of value implementation within a framework of order than would be possible if each of the subsystems involved had to go it alone as radically autonomous units. Basically, polarization may be said to stem from this phenomenon.

Given the valuation of a major type of achievement, functioning, or whatever, greater gains can be attained in the short run by freezing the problem within a relatively restricted framework of order, and insulating the system of immediate concern from the interferences and potentialities of involvement in a wider system. To adopt an economic term, the tendency to exploit this possibility of short-run effectiveness may be called "protectionism."

In this sense, the alternative to protectionism involves the risks which are a concomitant to commitment to a higher-level, more extensive system of order. In large measure, this greatly enhanced level of risk may be attributed to competitive activities, which might otherwise be excluded. Understandably, there is strong motivation to avoid such competition by operating only within the limits of a less extensive system. On the other hand, however, the potentialities of higher value implementation are equally valid arguments in favor of the more extensive system in the long run, provided certain conditions of their implementation can be realized.

In any event, we cannot fail to recognize the presence of the primary ingredient of integration as opposed to polarization: common values obtain at a certain level of the general societal system. Moreover, it is a genuinely common, albeit incomplete, system of values at the level where main conflicts come to a head. However, values constitute only one component of institutionalized order; the problem, therefore, is to strengthen the other components to the point where they begin to outweigh the divisive elements.

With regard to values, at present polarization involves those parts of the world community which have reached certain levels of attainment, as opposed to those which have not yet achieved these levels of attainment. Thus, the have-nots are faced with the problem of catching up with the haves. With respect to political power, the Communist bloc has in fact caught up, at least to some extent. With special reference to the command of military force, it is now for all practical purposes the equal of the free world. However, there is a considerable gap between the West and the Communist bloc in the economic sphere, and this is particularly evident in the standard of living of their respective populations.

In summary, then, insofar as polarization is structured about national political units, the leadership of the have-not (Communist) bloc has achieved substantial equality with respect to one component of a larger system of productivity and political effectiveness, namely, with respect to military power. But it has accomplished this by following a protectionist policy, in that other potentialities—both internal and external—have been subordinated to a restricted goal. Internally, on an economic level, the Communist bloc has used authoritarian trusteeship to concentrate its resources on building up the ingredients of national power, at the expense of the living standards of the masses,[4] and it has denied subgroups within its society a share of the power which they could exercise in a pluralistic political system. Externally, it has become oriented to protective control within its own sphere of influence, in terms of the doctrine of absolute sovereignty. However, this dual protectionism has been counteracted on the non-Communist front by a strong measure of what might be called "defensive protectionism," which is not only military, but ideological and political in the large sense, and to some extent economic as well.

In terms of ideology, the greatest threat of Communist protectionism stems from its all-encompassing goal of definitive ultimate victory for the socialist cause (although Khrushchev's famous dictum, "We will bury you," has been interpreted to imply economic superiority rather than military conquest). The counter ideology, of course, postulates the necessity of stamping out the "Communist evil." Clearly, definitive victory for either side is not the only possible choice. We have another alternative, namely, the eventual integration of both sides—and of uncommitted units as well—in a wider system of order.

In addition to common values, there are three other essential components of institutionalized order.[5] The first of these comprises a set of minimum rules through which the implications of these values are defined in practice within the system. The second component is the structure of interests, which must be differentiated at appropriate levels. The third is an ideology in which the system of reference is defined as an empirical entity, rather than an ideology concerned merely with value patterns which define directions of desirability.

The existence of a common set of values may be considered the focal point for change. Three principal factors concerning these values may have a bearing on the direction of policy. The first of these is the failure to recognize the existence of such a value consensus. This lack of awareness may be due to the fact that value commitments have come to be fused with the protectionist elements of respective ideologies and practical policies. Thus, the opposition contends that only a rigid formula of socialist organization is morally acceptable; on our own side, "free enterprise" is said to be the basic moral issue with which there can be no compromise.

Obviously, this is a fundamental and delicate problem. Essentially, the task of disentangling values from other components implies that many issues which have at some point been treated as fundamental moral issues must be downgraded. Once again, the internal party system may provide a helpful point of reference. A political party may, with justification, be committed to the particular policies it favors, which are in direct contrast to those advocated by the opposition. But, in a broader sense, the party system also implies the existence of a set of value commitments of a higher order which are shared by both parties; moreover, institutional considerations must supersede party differences. In the United States, for example, loyalty to the Constitution presumably supersedes party interests, no matter how important. Admittedly it is extremely difficult to maintain this perspective in the midst of a highly emotional ideological conflict. However, it is an easier task for those whose superior positions have been established than it is for groups in the process of achieving status. My first policy recommendation, therefore, is that every effort be made to promulgate carefully considered statements of value commitments which may provide a basis for consensus among both have and have-not nations. This would require that such statements be dissociated from the specific ideological position of either of the polarized camps.

In all probability, this will also require increasing recognition of the significant status of a rather large and growing neutral group of political units not firmly committed to either side. When a nation withdraws its potential support from the forces with which it has previously been allied, whether tacitly or overtly, it is inevitable that this action must permit—and promote—neutralism. And, of course, neutralism itself can fulfill a protectionist function, in that it may incorporate a cynical approach which may have the effect, whether deliberate or not, of playing one side off against the other. At the same time, under the proper conditions, neutral forces may evince more interest than would be possible for so-called committed factions in those elements of order which transcend polarization. Although this opinion requires substantial qualification, it would seem that in this frame of reference India has come closer to achieving the position of a moral leader than any other national unit, with the possible exception of Sweden. Here again, the intranational system may serve to point up the significance of neutralism. In successful two-party systems there is likely to be an important uncommitted sector of the electorate, an independent vote. As has been noted frequently, this uncommitted sector can serve as an important check on tendencies toward extremism on either side, since the effect of such extremism is to alienate the neutral groups, and hence to throw the balance in the direction of the opposition. In summary, then, we must clarify the nature of universally held value commitments, and promulgate their effective recognition. This in turn involves maximal dissociation from the defensive ideological positions and practical policies specific to either side. Admittedly, the accomplishment of such dissociation will depend on a high level of national self-criticism and self-discipline. The proper application of social science should prove valuable in this connection.

The third factor concerns the level at which value commitments are stated. Throughout this paper I have emphasized the fact that the Communist bloc and the nations of the free world do, in fact, share certain values in common. However, this should not be interpreted to imply that these common values have ultimate standing. At present, they might best be considered as relative; however, the repudiation of value absolutism does not imply the kind of relativity which would rule out the possibility of a common measure.

To illustrate, at one phase of Western history, religion (in the historic-formal sense) was the primary focus of political conflict. Beginning with the Thirty Years War, Western Christendom has undergone a gradual process, in the course of which religious tolerance has come to be institutionalized. I cannot describe the various stages of this process here, but I think my readers will agree that it has made its greatest progress in the United States, with denominational pluralism and the separation of church and state. In a sense, the recent election of a Roman Catholic to the presidency has put a seal on the pattern.

One of the notable facts about the world situation is the broad renunciation on the part of religious groups of any attempt to further their interests through proselytizing crusades. Even in the nineteenth century the degree to which Christian missions were politically implemented by Western interests requires careful examination. Whatever level of support did exist at that time has diminished notably since; nor is this development due entirely to anticolonialism. Conversely, acceptance of the Hindu or Buddhist religion by the West is not considered a prerequisite for the maintenance of friendly relations with India or Burma. Even Islam, the non-Christian religion which is most predisposed to militant proselytizing, has not stressed this. Many other issues are involved, but the significant fact is that current polarization has taken shape at secular political levels, with only one side making a point of militant secularism. There is a lesson to be learned here, namely, that it is somewhat dangerous to be dogmatic about the exact level at which a relatively stable value consensus can be attained. It is my opinion that this value consensus will vary with time and circumstances. In addition, I think an important parallel can be drawn between the present situation and the tensions which grew out of the Peace of Westphalia, at which time the formula *cuius regio, eius religio* was established, which provided for the institutionalization of religious liberty between political units, but not within them.

To return to our present concern with political liberty, and more specifically with the generalization of the implications of a value commitment to this end, it has been claimed vociferously that autonomy is the fundamental right of territorial political units. Why should such autonomy be confined to this level of social organization, and not be extended to liberties within the political unit? Indeed, I do not believe that such a limitation is really defensible as a value position on any terms; and in fact it is not defended by the Communists on those grounds, but on ideological grounds. Their argument, which stems from the Marxist concept of stage of development, is based on the allegation that the masses cannot be permitted freedom from the tutelage of the party until the final stage of the revolution. Presumably, the "withering away of the state" (and also of the party) will bring with it a level of individual freedom—both political and in other contexts as well—which will far exceed the freedom attained by bourgeois societies. We are all familiar with this theoretical approach; I have restated it here to bring into focus one essential point, namely, that freedom is valued, however distorted the means for attaining it. We can therefore conclude that political freedom at the associational and individual levels—subject, of course, to adequate institutional regulation—constitutes an essential component of the central value complex under discussion, and that the failure of the Communist camp to recognize this component in internal matters represents a basic ideological issue which merits special treatment. From a practical point of view, we are confronted with overwhelming evidence of the importance of emphasis on the existence of a value consensus. We can establish this fact effectively only if we enunciate these values directly and if we are particularly careful to avoid ideological commitments, which are specific to particular levels of society.

The Common Observance of Procedural Norms

In the present frame of reference, norms may be defined as patterns of desirable behavior which implement values in a variety of contexts, which are differentiated according to the particular functions of the agencies concerned and the specific situations in which they operate. The agencies of primary importance for purposes of this discussion are governments; the specific situation with which we are concerned is their relationship to each other, as this bears on the question of international order or, in its broadest sense, on the question of international law.

By way of preliminary comment, I would point out that there has been considerable development, and relatively good implementation, of norms in a wide variety of spheres other than those which involve the more direct relationships between governments. I refer to the regulation of international trade, to the conventions which enable the international circulation of persons and information and the like, and to the rules which have been established for conduct on the high seas, which is outside the territorial jurisdiction of any single government. There have been certain breaks in this legal order across the line of the iron curtain, of course, and recently censorship regulations and restrictions have been imposed on persons leaving the Union of South Africa. Nevertheless, this is a component of existing order which is not to be underestimated, and which is capable of gradual extension, without incurring major controversy in the process. One of the positive heritages of colonialism lies in the fact that European standards have been extended rather widely. Perhaps in this light the restrictive policies maintained by the Communist countries[6] may be viewed as a defensive maneuver. Thus, it becomes all the more important for the countries of the free world to maintain high standards in this respect. The McCarthy episode in American history was severely damaging precisely for this reason. The continuing presence of such protectionist elements in the nations of the free world should be overhauled very thoroughly.[7]

However, our discussion of the more immediately relevant category of norms—those which concern direct relations between governments—must encompass the whole complex of diplomatic usage, protocol, and immunities. Of course, under extreme stress, these break down.

The organization of the United Nations (and I refer to the League of Nations as well) may be viewed as an extension of a trend with deep historical roots. The central characteristic of this trend is the attempt to establish consensus at the procedural level. That is, the institutionalization of procedures is considered the focal growing point of systems of order at the level of norms, a feature which is shared both by legal systems, in the more technical sense, and by political systems. This is not to say that the common observance of general procedural norms will inevitably obviate conflicts as to standards of fairness, or those which refer to opportunity or methods of treatment of the case. Of course, such a procedural system undercuts the absolutism of commitment to goals by introducing problems attendant to settlement or compromise. However, there are different kinds of compromise. For our purposes, the important type is the promotion of integration, in terms of a higher normative level.

Of course, in part, procedural systems also enable coercive sanctions to enforce their norms. But coercive sanctions constitute only one component of the sanction system, and our crucial concern here does not involve the identification of specific sanctions. Rather, I wish to underscore a more basic issue, namely, the acceptance of procedural obligations.

I believe that this willingness on the part of its members to abide by the rules of procedure constitutes the central significance of the United Nations. For, in this sense, it is the embodiment of the world community. Clearly, the range within which one might compare the

United Nations to a court of law is still very limited (though it certainly should be capable of extension). But, short of a court of law, the United Nations may be likened to a forum in which the participants are obliged to provide for the public statement of a case, and to permit a hearing for the opposition's objections to the case, as stated. Participation at either level implies recognition of the legitimacy and power of judgment by world opinion.

It is to be expected that those who are deeply committed to particular goals will be extremely ambivalent about the acceptance of procedural norms, for such acceptance carries with it the risk of defeat without all-out struggle. In light of the reluctance of the Communist bloc to compromise, the behavior of Khrushchev and his cohorts in the early fall of 1960 was significant, not because of their attempts to disturb the orderly procedure of the United Nations, but because they deemed it so important to play the game. They demanded that structural changes be made in the procedural system and in fact threatened to walk out if these demands were not met. Quite apart from the validity of these demands, I believe that the fact that polarized conflict was brought within the framework of orderly procedure was of fundamental significance, and that every effort should be made to maintain and develop this pattern. Of course, this will require shrewd assessment of the degree to which pressure can be exerted without precipitating an explosion which might wreck the whole system. Despite the problem it may pose, the existence of a procedural forum to which there is an important degree of commitment on both sides constitutes one of our most precious assets.

The significance of the United Nations as a forum will emerge in sharper focus if its similarity to a democratic electoral system and a court of law is underscored. The latter does not guarantee a satisfactory outcome for either party, or even a just outcome, but rather a fair trial. The former does not guarantee that the outcome of an election will be good for the country from the point of view of either party, but rather that the incoming administration will have the adequate support of the electorate, according to procedural rules, and thereby be enabled to take the crucial step from the status of party leadership to leadership of the polity as a whole.

Obviously, then, reliance on procedural norms inevitably means increased risk to particular partisan goals. If we expect the Communist camp to submit their vital interests to procedural norms, we must, as a corollary, accept the possibility that adherence to these norms will result in the defeat of our own interests in many instances.

In other words, the development of new systems of norms of a higher order necessarily involves the institutionalization of a willingness to take risks relative to particular goals, even very important goals. Although these risks can be confined with certain limits, they cannot be eliminated entirely. Nevertheless, this is the price we must pay for increased freedom, for the resolution of the impasse which results from the protectionist policies of antagonistic elements.[8]

The Pluralistic Structure of Interests

The third basic component of the institutionalization of a new system of order derives from the structure of what I referred to earlier as "interests." My speculations regarding this component bear a close relationship to the preceding discussion of the role of procedural norms. However, other considerations are involved as well. We are concerned here with the level of differentiation within the system of interests, with the so-called problem of pluralism.[9]

The core of the problem is contained in one facet of the contrast between the Communist system, as it operates within the current climate of polarization, and the free world. I refer to the monolithic tendency of the Communist system, that is, its tendency to include as many aspects as possible of the society in question within a single system of highly centralized control, and hence to conceive of policy as an all-or-none commitment to complete success, as defined in terms of its broad goals, rather than as a commitment to attempt to integrate differentiated subinterests either internally or externally. The applicability of this definition to a national society, such as the Soviet Union, and particularly with regard to its relationship with other members of the Communist bloc, requires extensive qualification. Nevertheless, when one considers the quality of the international coalition of the free nations, whose solidarity is continually in question, the difference is striking. Furthermore, in this sense, the liberal societies are far more pluralistic internally, in ways which are undoubtedly familiar to the reader.

One of the basic attributes of a political system which has achieved a minimum level of stability is its capacity to resolve conflicts of interest; this in turn involves the structure of the system of interests. Typically, situations which require political decision-making are continually shifting. Policy issues hinge on a particular element, specific to a given situation; hence, issues change as a consequence of situational change.

In such a system, a monolithic bloc which is capable of staking its whole position on a particular issue, which has grown out of a specific situation, has a built-in short-run advantage because it can afford to apply a kind of pressure that less monolithic systems cannot risk. But this short-run advantage is gained at the expense of an element of instability in the large system which is essentially a feature of rigidity, on the one hand, and of an unreadiness to contemplate drastic change, with the knowledge that such change may cause the breakdown of the whole system, on the other.

Polarization in a stable two-party system does not constitute a fundamental threat because any such disruptive tendency is counteracted by an underlying structure of pluralistic, and hence crosscutting, solidarities. As a function of shifting situations which need to be dealt with, different balances among these structured interests can be mobilized; in other words, the sponsorship and motivation of a party are not constant, but vary, within limits, according to the situation. Interest components are enfranchised in that they have a realistic choice among a variety of alternatives to which they can lend their support. Consequently, it is exceedingly important to distinguish between polarization within monolithic blocs and polarization within a pluralistic infrastructure.

The cold war might be likened to the former type of polarization. On the one hand, the goal of the Communists is limited to the achievement of equal status. At the same time, however, in line with their deep ambivalence, they claim the right to achieve complete supremacy over the other camp. If this radical polarization is to be mitigated, our major task is to identify the process which might enable a shift in the direction of the pluralistic type of polarization, as conceptualized by the party system, and to determine the extent to which such a shift is in fact in progress.

In such a system issues must be dealt with one at a time, without too frequently posing broad questions of "confidence." Of course, in certain situations, it is possible for pluralization to operate directly between the principal protagonists. For example, in the field of cultural exchange, there has been a genuine mutual appreciation of the achievements of both sides in the natural sciences and the arts. In this area, solidarity stems from a devotion to, and recognition of, common standards. Quite possibly, the use of scientific experts to thresh out the technical problems of nuclear arms inspection would constitute a valuable application of this principle.

However, in all probability, it is with respect to pluralism that the existence of a substantial neutral bloc is most important. The process of decision-making in the world community requires that particular emphasis be placed on the expectation that the combinations in favor of one policy will differ from those which favor another. For example, it is inevitable that a major unit, such as the United States, will find itself allied with certain nations with respect to certain issues, and that these same allies may become their opponents on other issues. Ultimatums ("you are either for or against us all along the line") must be avoided at all costs. The direction of development should be pluralistic in this sense. To paraphrase the wording used by one important group of students of internal political process, the flexibility essential to the orderly adaptation of a system to variant situations involves the phenomenon of "cross-pressuring"; that is, it requires the participation of groups which have predilections in either of two alternative directions, and with respect to which the balance of interest may be expected to shift.[10]

What I have called the pluralistic structure of interests is an important ingredient of stability because it fragments the pressures which can influence the system at any one political decision point. In other words, a strong vested interest in the functioning of the larger system, as well as normative commitments, will serve to prevent untenable situations which require an ultimate and irreversible decision—in the extreme case, a declaration of war. Clearly, this implies the acceptance of the risk which is a concomitant of the subservience of individual interests to the procedural system.

One aspect of the significance of mutual nuclear deterrence is particularly relevant at this point. Nuclear war, with all of its implications of destruction for both sides, may well be the price to be paid for pressing a partisan case to the limit, so to speak. When relatively extreme measures are under consideration, a process does seem to obtain wherein the costs are counted—however subtle this process may be. Policy is thus deflected away from impulsive ultimatums to more particularized issues. This process can therefore be considered to represent one factor operating in the direction of the fragmentation which favors a pluralistic structure of interests. Moreover, it is applicable to neutral nations as well, in that the efforts on the part of the major parties to gain the allegiance of neutrals lead to a sort of stalemate which, in turn, prevents them from pushing coercive threats to extremes. Thus, competition is oriented toward the advantages of alliance for neutral nations, rather than threats of the dire consequences of political or ideological divergence.

The Positive Function of Ideology

For present purposes, ideology refers to the formulation of an evaluative, empirical, cognitive picture of the system in question, including the form this system may possibly take in the future. It is prerequisite of stable institutionalization that there exist a strong correlation between the implications of the value system and the diagnosis of the empirical system. Moreover, those processes which will enable a closer relationship between the empirical system and value requirements must be clearly envisioned.[11]

Those who tend to treat realistic interests as the primary basis of conflict also tend to downgrade ideology to the status of an epiphenomenon which can be safely ignored. While in some respects the Communist camp appears to assert this view with great vehemence, at the same time, in another context, they insist with equal vehemence on the importance of maintaining ideological correctness. However, among the "free" nations, too, there is a school of so-called realists who profess to believe that ideology is of little consequence. In my opinion, this constitutes a serious error.

Ideology has a dual functional significance. On the one hand, it is an educational mechanism. By enlisting the fervor which accompanies a sense of mission, it greatly facilitates the process of commitment which is an essential ingredient of institutionalization. With respect to the Communists, this involves institutionalization of the values described above, which may be summarized as the trend toward modernization. That is, a radical break with the reactionary past of the societies in the enemy camp is emphasized and dramatized. Indeed, Lenin advocated the extension of this function well beyond the earlier Marxist position, in that he stressed the importance of moving directly from what Marxists called feudalism to socialism, and omitting the intermediate bourgeois capitalism stage. In this light, Communist ideology may be interpreted as a statement of the symbolic values of modernization in which symbolic, covert gestures of reconciliation are made toward both the past and the future, within the framework of expected conflict.

The first of these gestures involves the attempt to preserve the integrity of the premodern system; and I believe that this is the primary significance of the symbol, socialism. In essence, the purpose of this device is to assure us that the process of differentiation which is inherent in modernization need not jeopardize the integrity of preindustrial community solidarity, provided the transition is carried out in such a way as to prevent the aggressive maneuvers of private interests, which are not bound by loyalty to such a community. Thus, this mechanism may be considered to facilitate recognition and acceptance of the risk-taking necessary for industrialization by asserting that these risks are limited to spheres of a lower order.

I would further interpret this aspect of Communist ideology as primarily defensive or protectionist in character, and hence to apply in a context which is not directly relevant to the polarized conflict. It is also very closely associated with basic anxieties about political democracy, since presumably this democracy would weaken preventive control over centrifugal tendencies in the community. The obverse of this, of course, is the defensive component of the counterideology, that is, the compulsive attachment to the free-enterprise formula, the fear of "creeping socialism," and the tendency to invoke authoritarian political measures, allegedly in order to safeguard our freedom.

The second component of the dual function of ideology concerns the inferior status of the rising elements, relative to those elements which are already well established. In a psychological sense, the attitude of these rising elements might be viewed as defensive; in our own frame of reference, it might be considered a variation of protectionism. Here, precisely because the core elements of the free world have already at least partially achieved the goals to which the developing nations aspire, there is a strong motivation to derogate these attainments. In ideological terms, the aim of these underdeveloped nations is not to achieve parity, but to supplant certain well-established elements of the "superior" society, for example, to substitute socialism for capitalism. The primary function of ideology in this instance is to emphasize the unique character of the socialist contribution. One rather oversimplified solution immediately comes to mind, namely, the use of opposition to maximize motivation, to define achievement as victory rather than mere goal attainment. Of course, here again the reaction of the counterideology must be considered, that is, the automatic tendency to define the success of those developing societies which are Communistically oriented as a defeat for the free world.

The direction of desirable change seems clear: ideological stresses must be minimized; those aspects of the situation which demonstrate an interest in order which transcends polarity must be underscored. One of the main themes here concerns those features which all industrial societies share in common, in contrast with previous economic and social organizations. An exposition of such features would necessarily focus on the standard of living of the masses—for obvious reasons a very sensitive area for the Communists. The features of social organization as such, particularly the differentiation of collectivities and roles, would constitute another area of focus. Still another concerns common elements at the cultural level, notably science and the arts.

This discussion has been based on an important assumption, which may seem rather vulnerable at this point. I refer to the assumption that one side has achieved a position of relative superiority in relation to the important values. The Communist goals, in terms of catching up and surpassing, may be taken as tacit proof of the validity of this assumption; however, on the other hand, their vehement assertions of the superiority of socialism and their irrational accusations of imperialism would appear to deny such gains. Thus, we must consider whether there is any prospect of dissociating these values from partisan considerations. If no such possibility exists, we must accept the fact that partisanship (as opposed to the mutual unmasking of ideological biases) cannot be transcended.

The fact that common values exist which have deep roots in the great traditions of all Western culture is one focus of leverage for such dissociation. Procedural norms and the pluralistic differentiation of interests constitute mechanisms which operate in the same direction. And we have another very important resource, namely, the contribution of social science. Insofar as the development of knowledge in this sphere is genuine and not spurious, it involves the institutionalization of norms of technical competence and genuine objectivity. To date, this process has been slow, halting, and difficult, but significant progress has been made and, hopefully, will continue in the future. On the basis of a realistic assessment of the current status of industrial societies and possible future trends of development, we can detect an element of common ground. Obviously, this mechanism will not produce dramatic consequences in immediate crisis situations, but its long-run importance should not be underestimated.[12]

Summary and Conclusions

The foregoing discussion may be summarized in a series of propositions:

1. Polarization, which is the salient characteristic of the world community at present, constitutes the primary threat to peace. However, at the same time, polarization attests to the existence of a world community and thus presents certain opportunities for the development of a more stable order within that community.

2. An effective two-party system within a relatively stable national polity constitutes a theoretical model which, while it is far from precisely applicable, is sufficiently similar to world bipolarity to provide significant clues as to methods for achieving world order.

3. The formulation of common value commitments which transcend partisan differences is one of the most important prerequisites of international order. It is my contention that, at a certain level, such a base does in fact exist in the world community, specifically with regard to the importance attached to economic development and

political autonomy. This basic uniformity needs to be clearly asserted in contexts which can be dissociated from divisive ideological particularities.

4. As they are presently conceived, value concepts are too general to influence political behavior. They must be spelled out in concrete terms. Moreover, it is particularly important that they be defined in terms of norms at the level of the procedures through which they can best be implemented. A consent on the part of the opposing factions to adhere to the rules of procedure implies the assumption of risk that one's particular goal may be jeopardized, that one's adversary may be victorious with respect to particular issues. Obviously, the stronger the commitment to a particular goal, the more difficult it will become to accept this procedural risk. However, there are considerable compensations for the acceptance of such risks; these risks enable gains which would be prohibited, or at least greatly deterred, by a go-it-alone policy. At many different points in the development of social structures, this has been accomplished by processes of differentiation. It can be promoted deliberately in many ways.

5. One of the main threats to stability stems from the monolithic concentration of interests on partisan all-or-none goal striving. The mitigation of this threat is, in part, dependent on the differentiation of interests in a pluralistic direction, so that a sufficiently important proportion will cut across the lines of partisan division. Procedural mechanisms tend to favor this process of differentiation and hence to increase pluralism. In this connection, the existence of sufficiently strong neutral elements which can form particularized ties in either direction is important. Under the proper conditions, neutralism should not be deplored, but welcomed.

6. Ideology is essentially a defensive or protective mechanism. However, it does have important positive functions in a world community, in that it cushions the inevitable severe strains which are inherent in the process of modernization. However, its tendency toward intransigence must be counteracted. This may be accomplished by dissociating value consensus from ideological difference, on the one hand, and, on the other hand, by objective scientific diagnosis of empirical situations, which tend to be presented in selected and distorted versions in ideological discussion.

7. Progress toward institutionalizing the normative framework of the world community, and the attendant web of pluralistic interests, depends on a balanced combination of various measures which are in accord with inherent trends, rather than one dramatic set of measures. Acute crises may be handled by single dramatic measures, but this balance is essential to our prospects over the long term.

It is my opinion, therefore, that Western policy should include each of the four components formulated in propositions 3 through 6 above. These include, first, the assertion of common values in ways which minimize the self-righteous implication that only we are true to these values, that our opponents are not; second, the promotion of procedural innovations, even though by so doing we are likely to suffer defeat on particular issues; third, the promotion of those opportunities which are likely to develop ties of solidarity both with iron curtain countries on specific divergent issues, and, above all, with neutral nations, even though they may be dealing simultaneously with the opposition in regard to other issues; and, finally, the use of social science to develop the most competent analyses possible at the present state of our knowledge of social and political systems throughout the world.

The hypothesis put forth in this paper lacks specificity because it stresses the balance between a plurality of factors. Moreover, it must be regarded as a preliminary sketch, rather than the sum of a carefully developed set of proposals. I have stated repeatedly that under the proper conditions a given factor, such as the establishment of procedural norms, or the pluralization of interests through the appeal to neutral elements, might be expected to work in the desired direction. A few suggestions as to these "proper conditions" have been delineated in the course of the discussion. But space forbids a full description of such conditions at the desired level of concreteness. (To a great extent, they probably are not known and can only be elucidated through further research.) In conclusion, then, the foregoing discussion does not purport to provide an infallible prescription for effective foreign policy. Rather, it purports to outline a theoretical framework within which, given the proper specification, a type of policy which has a better chance for success could be formulated. The careful delineation of such a policy would require a great deal of theoretical and empirical groundwork, which would obviously extend far beyond the limits of this paper.

NOTES

1. Cf. S. M. Lipset, *Political Man* (Garden City, N.Y.: Doubleday, 1960), and my review article in *World Politics* (October, 1960).

2. See Walt W. Rostow, *Theory of Economic Growth* (Cambridge: Cambridge University Press, 1960).

3. See Robert N. Bellah, *Tokugawa Religion* (Glencoe, Ill.: The Free Press, 1958).

4. See Alexander Gerschenkron, "Problems and Patterns of Russian Economic Development" in Cyril Black (ed.), *The Transformation of Russian Society: Aspects of Social Change Since 1861* (Cambridge, Mass.: Harvard University Press, 1960), pp. 42–72.

5. This is a scheme developed by the author in various publications. See, in particular, "An Approach to the Sociology of Knowledge," *Proceedings of the Fourth World Congress of Sociology, IV* (1961).

6. For example, their refusal to participate in the international copyright convention.

7. For example, the proposed repeal of the Connally amendment to the World Court Statute.

8. An excellent example of a suggestion for a procedural device outside the framework of the United Nations is T. C. Schelling's proposal of a "special surveillance force." See pp. 87–105 of the present volume.

9. See William Kornhauser, *The Politics of Mass Society* (Glencoe, Ill.: The Free Press, 1959), and my review article in *World Politics* (October, 1960).

10. See Bernard Berelson, Paul F. Lazarsfeld, and William McPhee, *Voting: A Study of Opinion Formation in a Presidential Campaign* (Chicago: University of Chicago Press, 1954).

11. See Parsons, "An Approach to the Sociology of Knowledge," *op. cit.*

12. At the International Sociological Congress at Stresa, Italy, in September, 1959, the leader of the Soviet Delegation, Professor P. N. Fedoseav, stated that his colleagues proposed to demonstrate the superiority of socialism by empirical research. This constitutes submitting one's case to an objective judgment, that of competent peers, with the implicit possibility that one may be shown to be wrong. It is another version of the supercession of intransigent assertion of particular goal-commitments, by acceptance of a procedural mechanism, including exposure to the risks inherent in such a system.

THE ROLE OF LAW IN BUILDING PEACE

By ARTHUR LARSON

MOST CURRENT OR RECENT DISPUTES of major proportions have involved legal questions of a kind which could be handled by judicial and arbitral procedures if the nations of the world, including the United States, would accept these procedures. This is not to say that in today's imperfect world these disputes are in fact going to be settled in court. The point is that by their inherent quality and nature, they are of a kind which could be so handled in whole or in part, if the parties would agree to this method of handling.

The Suez dispute centered around the alleged breach of Egypt's agreement with the Universal Suez Company and the Treaty of Constantinople of 1888. This alleged violation of legal rights was the kind of question that could have been appropriately submitted to the International Court of Justice, just as the nationalization of the Anglo-Iranian Oil Company, an event which also threatened to precipitate war in the Middle East, was submitted.[1]

The present Suez dispute, which takes the form of objections by Israel to Egypt's practice of blocking and searching Israel-bound shipping desiring to transit the Suez Canal, consists of a number of questions which are almost all legal in character. All the parties to the dispute, in their presentations to the United Nations, began by invoking their rights under international law. Egypt has accepted the compulsory jurisdiction of the International Court on questions involving the Treaty of Constantinople of 1888, and there seems to be no reason why a country which was a party to that treaty (which would not include Israel) should not in an appropriate case take this question to the International Court.

Another judicable dispute causing tension in the Middle East is the controversy on whether the Gulf of Aqaba and the Straits of Tiran are legally waters open to innocent passage by Israel-bound cargo.

The Berlin crisis involves several specific legal disputes. The principal legal questions concern rights of access under various agreements and under doctrines such as easement of necessity, and the Soviet claim of right to transfer its obligations under the Four-Power Pact to East Germany, as well as the legal effect of any such attempt to transfer on destruction of Western rights of access and of Soviet obligations generally.

Claims of expropriations of private property and of interference with international investment are intrinsically susceptible of judicial or arbitral determination. Boundary disputes are generally amenable to judicial or arbitral settlement. The International Court has already handled several such disputes. The boundary dispute between China and India, which has all the potentialities of a major source of tension, is in this category. Aerial incidents are also amenable to Court treatment, and several attempts to bring them into court have been made by the United States.[2]

It is clear, then, that many of the disputes threatening world peace today are in whole or in part the kind of disputes that judicial and arbitral processes could help settle peaceably. Sometimes, of course, there are mixed questions of law and diplomacy in a controversy. For example, the Berlin question is a mixture of disputes over present rights under existing agreements. which are judicable questions, and disputes over what changes should be made in any new regime that might be set up for Berlin and Germany, which questions are obviously political and diplomatic. But this does not mean that the judicial process would not make an important contribution. In such mixed questions, the judicial process could put to rest questions about existing legal rights, and could forestall arbitrary one-sided action in disregard of present agreements and rights, such as was threatened by Premier Khrushchev in the Berlin situation. While peace and order were thus being kept, any needed changes could be worked out by political means. In addition, and in a more general sense, the gradual strengthening of the judicial process in the world would serve to enhance the "habit of law" and the general atmosphere around the world of resort to peaceful settlement of disputes under law, as against impulsive and highhanded disregard of legal rights and procedures.

What are the building blocks of the law structure of peace? There is no mystery about them; they are the same as the familiar parts of any legal system worthy of the name:

1. A body of law that is accessible, up-to-date, and capable of deciding the disputes that cause tension in the world as it is today.

2. Machinery to apply that law—machinery which also is ac-

cessible, up-to-date, and adapted to settling the kind of disputes that today's world produces.

3. Acceptance of that body of law and the machinery by the persons affected—and here we must remind ourselves that most people of the world do not regard the present international law and court as *their* law and *their* court.

4. Compliance with the decisions of international tribunals once they are rendered.

The Body of Law

The task divides itself into two parts: making existing law accessible, and going beyond existing law to create a kind of law that will be usable by, and acceptable to, not just Western Christendom but the more than one hundred nations that now must be reckoned with.

As to accessibility, we face at once a stark axiom. Nonaccessible law is nonexistent law. Philosophers may debate whether there is really a sound when a tree crashes in a wilderness and the sound is not heard by any living creature. But lawyers know that for all practical purposes there is really no law when the law cannot be found and therefore is never heard by any judge. The objective is clear enough: the materials and evidences of international law should be published, annotated, indexed, and cross-referenced to the same extent as domestic materials. But where is the Shepard's Citator of international law? the key-number system? the regional reporter system? the annotated statutes? the Federal Register? the L.R.A. and A.L.R. and C.J. and A.J. and W. & P. and U.S.C.A. and N.C.C.A.? Not to mention the endless list of loose-leaf publications that keep lawyers poor, publishers prosperous, and secretaries frantic.

This relatively unglamorous piece of work, which could keep hundreds of scholars and lawyers busy for years, may seem a far cry from prophetic visions of a world that lives under law—and yet how can a world live under law until it can first find out what the law is?

Here is a task in which universities, bar associations, publishers, and governments can join. Since a task of such magnitude must be spread over years, the best approach may be to begin with areas of law where accessibility of law would now have the most to contribute to relieving of tensions. A good example is the need to compile and annotate all the law bearing on international rivers—so that authoritative guidance will be at hand to aid in the settlement of the many festering disputes on rights in international waters.

But even if all existing international law were accessible, this would only be a beginning. International law must be adapted to today's world, both as to content and as to universality of acceptance.

As to both needs, great promise lies in the "general principles" clause of the Statute of the International Court. This Statute lists as one of the major sources of international law "the general principles of law recognized by civilized nations." Think of the vast treasures of legal principle to which this clause invites us. The clause tells us that if we look at the internal legal principles of the world's various systems and find a common thread of principle, that thread becomes elevated to the status of binding international law.

For an example of how this approach can enrich the content of world law and adapt it to contemporary needs, the first project undertaken at the Duke Law School's World Rule of Law Center may be cited.

The idea of this project had its origin in an interview I had with the late Premier of Iraq, Nuri As-Said. I was no sooner inside the door than Nuri said: "I want some jamming equipment." I muttered something about Americans believing in free communication, but he repeated, "I want jamming equipment. I've got to jam Nasser. Let me tell you why. A few weeks ago Cairo broadcast a news report that I, Nuri, with my own hands, had murdered four Moslem holy men in the holy temple itself. What happened? Rioting, bloodshed, killing all over the place. I need that jamming equipment."

He never got it. But one couldn't help reflecting: if this is to be a world of law, is this kind of thing legal? Isn't international use of words to cause serious harm generally illegal? Isn't incitement to murder in itself an offense under the general principles of civilized nations? Is the offense any less because it is international—or because it is electronic, and therefore superficially novel?

We are hoping, through this project, to find in international law (including "general principles" law) some contributions toward a legal solution of this modern problem. To the extent we find present law deficient, we hope to draw and offer a voluntary code of ethics for international broadcasting.

Another example of how the "general principles" approach can help lay the legal foundations for peace is our newest project at the Center, called "Sovereignty Under the Law."

It is all too easy to assume that in this age of aggressive nationalism, each sovereign of the world's hundred-odd nations is considered by his legal system to be the only source of law and therefore above the law. If this were so, obviously the chance for acceptance of a concept of real supranational law would be slim indeed.

However, if we look at the deepest wellsprings of legal tradition in all parts of the world we find almost universal agreement that the sovereign is not above the law—he is under the law. This is not surprising when it is remembered that most major legal systems have religious origins. In a Moslem country, for example, no temporal sovereign could say, "I am above the Law of Islam."

The most familiar illustration is an Old Testament story which we all know, but whose legal significance we may never have appreciated: the story of King Ahab and Naboth's vineyard, in I Kings 21.

All King Ahab wanted was to acquire a nearby vineyard belonging to Naboth. Ahab was king of Israel. Naboth was just a plain citizen. Ahab was quite reasonable—he was even willing to pay for the vineyard. But Naboth invoked the Jewish Law of Inheritance, which was above both king and commoner. "The Lord forbid it me, that I should give the inheritance of my fathers unto thee," said Naboth. What did Ahab say? Did he say, "I'm the sovereign around here. I make the laws"? He did not. "He laid him down upon his bed, and turned away his face, and would eat no bread."

At this point entered Jezebel. In one scornful phrase Jezebel summed up the attitude of all those before and since who have thought that the sovereign was above the law: "Dost thou now govern the kingdom of Israel?" Jezebel was what you might call an early type of legal positivist. And we all know what happened to Jezebel. The searing wrath of Jehovah, the appalling punishments visited upon one who would defy the law of Israel, leave no doubt where this particular legal tradition stands on the question of sovereignty under the law.

Our own tradition, of course, is epitomized in the historic colloquy between James I and Lord Coke. The king accused Coke of saying that the king was under the law, "which it were treason to affirm." Coke, in the teeth of this far from subtle threat, stood his ground and said: "The king ought not to be under any man, but under God and the law."

Of course, there is plenty of evidence of a contrary view in some times and places. But the interesting fact is that both the *oldest* traditions and the *newest* legal developments are on the side of placing sovereignty under the law. The progressive abandonment of sovereign immunity is one evidence of this, as is the formation of transnational communities like the European Economic Community. Of great significance also is the appearance in the most modern constitutions, such as those of France, the Netherlands, and West Germany, of provisions expressly stating that international law in the form of treaties takes priority over national laws.

What we hope to discover in our project is whether we can show the nations of the world, including the many newer nations, that on the strength of their own deepest legal traditions they can accept without strain or loss of national pride a legal obligation higher and broader than their own local jurisprudence.

In addition, the body of world law can be enriched and modernized by deliberate jobs of research that do the spadework necessary for treaties and codification in such areas as the interpretation and termination of treaties, harms to persons and property, protection of private international investment, the law of international rivers, disarmament, space law, sea law, and the Law of Antarctica. Exciting projects in such areas as these are already in progress at a number of schools and research centers. One thing is clear: there is plenty of work for everyone.

The Machinery of Law

The International Court of Justice at The Hague is, in the words of its Statute, the "principal judicial organ" of the United Nations. In fact, it is the only one. Since the present Court plays such a key role in the future of world rule of law, it has become imperative for everyone to learn more about it. Lawyers agree that, by any familiar objective tests, this is a good court. It numbers among its fifteen judges some of the finest international lawyers in the world.

The Court is hampered by cumbersome procedures and practices —but these are not beyond remedy, and one fertile field of study will be proposals for their revision in the interests of efficiency. The Court's opinions are generally excellent in legal reasoning, scholarship, and judicial integrity. The Rule of Law Center at Duke University has a detailed two-year study of the Court in progress. We have just made an exhaustive check of the opinions and votes of all the judges in the Court's history. There is plenty of evidence, if any were needed, to show that these judges really think and decide as judges—and not as politicians, as some uninformed critics seem to fear they might.

The most direct proof is the fact that judges not infrequently have voted against their own countries when they thought their own country was wrong on the law. Indeed, they have done so in 24 out of 103 votes involving their countries. It might be of passing interest to note that in the recent *Interhandel* case the Soviet judge, Kojevnikov, not only voted in favor of the United States on three of five issues but wrote a separate opinion more strongly in favor of the United States position than that of the majority—while the

United States judge voted against the United States on one of these issues.

What is needed, then, is not to displace the present World Court, but to make a thorough study of how it can best be supplemented with a complete world-wide system of regional or lower courts, arbitration tribunals, claims courts for private litigants, and—since there will always be disputes that are political and nonjudicable in character—mediation and conciliation agencies. As matters now stand, it is as if you had to run to the Supreme Court in Washington to litigate every smashed fender or unpaid alimony claim.

Acceptance of the Law

Now, say you have a workable body of law and efficient machinery to apply it—what good is all this if it is not accepted by the parties affected? The third component, then, must be acceptance of the system.

At once we encounter the unhappy fact that less than half the members of the United Nations have accepted the obligatory jurisdiction of the World Court, and some of these have interposed reservations so severe as to render their acceptance largely illusory. The problem of our own "self-judging" reservation, under which we reserve the right unilaterally to declare a controversy domestic and hence outside the Court's jurisdiction, is by now becoming quite well known. Its repeal was called for repeatedly by President Eisenhower and other top members of his administration, by President Kennedy and the present administration, by the American Bar Association, and by many state and local bar associations. It is not necessary by this time to elaborate upon the issues. There is one point, however, the matter of reciprocity, that has never been sufficiently stressed, and which is important because it should convince even those who are impatient with arguments based on legal ideals or world leadership toward peace, and who want to get down to cold-blooded national self-interest.

Such people assume that the function of the self-judging clause is to throw up a wall against possible loss to ourselves as defendants. In fact, the principal effect is to throw up a wall against all possible remedies for ourselves as plaintiffs. Let us remember Robert Frost's well-known lines:

> Before I built a wall I'd ask to know
> What I was walling in or walling out

We are not merely walling the other fellow out of court. We are walling ourselves out, whenever we have a valid claim. France learned this lesson the hard way in the Norwegian loans case. Norway had floated loans payable in gold in France, and later went off the gold standard. France, on behalf of the investors, brought a case against Norway insisting on payment in gold. France had a self-judging clause like ours. Norway did not. The Court held that, as a matter of reciprocity, Norway could exercise France's claimed reservation and call the transaction domestic. Result: financial loss in cold cash to citizens of France. Cause: a supposedly protective clause interposed by France. Sequel: France last year repealed her self-judging clause. Will we similarly have to subject innocent Americans to severe financial loss before we learn our lesson?

After all, we need the protection of law more than any other country. We have billions invested within other countries' boundaries, with the ever-possible danger of damage, confiscation, or discrimination. We have hundreds of thousands of tourists abroad, always in danger of personal injury and property damage. We have foreign bases, communications installations, transportation facilities, and economic and technical aid projects. The chances of our needing, as plaintiffs, the help of the Court are many times as great as the chances of our appearing as defendant. In an oblique commentary on the even-handedness of the law, Anatole France said, "The law forbids both the rich and the poor to sleep in the park." But the poor man most needs the park, just as we most need the Court. In both cases, it is the party with the greatest need that would profit most by repeal of the restrictive law.

The depositing of a new good-faith acceptance of the Court's jurisdiction is an important move in the over-all drive toward international rule of law, since it will show the world we mean business when we talk of rule of law.

Acceptance of a world legal system may come about in various ways in addition to general acceptance of the World Court's jurisdiction. Indeed, in the case of the Communist countries, the best hope for a beginning may be the possibility of entrusting particular matters to the Court, or a panel of it, or some other tribunal. Suppose, for example, we reach the day when a real disarmament treaty is found desirable by the Soviet Union. Obviously such a treaty must contain a procedure for settling disputes as to its interpretation—since otherwise the treaty would collapse in a welter of misunderstandings and recriminations within a matter of months. Only a judicial tribunal can ultimately do the dispute-settling job in the time available. All future treaties should contain a clause submitting disputes on interpretations to an international court, as we have done in our last sixteen commercial treaties. If we insist on this clause as a matter of regular policy, we can go a long way toward bringing important areas of potential conflict within the framework of peaceful legal settlement.

Compliance with the Law

The fourth component of the law structure of peace is compliance with the decisions of international tribunals once they are rendered. It is a curious fact that although many people worry more about this item than any other, in practice it may prove to be the least worrisome of all. History demonstrates that with very few exceptions the decisions of international tribunals have always been obeyed. This seems to indicate that, if we can bring nations to the point where they so far accept the body and machinery of the law that they allow a case to go to decision, by that time it becomes unthinkable to flout the judgment after it is rendered. This is a fact of immense significance as we set up our scale of priorities for action. It should help to reassure those people who fear that a world legal system will be ineffectual unless backed by a world army, navy, and air force.

If the record of compliance with international decisions is at least as good as that with domestic decisions, and perhaps better, why is it that some critics go about sneering at international law and saying that it is something no one pays any attention to? I think the answer lies in a failure to distinguish between decisions of tribunals and unilateral assertions of legal rights. We allege that Country X has repeatedly broken treaties. We conclude that Country X is lawless and has no respect for international law. But does Country X admit this? Certainly not. It will give you some formula to show that it did not really break the treaty, but merely "interpreted" it. We may be positive we are right. But as long as matters are in this posture, it is impossible to say with impartiality and finality that Country X has broken international law. But let the case go to Court, let the law be applied to the particular facts—and then, when the rights and wrongs have been authoritatively settled, we shall have an unassailable test of the degree of compliance with law.

The record of compliance judged on this basis, then, is one reason why many feel that we can and should build up the structure of law without waiting for the day to come, if it ever comes, when some kind of global political authority comparable to national governments will stand behind the decisions of international judicial tribunals. Meanwhile, of course, we should study every possible means of strengthening measures short of force to ensure compliance, including public opinion, multilateral treaties, and diplomatic and economic sanctions.

The specific job of building the law structure of peace may seem to be a task of almost insuperable difficulty. But, difficult or not, we must try. Rousseau, in his book on education called *Emile,* wrote: "The best way to teach Emile not to lean out of the window is to let him fall out. Unfortunately, the defect of this system is that the pupil may not survive to profit by his experience." The world has been learning about international relations for centuries by a process of periodically falling out the window. The injuries have been severe, but never quite fatal. But we all know that one more fall will be our last. We must profit by our experience, for we will not be given another chance.

There is one factor that was never present before. The shadow of the H-bomb is over us all. Perhaps the mutual realization of capacity for mutual annihilation will telescope history and enable us to achieve a degree of progress in decades that in other times might have taken centuries.

NOTES

1. See *Anglo-Iranian Oil Company Case* (United Kingdom v. Iran), *ICJ Reports for 1951,* p. 89; *ICJ Reports for 1952,* p. 93.
2. See cases Nos. 22, 23, 25, 28, 36, 40, and 44 of the International Court's General List, *ICJ Yearbook for 1958–1959,* pp. 70–84.

CONSTRUCTING RULES THAT AFFECT GOVERNMENTS

By ROGER FISHER

AN EXPLICIT PREMISE of this paper is that arms control requires rules—that the task at hand is to design, create, and maintain rules that effectively restrain governmental conduct. In the light of rapidly changing technology and political conditions one might suggest that nations should not be tied up by rules but should be left as free as possible to alter their conduct quickly to meet new circumstances as they arise. That suggestion must be rejected. The problem is to create order out of chaos, and the essence of order is rules. Just as collisions on the highways are reduced by such rules as driving on the right, so the chaotic conditions of the arms race are reduced by rules restraining governments.

Much discussion of arms control rests on the assumption that the only way of creating rules to limit the arms race is to negotiate a treaty. It is suggested here that in fact there are a variety of ways in which restraints upon governmental conduct may be created. To appreciate the spectrum of rule-creating procedures, one must understand what it is that causes a government to respect a rule.

Why Governments Comply with Rules

Before turning to international rules that may guide governmental behavior, it should first be recognized that within a country the laws that restrict governments are quite different from the laws that restrict individuals. If one makes a contract with an individual and he breaks it, there is a third party, the government, which will use the superior force of the state to make that individual either comply with his contract or pay damages. If the individual does not pay, his property may be seized by the sheriff and sold. But if one makes a contract with the government, and the government does not pay, there is no third party to make the government do so. All that a court can do is to say that the government ought to pay. If the government does in fact comply with court decisions and with the Constitution, it is not because of the physical power of any marshal or sheriff.

The same is true of rules in the international field. Short of world government, there will be no superior force to compel compliance by the major powers with such rules as may be applicable to them.[1] Governments comply with treaties and other international rules as they do with constitutions and other domestic rules by a process of composite self-restraint.

If, having signed an arms-limitation treaty, State A decides that it now wants to abandon that approach and go full steam ahead in the arms race, there is no way to "enforce" the treaty. The most that State B can do is also to go full steam ahead in the arms race or take actions that are even more warlike. Short of world government, there is no physical control in arms control. If an arms-control rule is broken, the most that the community can do is to destroy the rule; it cannot, as it can in the case of a violation of a municipal ordinance against carrying guns, re-establish the rule. Any country, certainly a major power, acting as a unit, is physically free at any time to terminate a rule restricting its conduct, no matter how clearly it was written or how many times it was signed. In some ways a treaty is just a scrap of paper. A treaty cannot be iron-clad. It is eggshell thin, within the power of a state to smash it, and all the king's horses and all the king's men cannot put it back together again. And a treaty, like an egg, is kept from getting smashed by the enlightened self-interest of those who deal with it, not by anything inside it.

Among the limitless considerations which affect a governmental decision there appear to be four basic factors which tend to cause a government to respect rules—rules which it, as a unit, always has the physical, factual ability to violate.

1. Apprehension of action by "the other side." One factor causing governments to respect rules is the apprehension of the action which would be taken by those directly benefited by the rule—those on the other side of the rule. The decision of the United States government to respect the constitutional limitations on its power is influenced by an apprehension of what the people of the United States might do if the Constitution should be ignored. Similarly, the United States respects a treaty by a process of self-restraint which is influenced by a fear of what the other party to the treaty might do.

In the case of nontreaty rules, and even in the case of treaties such as those governing the Panama Canal, to divide governments into those on one side of the rule, those on the other side, and third states fails to reflect the true diversity and is obviously a simplified model. But for any given act by the United States, even such diverse countries as Egypt, China, India, Brazil, France, and the USSR can probably be divided among those "on our side," those who might take prompt action hostile to us, and those with whom our primary concern would be the long-range effects.

The deterrent effect of the fear of retaliatory action by those on "the other side" is well known. It supports not only rules against the use of gas, but rules establishing diplomatic immunity, rules keeping arms out of the Antarctic, and most other rules limiting the behavior of one government with respect to another.

2. Apprehension of the effect on third parties. A government is concerned not only with what the party most directly affected by the breach of a rule might do, it is also concerned with the effect of the breach on others. In the international sphere, this concern is usually with what is called "world public opinion." Should the United States resume U-2 flights over the Soviet Union, one category of consequences that we would fear would be the steps that the Soviet Union might take, such as to hit with rockets the bases or carriers from which the planes had taken off. A whole additional range of feared consequences would be, for example, political action in the United Nations and the loss of confidence in us by other countries.

If a government were convinced that it would have to violate an undertaking in order to maintain a military position necessary for survival, it would no doubt do so, and hope that it could justify its action to the world. But in some circumstances the views of third states may be more feared than retaliatory action. Presumably the Soviet decision to respect the rule of nonintervention in the Congo was brought about in significant part by concern for the views of third states. In a world in which actions speak louder than words, governments which engage in progaganda weigh the effect of their actions on third states.

3. Individual morality. In addition to the two types of external consequences that may cause a government to respect a rule, there are two internal factors which tend to work in the same direction. The first of these is that by and large man is a moral creature who must convince himself of the "rightness" of a proposed action. However evil we may think particular governments or individuals to be, we cannot ignore the extent to which people's behavior is influenced by their own notions of what they "ought" to do, independent of their judgment as to what the rewards or punishments might be for the particular act.

The fact that a government cannot afford to trust a potential enemy does not make the morality of individuals an unimportant consideration in arms control. Rules will have greater practical strength when they are reinforced by the moral principles of the individuals in the governments affected. We could expect rules against the assassination of officials of a foreign government to be respected for reasons going beyond a cold calculation of the consequences. On the other hand, rules requiring officials of one country to inform upon their colleagues might be violated because of moral scruples, despite a recognized theoretical advantage in compliance. Moral strength may depend not only on the substance of rules but also on the process by which they were established. When solemn promises are given or rules of recognized authority established, many government officials will tend to respect them because of their belief that they "ought" to, without basing each day's continued compliance upon a Machiavellian weighing of the pros and cons.

4. Institutional resistance to breaking rules. The second internal factor affecting a governmental decision to comply with rules is the restraint that results from the fact that a government is not a single unit but an elaborate political structure involving a great many people. Once a rule is established and a government is complying with it, any breach requires a change in governmental direction. Sheer inertia will tend to keep the government doing what it was doing before. Any change of policy requires recommendations, conferences, memoranda, and some kind of collective decision.

In particular, a decision to break a rule will have to overcome the individual moral notions of those who might think the rule should be respected. It will also involve attempts to reconcile differing appraisals of what the external consequences of the breach would be.

Finally, a government is a structure that is held together and operates on the basis of rules. The entire power of a government depends upon the officers and employees within it continuing to function in accordance with an elaborate scheme of rules. The government's ability to break a rule depends upon whether that particular rule can be sorted out and ignored, leaving respect for the other rules intact. Within the United States the government is not free to ignore decisions of the Supreme Court or to ignore the Constitution without jeopardizing the whole governmental structure. For many government officials direct respect for the Constitution would outweigh respect for a Presidential request to ignore the Constitution. Currently, treaties and other international rules are not so interwoven into the governmental fabric. But in the future, government officers may acquire a higher loyalty to an international rule, particularly to a rule that seems to them essential for world survival, than the loyalty which they have to the request of a superior. The critical point comes when the government officer considers the international rule as applying directly to him, rather than as applying to him only through the governmental chain of command. Once an individual official recognizes a direct duty to the rule, that government's freedom to break the rule is seriously reduced. Such a rule has become an element in the structure of a government which depends for its strength on respect for rules.

If the above analysis is correct, rules governing governments can be created by any process which defines a norm of governmental behavior and which marshals in support of that norm one or more of the forces which tend to bring about governmental compliance: fear of retaliatory action, fear of the effect on public opinion, the moral views of government officers, and institutional resistance to breaking rules.

The durability of a rule will depend upon the strength of the forces behind it. This strength will depend to some extent upon the rule-creating process. An act of acceptance by a state will create a moral commitment of some of its officers, will set up institutional resistances to change, and will require a state to consider the effect of a breach upon public opinion. The same forces will support any rule that is created by a process which makes it "law." The more solemn and formal the procedure is, the greater the commitment. Also, because of the force of public opinion, a rule accepted as binding by most of the countries of the world is by that fact alone a rule with which every other state must reckon. Public opinion and moral scruples will be less upset if the rule is in a form which can be "terminated" without "breaking" it, although the consequent action to be expected from the other side would often be the same.

The retaliatory action to be expected depends in part upon whether the rule was being respected by the other side and, if not, what an appropriate response to a breach would be. (There are rules about breaking rules: concern for public opinion, moral scruples, and the fear of further retaliation tend to deter one government from retaliating more than in an amount justified by the original breach.)

Because democratic institutional arrangements require clearing a decision with so many people, the less autocratic a government, the greater the strength of a rule accepted by it. Even in a democracy, however, the possibility of a secret breach reduces substantially all the forces which tend to support compliance. Fears of consequential action by the opposing party and an adverse public opinion are discounted to the degree that it is thought that the secret can be kept. Moral and internal resistances to breaking the rule exist only among the reduced number who are privy to the secret.

The strength of public opinion will further depend upon such factors as how clear it is that there is a rule, how clear it is that the rule applies to this case, and the extent to which the rule is easily understandable and appeals to common sense. An arbitrary rule will not have the strength of one that has a rational, historical, or geographic basis.

From such considerations it is apparent that the forces that produce governmental compliance with legal rules, including treaties, are also available in support of nonlegal rules of governmental behavior. Although the breach of a rule recognized as legally binding will usually involve more moral and institutional resistance and more of an adverse effect on world public opinion than in the case of a rule not considered to be one of law, this need not always be so. And the retaliatory considerations may be just as great in the absence of a treaty as with a treaty. Arms control need not be limited to rules that are thought of as legal.

Methods of Creating Arms-Control Rules

The science of game theory has shown that an understanding of international relations may be acquired by comparing the rules of governmental conduct to those of a game. In such terms, what we are concerned with here is the kind of a game in which one makes up the rules as one goes along. Take, for example, a situation in which several boys are starting to throw snowballs at each other. How does it become understood that the activity is to be limited to a snowball fight, and that neither side is to grab boys on the other side, or to wrestle with them, or to punch them in the nose? If one player thinks there ought to be a rule against putting stones in the snowballs, what is the best means of getting the rule established? Should he build up a reserve of snowballs with stones in them and agree to give them up in exchange for an agreed adoption of the rule, or should he promptly declare: "No stones in snowballs!"?

What we need to become is experts in the art of creating new rules to the game while the game is being played. There is scope for ingenuity. The other players do not have a veto over all the ways of creating rules. The following are suggested, in roughly ascending order in terms of the clarity and strength of the resulting rule, as illustrative types of processes for the creation of arms restraints.

Engaging in a course of conduct. A single nation may create a norm by a uniform course of conduct which conforms to that norm, even though the implied rule which it is respecting is never made explicit. A series of precedents creates a rule. The more years that go by without maneuvering near the Soviet border, the more unusual and hence provocative such an act would be. A pattern of conduct may tie a country's own hands.

If many nations follow a similar course of conduct, the rule that is established may affect not only themselves but all nations. If most nations conduct their military affairs consistently with certain restraints, those restraints tend to turn into custom. And the violation of custom involves, to a lesser degree, the same considerations of external consequences and internal restraints that are involved in breaking a rule recognized as binding.

Articulating a rule. Making explicit a particular norm may create a rule as to whether or not that norm reflects a contemporaneous course of conduct. If the articulation does define a course of conduct, it adds strength to any rule established by the conduct itself. Consider, for example, rules about testing long-range missiles. If the United States were to test a missile by firing it directly toward the Soviet Union but so arrange the missile that it would alter course and drop into the sea thirteen miles off the Soviet coast, would this violate any existing rule? So far as I know, neither country tests its missiles by firing them toward the other, but no rule against it has been mentioned. When the first person, looking at the specific facts on missile testing, articulates the concept of not shooting missiles toward the other country, the rule begins to take life. A significant fact about a rule is the frequency and extent to which the underlying concept is articulated, repeated, and accepted as a valid concept, whether or not it is accepted as a rule to be followed.

To some extent, the process of creating restraints through effective articulation is in the field of propaganda. But drawing lines is not simply a matter of words. The line articulated should reflect a concept that has internal validity, has a physical, practical, or historical basis, is readily understandable, and distinguishes a pattern of restrained conduct from a pattern of conduct that is meaningfully different and less restrained. Before countries can respect lines, the lines must be created, and some lines will work better than others. Through study and effort, valid concepts of arms restraint can be articulated.

A country is not only able to tie its own hands by making articulate the restraints it is respecting, it can also tie the hands of the other side. If there is conduct in which we are not engaging and in which we would like the Soviet Union not to engage, defining the line we have not crossed in terms that appeal to common sense and public understanding would, by that fact alone, cause the Soviet Union at least to pause at that line and appraise the consequences of crossing it. Such articulation by one side makes it increasingly easy for the other side to recognize the line as a convenient place to maintain a *modus vivendi* if it wishes to do so. Equally possible, though more difficult, is the articulation of rules which the other side is currently not respecting but which thereafter it will be persuaded to respect by the feared external consequences of not respecting it, the moral views of its officers, or both. Articulation can most effectively be done, perhaps, by governments, but it can also be done by organs of the United Nations, by private citizens, and by public and private groups.

Making a unilateral promise. A course of conduct, or the articulation of a course of conduct, contains at most an implied promise. Unilateral restraints can also be created by express promises. A country may undertake on its own to behave in a certain way. The United States might, for example, promise never to place a nuclear warhead in a satellite or might promise not to fly any of its military aircraft within fifty miles of the Soviet Union. Either of these promises would create a rule which would have a significant restraining influence on the future conduct of the United States. Breach of the rule would require overcoming appreciable internal resistances to going back on a promise—and some concern over the external consequences of the breach.

Unilaterally limiting capability. A promise of future conduct can be made absolutely binding for a while by a country's limiting its physical capability to act contrary to its promise. Switzerland may promise never to use nuclear weapons and may so conduct its affairs, by not training personnel and by not producing any nuclear weapons, that at any given time the world is sure of what Switzerland's conduct will be for some time in the future.

Another illustrative restraint in this category would be the unilateral disarmament of weapons that do not presently seem decisive. The total elimination of existing nuclear stockpiles seems extremely difficult, inasmuch as it is not subject to verification. On the other hand, the military risk of unilaterally disarming types of middle-grade weapons, like poison gas, would be comparatively slight. It need not be conditioned on reciprocal action by the other side; to the extent that it was not, the deterrent for the other side's using the "prohibited" weapon would depend upon a credible fear of a retaliatory use of bigger or worse weapons among those which were retained.

If two men, A and B, each armed with their fists, a knife, and a gun, are hostile and become involved in a fight, it might make sense for A to throw away his knife. Such a move would create a rule against using knives and would have a tendency to keep any fighting at the fisticuff level. A new pressure would have been created against B's using his knife. If B should pull his knife, A might have no reasonable choice except to draw his gun, and, if B is going to get into a gun fight, he would not want to start it with a knife but would want to be the first on the draw. (Of course, there is always the danger that A may end up being shot by quick-drawing B, or having to fight B's knife with his fists, having in turn been deterred by other factors from using his gun. But the example does suggest how a unilateral limitation on capability can create rules for the other side.[2])

It should be noted that in the rule-creating processes considered so far, the restraint is created unilaterally[3] without any aspect of agreement. The rule, which a state may be caused by the factors previously discussed to respect, is established without a treaty or even a tacit understanding. To be sure, the restraint is effective only if the restrained state "voluntarily" complies, but the forces, such as world public opinion, tending to cause such compliance are basically the same as those which would tend to cause compliance with rules that had been agreed upon.

Unilateral action plus United Nations articulation. Still without any acceptance by the other side, either the Soviet Union or the United States might be able to tie the other's hands quite effectively by a resolution of the General Assembly recommending a particular restraint for all countries. The United Nations, to a very real degree, has legislative powers. The rules it "enacts" can have the same types of compulsion behind them as do treaties and general rules of international law. They may be stronger or weaker, but this will depend upon many factors, including the inherent merit of the rule. It may sometimes be easier for a country to explain to the world why it had to break a bilateral promise than to explain why it had to act contrary to the expressed consensus of the world. Working through the United Nations has its risks. The United Nations might recommend a rule we would be unwilling to abide by, for reasons, for example, such as the difficulty of verifying compliance. But a country's day-to-day concern that particular rules might not be to its liking should not obscure its fundamental and long-range interest that there be rules.

Unilateral but reciprocal self-restraints. One process for limiting the arms race is for each side to demonstrate self-restraint. The more self-control one side undertakes, the more self-control the other side can afford to undertake, and vice versa. This is the process by which limited wars are limited. The process would seem equally applicable to limiting preparations for war. Although no clear line can be drawn between the case in which the restraining influence is established by the act of one side (but respected by the other) and the case in which the rule is established by the reciprocal acts of the two sides, the core concepts should be distinguished. In the first, the restrained government finds itself trapped by world public opinion and other forces in support of a rule announced and respected by the other side. In the second, rules are established by a deal—by a tacit agreement under which, as under an express agreement, performance is exchanged for performance. The essential difference between unilateral but reciprocal self-restraints and bilateral agreements would appear to lie in the fact that one side takes the first step without having the promise of the other side that it will take any step whatever.

There are infinite variations on the process. The continuance of the action taken by the first state may be made, expressly or impliedly, contingent upon the over-all restraint exercised by the second state, or upon the second state's demonstrating that it is subjecting itself to the identical restraint. The United States, for example, may conclude that it will not engage in an all-out nuclear shelter program so long as the Soviet Union does not launch such a program. Another form of reciprocal self-restraint is the case in which the second state adopts a quite different restraint which may be considered an appropriate quid pro quo. Examples of such reciprocal restraints may be taken from the limited-warfare area. In Korea, United Nations troops did not fight across the Yalu, and North Korean forces did not bomb Pusan harbor or Japan.

The process of unilateral self-restraint, contingent upon reciprocal self-restraint, lends itself more readily to some kinds of rules than to others. It would seem easiest when the action being restrained is action in which neither side has yet engaged, and when compliance with the rule is subject to ready verification at any time by the other side. The process seems least useful when the first step taken by one side would require a major shift in conduct from that in which it is currently engaged and when the risks are such that if the other side did not follow suit, the first state would feel obliged to shift back to its original course of conduct. The United States could hardly scrap all its long-range missiles and promise not to have any in the future, conditioned on the Soviet Union's doing likewise. Should the Soviet Union fail to follow suit, the United States would promptly have to re-create its whole missile program.

A major difficulty with the unilateral approach lies in the very fact that the determination of what step shall be taken and what reciprocal action will be deemed satisfactory is made by only one country. If we assume that the first state is seeking a fair and equivalent restraint on both sides rather than seeking to gain a military advantage, it still may not have appraised the risks and benefits in the same manner as does the other side. Unless there is a good deal of negotiation and communication between the two sides, the one will not know what is bothering the other, what steps each side thinks it can undertake, and what steps it considers equivalent.

The measurement of the respective military positions of the Soviet Union and the United States is not so fine that any single step of a modest sort could be said to alter the balance. The gamble that one side takes in not attempting a few unilateral steps toward military restraint is probably greater than the military risk those steps would involve. But a basic issue that must be faced in suggesting that a particular step be undertaken unilaterally is whether the first state would do better to hold out and get a promise of something in exchange for the restraint that it is adopting. In resolving this issue, it must be recognized that to rely wholly on bilateral agreements gives the other side a veto power over the creation of rules in support of which one may rally world public opinion.

Forces similar to those that would persuade the other side to honor an agreement once signed can be brought to bear through unilateral action. A series of unilateral steps by the Soviet Union—disarmament through deeds, not words—would bring some pressure on the United States. Also, the United States could be expected to take steps simply in order to encourage the Soviet Union on. We would far rather see their defense budget go down than up. And any encouragement, to be effective, would have to be demonstrated. If this analysis is correct, it is equally valid with the roles of the countries reversed.

One side can tailor a unilateral restraint on its own conduct to get the maximum effect toward military stability with the minimum interference with strength it considers essential. It can recognize that the other side, in whatever reciprocal action it may take, may have to tailor its restraints similarly. The process is thus well suited to situations in which the identical rule would affect the two sides quite differently.

Where one side judges the action it can afford to take on the basis of the actions which the other side has demonstrated it is taking, there is no necessity of negotiating first the promised performance, and then the promised inspection. Of course, neither side will rely on what the other says it is doing. But neither could it rely on what they promised to do if there were a treaty. In either case, it must judge from day to day what military preparations it must make and what restraints it can afford to exercise in the light of what the other side has demonstrated its performance to be.

The bilateral or multilateral negotiation of mutual obligations. The process of negotiating an international agreement is well understood. It has the great advantage of disclosing, at least in part, the relative interests and positions of the two or more sides. In the negotiating process, the full pressure of the bargain can be brought to bear: "I won't unless you will." If a treaty is concluded, obligations are defined that are acceptable to both sides. A government that concludes an arms-limitation treaty will be more firmly committed to that policy than if comparable actions were taken unilaterally. Therefore, it is easier to take bigger first steps, since it is quite likely that the other side will take the first step it has agreed to take.

The negotiation of a reasonably detailed, general, over-all disarmament agreement is an extremely complicated task. Any comprehensive treaty would require the participation not only of the United States and the Soviet Union but also of Communist China and many other countries of the world. Once a treaty was negotiated, there would be ratification problems, of which obtaining the advice and consent of two-thirds of the United States Senate would not be insignificant.

After a treaty has been negotiated, signed, and ratified, each side has the bare promise of a potential enemy which it is physically free to ignore at any time. Each side will be under pressure to construe the agreement favorably to itself and to take all military action which it can legally take up to the edge of the agreement. We, in the United States particularly, tend to believe that if a proposed action is legal it is all right to take it. However comprehensive a disarmament agreement might be, it could not preclude the possibility of the opposing sides' conducting an arms race around its edges. If the two sides did not conduct such a limited arms race, it would be because of self-restraint—restraint which, perhaps, they could have exercised without the treaty.

A quite different kind of treaty might be one which simply tried to set the tone for a joint policy of arms limitation. A joint declaration by the heads of state that each side would adopt a policy of limiting its weapons and of demonstrating to the other side that it was not preparing a surprise attack might be quite useful, if it was not taken as a substitute for action.

Assuming that a comprehensive arms-control treaty is sufficiently valuable so that great effort should be made to obtain one, regardless of the difficulties and regardless of the substantial chance that it could never be obtained, the question still remains: Should each country put all its arms-control efforts in the treaty framework? Should it accept the policy of all-out defense while trying to negotiate an arms-control treaty? Should each side assume that it is safer to exercise no self-control, except along lines agreed to by the other?

Conclusion

Within a country, the line between legal rules and other rules is fairly sharp. In general, a rule which is legally binding upon an individual has not only such moral force as it may carry with it, but also the superior physical force of the state behind it. In the international sphere, and more broadly in the sphere of rules that regulate governmental conduct, the line between legal rules and nonlegal rules still exists, but the consequences of that line are quite different. Legal rules carry with them a greater sense of "ought" than do other rules. But the same forces which persuade a government to comply with a legal rule can be marshaled in support of other rules.

Those who are concerned with reducing the risk of catastrophic war by developing rules of governmental conduct should not confine their activities to the attempt to create legal rules, whether through an international treaty or otherwise. The technical possibilities of desirable rules should be explored in the widest way. We should work out potential rules of governmental conduct, having in mind not only the military aspects but also factors such as ease of comprehension and appeal to common sense, which add strength to a rule. And for each potential rule all possible avenues for establishing that rule as one to be accorded respect should be explored.

NOTES

1. Although the discussion is directed at the problem of controlling the major powers, most of the discussion is equally applicable to the small powers. A big power cannot automatically compel a small power to respect a rule. For example, the United States may not be free to compel Cuba to respect the international law protecting foreign investments.

2. It has been suggested that this example also illustrates how such gaps in capabilities may create strong pressures on the other side to exploit the gap or to pre-empt the use of more potent forces. Such limitations must be selected with care.

3. Some discussions of "unilateral" measures fail to recognize that the number of states restrained by a rule may not be the number involved in creating the rule. A rule which binds only one country may have been established by treaty, and a rule that creates a restraining influence on two or more states may have been created by the unilateral act of a single state.

NEUTRALISM AND THE UNITED NATIONS

By LOUIS B. SOHN

FOR FIFTEEN YEARS the United Nations has been a pliable instrument in the hands of the United States and her Western allies. Both the Soviet bloc and the neutralists could seldom command the one-third of the votes needed in the General Assembly to block a decision. In the Security Council only the Soviet veto could stop a Western proposal, as the non-Western nations could never muster more than three or four votes out of eleven. While the Western nations have ordinarily used their preponderant majority for the strengthening of the powers of the United Nations, they have sometimes abused it in order to score mere propaganda victories. The rights of the minorities were not always respected.

With the admission of seventeen new members to the United Nations in 1960, and of a few more in 1961, the balance of power in the General Assembly has changed drastically and the Afro-Asian group has acquired decisive strength. A nation disliked by that group (e.g., Portugal or Belgium) can no longer be elected to the Security Council or to any other organ of the United Nations. To the extent that the Afro-Asian group stands united, it can prevent any action by the General Assembly, and even if it should split into two almost equal groups, it may still add more than twenty votes (i.e., more votes than are in the possession of the Latin American group) to either side of the issue, a number frequently sufficient to defeat any proposal requiring a two-thirds vote of the Assembly. In view of customary absences and abstentions less than 35 votes (out of 104) are usually required to block a decision.

Small Nations and Peace

Some people believe that this new situation is a dangerous one, that it is going to lead to constant impasses and will weaken the United

Nations. It is somehow assumed that the new members are not going to behave rationally, that they will abuse their new-found power and that the interest of the world community will, in consequence, suffer. One has to admit that some of these new countries acquired their independence so fast that they will require a period of adjustment before becoming completely responsible members of the family of nations. But even the least experienced nation realizes quite quickly that in the dangerous world of power politics and cold war, the United Nations constitutes its best hope for survival, stability, and peace. It is almost pathetic to see the exuberant faith of the delegates from the new nations in the omnipotence of the United Nations, their impatience with technicalities and jurisdictional obstacles, and their eagerness to have the United Nations adopt an active role in the removal of all injustices and inequalities in the world. More than the old, sophisticated veterans of the cold war, they take the ringing preamble to the Charter seriously and are willing to support all proposals which would bring closer the realization of the great goals accepted therein.

It is not the irresponsibility of the small nations, old and new, which constitutes the greatest danger to peace. Their quarrels can, of course, cause trouble. But as long as great powers stay out of these quarrels, and instead help the United Nations to solve the disputes between small states, such disputes cannot present a real threat to peace. It is only when the quarrel involves one or more of the big powers or one of their close allies that the danger to peace becomes imminent. Long-range rockets and nuclear weapons are still exclusive perquisites of great powers. Only these nations have in their hands the power to annihilate each other and to obliterate the rest of humanity in the process. Death-carrying particles thrown into the air by nuclear explosions do not respect boundaries or the most solemn declarations of neutrality. No longer can the neutrals receive important gains from wars between other powers; no longer are wars sources of fat profits for the neutrals. On the contrary, a war between great powers in the future would mean disaster not only for the belligerents but for the neutrals as well. The small nations seem to realize this fact much better than the big ones, and this is the main reason why they have grown impatient with the ineffective disarmament negotiations conducted by the big powers. The smaller nations might be right in thinking that only by the addition of their representatives to the negotiating committees can a way be found out of the present morass. The smaller nations much more than the larger ones are interested more in peace than in gaining a temporary advantage; they are more likely to reach a solution which would be fair to all concerned.

This interest in peace is common to all small nations, not only to the so-called neutralist ones, but also to those who are allied with the United States or the Soviet Union for purposes of defense or for economic reasons. One can easily observe that most Latin American nations, despite their close links to the United States embodied in the Rio Pact and the Bogota Charter of the Organization of American States, have shown great independence on such issues as peace, disarmament, economic development, or colonialism. Some NATO nations other than the Big Three have also shown an independent spirit and have often been ahead of the major powers in presenting constructive proposals. The Canadian initiative in the Suez crisis is but one of many effective contributions by those nations. While the spirit of independence is less apparent among the Eastern European nations, even they do not entirely lack constructive ideas. The Rapacki plan for nuclear disarmament of Central Europe, originated by the Polish foreign minister, is a prime example of a proposal coming from a smaller nation which later was endorsed, with some reluctance, by the Soviet Union.

Are Neutralists Really Neutral?

On the other hand, the independence of some of the neutralists does not appear to an impartial observer as clear as may be desired. It would be quite proper for neutralists to abstain on all votes relating to cold war issues, raised for propaganda purposes by one side against the other, but there is a tendency on the part of quite a few neutralists to be more receptive to the propaganda moves of the Soviet Union than to those of the Western powers. They seem to be particularly afraid of supposedly "sinister" designs of Western "colonialist" powers and of their allies, despite the excellent record of these powers in granting independence to more than thirty colonial territories. On the other hand, they have accepted with a mere shrug of the shoulders the extension of the Communist empire to many proud and previously independent nations. Somehow imperialism within the same racial group and over territories connected by land with the nation extending its empire seems to be more acceptable to these neutral nations than an attempt by a colonial power to dominate other races in territories across the sea. While there might be some valid reason for making these distinctions, this not completely neutral attitude of some neutralists has resulted in a condemnation of such pseudoneutralism by many official and unofficial statements in the West. It has also led to a disinclination to believe that true neutralism really exists and to a frequent complaint that many of the neutralists are neutral "against" the Western powers.

The Impartiality of the Secretary-General

A similar problem of allegedly non-neutral behavior has arisen in another area. Despite the great effort of the late Mr. Hammarskjold, Secretary-General of the United Nations, to act as an impartial international official, the Soviet Union has complained that in the Congo crisis he had sided with the colonialist powers and the NATO countries. To remedy this situation the Soviet Union has proposed that the Secretary-General be replaced by a group of three persons representing, respectively, the Western powers, the socialist states, and the neutralist countries. If it should be required that this collective executive body should function by unanimous vote only, this might result in a paralysis similar to that engendered by the Soviet veto in the Security Council. Even if that new organ should be allowed to function by a majority vote, there would still be the difficulty caused by the fact that the neutralist member would have to obtain the approval of one of the antagonists before any action could be taken. At present, the Secretary-General can assert his independence from both sides and can adopt impartial and objective decisions, dictated by his understanding of the common interests of the United Nations; he can, and frequently does, take steps that are objected to at one point by one side, at another point by the other side, and sometimes by both. This freedom of maneuver would disappear if all the decisions of the neutralist member of the triumvirate should require the concurrent vote of at least one other member of the group.

This system could work only if the executive group were enlarged to five, including in it three nationals of neutralist countries in addition to the representatives of the two sides in the cold war, and if it were possible to require that all decisions be made by a majority of three. In this case the neutralist members of the group would be able to make decisions without having to appease one or the other of the non-neutralist members. The situation could be further improved by the selection of the non-neutralist members not from the main antagonists but from the smaller nations allied with them. It would not be necessary to abolish the post of the Secretary-General, as one of the three neutralists might occupy that post, while the four other members of the executive group would function as undersecretaries. It would be prescribed, however, that certain major decisions of the Secretary-General would require the concurrence of at least two of the undersecretaries.

Precedents in International Arbitration

The solution proposed here finds an analogy in the rules adopted for the creation of international arbitral tribunals. The first Hague Convention for the Pacific Settlement of International Disputes of 1899 provided that in constituting an arbitral tribunal each party shall appoint two arbitrators and these latter together shall choose an umpire. In 1907, the second Hague Convention on this subject revised this rule to oblige each party to appoint only one of its two arbiters from among its own nationals. This proved still unsatisfactory, and the Geneva General Act for the Pacific Settlement of International Disputes of 1928 provided that each party shall nominate only one member of the arbitral tribunal, and that three neutral members be chosen either by common agreement or through one of the methods for impartial appointment outlined in the Act. The draft articles on arbitral procedure, prepared by the International Law Commission and noted by the General Assembly of the United Nations in 1958, also express a preference for a tribunal of five, designated either by the parties or by the president of the International Court of Justice. The reasons usually given for the adoption of these rules on the composition of an arbitral tribunal are similar to those given above with respect to the Secretariat of the United Nations, i.e., that the neutral members should be able to arrive at an impartial decision without dependence on the concurrent vote of one of the arbiters representing the parties.

Which Nations Are Neutralist?

Returning to the question of the structure of the United Nations, it might be possible to provide a better role for the smaller and neutralist nations if an agreement could be reached with respect to the nations belonging to this group. The principal imbalance in the United Nations in its early years resulted from the fact that the Communist nations had usually only five or six votes at their disposal while the United States could easily count on some thirty Western European and Latin American votes. The will of the United States thus became the will of the United Nations and what was good for the United States became almost automatically good for the United Nations. A nation which refused to support the United States point of view could thus be accused of opposing the United Nations as well, and the idea became current that neutralists are those nations which, though they do not belong to the Soviet bloc, usually vote against the United States or at least abstain on crucial votes.

One cannot contend that the interests of the United States have always, without exception, coincided with those of the United Nations as a whole. But in a preponderant number of cases, United States policy was sufficiently enlightened to justify its identification with the policy which the United Nations should have objectively pursued in these cases even if there were no pressure by the United States. Consequently, in such cases as Korea, Hungary, and Tibet, many neutralist nations were persuaded to vote with the United States, and a new concept of neutrality started to emerge.

Positive Neutralism

A nation can be neutralist as between the United States and the Soviet Union and may refuse to join one of the two major military blocs, but it cannot remain neutralist in its relations with the United Nations. Where the future of the United Nations itself is at stake, where a positive decision needs to be taken to enable the United Nations to survive, where inaction would diminish the possibility of future reliance by a small state on United Nations assistance, a nation cannot hide behind its neutralism. It has to accept responsibility for United Nations action, it has to help in framing a resolution acceptable to a preponderant majority of member nations, and it has to bear its share of the burden for the execution of the final decision of the competent United Nations organ. President Wilson said in 1915: "The basis of neutrality is not indifference; it is not self-interest. The basis of neutrality is sympathy for mankind." In modern terms, the noncommitted nations should embrace positive neutralism in aid of United Nations action rather than negative neutralism which is characterized by a refusal to support United Nations decisions. If positive neutralism can grow further to complete fruition, it may become a new important factor in the conduct of United Nations affairs.

In defining a positive neutralist, the old criteria of ties with military alliances ought to be discarded. In the world of intercontinental ballistic missiles and Polaris submarines, old military bases and the systems of alliances built upon them have lost their meaning. Economic and social changes of tremendous scope are sweeping one country after another, and governments can no longer be propped up by lavish military assistance. If wholesale shifts from one bloc to another are to be avoided, if wars arising from too sudden shifts in political and military balance are to be prevented, unilateral activities directed toward provoking or suppressing revolutionary changes need to be prohibited. But the very process of change cannot be stopped; it can only be diverted into more peaceful rather than violent channels. This can be done only if the whole problem is taken out of power politics and brought before the only forum in which a sympathetic judgment of an impartial arbiter can be obtained—the United Nations. But to do this job well the United Nations must grow up to its new responsibilities and if need be it must so adapt its structure that it could perform its new functions in a more efficient and unbiased manner.

It is submitted that the strengthening of the United Nations will require, in the first place, the strengthening of the truly neutralist group of nations and its enlargement to the maximum possible extent. To accomplish this, it would seem desirable to restrict the opposing camps to only those nations which seldom pursue independent policies and follow the leaders of their bloc in almost every instance; all other nations should be permitted to join the noncommitted group. The goal should be to balance the two opposing camps by giving them about equal strength in the General Assembly, at the lowest possible level, and to allow other nations to be freed from their bondage to the military alliances.

The Communist bloc in the United Nations includes at present ten nations: the Union of Soviet Socialist Republics, the Byelorussian S.S.R., the Ukrainian S.S.R., Albania, Bulgaria, Czechoslovakia, Hungary, the Mongolian People's Republic, Poland, and Rumania. If the principle could be adopted that, pending the unification of their nations, the Communist and non-Communist parts of the four divided countries should be admitted as separate members of the United Nations, four new members would be added to the Communist bloc: People's Republic of China, Democratic German Republic, People's Republic of Korea, and Democratic Republic of Viet-Nam. Thus, the total number of closely-tied Communist countries would be fourteen (or fifteen, if Cuba should become fully a Soviet satellite). Yugoslavia has shown enough independence to be omitted from this group, and though a Communist nation she can be properly considered as a neutralist.

The North Atlantic Treaty Organization constitutes the core of the Western alliance system. Besides the Big Three (United States, United Kingdom, and France), eleven other United Nations members belong to this organization: Belgium, Canada, Denmark, Greece, Iceland, Italy, Luxembourg, Netherlands, Norway, Portugal, and Turkey. If both Germanies should be admitted to the United Nations, the Federal Republic of Germany would have to be added to this group, which would then total fifteen members.

While almost thirty other nations are linked with the United States by various security treaties, practically all of them have shown an increasing amount of independence and it should not require a great effort for them to assert their freedom to vote as they please in United Nations debates. The record of Japan on disarmament, of the Philippines and Mexico on colonial questions, of Brazil and Uruguay on economic questions, to mention just a few examples, should make clear to an impartial observer that none of these countries considers it necessary to follow the leadership of the United States on all issues, and that they are able to vote differently whenever they consider the United States position not in the best interest of the United Nations. It is true that they still depend on the United States for assistance in case of aggression, but so does the rest of the non-communist world. The United States has explicitly promised her protection to several nations through the Eisenhower Doctrine, without requiring an express treaty with those nations. The time might soon arrive for the United States to replace its network of security obligations of varying degree by one straightforward commitment to come to the assistance of any nation against which an act of aggression is being committed regardless of the identity of the aggressor. The United States has done this already in Korea and Lebanon, and it has in fact agreed in the United Nations Charter to "give the United Nations every assistance in any action it takes in accordance with the present Charter."

Before the decision was made to embark on the perilous road of treaties for collective self-defense, the Commission to Study the Organization of Peace made a proposal in 1948 that the United States sponsor instead a treaty open to all members of the United Nations to make available military forces for joint action under the auspices of the United Nations at the request of either the Security Council or the General Assembly, acting by two-thirds vote including at least three of the permanent members of the Security Council. The "Uniting for Peace" Resolution adopted by the General Assembly in 1950 on United States initiative empowered the General Assembly to recommend in certain circumstances collective measures, including the use of armed force when necessary. It further recommended that each member maintain special forces for service as United Nations units "upon recommendation by the Security Council or General Assembly." Even though it was the principal author of this resolution, the United States refused to give an official pledge to make its forces available to a United Nations command; only a few smaller nations expressed willingness to provide United Nations contingents. The United States could still redeem its original promise and replace its network of treaties and unilateral declarations by a pledge to come to the assistance of any nation attacked in violation of the Charter and to make specified contingents available for the defense of any such nation. The use of these troops might be conditioned upon a decision of the Security Council or of a two-thirds majority of the General Assembly, including at least eight of the twelve largest nations of the world, thus ensuring that the United States will not be the only major power backing the decision of the General Assembly. Alternatively, the pledge of the United States might be conditioned upon similar pledges by other nations totaling at least double the number of forces pledged by the United States. Once such a pledge should come into force, there would no longer be any need for the various collective security treaties and they might be cancelled.

This new approach would have a double result: It would strengthen the United Nations, and it would terminate the formal ties which make it difficult to consider certain nations as neutrals. These nations would then be permitted to join the noncommitted group, would bring to it a variety of new points of view, and would enable it to exercise its mediating role between the two blocs in a more effective manner. At present, the neutralist group is handicapped, in approaching the problems before the United Nations objectively and impartially, in that it can muster the necessary two-thirds majority only by cooperating with one bloc or another. With the admission of the divided countries and of a few new nations, and with a shift of some thirty nations away from military alliances, the new neutralist group might command some eighty votes out of about one hundred and ten. It would thus possess a majority sufficient to deal with any situation submitted to the United Nations, provided it is motivated by the good of the United Nations as a whole rather than by selfish interests of some of its members. The unity of the enlarged neutralist group can be maintained only as long as its members work toward the common goals so ably described in the preamble to the Charter. Each important decision adopted at the initiative of this group must represent a reasonable compromise between conflicting points of view both within and outside the group. If this should be its lodestar and if the public opinion of the world can become convinced of the honesty and impartiality of its efforts, the great antagonists of today might have to bow to this joint pressure of the large majorities in the General Assembly and of a supporting public opinion, and a way might be found out of the present dangerous impasse.

The effectiveness of this approach would depend, of course, on the actual independence of the neutralist countries. As long as their very existence is conditioned on economic support by one of the major powers, the small nations must swallow their pride and support the position taken by their benefactors whether they like it or not. Only through a shift in present methods of economic and technical assistance could a remedy be found to this undesirable trend. If the United

States really wants to make it impossible for the Soviet Union to use economic assistance as a weapon of subversion, it must, as in the Congo case, insist that all assistance should be channeled from now on through international organizations and should abandon its own bilateral assistance programs. Once the possibility of economic pressure in crucial voting situations is thus removed, the neutralist nations would be able to vote according to their convictions and to establish a common front against any nation threatening to violate the basic principles of the Charter of the United Nations.

Enlargement of the Security Council

The proposals thus far presented, with respect to the Secretariat and the General Assembly, do not require any changes in the Charter of the United Nations. A strengthening of the Security Council would require, however, a change in the Charter. To increase the neutralist element in the Security Council and to establish a balance between the Western and Communist blocs it will be necessary to increase the membership of the Security Council to seventeen. Such enlarged membership would provide enough room for four members each from the two opposing blocs and would still leave control in the hands of nine neutralist members. Once this is accomplished, it might be possible to abolish the veto, as the danger that the Security Council would be used by one side in the cold war against the other should no longer exist.

Other Desirable Changes

Similarly, the membership of the International Court of Justice should be increased to seventeen, to be divided in the same manner as the membership of the Security Council.

Finally, if new treaties should solve such problems as disarmament, peaceful uses of atomic energy, joint exploration of space, and international police force, it would seem desirable to lodge the controls of these new activities not in the hands of a single director or commander, but in groups of five, each composed of one representative of the West, one representative of the Soviet bloc, and three nationals of neutralist countries.

Conclusions

On the basis of the foregoing considerations it is suggested:

1. That the neutralist group in the General Assembly be enlarged to include, besides the present African, Asian, and European neu-

tralists, all nations other than those which are parties to the NATO Pact or which are closely allied to the Soviet Union or the People's Republic of China; and that positive neutralism favorable to United Nations actions for peace be substituted for present negative neutralism.

2. That the executive group in the United Nations be enlarged to five persons, to include besides a neutralist Secretary-General two neutralist undersecretaries, an undersecretary from the NATO powers, and an undersecretary from the Soviet bloc; and that all major decisions require the concurring votes of three members of this group.

3. That the membership of the Security Council be increased to seventeen, four members coming from the NATO Powers, four from the Communist bloc, and nine from the neutralist nations.

4. That the membership of the International Court of Justice be similarly revised.

5. That the executive direction of new agencies of the United Nations, such as an international police force, disarmament inspectorate, or the agency for peaceful exploration of space, shall be entrusted not to single individuals but to groups of five persons, each composed of one person from the NATO group; one from the Communist bloc, and three from the neutralist nations.

If all these reforms could be accomplished, both sides might trust the United Nations sufficiently to agree to confer upon it additional powers enabling it to realize effectively the goals of the Charter. Thus, through an increase in positive neutralism and through a more adequate neutralization of the United Nations, the dreams of the framers of the Charter might be given concreteness and the purposes of the Charter might be given substance.

EDITORS' EPILOGUE

A PSYCHOLOGICAL BASIS FOR PEACE

By MORTON DEUTSCH

I SHALL ASSUME the truth of the following propositions:

(1) A large-scale nuclear war would achieve a result that no sane man could desire.

(2) When a small war occurs, there is a risk that it may turn into a large war; this risk would be considerably increased by the use of nuclear weapons. In the course of many small wars, the probability of a great war would become almost a certainty.

(3) The knowledge and capacity to make nuclear and other weapons of mass destruction cannot be destroyed; they will exist as long as mankind exists.

(4) Any war in which a nuclear power is faced with the possibility of major defeat or a despairing outcome is likely to turn into a large-scale nuclear war even if nuclear disarmament has previously occurred.

(5) A hostile peace will not long endure.

From these propositions it follows that, if mankind is to avoid utter disaster, we must see to it that irrational men are not in a position to initiate nuclear war, we must find alternatives to war for resolving international conflicts, and we must develop the conditions which will lead conflicting nations to select one or another of these alternatives rather than resort to war.

My discussion in this paper centers primarily on the question: How do we take the hostility out of a hostile peace? This question proliferates into other, related questions: How do we prevent the misperceptions and misunderstandings in international relations which foster and perpetuate hostility? How do we move from a delicately balanced peace of mutual terror to a sturdy peace of mutual trust?

How do we move in the direction of a world community in which law, institutions, obligations, and simple human decencies will enable mankind to enjoy a more amiable life? These are the central questions which must be answered if the world is to avoid disaster. The world will never again be in a position where it cannot destroy itself.

It is well for me to emphasize that opposition to war as a means of conflict resolution does *not* connote an opposition to controversy among nations. Controversy is as desirable as it is inevitable. It prevents stagnation, it is the medium through which problems can be aired and solutions arrived at; it is the heart of social change. Our objective is not to create a world in which controversy is suppressed but rather a world in which controversy is civilized, is lively rather than deadly.

I do not pretend to have answers to the difficult questions I have raised. I raise them because I have something relevant to say and because I believe it is important to confront the fundamental questions. Too often we are distracted from them by short-run urgencies. You may well ask what a psychologist can say that is relevant. A wide reading, however, of acknowledged authorities in the study of war and international relations has convinced me that the dominant conceptions of international relations are psychological in nature. Such psychological concepts as "perception," "intention," "value," "hostility," "confidence," "trust," and "suspicion" recur repeatedly in discussions of war and peace.[1]

I wish to make it clear that what I have to say in this paper is *not* based upon well-established, scientifically verified, psychological knowledge. As psychologists, we have only meager, fragmentary knowledge of how to prevent or overcome distortions in social perceptions, of how to move from a situation of mutual suspicion to a situation of mutual trust, of how to establish cooperative relationships despite intense competitive orientations, of how to prevent bargaining deadlocks. I take it for granted that we need more and better research before we may claim to speak authoritatively on these matters. However, my intent here is not to outline the research which is needed but rather to discuss these urgent matters as well as I can.

Is War Inevitable?

Is it possible that war is inevitable, that the psychological nature of man is such that war is an indispensable outlet for his destructive urges? True, there have been wars throughout human history and men have found outlets for psychological drives of all kinds in war—sadistic, masochistic, creative, heroic, altruistic, adventurous, and so on. Yet, as Jerome Frank[2] has pointed out, the historical prevalence of a behavior pattern is not proof of its inevitability. Human sacrifice in religious rites, slavery, sorcery, and certain forms of child labor have largely disappeared in modern industrialized nations, although such practices have existed throughout human history.

William James recognized that war and the military spirit produced certain virtues which are necessary to the survival of any society. However, he went on to point out that militarism and war are not the only means for achieving the virtues of self-discipline and social cohesiveness, that it is possible to find alternative means for achieving the same psychological ends.[3] (It is of interest to note that James's suggestion for a moral equivalent to war was a "Peace Corps" of youth enlisted in an army against *Nature.*) The view that alternative means for satisfying psychological motives can always be found is, of course, a basic concept in modern psychology. Egon Brunswick went so far as to elevate "vicarious functioning" (i.e., the equivalence and mutual intersubstitutability of different behaviors in relation to goal achievement) to the defining criterion of the subject matter of psychology.[4]

Man's make-up may always contain the psychological characteristics which have found an outlet in militarism and war. There is no reason, however, to doubt that these characteristics can find satisfactory outlets in peaceful pursuits. Aggressiveness, adventurousness, idealism, and bravery will take a peaceful or destructive outlet depending upon the social, cultural, and political conditioning of the individual and upon the behavioral possibilities which exist within his social environment. Some may assert that war provides a more natural, spontaneous, or direct outlet for hostility and aggressiveness than any peaceful alternatives. Such an assertion is based upon a fundamental misconception of war. War is a highly complex, organized social activity in which personal outlets for aggression and hostility are primarily vicarious, symbolic, indirect, and infrequent for most of the participants. This is especially true for the highly mechanized warfare of modern times which largely eliminates the direct physical contact between the aggressor and his victim.[5] Moreover, it is evident that no matter what his psychological make-up, an individual *per se* cannot make war. War-making requires the existence of complex social institutions necessary to organize and maintain a "war machine." This is not to say that a war machine cannot be activated by the decisions of strategically placed individuals. Obviously, one of the great dangers of our era is that a small group of men have the power to create a nuclear holocaust. Even a strategically placed individual can activate a war machine only if it exists; the mass of people, not being strategically placed, cannot directly activate a war no matter what their psychological predispositions. It is relevant to note here that research by T. Abel[6] indicates that warlike attitudes in the populace tend to follow rather than precede the outbreak of war.

The impersonal character of modern war, as Erich Fromm has pointed out,[7] makes it difficult for an individual to comprehend fully the meaning of his actions as he kills. It is easier for most people to kill faceless symbols of human beings at a distance than to kill people with their bare hands. The psychological danger of modern, impersonal war is not that it is a good outlet for aggression but rather, to the contrary, that it does not permit the button-pusher to appreciate fully the destructive nature of his actions. Were he to do so, his destructive actions might be inhibited rather than encouraged.

Misperceptions Which Lead to War

Neither war nor peace is psychologically inevitable. Exaggeration of the inevitability of war contributes to a self-fulfilling prophecy; it makes war more likely. Exaggeration of the inevitability of peace does not stimulate the intense effort necessary to create the conditions for a durable peace, for a stable peace has to be invented and constructed. There is nothing inevitable about it.

A fundamental theorem of the psychological and social sciences is that man's behavior is determined by the world he perceives. Perception is not, however, always veridical to the world which is being perceived. There are a number of reasons why perceptions may be distorted. I would like to consider five common causes of misperception, to illustrate the operation of each in international relations, and to indicate how these misperceptions can be counteracted or prevented.

1. *The perception of any act is determined both by our perception of the act itself and by our perception of the context in which the act occurs.* The contexts of social acts are often not immediately given in perception and often they are not obvious. When the context is not obvious, we tend to assume a familiar context—i.e., a context which is the most likely in terms of our own experience. Since both the present situations and past experiences of the actor and the perceiver may be rather different, it is not surprising that they will supply different contexts and interpret the same act quite differently. Misunderstandings of this sort, of course, are very likely when the actor and the perceiver come from rather different cultural backgrounds and are not fully aware of these differences. The stock conversation of re-

turning tourists consists of amusing or embarrassing anecdotes based upon misunderstandings of this sort.

Urie Bronfenbrenner's first-hand observations[8] lead him to conclude that the Soviets and Americans have a similar view of one another; each says more or less the same things about the other. For example, each states: "*They* are the aggressors"; "*their* government exploits and deludes the people"; "the mass of *their* people is not really sympathetic to the regime"; "*they* cannot be trusted"; "*their* policy verges on madness"; etc.

It is my contention that mutual distortions such as those described above arise, in part, because of an inadequate understanding of the other's context. Take, for instance, the Soviet Union's reluctance to conclude any disarmament agreement which contains adequate provisions for international inspection and control. We view this as a device to prevent an agreement or to subvert any agreement on disarmament which might be worked out. However, as Joseph Nogee has pointed out:

> Under present circumstances, any international control group reflecting the realities of political power would inevitably include a a majority of non-Communist nations. Decisions involving actual and potential interests vital to the USSR would have to be made continuously by a control board the majority of whose members would represent social and economic systems the USSR considers inherently hostile. Any conflicts would ultimately have to be resolved by representatives of governments, and it is assumed that on all major decisions the capitalist nations would vote as a bloc. . . . Thus, for the Soviet Union, representation on a control board along the lines proposed by the West would be inherently inequitable.[9]

I may assert that one can subjectively test the creditability of the Soviet position by imagining our own reactions if the Soviet bloc could consistently outvote us at the United Nations or on an international disarmament control board. Under such conditions, in the present world situation, would we conclude an agreement which did not give us the security of a veto? I doubt it. Similarly, one can test the creditability of the American position by imagining that the Soviet Union had experienced a Pearl Harbor in a recent war and that it had no open access to information concerning the military preparations of the United States. Under such circumstances, in the present world situation, would it be less concerned about inspection and control than we are? I doubt it.

The distorted view that "the mass of their people are not really sympathetic to the regime" is also based upon an inadequate view of each other's total situation. In effect, we ask ourselves if Soviet citizens had the choice between (a) living in Russia if it were like the United States with its high standard of living and its political system of civil liberties, and (b) living in the present-day Soviet Union, which would they choose? We think the answer is obvious, but isn't it clear that the question is wrong? The relevant comparison for them is between their past and their present or future: their present and future is undoubtedly vastly superior to their past. Similarly, the Soviet view is that a comparison of (a) Soviet society with its full employment and expanding economy with (b) capitalism in a permanent depression crisis would favor the Soviet Union. Perhaps it would, but is this the relevant comparison?

How can we prevent and overcome distortions and misunderstandings of this sort? Obviously, more communication, a great increase in interchanges of scholars, artists, politicians, tourists, and the like might be helpful. However, I think we should take cognizance of the findings of the vast body of research on intergroup contact: casual contact of limited duration is more likely to support deeply rooted distortions than remove them. To have any important effect, contact must be prolonged, functional, and intimate.

I suggest that the most important principle to follow in international communication on issues where there is controversy is one suggested by Anatol Rapoport.[10] He advocates that each side be required to state the position of the other side to the other side's complete satisfaction before either side advocates its own position. Certainly the procedure would not eliminate all conflict but it would eliminate those conflicts based upon misunderstanding. It forces one to place the other's action in a context which is acceptable to the other and, as a consequence, prevents one from arbitrarily rejecting the other's position as unreasonable or badly motivated. This is the strategy followed by the good psychotherapist. By communicating to the patient his full understanding of the patient's behavior and by demonstrating the appropriateness of the patient's assumptions to the patient's behavior and past experiences, he creates the conditions under which the current validity of the patient's assumptions can be examined. The attempt to challenge or change the patient's behavior without mutual understanding of its assumptions usually produces only a defensive adherence to the challenged behavior.

2. *Our perceptions of the external world are often determined indirectly by the information we receive from others rather than by our direct experiences.* Human communication, like perception itself, is always selective. The perception of an event is usually less detailed,

more abstract, and less complex than the event which is perceived; the communication about an event is also likely to be less detailed and less complex than its perception. The more human links in the communication of information about any event, the more simplified and distorted will be the representation of the event. Distortion in communication tends to take characteristic forms: on the one hand, there is a tendency to accentuate the unusual, bizarre, controversial, deviant, violent, and unexpected; on the other hand, there is a tendency for communicators who are communicating to their superiors to communicate only that information which fits the preconceptions of their superiors.

If we examine our sources of information about international affairs, we see that they are particularly vulnerable to distorting influences. There are only a small number of American reporters in any country; they do not necessarily work independently of one another. They are under subtle pressure to report items which will catch the reader's interest and conform to their publisher's viewpoint. In a period of hostility between nations, these conditions are not conducive to getting a clear understanding of how events are perceived by the other side.

I suggest that we should recognize the dangers inherent in not perceiving the other side's point of view on a continuing basis. Recognizing these dangers, shouldn't we offer to make arrangements with the Soviet Union whereby we would each be enabled to present our own point of view over the other's radio and television and in their leading newspapers? Suppose the Soviet leaders are afraid to participate on a reciprocating basis; should we make the offer anyway? My answer is in the form of a question: do we have anything to lose by understanding their viewpoint as well as we can; wouldn't "truth squads" adequately protect us from deliberate attempts to mislead us?

3. *Our perceptions of the world are often very much influenced by the need to conform to and agree with the perceptions of other people.* Thus, in some communities it would be difficult for an individual to survive if he perceived Negroes as his social equals or if he perceived Communist China as having legitimate grievances against the United States. If he acted upon his perceptions he would be ostracized socially; if he conformed to the perceptions of other people without changing his own perceptions, so that they were similar to those prevalent in his community, he might feel little self-respect.

It is my impression that most social and political scientists, most specialists in international relations, most intellectuals who have thought about it, and many of our political leaders personally favor the admission of Communist China into the United Nations and favor our taking the initiative in attempting to normalize our relations with Communist China. Yet conformity pressures silence most of us who favor such a change in policy. The strength of these conformity pressures in the United States on this issue is so great that it is difficult to think of Communist China or to talk about it in any terms except those which connote absolute, incorrigible evil. I believe this is an extremely dangerous situation, because without a fundamental change in United States-Chinese relations the world may be blown up shortly after China has acquired a stockpile of hydrogen bombs; this may take less than a decade.

How can we break through the veil of conformity and its distorting influences? Asch's insightful studies of conformity pressures point the way. His studies reveal that when the monolithic social front of conformity is broken by even one dissenter, other potential dissenters feel freer to break with the majority.[11] The lesson is clear: those who dissent must express their opinions so that they are heard by others. If they do so, they may find more agreement than they anticipate.

4. *A considerable body of psychological research*[12] *indicates that an individual attempts to perceive his environment in such a way that it is consistent with his self-perception.* If an individual feels afraid, he tends to perceive his world as frightening; if he feels hostile, he is likely to see it as frustrating or unjust; if he feels weak and vulnerable, he is apt to see it as exploitative and powerful; if he is torn by self-doubt and self-conflict, he will tend to see it as at odds with him. Not only does an individual tend to see the external world in such a way as to justify his feelings and beliefs but also so as to justify his behavior. If an individual is a heavy smoker, he is apt to perceive cigarette smoking as less injurious to health than does a nonsmoker; if he drives a car and injures a pedestrian, he is likely to blame the pedestrian; if he invests in something (e.g., a munitions industry), he will attempt to justify and protect his investment. Moreover, there is much evidence that an individual tends to perceive the different parts of his world as consistent with one another. Thus, if somebody likes you, you expect him to dislike someone who dislikes you. If somebody disagrees with you, you are likely to expect him to agree with someone else who disagrees with you.

The danger of the pressure for consistency is that it often leads to an oversimplified black-white view of the world. Take, for instance, the notions that since the interests of the United States and the Soviet Union are opposed in some respects, we must be opposed to or suspicious of anything that the Communists favor and must regard any nation that desires friendly relations with the Soviet Union as opposed to the United States. If the Soviet Union is against colonialism in Africa, must we be for it? If nations in Latin America wish to establish friendly, commercial relations with the Communist nations, must we feel threatened? If Canada helps Communist China by exporting food to it, must we suspect its loyalty to us? Are nations which are not for us necessarily for the Communists? The notions expressed in affirmative answers to these questions are consistent with the view that the conflict between the United States and the Soviet Union can only be ended by total defeat for one or the other. But is it not possible that the conflict can be resolved so that both sides are better off than they are now? Recognition of this latter possibility may suggest that what benefits the Soviet Union does not necessarily harm us, and that nations with amicable relations with both the United States and the Soviet Union may be an important asset in resolving the cold war before it turns hot.

The pressure for self-consistency often leads to rigid, inflexible positions because it may be difficult to change a position that one has committed oneself to publicly without fear of loss of face. To some extent, I believe this is our situation vis-à-vis the admission of Communist China to the United Nations and with regard to our policies toward Cuba. We are frozen into positions which are unresponsive to changing circumstances because a change in our positions would seem to us to be admission of mistaken judgment which could lead to a loss of face.

What can we do to avoid the "consistency of little minds" and the rigidities of false pride? These dangers to accurate perception are most likely when an individual feels under threat, when his self-esteem is at stake. I think in such circumstances it is prudent to seek the advice and counsel of trusted friends who are not so emotionally involved in the issues. Thus, I think it would be wise to consult with such nations as Canada, France, and Great Britain on our policy toward Cuba and Communist China precisely because they do not have as deep an involvement with these countries as we do. Similarly, consultation with more or less neutral nations such as India, Sweden, Austria, and Nigeria might prevent us from developing an oversimplified view of the nature of our relations with the Soviet Union.

5. Ichheiser has described a mechanism, similar to that of projection, which leads to misunderstandings in human relations: the *mote-beam mechanism.*[13] It consists in perceiving certain characteristics in others which we do not perceive in ourselves. These characteristics are perceived as though they were peculiar traits of the others and, hence, the differences between the others and ourselves are accentuated. Since the traits we are unable or unwilling to recognize in ourselves but are willing to recognize in others are usually traits

we consider to be undesirable, the mote-beam mechanism results in a view of the other as peculiarly shameful or evil. Thus, although many of us who live in the North easily recognize the shameful racial discrimination and segregation in the South, we avoid a clear awareness of the pervasive racial discrimination in our own communities.

Similarly, in international relations it is easy to recognize the lack of political liberties in the Soviet Union, their domination of the nations in Eastern Europe, their obstructiveness in the United Nations, etc., but it is difficult for us to recognize similar defects in the United States: e.g., the disenfranchisement of most Negro voters in many states, our domination of Latin America, our unfair treatment of the American Indian, our stubbornness in the United Nations in pretending that the representative from Taiwan is the representative of mainland China. Since the mote-beam mechanism, obviously, works on both sides, there is a tendency for each side to view the other as peculiarly immoral and for the views to mirror one another.

What can be done to make the mote-beam mechanism ineffective? The proposals I have made to counteract the effects of the other type of perceptual distortions are all relevant here. In addition, I would suggest that the mote-beam mechanism breeds on a moral-evaluative approach to behavior, on a readiness to condemn defects rather than to understand the circumstances which produced them. Psychoanalytic work suggests that the capacity to understand rather than to condemn is largely determined by the individual's sense of self-esteem, by his ability to cope with the external problem confronting him, and by his sense of resoluteness in overcoming his own defects. By analogy, I would suggest that we in the United States will have less need to overlook our own shortcomings or to be fascinated with the defects of others to the extent that we have a thriving society which is resolutely overcoming its own problems of racial prejudice, economic stagnation, and lack of dedication to common public purposes.

While distortions in perception are very common for the reasons I have outlined above, it is also true that in many instances everyday experience provides a corrective to the distortions. When reality is sufficiently compelling, and when the contact with reality occurs with sufficient frequency, the distortions will be challenged and may yield. However, there are circumstances which tend to perpetuate and petrify distortions. Let me briefly describe three major reasons for the perpetuation of distortions:

1. *A major psychological investment has been made in the distortion.* As a consequence, the individual may anticipate that giving

up the investment will require drastic personal reorganization which might result in personal instability and the loss of social face and might precipitate unknown dangers.

We have to recognize that a disarmed world, a world without external tensions to justify internal political policies, a world without violence as a means of bringing about changes in the *status quo* would be an unfamiliar world, a world in which some would feel that their vested interests might be destroyed. For example, I am sure that many military men, scientists, industrialists, workers, and investors fear a disarmed world because they anticipate that their skills and knowledge will become obsolete, or they will lose social status, or they will lose financially. These fears have to be dealt with constructively or else they may produce defensive adherence to the views which justify a hostile, armed world. I suggest that we must carefully plan to anticipate the psychological difficulties in the transition to a peaceful, disarmed world. As a basic strategy to overcome some of these difficulties, I would recommend that we consider a policy of *overcompensating* those who might be adversely affected by the change. We want to change the nature of their psychological investment from an investment in military pursuits to one in peaceful pursuits.

2. *Certain distorted perceptions perpetuate themselves because they lead the individual to avoid contact or meaningful communication with the object or person being perceived.* This is especially true when the distortions lead to aversion or hostility toward the object being perceived. Newcomb has used the term "autistic hostility" to label this self-perpetuating process.[14] Autistic hostility in international relations is exemplified in our relations with Communist China. Here, hostile attitudes produce barriers to communication which eliminate the possibility of a change in attitudes. The best antidote would seem to be repeated attempts at communication which followed the rules of procedure suggested by Anatol Rapoport.[15]

3. Robert Merton has pointed out that distortions are often perpetuated because they may evoke new behavior which makes the originally *false* conception come true.[16] The specious validity of the self-fulfilling prophecy perpetuates a reign of error. The prophet will cite the actual course of events as proof that he was right from the very beginning. The dynamics of the self-fulfilling prophecy help to explain individual pathology—e.g., the anxious student who, afraid he might fail, worries so much that he cannot study, with the consequence that he does fail. It also contributes to our understanding of social pathology—e.g., how prejudice and discrimination against the Negro keeps him in a position which seems to justify the

prejudice and discrimination. So too in international relations. If the representatives of East and West believe that war is likely and either side attempts to increase its military security vis-à-vis the other, the other side's response will justify the initial move. The dynamics of an arms race has the inherent quality of a *folie à deux,* wherein the self-fulfilling prophecies mutually reinforce one another.

The Conditions for Mutual Trust

In the preceding section, I have attempted to indicate some of the sources of misperception in international relations and some of the conditions which tend to perpetuate the distortions or make them come true. Our present international situation suggests that the distortions have come true. The East and the West are in an arms race and in an ideological conflict in which each side, in reality, threatens and feels threatened by the other. How can we reverse this hostile spiral which is likely to result in mutual annihilation?

As I present some specific proposals, I will indicate the psychological assumptions underlying them, assumptions which come from theoretical and experimental research I have been doing on cooperation and competition, interpersonal trust and suspicion, and interpersonal bargaining.[17]

1. *There are social situations which do not allow the possibility of "rational" behavior so long as the conditions for mutual trust do not exist.* Let me illustrate with a two-person game that I have used in my experimental work on trust and suspicion. In this game, each player has to choose between pressing a red button and a green button: if both players press the red button each loses $1.00; if both players press the green button, each wins $1.00; if Player A presses the green button and Player B presses the red button, A loses $2.00 and B gains $2.00; and if Player B presses the green button and Player A presses the red button, B loses $2.00 and A gains $2.00. A superficial rational calculation of self-interest would lead each player to press his red button since he either wins as much as he can or loses as little as he can this way. But if both players consider only their self-interest and press their red buttons, each of them will lose. Players oriented toward defeating the other player or to their self-interest only, when matched with similarly oriented players, do in fact choose the red button and do end up losing consistently.[18]

I believe our current international situation is in some respects similar to the game I have described. A characteristic symptom of such "nonrational situations" is that any attempt on the part of any individual or nation to increase its own welfare or security (without regard to the security or welfare of the others) is self-defeating. In such situations the only way an individual or nation can avoid being trapped in a mutually reinforcing, self-defeating cycle is to attempt to change the situation so that a basis of mutual trust can develop.

Comprehension of the basic nature of the situation we are in suggests that *mutual security* rather than national security should be our objective. The basic military axiom for both the East and West should be that *military actions should only be taken which increase the military security of both sides; military actions which give a military superiority to one side or the other should be avoided.* The military forces of both sides should be viewed as having the *common* primary aim of preventing either side (one's own or the other) from starting a deliberate or accidental war. Awareness of this common aim could be implemented by such measures as regular meetings of military leaders from East and West, the establishment of a continuing joint technical group of experts to work together to formulate disarmament and inspection plans, and the establishment of mixed military units on each other's territory.[19] The key point we must recognize is that if military inferiority is dangerous, so is military "superiority"; it is dangerous for either side to feel *tempted* or *frightened* into military action.

2. *Our research indicates that mutual trust is most likely to occur when people are positively oriented to each other's welfare—when each has a stake in the other's doing well rather than poorly.* Unfortunately, the East and West, at present, appear to have a greater stake in each other's defects and difficulties than in each other's welfare. Thus, the Communists gloat over our racial problems and our unemployment and we do likewise over their agricultural failures and their lack of political liberties.

We should, I believe, do everything possible to reverse this unfortunate state of affairs. First of all, we might start by accepting each other's existence as *legitimate* and by rejecting the view that the existence of the other, per se, is a threat to our own existence. As Talcott Parsons has pointed out,[20] there is considerable merit in viewing the ideological battle between East and West in the world community as somewhat akin to our own two-party system at the national level. An ideological conflict presupposes a common frame of reference in terms of which the ideological differences make sense. The ideologies of East and West do share many values in common: technological advance, economic development, universal education, encouragement of science, cultural progress, health advances, peace, national autonomy, and so forth. We must accept the possibility that one side or the other will obtain an advantage on particular issues when there is a conflict about the procedures for attaining these objectives. But this is not catastrophic unless each side views the conflict as an all-or-none conflict of survival.

To establish a basis for mutual trust we, of course, have to go beyond the recognition of each other's legitimacy to a relationship which promotes cooperative bonds. This would be facilitated by recognition of the profound human similarities which link all mankind together. The human situation no longer makes it feasible to view the world in terms of "we" or "they"; in the modern era, our destinies are linked objectively; the realistic attitude is "we" *and* "they." More specifically, I think our situation would be improved rather than worsened if the people in the various Communist nations had a high standard of living, were well educated, and were reaping the fruits of the scientific revolution. Similarly, I think we would be better off rather than worse off if the political leaders of the Communist nations felt they were able to provide their citizenry with sufficient current gratifications and signs of progress to have their support, and if they were sufficiently confident of their own society not to fear intensive contacts with different points of view.

The implication of the above calls for a fundamental reorientation of our foreign policy toward the Communist nations. We must initiate cooperative trade policies, cooperative research programs, cooperative cultural exchanges, cooperative loan programs, and cooperative agricultural programs, and we must not be concerned if, at first, they appear to benefit more than we. We are, after all, more affluent than the Communist nations. Our objective should be simply to promote the values of economic well-being, educational attainment, and scientific and industrial development which we share in common and which we believe are necessary to a stable, peaceful world. Let me emphasize here that I think this is especially important in our relations with Communist China. (It amazes me constantly that so little public attention is given to the extraordinary dangers involved in allowing our current relations with Communist China to continue in their present form.) The Communist nations (especially China) are likely to be suspicious of our motives, may even rebuff our initial attempts to establish cooperative relationships, and will undoubtedly not feel grateful for any assistance they may receive. These reactions are all to be expected because of the present context of international relations. Our policy of cooperation must be a *sustained* policy of *massive reconciliation* which does not reciprocate hostility and which always leaves open the possibility of mutual cooperation despite prior rebuff. In my view, we must sustain a cooperative initiative until it succeeds; in the long run, the alternative to mutual cooperation is mutual doom.

My rationale here is very simple. We have no realistic alternative but to coexist with the Soviet Union and Communist China. Coexistence among nations will be considerably less dangerous if we each recognize that poverty, illiteracy, economic difficulties, internal strain, and crisis in a nation are likely to produce reckless, belligerent international policies rather than peaceful ones. After all, the delinquents and criminals in our local communities rarely come from those segments of our populace that are successfully dealing with their own internal problems or that are well integrated into and accepted by the broader community.

3. *To induce a cooperative orientation in another and to develop adherence to a set of rules or social norms for regulating interaction and for resolving disputes, it is necessary* (*a*) *to demonstrate that one's own orientation to the other is cooperative;* (*b*) *to articulate fair rules which do not systematically disadvantage the other;* (*c*) *to demonstrate one's adherence to these rules;* (*d*) *to demonstrate to the other that he has more to gain* (*or less to lose*) *in the short and long run by adherence to the rules than by violation of them; and* (*e*) *to recognize that misunderstandings and disputes about compliance will inevitably occur and hence are not necessarily tokens of bad faith.*

The importance of a cooperative orientation to the development of mutual trust has been discussed above; it is reiterated here to emphasize the significance of a cooperative orientation in the development of any workable system of rules to regulate international relations. In discussion and negotiations concerning arms control and disarmament, there has been much emphasis on developing rules and procedures for inspection and control which do not rely upon cooperative orientations; surveillance of the other's actions is to replace trust in the other's intent. I think it is reasonable to assert that no social order can exist for long without a minimum basis of mutual trust; surveillance cannot do the trick by itself. This is not to deny the necessity of surveillance to buttress trust, to enable one's trustworthiness to be confirmed and one's suspicions to be rejected. However, I would question the view which seems to characterize our approach to arms-control negotiations: namely, the less trust, the more surveillance. A more reasonable view might state that when there is little trust the only kinds of agreements which are feasible are ones which allow for simple, uncomplicated, but highly reliable techniques of surveillance. Lack of trust between equals, paradoxically, calls for but also limits surveillance when the negotiations are not part of an effective community.

The inducing of adherence to rules to establish orderly relations among nations requires fair rules. It is easier to state the characteristics of an unfair than a fair rule: a rule is unfair if the party favoring it would be unwilling to accept it, were he in the situation of the other side. The history of disarmament negotiations suggests that neither the Soviet Union nor the United States has been interested in proposing fair rules. Nogee asserts: "Every plan offered by either side has contained a set of proposals calculated to have wide popular appeal. Every set has included at least one feature that the other side could not possibly accept, thus forcing a rejection. Then the proposing side has been able to claim that the rejection is opposed to the idea of disarmament *in toto*. The objectionable feature may be thought of as the 'joker' in every series." He further points out: "Disarmament negotiations themselves have become a weapon in the cold war. Speeches made in commission, committee, and Plenary Assembly have more often been designed to influence different segments of opinion than to reach an accommodation with the other nations represented at the conference table."[21]

How can the formulation of fair rules be facilitated? A suggestion by Bertrand Russell is pertinent here.[22] He proposes the formation of a conciliation committee composed of the best minds from the East and West, with some of the leading thinkers from neutral nations also included. Such a committee, meeting together in quiet, unpublicized deliberation, might be given the responsibility of formulating rules which would be acceptable to both sides. The hope is that, with sufficient time, intelligent men of good will whose perspectives reach beyond the cold war may be able to formulate rules that are fair to all mankind.

Fair rules for certain matters, of course, do already exist. Some of these rules are written in the Charter of the United Nations, some in the decisions of the International Court of Justice at The Hague, some in the legal traditions which have governed various aspects of international relations through the centuries (e.g., the international postal system, international trade, "freedom of the seas," ambassadorial rights). As Arthur Larson has pointed out,[23] there is much need for legal research to make the existing body of international rules accessible and up to date and establish a legal machinery which is also accessible and adapted to settling the kinds of disputes that today's world produces. In addition, there is a need to induce acceptance of the body of law and legal machinery by the persons affected.

How to induce acceptance of such rules once they are formulated? It seems clear that if we wish to induce others to accept fair rules, our own course of conduct must exemplify supranationalistic or universalistic values; it must constantly indicate our willingness to live up to the values that we expect others to adhere to. We must give up the doctrine of "special privilege" and the "double standard" in judging our own conduct and that of the Communist nations. Can we really convince others that we are for international law when we reserve the right (in the so-called Connally reservation) unilaterally to declare a controversy to be a domestic matter and hence outside the World Court's jurisdiction? Can we really be persuasive when we reserve the right to intervene unilaterally against the establishment of a Communist nation in the Western hemisphere but deny a similar right to the Soviet Union and China with regard to Western-oriented nations near their borders? Do we promote international order when we use our power in the United Nations to prevent the admission of the most populous nation in the world and, thus, exclude it from discussion of matters which relate to its interests? We only undermine the possibility of establishing a world rule of law by declaring our sovereign interests to be above the law. The deepest legal traditions in all parts of the world rest upon the view that the sovereign is not above the law—he is under the law.

Would adherence to universalistic values and international law on our part allow a violator of fair rules of international conduct to profit and thus encourage his violation? Certainly it makes no sense to encourage violations. However, an effective system of rules clearly defines what a violation is, specifies the procedure for ascertaining whether an act is a violation, prescribes the sanctions to be invoked against violations, and indicates the rights of self-defense or redress to the aggrieved party. Such a system presumably deters violation by making it unprofitable, but it also limits and controls the response to violation so that it is appropriate and under law. We must, of course, be prepared to discourage violations of fair practices and to defend ourselves against them, but we cannot afford to do so in disregard of the universalistic values we espouse.

I suggest that our *attitude* toward violations should express, simultaneously, firm resistance to violations when they occur and clear receptivity to the possibility of renewing cooperative relations. Recriminations and a punitive, self-righteous attitude toward violations are unlikely to encourage the development of a desire for normal, civilized relations. Retaliation (counterthreat in response to threat, counteraggression in response to aggression) tends, rather, to nourish and intensify an existing or incipient hostile spiral. Policy guided by the need to demonstrate that one is "man enough" to be tough, that one isn't "chicken," tends to change situations where there is room for negotiation into competitive struggles for "face." Once this occurs it becomes difficult indeed to make concessions without a severe loss of self-esteem.

4. *Mutual trust can occur even under circumstances where the parties involved are unconcerned with each other's welfare, provided their relations to an outside, third party are such that this trust in him can substitute for their trust in one another.* This indirect or mediated trust is, of course, a most common form of trust in interpersonal relations. Since we exist in a community in which various types of third parties—the law, the police, public opinion, mutual friends—can be mobilized to buttress an agreement, we can afford to be trusting even with a stranger in most circumstances. Unfortunately, in a bipolar world community which does not contain powerful "third parties," it is difficult to substitute mediated trust for direct trust.

There are two policy implications of this fact which I would like to stress. The first is the importance of encouraging the development of several strong, neutral groups of nations and the development of a strong, neutral United Nations that might mediate in conflicts between East and West. We must, of course, be aware of the dangers of a *tertius gaudens,* in which a third party would attempt to play East and West off against one another to its own advantage. However, what I am suggesting is not a third bloc but rather a group of diverse, independent nations with crisscrossing interests that have the common objective of developing and maintaining an orderly world. In a neutral United Nations,[24] with a large group of independent voters, we would sometimes find ourselves on the losing side. But can we afford a United Nations in which the other side has little chance of ever winning a dispute with us?

The second implication follows from the realization that strong, responsible independent nations and a strong neutral United Nations do not yet exist and will take time to develop. Where no strong external community exists, it is important to recognize that bargaining—the attempt to find a mutually satisfactory agreement in circumstances where there is a conflict of interest—cannot be guided by a Machiavellian or "outwitting the other" attitude. Where no external community exists to compel agreement, the critical problem in bargaining is to establish sufficient community between the bargainers so that a mutually satisfactory agreement becomes possible: the question of who obtains the minor advantages or disadvantages in negotiation are trivial in comparison to the question of whether an agreement can be reached which leaves both parties better off than a lack of agreement. I stress this point because some political scientists and game theorists, misled by the fact that bargaining within a strong community can often fruitfully be conducted with a Machiavellian attitude, unwittingly assume that the same would be true where no real community exists.

In concluding this section, let me quote from a monograph on the *Causes of Industrial Peace* which lists the conditions that have led to peaceful settlement of disputes under collective bargaining:

1. There is full acceptance by management of the collective-bargaining process and of unionism as an institution. The company considers a strong union an asset to management.
2. The union fully accepts private ownership and operation of the industry; it recognizes that the welfare of its members depends upon the successful operation of the business.
3. The union is strong, responsible, and democratic.
4. The company stays out of the union's internal affairs; it does not seek to alienate the workers' allegiance to their union.
5. Mutual trust and confidence exist between the parties. There have been no serious ideological incompatibilities.
6. Neither party to bargaining has adopted a legalistic approach to the solution of problems in the relationship.
7. Negotiations are "problem-centered"—more time is spent on day-to-day problems than on defining abstract principles.
8. There is widespread union-management consultation and highly developed information-sharing.
9. Grievances are settled promptly, in the local plant whenever possible. There is flexibility and informality within the procedure.[25]

This is in accord with our discussion of the basic conditions for world peace: namely, the necessity of developing attitudes which consciously stress mutual acceptance, mutual welfare, mutual strength, mutual interest, and mutual trust and the necessity of developing approaches to disputes which consistently emphasize full communication, willingness to negotiate, and specific issues rather than the ideological frame of reference of the parties in dispute.

The Conflict Between East and West

Underlying my discussion throughout this paper has been the thesis that the conflict between East and West can be resolved peacefully. This thesis grows out of the assumption that the only alternative to peace is mutual catastrophe. The conflict must be resolved peacefully, but can it be?

Public statements of the leaders of the two blocs define the conflict as a confrontation of two mutually irreconcilable ideologies; and we must acknowledge that basic ideological differences do exist. On the other hand, it must be borne in mind that neither the United States nor the USSR closely resembles its ideological "ideal type." Neither Adam Smith nor Karl Marx would recognize his offspring.

But the conflict of the cold war has intensified our perception of ideological differences, while at the same time reducing our ability to perceive similarities. Thus, we in the West see a conflict between "free societies and a totalitarian system that is attempting to dominate the world." At the same time, our counterparts in the East see a conflict between "a system that represents the interests of the masses of the people and the imperialist, capitalist ruling cliques that wish to continue their exploitation of the people." Both descriptions are essentially mirror images of each other, each side claiming that their side stands for just, universalistic values opposed by the other side. We in the West, however, see human justice as being threatened by the expansionist tendencies of the East, while the leaders in the East see human justice being thwarted by the West's attempt to maintain the *status quo* and to stem (what they consider to be) the natural tide of history.

The dominant theme of Freudian psychology is that the manifest life of the mind—what men know or pretend to know about the motives of their behavior—is often merely a socially acceptable rationalization of their unrecognized or latent motives. The difference between the manifest and latent content of behavior results from the need to present one's behavior to one's self, as well as to others, so as not to lose social or self-esteem. This need to "maintain face" can, of course, in turn be a determinant of behavior. I suggest that although there are basic ideological differences between East and West, the intensity of the ideological struggle primarily reflects an anachronistic power struggle between nations that have defined their prestige and security in terms of world leadership. The ideological differences within the West (e.g., between the United States and Portugal) or within the East (e.g., between Russia and China) are often as gross as those between East and West.

Traditionally, the quest for world power has been closely bound to strivings for national security, economic dominance, and international prestige or influence. The quest for power has commonly taken the form of the attempt to establish military supremacy. In previous sections of this paper, I have stressed the anachronism of the drive for military supremacy in the age of missiles and hydrogen bombs. Similarly, I believe the more powerful nations are beginning to recognize that the best opportunities for economic exploitation will arise from scientific research and development rather than from colonial domination, Eastern or Western style.

However, the quest for international prestige and influence is, I believe, a reasonable one for all societies. Hence we must find alternative social institutions and processes to militarism and war, by which this quest can be pursued. Amitai Etzioni has suggested a number of criteria which are relevant to the kinds of social institutions which should be created. Namely, the international competition for prestige should involve many different kinds of contests which are repeated at frequent intervals so that defeat is never *total* or irreversible. Moreover, he proposes that there be many different contestants in every contest so that competition is diffuse rather than sharply focused and that competition be centered about achievements which represent genuine accomplishments of which all mankind can be proud.[26]

More specifically, I suggest that the United Nations (or some other organization which includes Communist China) organize a series of periodic international contests which would enable the different nations of the world to reveal their achievements and progress in such fields as art, music, literature, the various sciences, space exploration, education, economic development, agriculture, sports, ballet, the theater, cooking, architecture, medicine, women's fashions, the domestic arts, children's books, and so on. The contests should be diverse enough to permit each national culture to display its unique attainments. The rules should require that the knowledge, skills, and techniques of the contest winners be made freely available to every nation. Awards might be granted on two separate bases: the relative level of absolute achievement and the relative amount of progress since the last contest. It is assumed that the societies who win many contests will be the ones who are effective in developing a culture that is richly creative and a populace that is educated, talented, and resourceful. There are, of course, difficulties in implementing such a proposal, in developing contests and rules which are not stacked for or against any nations. However, since the kinds of contests I am proposing already exist within many nations, there is a vast body of experience which can be drawn upon to develop workable rules.

I suggest that the United States, with the co-sponsorship of the Soviet Union, take the initiative in submitting such a proposal to the United Nations. If we are to engage in international competition for prestige and influence, let it be in peaceful rather than in militaristic pursuits, let it be in achievements from which all mankind can profit, let it be in activities which promote the recognition of the common values of mankind.

I conclude with an Intellectual's Manifesto: *Intellectuals, Scientists, Scholars, and Academicians of the world, unite; we have nothing to lose but our ideological blinders. The problems besetting the world are too serious to permit our work to be beclouded by dogma or narrowly conceived national interest. We cannot afford to let the slogans and categories of ideological conflict dominate our intellectual analysis. We must be free to view the great problems of our time—the nuclear arms race, the tremendous disparities in standards of living among the nations of the world, racial prejudice, ideological intolerance, and the rapid increase in the world's population—in a way that allows us to take advantage of the explosion in knowledge now taking place. Let us begin to replace dogmatic, ideological assertion with an open-minded, objective, factual test of our theories and hypotheses about economic development, social change, and the development of creative, responsible people. Only by so doing will our common objectives of creating a saner, comelier, and more amicable life be achieved.*

NOTES

The views expressed in this paper do not represent, nor are they necessarily similar to, the views of any organization with which the author is affiliated.

1. Perhaps there has been too much psychologizing about these matters; there are, after all, critical differences between persons and nations. Not the least of these is the fact that in a deadly quarrel between people it is the quarrelers who are most apt to be killed, while in a deadly quarrel among nations, the decision-makers are rarely the ones who have the highest probability of dying. Be that as it may, I shall assume that there is some merit in viewing nations, like persons, as behaving units in an environment, and in conceiving of international relations in terms somewhat analogous to those of interpersonal relations.

2. See pp. 192–205 of the present volume.

3. See William James, "The Moral Equivalent of War," in his *Memories and Studies* (New York: Longmans, Green, 1911).

4. See Egon Brunswick, "The Conceptual Framework of Modern Psychology," in *International Encyclopedia of Unified Science* (Chicago: University of Chicago Press, 1952).

5. War is vastly overrated as an outlet for direct aggressiveness; it does not compare with the directness of reckless automobile driving, a boxing match, or a football game. War is defined to be such a good outlet *only* because of our cultural conditioning: the military toys children are given to play with; the identification of heroism and bravery with war in so many novels, television dramas, and films that we all are exposed to; the definition of patriotism in military terms in so many of our public ceremonials and holidays, and so forth.

6. Abel is cited in Jessie Bernard, "Parties and Issues in Conflict," *Conflict Resolution,* I (1957), pp. 111–21.
7. See pp. 178–191 of the present volume.
8. See Urie Bronfenbrenner, "The Mirror Image in Soviet-American Relations," *Journal of Social Issues,* XVII (1961), pp. 45–56.
9. Joseph Nogee, "The Diplomacy of Disarmament," in *International Conciliation,* No. 526 (Carnegie Endowment for International Peace, 1960), p. 275.
10. See pp. 246–262 of the present volume.
11. See S. E. Asch, "Studies of Independence and Conformity: I. A Minority of One Against a Unanimous Majority," *Psychological Monographs,* LXX (1956), Whole No. 416.
12. Much of this research is summarized in various articles in D. Katz, (ed.), "Attitude Change," *Public Opinion Quarterly,* XXIV (1960), pp. 163–365.
13. See G. Ichheiser, "Misunderstandings in Human Relations," *American Journal of Sociology,* LV (1949), Part 2, pp. 1–70.
14. See T. M. Newcomb, "Autistic Hostility and Social Reality," *Human Relations,* I (1947), pp. 69–86.
15. See pp. 246–262 of the present volume.
16. See R. K. Merton, "The Self-Fulfilling Prophecy," in *Social Theory and Social Structure* (Glencoe, Ill.: The Free Press, rev. ed., 1957), pp. 421–36.
17. See Morton Deutsch, "A Theory of Cooperation and Competition," *Human Relations,* II (1949), pp. 129–52; "The Effects of Cooperation and Competition Upon Group Process," *Human Relations,* II (1949), pp. 199–231; "Trust and Suspicion," *Conflict Resolution,* II (1958), pp. 265–79; "The Effect of Motivational Orientation Upon Trust and Suspicion," *Human Relations,* XIII (1960), pp. 123–40; "Trust, Trustworthiness, and the F Scale," *Journal of Abnormal and Social Psychology,* LXI (1960), pp. 138–40; and "The Face of Bargaining," a paper presented at the Nineteenth Annual Meeting of the Operations Research Society of America, Chicago, May 25, 1961; and M. Deutsch and R. M. Krauss, "The Effect of Threat Upon Interpersonal Bargaining," *Journal of Abnormal and Social Psychology,* LXI (1960), pp. 181–9.
18. See Anatol Rapoport's discussion of games in the present volume, pp. 247–250.
19. See H. C. Kelman's essay in the present volume, pp. 106–122.
20. See pp. 310–331 of the present volume.

21. Nogee, *op. cit.,* pp. 281 and 282.

22. See pp. 263–272 of the present volume.

23. See pp. 332–341 of the present volume.

24. For a proposal to neutralize the United Nations, see Louis B. Sohn's essay in the present volume, pp. 355–365.

25. National Planning Association, *Causes of Industrial Peace* (Washington: National Planning Association, 1953), p. 92.

26. See pp. 226–245 of the present volume.

TRANSNATIONAL FORUMS FOR PEACE

By WILLIAM M. EVAN

WHETHER A NUCLEAR WAR, limited or unlimited, will ever break out —as a result of a deliberate, "rational" decision or as a result of an accident—is unknown. What we do know with a fair degree of certainty is that in the years ahead the East and the West will be confronted with many dangerous stalemates of a political and military nature. How can such highly predictable stalemates be broken without triggering off a nuclear World War III?

The prevailing methods for breaking deadlocks in international relations are unreliable. Such a neutral "third party" mechanism as the International Court of Justice is as yet an ineffective instrument for resolving international disputes: more than half of the members of the United Nations have not accepted its compulsory jurisdiction;[1] and there are as yet no provisions for enforcing decisions of this tribunal. It is apparent that the longer the cold war continues and the more intense it becomes, the greater will be the need for a variety of mechanisms for the peaceful resolution of international conflicts. Transnational forums proposed in this paper would, in my opinion, contribute toward this end.

Assumptions About East-West Conflicts

Two pervasive assumptions with respect to the conflicts between East and West are: (a) that treaties between the major powers are essential to initiate a program of arms control or disarmament; and (b) that such treaties would be a direct product of negotiations between statesmen of East and West. In all likelihood neither of these assumptions is true.

With respect to the first assumption, as Roger Fisher points out elsewhere in this volume (pp. 342–354), the implementation of a bilateral or multilateral treaty ultimately depends on the self-restraint of the signatories engendered by "fear of retaliatory action, fear of the effect [of non-compliance] on public opinion, the moral views of government officers, and institutional resistance to breaking rules." One of his cogent conclusions is that unilateral actions for peace may prove as effective as bilateral or multilateral agreements for the development of mutually binding norms, of an informal or tacit nature, designed to regulate international relations.[2]

Similarly, Osgood in his penetrating essay in this book (pp. 161–177) argues for a program of "graduated" unilateral initiatives for peace which are not contingent upon any promise by an opponent to reciprocate, which are susceptible to verification so as to allay any suspicions as to the bona fides of the action in question, and which are designed to induce reciprocation from an opponent.

Given the level of international tension, mutual fear, and distrust, the likelihood of reaching bilateral or multilateral agreements on disarmament in the near future appears slim. For fifteen years multilateral negotiations for a disarmament treaty have failed. It appears to me that it is tacit agreements stemming from "graduated" unilateral actions for peace—rather than negotiations—that can pave the way for eventual bilateral or multilateral agreements.

The second prevailing assumption, that treaties on disarmament will be a direct product of negotiations by governmental representatives of East and West, has not been critically examined. This is due in part to the common belief that nation-states have always existed and that the principle of national sovereignty is inviolable. This assumption overlooks some vital considerations.

When a crisis arises in the relations between East and West, there are severe pressures on the statesmen engaged in diplomacy and negotiations. As the major spokesmen of the respective ideologies, they are generally compelled to advocate the most orthodox version of their systems of values. This prompts them to make pronouncements regarding political, military, or economic matters which may actually be at variance with policy positions they are willing to entertain or have already taken. Such discrepancy between pronouncement and policy position—which probably occurs both in the East and in the West—exacerbates the already difficult problems of negotiations between parties having conflicting interests and ideologies.

As part of the political rhetoric of the cold war, statesmen of East and West appear to be in agreement that there is a difference between "governments" and "peoples": The Soviet government tends to assert from time to time that the American *government* engages in war-provoking actions, but that the American *people* are peace-loving; the American government tends to assert from time to time that the Soviet *government* engages in war-provoking actions, but that the Soviet *people* are peace-loving. Rhetoric aside, actions for peace undertaken by *peoples,* as distinct from and in addition to those taken by their *governments,* may prove of critical value. To be sure, such action is much more feasible at the present in the West than in the East.

The Concept of Transnationalism

Actions undertaken by entities larger than nations or smaller than nations and outside the framework of nation-states, I shall call "transnational." This concept, partially based on Jessup's idea of "transnational law,"[3] subsumes modes of action of "supranational" and "infranational" bodies.

Associations of scientists and other professionals which periodically hold international meetings contribute, in however small a measure, to a greater mutual understanding between citizens of politically hostile countries. The Pugwash Conference is an example of an activity undertaken principally, if not entirely, by private citizens of different countries for the purpose of contributing to world peace. The high degree of agreement reached by the scientists at the Pugwash Conferences as to the potential dangers of a nuclear war and as to the desirability and feasibility of the suspension of nuclear tests and of disarmament in general may have induced the governments of East and West—it has been asserted—to convene the Geneva Disarmament Conference at an earlier date than it might otherwise have been convened. Private organizations such as CARE may directly or indirectly promote friendly and peaceful attitudes among the peoples of different countries. And trade initiated by businessmen of Western countries with some Eastern countries may be conducive to the reduction of the level of international tension.

Unofficial or private "diplomats" such as scientists and representatives of nonprofit and profit organizations, though lacking the power of policy-making, may well have special knowledge of relevance to international relations; and they are not as likely to be as sensitive to loss of "face" as are statesmen with official power and responsibility.[4] Indeed, in a grave international crisis unofficial diplomacy may lay the basis for a resolution short of a nuclear holocaust.[5]

Transnational actions for peace can become more significant, given more effective channels of communication. A potentially strategic channel for transnational action is already in existence—the United Nations—though it has scarcely been conceived as such. Some of the delegates to the 1945 U.N. conference at San Francisco may have been aware of the concept of transnationalism in light of the opening sentence of the Preamble of the U.N. Charter which reads, "We the peoples of the United Nations. . . ." However, the closing sentence of the Preamble, "Accordingly, our Governments . . ." is more descriptive of the underlying conception of the U.N. Charter. Thus far, the United Nations has been primarily an instrument for internation or intergovernment debate, negotiation, and action. A feasible proposal would be to extend the range of functions of the United Nations to facilitate transnational action. The addition of new organs of a transnational character would add other voices to those now heard in U.N. deliberations. A multiplicity of voices, especially in a crisis, may generate ideas for new alternatives and bring pressure to bear on governments to entertain new alternatives, thus facilitating the resolution of conflicts.[6] The new organs might consist of (1) a forum of supranational communities, (2) a forum of nongovernmental organizations, and (3) a forum of individual citizens of the United Nations.

A Forum of Supranational Communities

The first extension of the functions of the United Nations might be the establishment of an organ for supranational communities. The unit of membership would not be a nation-state, as is presently the case, but a regional entity with a federated or supranational structure. Such communities are brought into existence by a complex of forces—economic, political, cultural, military, etc.—and they may perform multiple functions. Although the rationale for such an organ in the United Nations would be to enhance the chances of world peace, it would be difficult and perhaps also undesirable to restrict membership only to supranational communities of a principally nonmilitary character. Beyond affording the representatives of these supranational communities an opportunity to deliberate on issues affecting world peace, this organ could also better marshal the full resources of the United Nations toward assisting in the economic development of the member communities. It is conceivable that as a result of the functioning of the proposed forum, some supranational communities of a predominantly military character may acquire other functions of a nonmilitary nature.

Since the end of World War II, there has been a revival of interest in European integration, particularly in the integration of the economies of the Western countries. One of the more successful supranational experiments was the European Coal and Steel Community[7] founded in 1952. Instead of establishing a common market for all the commodities of the member nations, this Community attempted "integration by sector"—coal and steel. The six member governments (Belgium, France, West Germany, Italy, Luxembourg, the Netherlands) pledged, among other things, to eliminate all tariffs, quantitative restrictions, discriminatory transportation rates, double-pricing practices, and other practices inconsistent with a competitive common market. This Community was to an extent the prototype for the European Economic Community established in 1958.[8] According to Benoit, the European Economic Community is more than a mere customs union in that it provides for: (1) free movement of labor, capital, and enterprise; (2) restraints on governmental or private actions which hamper competition within the Community; (3) the "harmonization" of policies regarding employment, social security, and wage levels; (4) the establishment of common operating agencies including developmental and adjustment funds; and (5) recognition of some sort of political goal and an aspiration toward an increasingly closer association among the member nations.[9] Although the immediate sphere of supranational activity is economic, the authors of the treaty and the officials of the Community are aware of the potential import of economic integration for political integration.[10]

It is noteworthy that there are efforts under way in Latin America and Africa to establish regional supranational communities similar to the European Economic Community.[11] The U.N. charter recognizes such regional arrangements and seeks to bring them into closer relations with the United Nations (Articles 52–54). The increase in such supranational communities would probably further the movement away from an unstable bipolar division of the world to a multipolar division, which would in all likelihood be considerably more stable. The growth of supranational communities would probably encourage supranational loyalties and, in turn, supranational types of actions for peace. The favorable disposition toward supranationalism in various countries, particularly in Europe,[12] may stimulate the further growth and strengthening of supranational communities. Daniel Lerner concludes, on the basis of a continuous seven-year survey among European leaders, that a European Defense Community integrated with a European Political Community is likely to emerge in the next few years, as the present leadership is replaced by Europeans of the World War II and postwar generations. He finds that the Europeans have passed "beyond nationalism"; the creation of European institutions of collective responsibility at the highest level would add together existing strands of European loyalty and then multiply their force by involving them in the effective functioning of the supranational European community.[13] It is also reasonable to expect that the establishment of a forum in the United Nations for supranational communities would accelerate the trend toward regional supranational communities and regional supranational loyalties.

A Forum of Nongovernmental Organizations

A second extension of the range of functions of the United Nations would entail the establishment of an organ for "infranational" entities in the form of nongovernmental or private organizations. By infranational entities, I mean groups with constituent members smaller than the nation-state. Nongovernmental organizations operate on either the national or the international level, or both.[14] Whatever the level of operations, they can potentially influence government policy—particularly in the West—either directly or indirectly.[15] In persuading policy-makers to take their views into account, they may exert direct influence on policy-making. To the same effect, they may engage in actions to mold public opinion by changing the climate of opinion or by making public opinion articulate. Apart from their capacity to influence policy-making, nongovernmental organizations can contribute expert knowledge useful to intergovernmental deliberations.[16]

In recent years the number of nongovernmental organizations, particularly at the international level, has increased markedly.[17] Examples include professional associations, trade unions, businessmen's associations, farmers' organizations, religious organizations, political organizations, social welfare associations, etc. According to the *1960–61 Yearbook of International Organizations,*[18] there are over 1,200 such organizations in existence. The burgeoning of international nongovernmental organizations in recent years is in large measure due to the establishment of the United Nations. Whereas nongovernmental organizations did not have official status under the League of Nations, under the U.N. Charter they do. The Economic and Social Council of the United Nations, according to Article 71 of the Charter, may call upon international nongovernmental organizations for consultation. Approximately 250 such organizations have some kind of consultative status with the Economic and Social Council.[19]

Similarly, the constitutions of the various specialized agencies of the United Nations provide for consultation with international NGO's, as nongovernmental organizations are known in U.N. parlance. More than any other specialized agency, UNESCO has relied on NGO's in the planning and executing of its activities. To date, it has established relationships with about 400 such organizations.[20] As part of its program to promote mutual understanding among nations, UNESCO has been instrumental in sponsoring the establishment of a relatively large number of NGO's. For example, in 1950 it was responsible for the establishment of the International Association of Universities, and between 1949 and 1952 it aided in the organization of international associations in economics, political science, psychology, sociology, and comparative law.[21] UNESCO also helped the International Council of Scientific Unions—the largest nongovernmental association in the field of natural sciences—to initiate the International Geophysical Year, one of the most extensive and successful efforts at cooperative research in the annals of the scientific community.[22]

Another factor in the recent growth of international nongovernmental organizations is the appearance of supranational communities. Since 1949 when the European Coal and Steel Community was being organized, many nongovernmental organizations, including trade associations, trade unions, and political parties, have come into existence.[23] The object of these organizations is to promote their group interests as part of the new supranational community. It is to be expected that as supranational communities grow in number so will the number of international NGO's.

In short, the fact that the United Nations already accords NGO's official status would make the establishment of a forum of NGO's that much easier. In view of the large number of such organizations, representation in the proposed forum would presumably be based on *types* of NGO's rather than on *individual* NGO's. The proposed forum would enable the representatives to air their views on any issue affecting world peace. The forum would also provide more opportunities than presently exist for exchanges of information among the various organizations and their memberships and for various joint endeavors.

A U.N. forum of nongovernmental organizations would undoubtedly stimulate the further growth of such associations. In addition, however, it would probably provide a countervailing force to the actions of governments, particularly in crisis situations. The potential value of such organizations in the modern world has been well expressed by an international civil servant and former NGO official: "At a time when governments are assuming increasing responsibilities for the welfare of their peoples, the role of voluntary organizations necessarily shifts in emphasis. The era of soup kitchens, orphanages, and private charities is fading. Today the NGO's have another primary objective—to be the conscience of the state and monitor its activities in the name of the people. . . . One of the greatest opportunities of the NGO's is to take the initiative with ideas and projects which governments are not yet ready to make their own. Here is one advantage the NGO's have over governments."[24]

A Forum of Individual Citizens

A third extension of the functions of the United Nations would be similar to the second discussed above in that it too would involve establishing a forum of an "infranational" character. In this case the unit of membership would not be an interest group such as a non-governmental organization but an individual in his capacity as a citizen of the United Nations.[25] To be sure, such a forum at the present time seems highly visionary. In all likelihood it could come into existence only after one or both of the preceding innovations in the structure of the United Nations have been made.

A United Nations forum of representatives of individual citizens from the various countries of the world presupposes that individuals would have dual citizenship, as is the case in a federal system of government. In the United States, for example, dual citizenship is institutionalized. As the first section of the Fourteenth Amendment to the Constitution states: "All persons born or naturalized in the United States and subject to the jurisdiction thereof, are citizens of the United States and of the State wherein they reside."[26] Since the state constitutions are on the whole consonant with the federal Constitution, the average American citizen generally suffers little conflict, a notable exception in recent years being the conflict engendered by the Supreme Court's school desegregation decision. The principle of federalism suggests the potential value of dual citizenship for all human beings in the world—one in their nation or tribe and one in the United Nations.

A tangible duty of all individual citizens of the United Nations, comparable to that of all citizens of nation-states, would be to pay a small yearly tax, the funds so collected to be used, for example, for the promotion of health and welfare facilities for all peoples, in particular for those in underdeveloped countries. Such a yearly tax, even if its primary purpose were to afford a symbolic expression of individual allegiance to the United Nations, could at the same time provide the United Nations, or the "forum of individual citizens," with an independent and politically stable source of revenue to finance its various operations. An annual per capita tax, for example, of one penny from each of the three billion people in the world would yield thirty million dollars. It is noteworthy that the Quakers' program of self-taxation on behalf of the United Nations has spread to various parts of the United States.[27] In this instance their commitment to supranational loyalties has led some Quakers to contribute voluntarily 1 percent of their annual income to the United Nations. Such a tax rate would probably be a burdensome obligation to impose on all individual citizens of the United Nations. If individual U.N. citizenship were to become a culturally supported institution, it might encourage the practice of voluntary "tax" payments in the spirit of the Quakers' payments.

Other kinds of duties of individual citizens of the United Nations are, of course, conceivable. Of major significance would be the duty to uphold all international agreements concerned with the prevention of war. This might entail, among other things, the duty to report any evidence of violation of disarmament or arms-control agreements, as has been suggested by Bohn (pp. 20–39), Melman (pp. 40–51), and Clark and Sohn.[28]

With regard to the *rights,* as distinct from the *duties,* of individual citizens of the United Nations, these might include an exchange of opinion and information regarding various international events. Through a specially elected body representing individual citizens of the United Nations, each citizen would have an opportunity to express his views on current international conflicts. In addition, two channels of communication might be provided: one from individual citizens to the United Nations; the other from the United Nations to all its individual citizens.[29]

The channel of communication from individual citizens to the United Nations might be via the postal system or preferably via a special supplementary U.N. postal system to prevent local censorship; in addition, the United Nations, with the aid of a system of communications satellites, could establish in the various communities of each country radio-transmitter stations to which every U.N. citizen would have access. A channel of communication from the United Nations to all of its individual citizens would require, among other things, radio and television facilities, again with the aid of a system of communications satellites, whereby special programs of information and opinion would be broadcast for the benefit of the individual citizens of all nations. Since in much of the world illiteracy is the rule, such media of communication, particularly television, could be of inestimable value in improving the lives of people.[30] In this connection, the development of a universally spoken "auxiliary" or second language, as discussed by Harris (pp. 299–309), could be of great value.

The justification for establishing the two channels of communication between individual citizens and the United Nations could, in part, rest on Article 19 of the Universal Declaration of Human Rights which was unanimously adopted by the General Assembly in 1948. It reads as follows: "Everyone has the right to freedom of opinion and expression; this right includes freedom to hold opinions without interference and to seek, receive and impart information and ideas through any media and regardless of frontiers."[31] Notwithstanding this provision of the Universal Declaration of Human Rights, the right to listen to broadcasts from abroad has by no means been universally institutionalized. In 1950 the General Assembly found it necessary to condemn the jamming of radio broadcasts.[32]

To protect the right of free speech the proposed forum for individual citizens of the United Nations would have to institutionalize a right to travel pursuant to a U.N. passport and a right to political asylum. There is already a precedent for a U.N. travel document in the "Nansen passport" issued by the League of Nations in the twenties and thirties for refugees and stateless people.[33] In addition to institutionalizing a U.N. passport, a forum of individual U.N. citizens would also have to work toward the elimination of visa barriers. Some progress toward visa-free travel has been made, on the initiative of the Economic and Social Council of the United Nations and among some of the Western nations, but much more remains to be accomplished.[34]

The effect of setting up a forum in the United Nations for individual citizens might be threefold. First, it could provide a vehicle for expression of independent opinion on the part of individual citizens of different countries. The expression of opinions of individual citizens of the United Nations, particularly if they diverge significantly from the opinions of representatives of the governments of their nation-states, might help break international stalemates by disclosing alternatives not otherwise likely to be articulated because of various constraints imposed on statesmen.

Second, such a forum of the United Nations would provide an organizational medium for generating loyalty to supranational communities and eventually to a world community. Human beings everywhere would gradually, perhaps in the course of several generations, enlarge their capacity for identification from their immediate circle of relatives and friends and their nation or tribe, to an all-inclusive social entity, namely, all mankind. The development of such a loyalty probably necessitates frequent and personal contact between individuals of many nations. The more prolonged and intimate the contact, the greater the likelihood of developing supranational loyalties. But even relatively impersonal contacts through exchange of correspondence and exchange of mass-media communications could be expected to have an effect. The exchange of large numbers of young people in educational programs and the establishment of national or international "peace corps" may serve to establish personal loyalties which go beyond national boundaries. Such personal loyalties may well lead to the development of loyalty to a world community.

Third, the growth of such transnational loyalties would foster the growth of transnational law, and the confluence of transnational (i.e., infranational and supranational) loyalties and transnational law may turn out to be two prerequisites for the emergence of something akin to a world community.

Relation of Proposed Organs to Existing Organs of the United Nations

The three new forums discussed above would be transnational channels of communication as distinct from the principal prevailing forum of nation-states in the United Nations, the General Assembly. It would appear to be desirable to establish the three forums on a level coordinate with that of the General Assembly. Like the General Assembly, as presently constituted, the proposed forums would not be legislative bodies. Rather, they would discuss major problems affecting world peace, pass resolutions, and make recommendations to the Security Council and to other U.N. bodies. The mere opportunity to ventilate issues in an international crisis, in four different forums, would probably increase the chances of generating new ideas as well as pressures favorable to the resolution of conflicts further away from the brink of a nuclear war than is possible in a single forum of nation-states.

The relation between the proposed forums and the Economic and Social Council, on the one hand, and the various specialized agencies, on the other, would also have to be clarified. Since the Economic and Social Council inquires into and deliberates on major world problems, the results of which it may communicate to the General Assembly and the Security Council, it would be important for the Economic and Social Council to function under the aegis of all four forums, the General Assembly as well as the three proposed forums. Accordingly, the structure of the Economic and Social Council would have to be changed so that its membership would comprise representatives from all four forums. With respect to the various specialized agencies some form of liaison with the new forums would be necessary, so that the agencies could avail themselves of the channels of communication of these forums in pursuing their objectives. Only after the relations between the General Assembly and the three new forums develop would it be possible to ascertain whether corresponding structural modifications would be necessary in the Security Council and in the Secretariat to take account of these new forums.

Establishing these new forums on a level coordinate with that of the General Assembly would require a revision of the Charter of the

United Nations. A great many proposals for revising the Charter have been put forth.[35] That there are formidable obstacles to amending the Charter, given the stringent provisions of Articles 108 and 109 and the attitudes of some of the member nations toward Charter reform, is well known. Such forums however, could be established preliminarily as "subsidiary organs," with an advisory function, by action of the General Assembly without Charter amendment (Article 22). Unless new ways—such as those presented here—are found to develop an *effective* world public opinion behind the United Nations, it may not evolve in its functioning so as to contribute adequately to world peace.

Conclusion

In the proposal outlined above for the development of transnational modes of action for peace an effort is made to explore a strategy of world peace which could supplement any others that may be employed. Just as unilateral actions for peace on the part of governments can create mutual and binding norms in international relations, so may transnational actions for peace increase the chances for breaking deadlocks in the relations between East and West.

The proposed forums in the United Nations would provide certain organizational mechanisms for restraining irrational (i.e., militaristic, in this context) actions of statesmen in crisis situations. The proposed organizational innovations in the United Nations would contribute to the growth of a pluralistic world community; no one nation or bloc of nations would be able to dominate the entire world.

Developing transnational mechanisms for peace involves complex problems of the relation between the elite values of a society and those of the masses or citizenry. To be sure, neither the elite nor the citizenry is homogeneous in value orientations. There are some components in the elite that are fully aware of the dangers of an all-out nuclear war. On the other hand, there are some elements in the citizenry that are not aware of these dangers and clamor for an aggressive policy vis-à-vis the potential enemy. What the balance of irrationality is between the elite and the masses of different countries is a problem for social science research, difficult as it may be.[36] It is reasonable to expect that under some circumstances the elite in fact may protect the citizenry from its own irrational impulses.[37] The converse, however, is also possible. As industrialization increases, bringing in its wake both a decline in the proportion of unskilled workers in the labor force and an upgrading in the level of education, the number of constituent groups in the citizenry capable of exercising some control over the elite will probably increase. In other words, as industrialization progresses in East and West, various components of the citizenry may increase their capacity for independent judgment and may be more likely to engage in actions, including those of a transnational nature, to promote peace.

In unindustrialized countries interest in transnationalism may develop only after nationalism, in its beneficent and transient forms, has had an opportunity to take root and afford underdeveloped societies an opportunity for self-determination. The institutions and ideologies of nationalism may, to a degree, facilitate the industrialization of a country. Probably only after a certain degree of industrialization is achieved are such new nations likely to be receptive to transnational ideologies and forms of organization. This is not to say that the new underdeveloped countries must undergo the same historical process, with respect to nationalism, as the developed countries did. These countries may become more receptive to transnationalism long before they have passed from the stage of beneficent nationalism, which aids in self-development, to the stage where, in some instances, nationalism —via chauvinism and imperialism—impairs the development of one's own society or of other societies.

How to establish transnational forums for peace is indeed a challenging question. Presumably, the initiative could come from supranational communities and particularly from nongovernmental organizations of various kinds. If, for example, the major international associations of labor,* management,† and science‡ were to become interested in proposals such as those presented here and in those of Clark and Sohn,[38] they could probably be instrumental in paving the way for a forum of nongovernmental organizations and in initiating discussions of such proposals in the United Nations.

The social scientist in his own way can make a contribution toward the development of transnational forums for peace by undertaking research, for example, on the relation between the values of elites and masses of various societies differing in degree of industrialization; attitudes toward transnationalism of various components in the elites and masses of different societies; problems of multiple loyalties; and problems of enlarging the size of the social unit to which people are loyal.[39] In addition, the social scientist—and, for that matter, the natural scientist, the humanist, and others, too—can

* International Confederation of Christian Trade Unions, World Federation of Trade Unions, and International Confederation of Free Trade Unions.

† International Organization of Employers, International Chamber of Commerce, and International Federation of Agricultural Producers.

‡ International Council of Scientific Unions and International Social Science Council.

experiment with ideas for peace, even if they are not salable in the immediate future.[40] The danger of nuclear war is much too great for people to leave the problem of war or peace entirely to generals and statesmen.

NOTES

The views expressed in this paper are those of the author only and do not in any way reflect the views of any organization with which he is affiliated. For valuable comments on the manuscript, the author wishes to thank the following individuals, none of whom, however, is in any way responsible for the opinions presented here: Alfred W. Blumrosen, Thomas A. Cowan, Sarah Evan, Harold B. Gerard, Robert M. Krauss, Daniel Lerner, Gerard R. Moran, and Rita Weisbrod.

1. Arthur Larson, *The International Rule of Law* (New York: The Institute for International Order, 1961), p. 29.
2. See also T. C. Schelling, "Reciprocal Measures for Arms Stabilization," in Donald G. Brennan (ed.), *Arms Control, Disarmament and National Security* (New York: George Braziller, 1961), pp. 174–5.
3. Philip C. Jessup, *Transnational Law* (New Haven: Yale University Press, 1956), pp. 1–6 ff.
4. Cf. Eugene Rabinowitch, "Science: The Only Common Enterprise?" in Harlan Cleveland (ed.), *The Promise of World Tensions* (New York: Macmillan, 1961), p. 125. See also Richard C. Snyder and James A. Robinson, *National and International Decision-Making* (New York: The Institute for International Order, 1961), pp. 68–9.
5. Rabinowitch, *op. cit.,* p. 123.
6. Cf. Snyder and Robinson, *op. cit.,* p. 69, for a discussion of an unpublished paper by Ithiel de Sola Pool entitled "Private and Public Diplomacy."
7. See, for example, Ernst B. Haas, *The Uniting of Europe* (Stanford, Calif.: Stanford University Press, 1958).
8. Emile Benoit, *Europe at Sixes and Sevens* (New York: Columbia University Press, 1961), p. 18.
9. *Ibid.,* p. 29.
10. *Ibid.,* pp. 240 ff.
11. *Ibid.,* pp. 260–4.
12. See, for example, Haas, *op. cit.;* William M. Evan, "An International Public Opinion Poll on Disarmament and 'Inspection by the People':

A Study of Attitudes Toward Supranationalism," in Seymour Melman (ed.), *Inspection for Disarmament* (New York: Columbia University Press, 1958), pp. 231–50.

13. Daniel Lerner, personal communication. See Daniel Lerner and Morton Gorden, "European Leaders Look at World Security" (Cambridge, Mass.: Massachusetts Institute of Technology, Center for International Studies, Report C/60–7, mimeo.).

14. Lyman C. White, *International Non-Governmental Organizations* (New Brunswick, N.J.: Rutgers University Press, 1951), p. 3.

15. Bernard C. Cohen, *The Influence of Non-Governmental Groups on Foreign Policy-Making* (Boston: World Peace Foundation, 1959), pp. 4, 20.

16. White, *op. cit.,* pp. 10–14.

17. Bertram Pickard, *The Greater United Nations: An Essay Concerning the Place and Significance of Non-Governmental Organizations* (New York: Carnegie Endowment for International Peace, 1956), p. 18.

18. (Brussels: *Union of International Associations,* 1961), pp. 237–1324.

19. Edwin A. Bock, *Representation of Non-Governmental Organizations at the United Nations* (Chicago: Public Administration Clearing House, 1955), p. 1.

20. Walter H. C. Laves and Charles A. Thompson, *UNESCO: Purpose, Progress and Prospect* (Bloomington, Indiana: Indiana University Press, 1957), p. 87.

21. *Ibid.,* pp. 90–91. 100–101.

22. *Ibid.,* p. 99. "The great success of the International Geophysical Year—it will take years to work up the enormous experimental material accumulated during its eighteen months—has encouraged an indefinite extension of many of its activities on an international basis; it has also stimulated a search for other areas, in which analogous cooperative programs would be possible and desirable. We are certain to see such projects multiply and become a permanent aspect of international life." Rabinowitch, *op. cit.,* p. 114.

23. For example, 58 nongovernmental trade associations were organized in this period. See Haas, *op. cit.,* p. 318 and chs. 9–11.

24. *Ibid.,* pp. 79–80.

25. "The citizens of the member Nations and of the non-self-governing and trust territories under the administration of member Nations shall be deemed to be citizens of the U.N. as well as of their own respective nations." Grenville Clark and Louis B. Sohn, *World Peace through World Law* (Cambridge: Harvard University Press, 1960),

pp. 14–15. In their comprehensive plan for world peace in the form of a proposed revision of the U.N. Charter, Clark and Sohn also provide for individual citizenship. However, they do not advance their proposal in terms of a new organ for individual citizens as is done in this paper.

26. In the historic United States Supreme Court decision in the Slaughter-House Cases in 1872, the Court stated: "It is quite clear, then, that there is a citizenship of the United States and a citizenship of a State which are distinct from each other and which depend upon different characteristics or circumstances in the individual." 16 Wallace 36 (83 U.S. 36), 408.

27. "The money . . . represented not only a token of the givers' 'obligation as world citizens' but of their 'willingness to be taxed and governed by a system of world law, and their desire to share in the economic betterment of other peoples and areas.' " "Quakers' U.N. Tax Spreads to Coast," *The New York Times,* October 2, 1960, p. 46.

28. Clark and Sohn, *op. cit.,* pp. 15, 267.

29. Cf. Melman, *op. cit.,* pp. 38–41, for a discussion of a similar two-way communication system as an inspection device for disarmament.

30. Cf. Alfred O. Hero, *Mass Media and World Affairs* (Boston: World Peace Foundation, 1959), pp. 146–8.

31. Quoted in George A. Codding, Jr., *Broadcasting Without Barriers* (Paris: Unesco, 1959), p. 71.

32. *Ibid.,* pp. 74–75. See also Quincy Wright, "Freedom and Responsibility in Respect to Trans-National Communication," *Proceedings of the American Society of International Law* (Washington, D.C.: American Society of International Law, 1950), pp. 95–107.

33. P. E. Corbett, *Law and Society in the Relations of States* (New York: Harcourt, Brace, 1951), pp. 165–6.

34. Daniel S. Cheever and H. Field Haviland, Jr., *Organizing for Peace* (Boston: Houghton Mifflin, 1954), p. 587.

35. By far the most systematic and detailed plan for Charter revision is that of Clark and Sohn, *op. cit.*

36. Cf. Ithiel de Sola Pool, *Communication and Values in Relation to War and Peace* (New York: The Institute for International Order, 1961).

37. See, for example, Samuel A. Stouffer, *Communism, Conformity, and Civil Liberties* (Garden City, New York: Doubleday, 1955), p. 57.

38. *Op. cit.*

39. de Sola Pool, *op. cit.;* Snyder and Robinson, *op. cit.*

40. David Riesman, "Private People and Public Policy," *Shenandoah,* X (Autumn, 1958), p. 64.

MAINTAINING PEACEFUL COEXISTENCE

By QUINCY WRIGHT

POLICIES FOR THE PREVENTION of World War III have approached the problem from the diverse points of view of promoting mutual terror and of promoting mutual trust. Advocates of the first point of view adhere to the idea of absolute national sovereignty and believe that the foreign policy of a sovereign state is determined by its national interests, that the overriding national interest of each is the preservation of its territorial integrity and political independence, and that the only available means for securing this interest is the development of national power in the form of armaments, economic potential, national morale, and alliances greater than those of any potential enemy.

People of this opinion may admit that such policies have in the past resulted in a rivalry in power-building which induces an arms race, augments mutual suspicions, and increases international tensions, usually ending in war. But under present conditions, they say, mutual trust across the iron curtain is impossible; and the cold war will not turn into hot war because each side possesses nuclear weapons and means of delivery capable of destroying the other. There is no direct defense against a missile-borne nuclear attack, and no effective means for protecting civilian population and economy. Each of the rivals is convinced that it would be unable to keep the other from retaliating with unacceptable force. From this point of view they believe the "peace of mutual terror," so named by Sir Winston Churchill, is possible and is the only kind of peace which is possible.

Advocates of the second point of view reject both of these conclusions. They do not believe it possible to maintain a balance of mutual terror indefinitely and they believe a greater degree of mutual trust is possible. I share this opinion.

The balance of mutual terror is extremely unstable. It is vulnerable to accident from alerted retaliatory forces; to pre-emption due to one side's conviction that the other is about to strike; to irresponsible action caused by the increasing strain on political and military officials or by the spread of nuclear weapons to inexperienced or revolutionary governments; and to the escalation of border wars or civil strife into general nuclear war through the insistence by each side that "there is no substitute for victory." Putting these factors together, C. P. Snow estimated in 1961 that nuclear war was inevitable within ten years unless radical changes in opinions and policies occur.[1]

A peace of terror is, in any case, unsatisfactory. The expense of increasing armament tends to prevent economic and social progress. The need to regiment opinion and economic activity tends to destroy individual freedom. And the superior capability of police states to direct economy, foreign aid, education, and propaganda toward power-building places free democracies at a hopeless disadvantage. Thus an arms race, if it does not end in nuclear war, will end either in the destruction of free democracies by subversive intervention and propaganda, or in the voluntary abandonment of their institutions by the democracies so that they can compete in power-building on a more even basis.[2]

Furthermore, it cannot be said that peace through mutual trust is now impossible. There is much evidence that the Soviet government has abandoned the policy of expansion through war, that the Western governments have not had such a policy since World War II, that each considers termination of the arms race a national interest, and that both are beginning to recognize that this can be achieved only with some measure of mutual trust.[3]

This optimistic opinion is supported by the general belief that all governments are capable, if they reflect, of moderating spontaneous reactions which defeat their interests and of adopting rational policies which further their interests. When each government is vulnerable to, and therefore dependent upon, its rival, all have an interest in maintaining general confidence that agreements will be observed. Consequently each can by analysis identify its national interest, in considerable measure, with the general interest in world stability.[4] All peoples have many basic desires in common, such as the opportunity to enjoy life, liberty, and the pursuit of happiness. It is a national interest of each state that particular national policies be pursued by means which will not sacrifice these basic desires. A peaceful reconciliation of conflicts of special national interests, therefore, seems possible, if states are prepared to act in accord with a concept of the world as a whole which provides such satisfaction to their special interests—arising from distinctive aspects of the geography, economy, history, tradition, and ideology—as is consistent with reasonable satisfaction of the common desires of all peoples.[5]

Solution of the problem of avoiding World War III should begin therefore not with proposals for armament or disarmament, inspection, information, political accommodations, or new forms of international procedure or organization, but with proposals for a world society, realization of which will seem both feasible and moderately satisfactory to leaders on both sides of the iron curtain.

Many concepts of a world society have been proposed but two have been most significant, that of a universal society of individuals and that of a universal society of states. The first implies a considerable synthesis of all value systems, the other a considerable geographic segregation of such systems.[6] Both differ from concepts of absolute national sovereignty which imply that peace can mean only an unstable balance of power or subordination of all nations to one in a universal empire.

The concept of a universal human society, which may be called "cosmopolitanism," has been developed by missionary religions (Buddhism, Christianity, Islam), by secular ideologies (Stoicism, democracy, socialism, Communism), and even by empires like Rome which have merged the national in the universal concept. The concept of a universal society of states, which may be called "internationalism," has been developed by systems of international law, international economics, international organization, and even international politics when nations have put stabilization of the balance of power ahead of national aggrandizement.[7] The difference between the two is limited in that both take a world point of view. Cosmopolitanism does not completely ignore the natural divisions of mankind into peoples of divergent tradition, economy, and culture; and internationalism recognizes that all men, in spite of national diversities, have much in common. The difference depends on the degree of communication among peoples, which influences the weight given to the common and divergent aspects of the various peoples, nations, states, and governments. With the progress of science and communications, it may be that a universal community in which all feel primary loyalty to mankind will eventually emerge. Today the differences of religion, ideology, culture, and nationality are so great and primary loyalties are so generally focused upon sovereign states, that political steps to realize a cosmopolitan society of universal scope are not feasible.[8] Political steps in this direction, in fact, have resulted in the past, and are resulting today, not in a cosmopolitan society, but in a rivalry of states each committed to the expansion of its particular ideology or religion, to polarization of power, and to an arms race producing a peace of terror and increasing the likelihood of a general war.[9]

A universal ideology for mankind may develop in time through free communication, but political support for particular ideologies induces strife which both segregates and ossifies ideologies. That is the significance of the principle—accepted in most free democracies—that church and state should be separated, reflected, indeed, in most religions, as indicated by the biblical precept "give unto Caesar that which is Caesar's." However intense may be a group's moral conviction of the rightness of its particular religion or ideology, it should in its own interest function within the universally accepted system of law and politics aimed at order and justice, and to that end limit its methods of missionary activity. But in the interest of progress each system should tolerate all religions and ideologies so functioning, and foster communication among them, without discrimination.

The opponents of a peace of mutual terror, therefore, usually support internationalism or what has been called "the peaceful coexistence of states," a phrase emphasized by the Soviet Union but consistent with the traditions of international law and democratic nationalism.[10]

Peaceful Coexistence

The first step in preventing World War III, if the foregoing analysis is correct, is to answer three questions concerning peaceful coexistence: (1) What does it mean? (2) Is it desirable? (3) If it is, what can be done to promote it? This essay will seek to answer these questions, with particular emphasis upon the last.

1. *What does peaceful coexistence mean?* There have been different interpretations of the term "peaceful coexistence" mainly because of uncertainty as to the entities which are to coexist. The obvious interpretation would identify these entities as sovereign states. Since the Peace of Westphalia in 1648, international law has assumed that the territorial state is the unit of political organization, that such states are sovereign and equal in law, that each is entitled to deal with internal questions including ideological questions at discretion, but that all are bound by the rules of international law. In time of peace these rules require mutual respect for territorial boundaries, respect for diplomatic immunities, observance of treaties entered into by proper procedures, and utilization of peaceful processes for the settlement of disputes. Traditional international law recognized war as the *ultima ratio regum,* although the Treaty of Westphalia itself urged the use of diplomacy and arbitration first.[11] In the twentieth century, states have by general treaties outlawed hostilities except in individual or collective self-defense; on invitation of a government in uncontested control of the state it represents and within which the force is to be used; or

under authority of an international organization with competence over the state in whose territory the use of force is recommended or required.[12]

This system, maintaining the coexistence of territorial states, has for three centuries been considered superior to the system of ideological unity which prevailed in Europe during the Middle Ages. That system led to the serious ideological wars between Christendom and Islam culminating in the Crusades, and to the post-Reformation wars between Catholicism and Protestantism culminating in the disastrous Thirty Years War of the seventeenth century, ended by the Peace of Westphalia.[13] Peaceful coexistence is accepted by the United Nations Charter, which "is based on the principle of the sovereign equality of all its members." The Charter also requires members to settle disputes peacefully and to refrain in their international relations from threat or use of force in a manner inconsistent with the purposes of the United Nations; and it forbids intervention by the United Nations, and *a fortiori* by states, in "matters which are essentially within the domestic jurisdiction of any state," with exception of situations in which the Charter itself provides for enforcement measures.[14] Reliable observance of these principles depends upon general agreement on the meaning of such key terms as domestic jurisdiction, subversive intervention, aggression, and defense; upon procedures for keeping international law up to date in a changing world, for settling disputes peacefully, for adjudicating legal claims impartially, and for assuring the security of all states by collective action under international authority; and, finally, upon the acceptance by all states of peaceful coexistence as a guide to policy. Such acceptance is implied by the provision in the Charter Preamble calling upon the peoples of the United Nations "to practice tolerance and live together in peace with one another as good neighbors."

These same principles have been given emphasis in the Orient by the *Panch Shila* or Five Principles proposed by India and accepted by twenty-nine Asian and African states at the Bandung Conference of 1955. They call for mutual respect for territorial integrity and sovereignty, nonaggression, noninterference in the internal affairs of others, equality of nations and races, and peaceful coexistence.[15] This concept of coexistence was accepted by Premier Khrushchev in his *Foreign Affairs* article of August, 1959, and by President Eisenhower —though he avoided use of that term—in many speeches, especially that of May, 1953.

Considering that the concept of peaceful coexistence of states has been so widely accepted, why has there been objection to the term? The answer seems to be that many statesmen, newspaper reporters, and other people assume that the Soviet leaders, in using the term peaceful coexistence, imply not peaceful coexistence among states recognized as sovereign, but peaceful coexistence between the ideologies of Communism and free democracy, and between the great power blocs, cemented by the Warsaw and NATO alliances, respectively dedicated to the promotion of these ideologies. They have assumed that such peaceful coexistence would result in continued denial of human rights within Communist states and indefinite continuance of dominance by the Soviet Union over the states of Central Europe and East Germany, and of dominance by Communist China over North Korea, North Vietnam, and Tibet, a situation disliked by numerous groups in the United States and elsewhere which sympathize with political exiles from these countries. These groups and many Americans assume that the total extinction of Communism is ultimately necessary, and that the satellites or "captive nations" must immediately be freed and given the opportunity for self-determination. In pursuance of this interpretation the editor of the periodical issued by the Assembly of Captive European Nations quoted Premier Khrushchev as saying on October 10, 1959, at Novosibirsk:

> Coexistence means continuation of the struggle between the two social systems—but by peaceful means, without war, without interference by one state in the internal affairs of another. We consider it to be an economic, political and ideological struggle, but not a military.[16]

Commenting on this under the heading "Khrushchev's peaceful coexistence," the editor writes:

> The liquidation of the cold war, as understood by the Soviets, means that the West should not challenge Soviet colonial possessions while the Communists pursue their ideological struggle against democracy and also challenge Western rights and positions whenever it suits them. . . . It automatically implies the recognition by the free world of the *status quo*. If the West recognizes as permanent the present subjugation of the peoples of East-Central Europe, she will be able to convince these peoples to reconcile themselves to their present situation. . . . It will also, the Soviets hope, bring about a slackening of the efforts of the West to build up its defenses.

It is clear that this interpretation of peaceful coexistence is inconsistent with the natural meaning of the term. It implies that ideological conflict is to be the main preoccupation of international politics and that all methods short of military force are to be used to maintain and expand the areas now under the competing ideologies, thus re-establishing the situation which existed during the long periods of strife between Islam and Christendom and between Catholicism and Protestantism. Yet a major objective of the makers of modern international law and the Peace of Westphalia was to end this very situation. Based on the proposition *cuius regio eius religio,* the Peace of Westphalia sought to relegate religious and ideological controversy to the domestic jurisdiction of states, each of which was equally sovereign and equally entitled to decide on this internal problem. President Eisenhower also supported this principle:

> Any nation's right to a form of government and an economic system of its own choosing is *inalienable.* . . . Any nation's attempt to dictate to other nations their form of government is *indefensible.*[17]

It is true that in the period before Westphalia ideological expansion was promoted by armed force, while Khrushchev interprets peaceful coexistence as inconsistent with the use of armed force for this purpose. He goes even further in saying that peaceful coexistence implies no "interference by one state in the internal affairs of another." If this were observed, his conception of peaceful coexistence would differ little from peaceful coexistence of sovereign states under international law; but his critics, observing the situation in the satellite states, and particularly the Hungarian incident of 1956, do not believe that Khrushchev really intends this, or that he intends to refrain from the use of armed force within the present Communist domain. In other words, his critics say he reserves a carte blanche within this area, suggesting abstention from military force and subversive intervention only across the line which now separates the great power blocs.[18]

If peaceful coexistence means maintenance of the *status quo*—political, ideological, social, and economic—by the authorities now in control in Moscow and Peking over the vast areas now under their effective authority, it runs counter to the principles of national self-determination of peoples and respect for human rights. On the other hand, if peaceful coexistence means recognition of the sovereignty of states under international law, it opposes dominance by one sovereign state over another and requires every state to observe the principles of international law and of the Charter defining limits to sovereignty such as those with respect to human rights and self-determination. It is true that international law has in the past recognized the sovereign right of states to make treaties and the propriety of treaties whereby a state places itself under protection or other control by another state, but in principle such treaties do not accord with the principles of the Charter unless freely made, and have been rapidly disappearing under the aegis of the principle of national self-determination.[19]

Recognizing the great difference between these two interpretations of peaceful coexistence, the term is used in this paper in the sense of peaceful coexistence between recognized sovereign states under international law as defined by custom and by the Charter and other treaties.

2. *Is general acceptance of peaceful coexistence desirable?* An affirmative answer to this question is suggested by the analysis presented in the first part of this essay, but a full answer requires consideration of the practical situation in which peaceful coexistence will be applied. What would be the probable consequences of general adherence to the conception of peaceful coexistence? It must be admitted that in the contemporary world practical application of this conception in the international law sense would not differ immediately from its application in the Soviet sense.

Acceptance of the territorial sovereign state as the basis of international relations hampers outside assistance to revolutionists because it implies that a *de facto* government which has existed for a considerable time must be assumed to be satisfactory to the people and capable of representing the state. Intervention in any form intended to upset such a government, even though it appears to lack popular support, is inconsistent with the mutual respect owed by states to one another and is therefore contrary to international law. The Soviet Union violated international law through various types of intervention, establishing satellite states in Europe and attempting to do so in Asia and Africa. The United States did the same by the Presidential proclamation of "Captive Nations Week" in July 1960 and 1961 and by the support given by the government to the attempted invasion of Cuba by Cuban refugees in April 1961.[20]

The acceptance of peaceful coexistence of sovereign states also tends to hamper the self-determination of colonies and minorities within the territory of recognized states, even though such colonies or minorities clearly manifest a desire for independence or affiliation with another state. The principle of "self-determination of peoples" as accepted in the United Nations Charter and increasingly recognized in international practice, even by President de Gaulle in reference to Algeria, has not been sufficiently defined to constitute a legal right of such peoples except in the case of trusteeship territories and perhaps in the case of a "non-self-governing territory" recognized as such by the administering power or the General Assembly.[21] The realization of self-determination practically depends upon negotiations between the sovereign state and the dissident people, assisted by such recommendations as may emerge from the United Nations and such pressures as may be brought by the peoples themselves.

Peaceful coexistence also offers obstacles to the development of effective international procedures to protect the human rights of the inhabitants of a state who are at the time its nationals. While the Charter seems to make respect for human rights a legal obligation of the members (Article 56), Covenants of Human Rights have not yet been concluded which clearly define these rights. The claims of some states such as the Union of South Africa that this matter is within their domestic jurisdiction has made many states hesitant to accept procedures to implement these rights. The United States, by announcing in 1953 that it would not enter into Covenants of Human Rights (apparently because of domestic difficulties), halted the United Nations effort to give legal protection to human rights.[22] The Security Council, it is clear, must consider movements for reform and even rebellion and insurrection as domestic matters in which it cannot "intervene," as was illustrated in the Congo in 1960, unless international peace and security is threatened (Article 39).

It thus appears that international law, based on the principle of peaceful coexistence of territorial sovereign states, may in practice permit autocratic and oppressive governments to continue, and may therefore hamper reforms envisaged by the Charter in favor of self-determination of peoples and human freedom. Leaders of the free world, while sometimes unenthusiastic about these reforms in their own territories, have insisted that they should be observed in territories under Communist control, and that they can be thus realized only by continued political and military pressure upon the Communist states accompanied by continuous incitement of dissident peoples within these states.[23] Such policies, however, mean continuance of the cold war or the ideological struggle; and they have had and will probably continue to have the following effects:

Cold war policies have consolidated the governments of the Communist bloc under the leadership of Moscow and have steadily improved its relative power position in relation to the free world. It has been the experience in most historical situations, and notably in that since World War II, that governments tend to unite against a common enemy. Furthermore, free democracies, necessarily decentralized, have been less capable (except perhaps during actual war) of developing, coordinating, and utilizing military, economic, and propaganda resources to augment political power in the game of international politics than have highly centralized autocratic governments.[24]

Cold war policies seem to have augmented the oppressiveness of the Communist governments in denying self-determination and the enjoyment of human rights in the areas they control, although there have been some relaxations since the death of Stalin, especially in Poland. It has been the general historic experience that high international tensions have led to centralization of government, regimentation of opinion, suppression of dissent, and oppression of peoples. Even in democracies, actual war or widespread fear of attack has often had these results. Tyranny thrives and democracy withers under high international tensions.[25] Under such conditions all states tend to become "garrison states."[26]

Cold war policies have also had the effect of encouraging revolts within the Soviet orbit in the illusory hope by the revolters of support from the free world. The actual result has been vigorous suppression of such revolts followed by even greater oppression. It is true that revolts against tyrannical and oppressive regimes and self-determination movements in the name of freedom have often been successful, but usually because of external support (such as that France gave the United States during the American Revolution) or support within the imperial state itself (such as that British Whigs gave to the American Revolution and the British Labor Party has consistently given to recent self-determination movements within the Empire). However, with the threat of nuclear war, external aid to such revolts within the Soviet zone is unlikely, as was evident in the Hungarian revolt of 1956; and with the control of opinion in the Communist states, internal support is less likely to manifest itself than has been the case in Empires in which the metropole has become democratic.

Finally, cold war policies have so expanded military appropriations in all states that economic progress has been hampered and human welfare neglected.

The world seems to face a dilemma. Restoration of the system of peaceful coexistence envisaged by international law and the United Nations Charter seems to require continuance of cold war pressures to liberate the satellites. Such continuance, however, tends to destroy the very system it is designed to restore; consequently, relaxation of tensions and peaceful coexistence between the existing power blocs seem to be called for. But such relaxation of tensions may serve to confirm the *status quo* within the Soviet orbit and militate against the development of democracy, self-determination, and peaceful coexistence within that area. Thus the argument pursues its circular course. Observance of the rule of international law forbidding intervention may frustrate the new international law which conceives the state as the instrument not of its government but of its people. On the other hand, intervention, ignoring that rule, has had that frustrating effect in even greater degree.

The problem can only be solved by determining, through historical and sociological studies, which of the effects attributed to termination of cold war is most probable. Will the independence of states, the liberation of the captive nations, the self-determination of peoples, and respect for human rights actually be better promoted by the continuance of cold war tensions? A thoroughly convincing answer would require extensive study, but the experience of the last ten years and a large body of historical experience support the conviction that the better solution is acceptance by the existing governments of all *de facto* states, under the assumption that such acceptance will result in relaxations which will gradually lead to establishment of governments of their choice by the people of these states, and to general respect for international law, human rights, and self-determination of peoples.

Democracy and freedom have grown under conditions of peace and in areas like England and the United States long protected by geography from military aggression. If the preceding analysis is correct, policies to promote and maintain peaceful coexistence of states should tend to restore trust among nations and create conditions preventing World War III, and at the same time forward the cause of democracy and freedom. "Peace," suggests Charles de Visscher, former president of the International Court of Justice, "will serve justice more than justice will serve peace."[27]

3. *What can be done to promote peaceful coexistence of sovereign states?* The United States should, I believe, direct its policy, and encourage other states and the United Nations to do likewise, toward: (a) reducing international tensions and liquidating the cold war; (b) stabilizing the balance of power; (c) strengthening the rule of law in international affairs; and (d) strengthening the United Nations. Policies to realize these four goals will be considered in the next sections. The first is a prerequisite to the others, for in international relations, the psychological precedes the mechanical. "Wars are made in the minds of men."[28] Governments act not because of situations or events but because of their interpretations of situations or events in the light of their ambitions and fears, often flowing from beliefs about the intentions and capabilities of others. Technological changes influence policy only indirectly through appraisals of their consequences and utilities; no mechanical arrangement or technological invention can secure peace. Peace programs must rather aim first at the beliefs and opinions of governments and peoples, especially their beliefs about one another. The object of the policies proposed, there-

fore, is to contribute to a more peaceful climate of opinion, making possible other steps to prevent World War III.

The Reduction of International Tensions

Among the steps to reduce cold-war tensions, summit conferences, cultural exchanges, abandonment of crusading slogans, social and economic cooperation, and avoidance of provocations and encouragement of conciliation have been suggested.

1. *Summit conferences.* Such conferences may promote mutual understanding and improve the atmosphere even if they do not immediately result in specific agreements. Some writers fear that in that event they will lead to disillusionment and make relations worse than they were before, but I believe this is to misunderstand the nature of the cold war conflict. There may be serious international conflicts because a state tends to encroach upon the vital interests or even destroy the independence of another state, as was the case with Hitler, and as may have been true at times with Stalin; but often conflict results from mutual fears due to misinterpretation. In such a case, the conflict is between the images which each state has of the other, rather than between the states as they see themselves or as an omniscient observer might see them. Insofar as such false images account for conflict, an improved atmosphere, in which each sees the values and policies of the other as they really are, would itself ameliorate conflict and create conditions in which tangible conflicts of interest or policy can be solved.[29]

While in the present situation differences of material interests undoubtedly exist, it appears that in recent years the cold war has rested to a considerable extent upon mutual fears. Each side fears that the other will interpret any move toward conciliation or compromise as a manifestation of weakness, and take advantage of it. Hence, each attempts to arm more effectively; and each, therefore, becomes more convinced of the aggressive intentions of the other. The cold war has developed from a process of spontaneous action and reaction, not from a calculation of causes and effects or a rational adaptation of means to ends. Governments have exhibited the "repetition compulsion" often observed by psychiatrists: "They keep repeating the very acts which cause trouble for them."[30] Seeking security, they increase their armaments; and although this reduces their security, they repeat the performance.

Direct personal contact among leaders may moderate such obsessions. Furthermore, summit conferences provide virtually the only means for estimating the mind of a dictator behind his facade of propaganda. It is true that such conferences may fail if not prepared for or followed up by lower levels of diplomacy, and if incidents augmenting tension are permitted to occur.[31] But with these qualifications, summit conferences can have great value in reducing tensions.

2. *International cultural exchanges.* Not only governments but peoples must have better mutual understanding if the atmosphere of international relations is to improve. Exchange of leaders of opinion, artists, students, farmers, newspaper correspondents, professional men, and others may have considerable importance in improving the atmosphere. Such direct contacts reduce the feasibility of propaganda designed to create false images.

3. *Abandonment of crusading slogans.* The atmosphere would surely improve if statesmen, legislators, and the press would use greater reserve in employing such slogans as "containment," "roll-back," "liberation," "encirclement," "liquidation of Communism," "burying of capitalism," "imperialistic policies," and "captive nations." It is difficult to see that such slogans have had any influence except to provoke counterslogans and increase tension. Action to support the slogans is precluded by the mutual fears of nuclear war. While it is to be expected that each side hopes and anticipates that its ideology will in the long run be accepted throughout the world, this is unimportant from the point of view of international politics, provided the time set for such achievement is measured in generations or centuries rather than years, and provided the instruments to be utilized are peaceful and legal. No one in the West can properly object if Communist governments make their system work so well in their territories that others will voluntarily accept it as a model, nor can those governments properly object if the Western nations so develop their system that it provides an even more alluring model.

The international issue should concern not the relative merit of ideologies or the long-run goals of governments, but the means employed to realize ideologies and to achieve goals. Armed invasion and subversive intervention can and should be prevented by international action, and the governments themselves should refrain from such methods if they honestly wish for peaceful coexistence.

4. *Social and economic cooperation.* The Soviet Union has joined most of the specialized agencies of the United Nations and cooperates in their activities. Such cooperation should be encouraged as another means of improving the atmosphere.

This might well extend to cooperation in technical and economic assistance to underdeveloped areas. Competition in this activity inevitably results in its being used as an instrument of political propaganda and thus extends the cold war into the underdeveloped areas which naturally utilize such competition to bargain between the great powers. The United States might well give a larger proportion of technical assistance and economic aid through the United Nations, and challenge the Soviet Union to do the same. Such cooperation would not only serve better to advance the economic welfare of these areas but would also contribute much toward reducing cold war tensions.

5. *Avoidance of provocation and encouragement of conciliation.* In dealing with international problems American opinion has considered "winning the cold war" the central policy. That policy has been devoted to building alliances and bases around the Soviet Union to contain it, and to developing more effective bombs, missiles, and other weapons systems to deter it from aggression by threats of massive retaliation. The result has been that the Soviet Union has done the same, even more efficiently. Hence the relative power position of the West has diminished as the Soviet Union has added China and other Asian and European states to its bloc, acquired the secret of the atom, developed superior missiles and satellites, and manifested greater effectiveness in winning favorable opinion among Asian, African and Latin American countries. This might have been anticipated from a study of history and an analysis of the conditions of success in an arms race.[32]

The United States and other countries might well adopt policies which moderate every proposed defense appropriation or action by consideration of its probable provocative effect, and which utilize every opportunity for conciliation and settlement of differences by bargain or compromise that does not have the character of appeasement in the sense of giving away rights of other states. Defense without provocation and conciliation without appeasement would seem suitable policies for reducing international tensions.[33]

Stabilization of the Balance of Power

It is too seldom realized that the stability of any political organization —whether a unitary state, a federation, an alliance, an international organization, or an unorganized state system—rests on some sort of equilibrium of internal forces. When the equilibrium in the United States Senate between the representatives of the diverse cultures of the North and the South was broken, the Civil War developed. Suitable policies of decentralization, *de facto* recognition, and disarmament might stabilize the balance of power.

1. *Decentralization of power.* A bipolar equilibrium is inevitably unstable if the power of each part is greater than that of the whole.

A two party system can promote stability when the state within which it functions is much stronger than any party; whereas this is not the case, as in some Asian and Latin American states, a two party system makes for instability. The out-party is tempted to utilize illegal and violent methods to gain power. In the world community, where international organizations are much weaker than each of the great states, this is notably true. When the European equilibrium became bipolarized between the Triple Alliance and the Triple Entente, World War I resulted; when it became bipolarized between the Axis and the Anglo-French bloc, World War II resulted. The bipolarization between the NATO and Warsaw blocs since World War II has been equally dangerous, though hot war has not yet resulted.

When all power is concentrated in two centers, each of which relies on its own armed forces for security, and there is no opportunity for diplomatic maneuvers to maintain balance by shifting external forces from one side to the other, each side necessarily considers the influence of time on its power position; and the side time appears to be against is likely to risk war because it fears that if it waits, the other side's superiority will eventually be so great that it will not be able to avoid destruction.[34]

Stability would be promoted by increasing the number of relatively independent centers of power, a tendency which has been observed during the last few years and could be expected to increase if international tensions were reduced. Decentralization of the great power blocs must, however, take place simultaneously. If one side greatly decentralized first, it would present an opportunity for successful aggression or infiltration by the other.

It seems probable that reduction of tensions throughout the world would augment the tendency of China and the Central European satellites to assert greater independence from Moscow, and of the Commonwealth led by the United Kingdom and Western Europe led by France to assert greater independence from Washington. Statesmen should prepare for these probable and not necessarily undesirable tendencies.

The problem is linked with the problem of the distribution of atomic weapons. The United States, the Soviet Union, the United Kingdom, and in lesser degree, France, have them. The acquisition of such weapons by China and perhaps by a Central European Federation led by Poland would undoubtedly increase the trend toward independence of these political centers. On the other hand, the wider distribution of atomic weapons is a danger in that it increases the probability of their accidental or irrational use precipitating atomic war. Agreement to limit the "nuclear club," involved in the problem of terminating the testing of nuclear weapons, would seem to be in the interests of peace. It should be recognized, however, that such a policy is in some measure incompatible with stabilizing the balance of power. For this reason, it might be more desirable to build checks and balances into the alliance systems so as to assure that while effective for defense, they cannot be used for aggression. Such checks were illustrated when Britain checked American aggressiveness in Vietnam in 1954, when the United States checked British and French aggressiveness at Suez in 1956, and when, apparently, the Soviet Union checked Chinese aggressiveness in the Straits of Formosa in 1958.

2. *Recognition of* de facto *states.* Decentralization of the power equilibrium would probably be aided by general recognition of all *de facto* states and their admittance to the United Nations. This is especially true of China and may also apply to Germany, Korea, and Vietnam. The fact that each opposing government in these states is recognized by some states as the government of the whole undoubtedly contributes to tensions in both Asia and Europe.[35] The balancing process in international affairs takes place through diplomacy, and is hampered by nonrecognition of important states. Furthermore, agreements for disarmament, inspection to maintain such agreements, and the functioning of collective security through the United Nations requires participation by all states with any substantial material power. The exclusion of major Communist states from the United Nations makes it unrepresentative of the world as it is, and impairs its capacity to function efficiently.[36] Finally, the collaboration of states in the United Nations has a socializing tendency, while ostracism has an opposite effect. The worse the record of a state, the more important that it be a member of the United Nations. The difficulties in the way of recognizing these states and admitting them to the United Nations, great as they are, should be faced by statesmen.

3. *Disarmament.* Disarmament refers to many types of international agreements and the effect of these various types of agreements is complicated. The power equilibrium would probably be stabilized by quantitative disarmament agreements in the form of a moratorium on budgets, effectives, or matériel, or even more, a proportional reduction of all these elements of military power. But it must be realized that reduction of armaments-in-being increases the importance of military potential, such as industrial plants and population. Thus reductions which actually maintain an existing power ratio are difficult to accomplish. Furthermore, the nuclear stalemate depends on each major power's retaining secure retaliatory power sufficient to prohibit attack. The peace of mutual terror cannot be

abandoned until the peace of mutual trust is assured in considerable measure.

Perhaps more important than quantitative reductions, for stabilizing the power equilibrium, is qualitative disarmament, reducing or eliminating weapons most useful for aggression and thus strengthening the relative power position of the defensive. Agreement prohibiting the use of nuclear weapons including tactical weapons and long-range missiles, except in direct retaliation against uses of these weapons by an aggressor, would therefore tend to stabilize the balance, although it would at the same time increase the effectiveness of conventional weapons.[37] While eliminating stocks of nuclear weapons would strengthen such an agreement, inspection to assure observance is probably now impossible. Elimination of missiles is more practicable. Excessive fears doubtless increase the instability of the balance of power. Such fears would be moderated by limiting nuclear tests to prevent lethal fallout and forestall the development of nuclear weapons by powers which do not now have them. Establishing reliable inspections to give warning of impending attack would have a similar effect.

The arms race tends to develop weapons and means of delivering them with increasing destructiveness. Increased destructiveness of weapons reduces the probability of deliberate nuclear war but preparations for retaliation and the tensions they develop tend to increase the probability of *accidental, pre-emptive,* or *irrational war. Nibbling aggression* with conventional armaments may be encouraged by confidence that atomic retaliation will not be used against it, yet it may develop into atomic war under the impetus of a leader who thinks there is "no substitute for victory." Similar danger may arise through the expansion of *civil strife* because of the intervention of third states.[38]

These complicated interrelations make it difficult to calculate the probability of agreement upon, or the effect of, any particular disarmament proposal. It appears, however, that disarmament should seek to stop the arms race, stabilize the balance of power, strengthen the relative power of the defensive, reduce military budgets so as to release funds for economic development, and reduce dangers to health from atomic fallout. The ending of nuclear testing should probably be the first step in a disarmament program.[39]

While suitable inspection is necessary to give assurance against violation of any disarmament agreement, it must be realized that there can be no absolute assurance through any feasible system in view of the wide distribution of atomic weapons and scientific know-how. A major sanction for disarmament agreements must always be good faith arising from confidence that all parties to the agreement regard its continued observance as a greater interest than any possible gain from violation. Such confidence grows out of an atmosphere of relaxation. Consequently, a reduction of tensions is a prerequisite to disarmament agreements. Such agreements may further reduce tensions, permitting further disarmament—thus initiating a process of action and reaction between material and moral factors making for peace. Such a process would be the opposite of an arms race. It implies general acceptance of the ultimate objective of general and complete disarmament, i.e., reduction of arms to what is necessary for domestic and international policing.

If mutual trust is to develop, there must be confidence that all take seriously their obligation to refrain from threat or use of force in international relations. A system of deterrence in which each retains a high level of armament inspires conviction that some plan to use arms, or at least to threaten such use, is an aid to diplomacy. Such a system seeks to make the use of arms both credible and incredible, and prevents mutual trust.

Strengthening International Law

A strong movement has developed in the American Bar Association for the "world rule of law."[40] It must be realized that in the shrinking world law is necessary for the functioning of the United Nations and indeed to define peaceful coexistence itself. Among steps to strengthen international law are the clear definition of such key terms as aggression, defense, subversive intervention and domestic jurisdiction, and improvement of procedures for developing and applying international law, especially through the International Law Commission and the International Court of Justice.

1. *Definition of aggression.* Collective security would work more efficiently if there were general agreement as to the meaning of "aggression" and the international procedures for dealing with it. The United States should modify its present policy and urge the General Assembly to develop such a definition. The matter has long been under discussion. Apparently it has failed to be resolved because some states have wished a more extensive and some a more restrictive definition than that implied by the Charter. The United States and some other states have wished the definition to include propaganda, infiltration, subversion, and other acts sometimes called "indirect aggression." The term "aggression," however, is used in the Charter to define threats or uses of force by a state, which justify other states in using armed force in individual or collective self-defense or the United Nations in organizing force against that state. It should be

clear that the term can include only the illegal threat or use of armed force in international relations. Surely the use of armed force should be permissible only against a state which has itself resorted to an illegal threat or use of armed force, and not against a state which is utilizing propaganda or other nonmilitary forms of subversion.

On the other hand, some states have wished a restrictive definition which would permit a state to use armed force after peaceful methods have failed, as a measure of reprisal to remedy an injury due to the alleged illegal behavior of another state. Great Britain and France tried to justify their invasion of Suez in 1956, and India its seizure of Goa in 1961, on this ground. Such an interpretation, however, would practically eliminate the bars against war which it was the main purpose of the Charter to erect.

It is difficult to find any justification in the Charter for either expansive or restrictive interpretations of aggression. The term was *not* intended to include acts against a state's territorial integrity or political independence not involving the use of armed force[41]; it *was* intended to forbid some uses of armed force which have in the past been considered permissible to remedy injustice. As used in United Nations debates the term "act of aggression" (Articles 1, 39), has included any "threat or use of force" in "international relations" (Article 2, paragraph 4); any "threat to" or "breach of" international "peace" (Article 39); and any "armed attack" (Article 51) directed by a government, or by unofficial groups in a state's territory with complicity or toleration of the government, against "the territorial integrity or political independence"[41a] of another state or "in any other manner inconsistent with the purposes of the United Nations" (Article 2, paragraph 4), in case the initiating or negligent government has been identified and its act is not expressly or implicitly permitted by the Charter. The only such permissions seem to be in case of a necessity for "individual or collective self-defense" (Article 51), in case of authorization by the United Nations (Articles 2, paragraph 5; 11, paragraph 2; 39, paragraph 42), or as an implication from sovereignty (Article 2, paragraph 1) by invitation of the state in whose territory the force is to be used.[42] While a definition of aggression is important to prevent aggression by inadvertence, collective security action by the United Nations, as by the League of Nations, has begun, not by determining the aggressor, but by a cease fire order addressed to both belligerents. If one refuses to accept this order it brands itself the aggressor. However, the basic concept referred to may be necessary if neither accepts the cease fire or if both accept it and claims to damages arise after fighting has ended.

2. *Definition of defense.* Military defense of a state's territory or

public agencies is permissible only if the defending state is the victim of an armed attack or the immediate threat of such attack. The right of defense seems therefore to be defined by the meaning of aggression and vice versa. The use of the term "collective self-defense" in the Charter suggests the importance of a definition of defense which would unequivocally establish the limits of defensive military action in the relations of allies. Collective self-defense could be used as an excuse for aggression if a state, alleging that an ally had been attacked, were justified in invading the territory of that ally on the basis of a general treaty declaring an attack on one an attack on all. The Soviet Union sought to justify its action in Hungary in 1956 on the ground that since Hungary was about to be the victim of aggression, the Warsaw Pact permitted the Soviet action. Certainly such invasion is justified only if the ally actually is the victim of aggression and if its established government has invited such assistance.[43]

3. *Definition of subversive intervention.* Sometimes called "indirect aggression" or "war mongering" (though not "aggression" as used in the Charter), subversive intervention operates by means of propaganda inciting to revolt, infiltration of official state agencies, establishment of fifth columns penetrating political parties and influencing opinion, and utterances or publications inducing contempt for the state or encouraging international or civil war. Such activities are disturbing to the peace and have long been considered violations of international law if directed or incited by another government. Certainly they militate against peaceful coexistence and have been condemned at times by resolutions of the General Assembly of the United Nations. The term "subversive intervention" should be clearly defined and procedures elaborated through the United Nations to prevent such activity. The problem of definition is difficult because too broad a definition (requiring governments to censor private utterances or publications) would invade the human right to freedom of speech and communication. The problem is similar to that faced by the Supreme Court of the United States in drawing a line between activities permissible under the First Amendment of the Constitution and those which Congress may properly penalize under the head of subversive utterances, sedition, or treason.[44]

4. *Definition of domestic jurisdiction.* The Charter forbids intervention in the domestic jurisdiction of states with the exception of enforcement measures by the United Nations. The International Court of Justice has defined domestic jurisdiction as inclusive of any exercise of authority by a state in which its discretion is not limited by any obligation of general international law or treaty, but incidents such as civil strife within a state's territory become matters of international

concern if the United Nations finds that they threaten international peace. In such circumstances they are not within the state's domestic jurisdiction and the United Nations can intervene as it did in the Congo, whether or not its action can be regarded as an "enforcement measure."[45] Since a state's obligations under general international law and treaties are to be interpreted and applied in final instance by suitable international procedures, only by such a procedure can it be determined whether a particular claim of authority by a state is within its domestic jurisdiction. Self-judgment on this, as in the American Connally Amendment, nullifies international law. Peaceful coexistence implies respect by each state for the domestic jurisdiction of others but it does not forbid protest and the invocation of suitable international action to compel a state to live up to its international obligations.

5. *Strengthening the International Law Commission.* Many additional aspects of international law need re-examination in the changing world situation, especially in order to give consideration to the views of justice of the many new states of Asia and Africa with religious and philosophical traditions somewhat different from the Classical and Christian tradition within which international law has developed in the Western world. International law must be acceptable to all states, not merely to those of the West.[46]

The law of the sea was in some measure codified by the 1958 Geneva international conference, acting on recommendations of the International Law Commission, but the limits of territorial waters remained to be defined. Other questions which need examination include a state's responsibility for injuries to aliens within its territory, especially regarding nationalizations; the implementation of human rights and self-determination; the law of outer space, the bed of the sea, and the polar regions; and the interpretation and application of treaties. Peaceful coexistence cannot be maintained unless the law which defines it is regarded by all states as being a substantial reflection of national interests and international justice under existing conditions of the world. The more rapidly the world changes, the more necessary are effective legislative procedures for international law. The International Law Commission should be strengthened as the major agency for initiating international legislation.

6. *The jurisdiction of the International Court of Justice.* Perhaps most important of all is the expansion of the jurisdiction of the International Court of Justice. Third-party adjudication is no less important for the rule of law than procedures for keeping international law up to date. The repeal of the Connally reservation to the World Court Statute is the first step in this direction. Under this reservation the

United States can avoid being sued, by declaring the issue within its domestic jurisdiction, but because the reservation applies reciprocally, it cannot sue any other state without the latter's consent. The rule of law implies that in disputes where both parties argue on legal grounds and diplomacy fails to achieve agreement, either should be able to compel the other to go before an impartial court for authoritative decision on the meaning and application of the law in that case. Claims of domestic jurisdiction seem particularly suitable for submission to the Court; the political organs of the United Nations might well follow the practice of the League of Nations in asking the Court for an advisory opinion on such claims unless they concern determination of threats to the peace, clearly a matter for the political organs of the United Nations. It is of course implied that the Court is impartial between the litigants, and there has doubtless been hesitancy among Oriental and Communist states in utilizing the Court because the majority of the judges come from countries with alien legal and ethical traditions. Both the composition of the Court and the character of the law it applies have a bearing upon a state's willingness to submit to its jurisdiction. However, if any state argues its case on legal grounds it should be prepared—if not to submit to the Court—at least to submit to a form of *ad hoc* arbitration assuring a tribunal in which it has complete confidence.[47]

It is true that in many important international disputes one or both parties seek not the application of existing international law but its change or an exception from it. Such demands are not susceptible of judicial settlement. If a state believes that its economic, political, military, or other interests require the other state to relax its insistence upon the law, the case can be settled by adjudication only if the law itself is sufficiently flexible to permit arguments of equity or of abuse of rights in cases where strict law would do an obvious injustice. In the main, then, conflicts of interest can be settled only by negotiation or conciliation. But when both parties to a dispute make claims of right, neither should be able to evade adjudication after reasonable attempts at negotiation have failed.[48]

Strengthening the United Nations

This problem has been widely studied, especially by the Commission to Study the Organization of Peace, and will not be discussed here except to emphasize its close relation to maintaining peaceful coexistence. By creating confidence in collective security, pacific settlement of disputes, and cooperation for economic and social development, a strong United Nations would have great influence in reducing fears and tensions in the world.

Of first importance to peaceful coexistence are the implementation of the Uniting for Peace Resolution of 1950 by earmarking national forces for international policing and establishing a small permanent United Nations police force, the improvement of the means of pacific settlement and the increase of United Nations economic and social services. These means can make it possible for all states to identify their national interests with maintenance of United Nations principles, procedures, and institutions. Progress in this direction has been marked by the establishment of United Nations forces at Suez and in the Congo, the development of the political initiative of the Secretary-General, and the expansion of United Nations agencies for economic assistance to underdeveloped nations.

The effectiveness of the United Nations depends upon progress in all the issues discussed in this essay: the reduction of tension, the stabilization of the balance of power, and development of international law. The United Nations cannot function effectively in a bipolarized world of high tension, in which many states doubt whether international law embodies international justice and whether the institutions for applying it will function impartially in specific cases. Progress in all these fields can be promoted by discussion in the United Nations itself, but depends also upon diplomacy among the great powers and action by existing governments in adapting their policies and developing opinion among their peoples to conform to the requirement of an interdependent and peaceful world of coexisting states.[49]

To assist in this work the United Nations might well seek to enlighten world public opinion on four basic distinctions.

1. "Collective security," organized in Articles 39 to 50 of the Charter and in the Uniting for Peace Resolution, should be distinguished from "collective self-defense" permitted to states by Article 51 of the Charter. The first envisages a policing action in which the agencies of the whole jural community enforce the law against a dissident member, while the latter implies action by a state or group of states to defend themselves against attack by an outside state or group over which they have no jurisdiction. The distinction between public police action and private self-defense is recognized in all legal systems, and is inherent in the idea of law. The frequent failure to make this distinction, as by referring to NATO as a "collective security" organization, has impaired the effectiveness of the United Nations. Collective security tends toward a world rule of law, but collective self-defense tends at best to a stable balance of power and at worst to an arms race.[50]

2. "Aggression" should be distinguished from "subversive intervention"; that is, the illegal use of armed force in international relations should be distinguished from other threats to the independence and security of states as by propaganda, infiltration, corruption, or other means of subversion. As already noted, the use of the term "indirect aggression" for subversive intervention has tended to confuse these very different types of offenses against international law. Only aggression can properly be remedied by use of military force whether under authority of the United Nations or as a measure of self-defense by a state or alliance. Military force is not an appropriate remedy against subversive intervention and if used will make the user itself the aggressor. Certainly subversive intervention is a danger. International law seeks to define the offenses against peace implied by the term, and the United Nations should contribute to preventing these offenses by such measures as monitoring radio communications and conducting investigations, but the prime defense against subversive intervention lies within each state in the exercise of its domestic jurisdiction. The difficulty lies in drawing the line between the human right to freedom of opinion and communication and the national right to freedom from propaganda, subversion, and incitement to sedition initiated outside its territory and actually likely to stir up internal trouble.[51]

3. Nuclear aggression should be distinguished from "nibbling aggression"; that is, the threat or initiation of major war should be distinguished from the threat or initiation of minor war. This is obviously not an easy distinction to make; with the present military technology, it appears to depend on whether or not nuclear weapons are used or threatened. Hence the great danger of the American threat to use "tactical nuclear weapons" against attack by conventional weapons, said to be necessary to compensate for the greater size of the land armies controlled by the Soviet Union. Tactical nuclear weapons are very likely to be countered by nuclear attacks on the bases from which they are launched and to result in general nuclear war. A stalemate can be maintained only if the use of nuclear weapons of any kind is prohibited except against actual nuclear attack. If nibbling aggressions are confined to conventional weapons, collective security forces using only such weapons can be mobilized to counter them by the procedure suggested in the Uniting for Peace Resolution of the General Assembly.[52]

4. "Self-determination" movements should be distinguished from "subversive intervention." The right of revolution is inherent in the Charter recognition of the principle of self-determination, as well as in the concept of democracy and government by consent of the governed. In principle, internal revolution is a matter within the

domestic jurisdiction of a state; other states are forbidden to intervene even on invitation of the government. Colonial powers in NATO have at times sought to agree upon common policies by which all the members would give assistance to maintain power in their colonies. They have sought to justify this on the ground that colonial disturbances proceed from subversive intervention by the Soviet bloc which it is a general object of NATO to prevent.

At the present time NATO extends only to protecting from aggression the home territories of the member states, with the exception of Algeria, originally regarded by NATO as part of the home territory of France. Subversive intervention may be dealt with by the United Nations and by action within its territory by the victim state.

Intervention by outside states to assist in the success or the suppression of revolution or colonial revolt would violate either the right of sovereignty or the right of revolution and self-determination inherent in the Charter. The United Nations, however, can properly intervene in civil disturbances, if human rights are violated, if the right of self-determination by peaceful process is denied, if subversive intervention from outside threatens the independence or security of the state, or if civil strife actually threatens international peace. But any such action by the United Nations should be preceded by careful investigation to determine whether any of these grounds for intervention exist, particularly whether unrest has been caused by outside aggression or subversive intervention, or by internal dissatisfaction with the government or demands for self-determination. Intervention by a state at the invitation of another to assist in suppressing subversive intervention is seldom necessary, and intervention in collective self-defense is not permissible unless the inviting state is the victim of aggression in the sense of actual or immediately threatened armed attack.[53]

The importance of these four distinctions has been generally recognized in the United Nations, but a number of states have failed to make them and public opinion should be more aware of them if peaceful coexistence is to be maintained.

Conclusion

If peaceful coexistence of states is assured there will be no third world war; but peaceful coexistence cannot be maintained unless people desire it more than they desire the immediate destruction of ideologies which they deem immoral. It implies the practice of tolerance and the observance of law. Relaxation of tensions, stabilization of the balance of power, strengthening of international law, and strengthening of the United Nations all would be forwarded by general restoration of confidence in peaceful coexistence. This has been recognized by the heads of all the principal states. Restoration of such confidence requires reconsideration in the West of the idea that Communist states are implacable in their quest for world dominance, inhuman in the methods they are ready to use, and insusceptible to any influence but force. It similarly requires reconsideration in the East of the idea that capitalist states are inevitably imperialistic and aggressive. It must be realized that governments are human and usually act on the basis of values inherent in their cultures and formulated as national interests. It must be assumed that a state's values are its own affair so long as they do not induce action which violates international law; that its national interests as it views them can usually be discovered by study of its values, its conditions, and its actions; that its foreign policy can be expected to reflect its values and its interests under the conditions it faces; and that unless dominated by passions or obsessions—the likely fruit of rising tensions—it will not deliberately act in a way obviously contrary to its interests as it perceives them.

Concentrating public discussion of international relations in terms of arms, the missile gap, or outer space tends to make the public and governments forget that international relations are human relations and that the values, interests, and policies of states are more important than military capabilities in predicting action. It is more important to know where a gun is pointed than its caliber, and the former depends on the mind behind the gun. Intentions and capabilities are undoubtedly related. Governments—being human—tend in the short run to employ their capabilities to further their interests, but in the long run—being human—they tend to modify their interests to take advantage of increased capabilities or to accommodate to declining capabilities.

Bismarck once said that political decisions should not be concerned with periods of more than three years. In such short-run policy-making, mutual understanding of national interests is of prime importance in predicting deliberate action. Technical studies of the arms race and capabilities of deterrence emphasizing the emergence of a missile gap in the 1960's provide no realistic information on the probability of deliberate war. The publicity given to such studies has tended to augment tensions and to engender military policies of alertness, considerably augmenting the probability of accidental, irrational, or pre-emptive war. To estimate the probability of deliberate war, study should be devoted primarily to psychological and political factors indicating national values, interests, policies, and intentions, and only secondarily to technological factors indicating capability.

So long as studies of public opinion, the policies of governments, and the attitudes of leading statesmen indicate that each side in the cold war believes that the other if attacked with nuclear weapons would have sufficient retaliatory force to cause considerable destruction to the attacker, and that each side has such confidence in its system that it believes time favors it in peaceful competition, there would seem to be little danger of deliberate aggression with atomic weapons.

The danger of nibbling aggression on frontiers is appreciable and tends to increase with the general conviction that atomic retaliation is too dangerous to employ against such aggression. The remedy for nibbling aggression, however, is not to make incredible threats of massive retaliation or to augment the arms race, but to organize collective security under the United Nations by earmarking ground forces available for use at all vulnerable frontiers.[54]

While studies and public discussion about the capability of weapon systems cannot be avoided, the public should be informed of the relative danger in a given situation of *deliberate,* as compared with *accidental, irrational,* or *pre-emptive* war, or the expansion of *nibbling aggression* or *civil strife.* The public should realize the great danger which lies in excessive preparation against deliberate war as in expensive programs of shelters or extreme readiness to retaliate against nuclear attack. The belief that war is inevitable may stimulate tensions or even induce the use of force, making it a self-fulfilling prophecy.

A public policy devoted primarily to the reduction of international tension, stabilizing the world's power equilibrium, developing international law, and strengthening the United Nations would establish conditions which would promote mutual trust, prolong peaceful coexistence, and prevent World War III.

NOTES

1. Address to the American Association for the Advancement of Science, New York, Winter, 1961.

2. John Foster Dulles, before he became Secretary of State, raised the question: "Who has been helped most by seeming to give our foreign policy a militaristic pattern—the United States or the Soviet Union? We have, perhaps, gained some military advantage. But we have paid a high price in moral and psychological disadvantages. Just how high that price is, we can only guess, for only a small part of the cost has been revealed." See his *War or Peace* (New York: Macmillan, 1950), p. 239. See also Quincy Wright,

"The U.S. Position in the World," *Challenge,* V (December, 1956), 13 ff. See also Notes 25 and 26 below.

3. Fred Warner Neal, "Coexistence and the Kremlin," *Bulletin of the Atomic Scientists,* XVI (September, 1960), pp. 283 ff. The inherent interest of revolutionists in destroying stability is said to have greatly diminished among the Soviet leaders because of their increasing interest in economic progress and the fruits of "socialist construction" dependent upon social and political order. This accords with the usual tendency of revolutionary regimes, including that of the United States in 1776, to become increasingly interested in stability with age.

4. Lewis F. Richardson, *Arms and Insecurity* (Pittsburgh: Boxwood Press, and Chicago: Quadrangle Books, 1960), pp. 12 ff.; and Quincy Wright, *A Study of War* (Chicago: University of Chicago Press, 1942), p. 1482.

5. Wright, *op. cit.,* pp. 1299 ff.

6. F. S. C. Northrop, *Philosophical Anthropology and Practical Politics* (New York: Macmillan, 1960), p. 435; Wright, *op. cit.,* pp. 978 ff.

7. Wright, *The Study of International Relations* (New York: Appleton-Century-Crofts, 1955), pp. 32, 42; and *A Study of War,* p. 965.

8. Wright, *The Study of International Relations,* p. 44: Wright, *The Strengthening of International Law* (The Hague: Academy of International Law, Recueil des Cours, 1959), pp. 26 ff.

9. Wright, *The Strengthening of International Law,* pp. 11, 106, 173; Wright, *A Study of War,* pp. 198, 690, 722, 763; Wright, *The Study of International Relations,* pp. 139 ff.; Wright, "International Law and Ideologies," *American Journal of International Law,* XLVIII (October, 1954), 616 ff.

10. Commission to Study the Organization of Peace, Twelfth Report, *Peaceful Coexistence, A New Challenge to the United Nations* (New York: American Association for the United Nations, 1960).

11. Treaty of Münster, 1648, Article 123, quoted in Francis B. Sayre, *Experiments in International Administration* (New York: Harper, 1919).

12. Wright, *The Strengthening of International Law,* pp. 146, 153, 163; A. Appadorai, *The Use of Force in International Relations* (Bombay: Asia Publishing House, 1958), pp. 82 ff.

13. See Notes 6 and 9 above.

14. U.N. Charter, Article 2.

15. A. Appadorai, *The Bandung Conference* (New Delhi: 1955); and Wright, *The Strengthening of International Law,* pp. 74 ff.

16. *ACEN News* (October, 1959), p. 2. In a speech to a general meeting of party organizations, published in Moscow on January 6, 1961, Premier Khrushchev said: "The policy of peaceful coexistence is thus, so far as its social content is concerned, a form of intense economic, political and ideological struggle between the proletariat and the aggressive forces of imperialism in the world arena." He said war was not necessary to achieve Communist victory, which was "inevitable by the laws of historical development," but would come if capitalist nations tried to resist. See the *Washington Post,* January 18, 1961. See also Appadorai, *The Use of Force in International Relations,* pp. 70 ff., and Note 10 above.

17. United States Department of State, *Bulletin,* XXVIII (April 27, 1953), p. 599.

18. See Note 3 above.

19. Wright, *The Strengthening of International Law,* pp. 171 ff.

20. Wright, "Subversive Intervention," *American Journal of International Law,* LIV (July, 1960), 521 ff.; "Intervention and Cuba," *Proceedings of the American Society of International Law,* 1961.

21. Wright, "Recognition and Self Determination," *Proceedings of the American Society of International Law* (April, 1954), pp. 23 ff.; *The Strengthening of International Law,* pp. 178 ff. In December, 1960, the General Assembly approved without dissent a resolution calling for the speedy emancipation of all colonies; *United Nations Review* (January, 1961) p. 7.

22. *Ibid.,* pp. 206 ff.

23. See Note 20 above.

24. Wright, *A Study of War,* p. 842.

25. *Ibid.,* pp. 826 ff.

26. Harold D. Lasswell, "The Garrison State," *American Journal of Sociology,* XLVIII (1941), 455 ff.; Wright, *Problems of Stability and Progress in International Relations* (Berkeley: University of California Press, 1954), pp. 273 ff.; Wright, *The Study of International Relations,* p. 176; and Note 25 above.

27. Charles de Visscher, *Theory and Reality in International Law* (tr. P. E. Corbett. Princeton: Princeton University Press, 1957), p. 328.

28. UNESCO Constitution, Preamble.

29. Wright, "International Conflict and the United Nations," *World Politics,* X (October, 1957), 24 ff.

30. Jerome Frank, "The Great Antagonism," *The Atlantic Monthly* (November, 1958), p. 59; and Richardson, *op. cit.,* p. 12.

31. Wright, "Legal Aspects of the U-2 Incident," *American Journal of International Law,* LIV (October, 1960), 836 ff.

32. See Notes 2 and 24 above.

33. See Note 29 above.

34. See Note 9 above.

35. Wright, "Non-recognition of China and International Tensions," *Current History,* XXXIV (March, 1958), 152 ff. See also Edgar Snow's interviews with Chinese Prime Minister Chou En-lai and Party Chairman Mao Tse-tung, "Red China's Leaders Talk Peace on Their Terms," *Look,* XXV (January 31, 1961), 86 ff.

36. John Foster Dulles, before he became Secretary of State, thought: "The United Nations will best serve the cause of peace if its Assembly is representative of what the world actually is" (Dulles, *op. cit.,* p. 190). The Soviet government's lack of confidence in the United Nations and its frequent use of the veto in the Security Council have apparently been due in part to its gross under-representation of the Communist third of the world's population in the principal U.N. organs (*ibid.,* p. 162).

37. Opinion is coming to recognize that tactical atomic weapons would not equalize inferior Western ground forces in Europe when the Soviet Union has such weapons, and that if general nuclear war is to be avoided use of all nuclear weapons should be prohibited. See Morton H. Halperin, *Nuclear Weapons in Limited War* (Cambridge: Harvard University Center for International Affairs, 1960).

38. Albert J. Wohlstetter, "The Delicate Balance of Terror," *Foreign Affairs,* XXXVII (January, 1959), 211 ff.; and Fred C. Iklé, "Nth Countries and Disarmament," *Bulletin of the Atomic Scientists,* XVI (December, 1960), 394.

39. The Soviet attitude in the spring of 1961 suggested that progress in these negotiations would be halted unless Communist China was brought in.

40. A special Committee on "World Peace through Law" was established in 1958 under the chairmanship of Charles S. Rhyne, a former president of the American Bar Association. See "The Role of Law Among Nations," *Digest of Proceedings of Regional Conference* (1959); and "*Background Information*" (1960), prepared by this Committee for the A.B.A.

41. That it included only uses of armed force and not nonmilitary intervention is indicated by Article 1, Paragraph 1 of the Charter which refers to "acts of aggression or *other* breaches of the peace." A "breach of the peace" implies military action and in the context of the Charter refers only to international peace, excluding civil strife.

41a. This phrase clearly refers to the *de facto* situation. A use of force by a state to occupy territory which it claims, but which is occupied by another state, on the basis of a cease-fire line as in Kashmir, Palestine, Germany, Korea and Vietnam, or on the basis of an opposing claim as in Goa and Kuwait, constitutes aggression. The Charter requirement that international disputes be settled by "peaceful means" forbids forcible self-help to remedy territorial occupations alleged to be unjust. Quincy Wright, *The Role of International Law in the Elimination of War* (Manchester: Manchester University Press; New York: Oceana Publications, 1961), pp. 13 ff., 63.

42. *Ibid.,* pp. 59 ff.; note 12 above.

43. *Ibid.* and Wright, *The Strengthening of International Law,* pp. 88 ff., 158 ff.

44. See Note 20 above; Wright, "The Crime of War Mongering," *American Journal of International Law,* XLII (January, 1948), 128 ff.; Wright, "International Law and Civil Strife," *Proceedings of the American Society of International Law* (1959), pp. 145 ff. Subversive intervention, as well as aggression, often has the character of a "crusade" to convert peoples to a religion or ideology believed to be "true" and beneficial to all, and thus seems morally justifiable to the crusaders. International law, however, does not distinguish the relative value of different religions and ideologies, but forbids illegal methods to expand any. It may, therefore, face sincere advocates of a particular doctrine with the dilemma of violating international law or seeming weak in their faith. Law, if it is to avoid oppression and preserve peace among peoples of diverse beliefs, must be tolerant of doctrines believed by some to be "wicked," so long as the adherents of these doctrines do not resort to violence or other illegal actions. It has been the belief of liberals that if law thus maintains a peaceful forum for the discussion of opposing doctrines, the better will eventually prevail. See Wright, "International Law and Ideologies," note 9 above; *A Study of War,* pp. 176 ff.; and *The Role of International Law,* p. 73 ff.

45. Incidents ignoring other obligations of international law, such as respect for the immunities of foreign official agencies in the state's territory, the exercise of due diligence to protect resident nationals of other states, and the fulfillment of specific treaty obligations, are also matters of international concern outside of the state's "domestic jurisdiction." See Wright, *The Strengthening of International Law,* p. 191.

46. *Ibid.,* pp. 59 ff., 127 ff.

47. *Ibid.,* pp. 251 ff.

48. *Ibid.,* pp. 237 ff.

49. Commission to Study the Organization of Peace, Reports 9 (*Charter Review Conference,* 1955); 10 (*Strengthening the United Nations,*

1957); 11 (*Organizing Peace in the Nuclear Age,* 1959); and 12 (*Peaceful Coexistence,* 1960).

50. See Notes 12 and 43 above; and Richardson, *op. cit.*

51. See Note 44 above.

52. See Note 37 above.

53. Wright, *The Strengthening of International Law,* pp. 171 ff.

54. General Maxwell D. Taylor, *The Uncertain Trumpet* (New York: Harper, 1959), pp. 130 ff.; Lieutenant General James M. Gavin, *War and Peace in the Space Age* (New York: Harper, 1958), p. 286.

Notes on Contributors

EMILE BENOIT—Associate Professor of International Business in the Graduate School of Business of Columbia University, author of numerous articles and *Europe at Sixes and Sevens.*

LEWIS C. BOHN—Political Scientist, independent consultant to research organizations on disarmament and national strategy, author of various articles and of a forthcoming book on the politics of peace.

C. WEST CHURCHMAN—Professor of Business Administration at the University of California, author of many books, including *Logic and Formal Science; Introduction to Operations Research; Theory of Experimental Inference;* and *Prediction and Optimal Decision: Philosophical Issues of a Science of Values.*

DAVID DAICHES—Professor of English and Dean of the School of English Studies at the University of Sussex, author of numerous books, including *New Literary Values; Literature and Society; The Novel and the Modern World;* and *A Critical History of English Literature.*

KARL W. DEUTSCH—Professor of Political Science at Yale University, author of various books, including *Political Community at the International Level; Nationalism and Social Communication; Political Community and the North Atlantic Area;* and *Foreign Policy in World Politics.*

MORTON DEUTSCH—Social Psychologist at the Bell Telephone Laboratories, Adjunct Professor of Psychology at New York University, Staff member of the Postgraduate Center for Psychotherapy, author of numerous articles on the conditions affecting cooperation, and coauthor of *Research Methods in Social Relations* and *Interracial Housing.*

AMITAI ETZIONI—Associate Professor of Sociology at Columbia

University, author of *A Comparative Analysis of Complex Organizations, The Hard Way to Peace: A New Strategy,* and editor of *Complex Organizations: A Sociological Reader.*

WILLIAM M. EVAN—Sociologist at the Bell Telephone Laboratories, author of many articles, including "An International Public Opinion Poll on Disarmament," and editor of *Law and Sociology: Exploratory Essays.*

ROGER FISHER—Professor of Law at the Law School of Harvard University, author of various articles, including "Bringing Law to Bear on Governments."

JEROME D. FRANK—Professor of Psychiatry at Johns Hopkins University, author of numerous articles relating to psychotherapeutic aspects of world tensions and *Group Psychotherapy.*

ERICH FROMM—Adjunct Professor of Psychology at New York University and Professor of Psychoanalysis at the National Autonomous University of Mexico, author of various books, including *Escape from Freedom; Man for Himself; The Sane Society;* and *May Man Prevail.*

RALPH W. GERARD—Professor of Neurophysiology at the Mental Health Research Institute of the University of Michigan, author of various books, including *The Body Functions; Methods in Medical Research;* and *Problems in Evaluation of Psychopharmacology.*

ROBERT GOMER—Professor of Chemistry at the University of Chicago, author of *Field Emission and Field Ionization,* and editor of *Structure and Properties of Solid Surfaces.*

ZELLIG S. HARRIS—Professor of Linguistics at the University of Pennsylvania, author of many books, including *Methods of Structural Linguistics.*

HERBERT C. KELMAN—Professor of Psychology at the University of Michigan, author of various articles and editor of a forthcoming book entitled *Imagery and Interaction in International Relations.*

ARTHUR LARSON—Professor of Law and Director of the World Rule of Law Center at Duke University and author of various books, including *Cases and Materials on the Law of Corporations; The Law of Workmen's Compensation;* and *When Nations Disagree.*

SEYMOUR MELMAN—Associate Professor of Industrial Engineering at Columbia University, author of *Dynamic Factors of Industrial Productivity; Decision Making and Productivity;* and *The Peace Race;* and editor of *Inspection for Disarmament.*

ARNE NAESS—Professor of Philosophy at the University of Oslo, author of *Erkenntnis und wissenschaftliches Verhalten; Interpretation and Preciseness;* and *Democracy, Ideology, and Objectivity;* coauthor of *Gandhis poltiske etikk.*

CHARLES E. OSGOOD—Professor of Psychology at the University of Illinois and Director of The Institute of Communications Research, and author of *The Measurement of Meaning,* and *Method and Theory in Experimental Psychology.*

TALCOTT PARSONS—Professor of Sociology at Harvard University, author of many books, including *The Structure of Social Action; Toward a General Theory of Action;* and *The Social System.*

G. I. POKROVSKY—Professor of Applied Physics at the Zhukovskii Engineering Academy in Moscow, author of various articles and *Science and Technology in Contemporary War.*

ANATOL RAPOPORT—Professor of Mathematical Biology at the Mental Health Research Institute of the University of Michigan, author of *Science and the Goals of Man; Operational Philosophy;* and *Fights, Games and Debates.*

DAVID RIESMAN—Henry Ford II Professor of Social Sciences at Harvard University, author of many books, including *The Lonely Crowd* and *Faces in the Crowd.*

BERTRAND RUSSELL—British philosopher, author of numerous books, including *A History of Western Philosophy,* and coauthor of *Principia Mathematica.*

T. C. SCHELLING—Professor of Economics and Associate of the Center for International Affairs at Harvard University, author of *International Economics* and *The Strategy of Conflict;* coauthor of *Strategy and Arms Control.*

LOUIS B. SOHN—Bemis Professor of International Law at the Law School of Harvard University, coauthor of *World Peace Through World Law.*

IVAN SUPEK—Professor of Theoretical Physics at the University of Zagreb and member of the Yugoslav Academy of Science and Art, author of works on theoretical physics, including *Teorijska fizikia i structura materije; Elektrische Leitfähigkeit der Metalle;* and author of novels and plays, including *Dvoje izmedu ratnik linija; The Great Pyramid; On the Verge of the Forest;* and *Atomic Island.*

QUINCY WRIGHT—Professor of Foreign Affairs at the University of Virginia, author of numerous books, including *Mandates Under The League of Nations; A Study of War; The Study of International Relations;* and *The Strengthening of International Law;* and *The Role of International Law in the Elimination of War.*

INDEX

E

N

Q

R

S

V

W